Putin Redux

This book builds on the strengths of the previous volumes by the same author to provide the most detailed and nuanced account of the man, his politics and his profound influence on Russian politics, foreign policy and society. However, this is not a new edition of the earlier books but is an entirely new work. The focus now is on the dilemmas of power since 2008. There is a brief biographical sketch of Vladimir Putin and much analysis of his ideas and policies, but the book now focuses on the systemic contradictions that have created a blockage on modernisation and a stalemate in politics. Putin's role as prime minister since 2008 and his political successes and failures, analysis of the implications of Putin's third term as president and the 2011–12 electoral cycle and the ensuing crisis which led to thousands protesting on the streets are at the centre of analysis.

This work assesses the achievements and failing of Putin's rule, but above all tries to make sense of contemporary developments. This is the definitive account of Putin and is essential reading for all scholars and students of Russian politics.

Richard Sakwa is Professor of Politics at the University of Kent, UK.

Putin Redux

Power and contradiction in contemporary Russia

Richard Sakwa

LONDON AND NEW YORK

First published 2014
by Routledge
2 Park Square, Milton Park, Abingdon, Oxon OX14 4RN

and by Routledge
711 Third Avenue, New York, NY 10017

Routledge is an imprint of the Taylor & Francis Group, an informa business

© 2014 Richard Sakwa

The right of Richard Sakwa to be identified as author of this work has been asserted by him in accordance with the Copyright, Designs and Patent Act 1988.

All rights reserved. No part of this book may be reprinted or reproduced or utilised in any form or by any electronic, mechanical, or other means, now known or hereafter invented, including photocopying and recording, or in any information storage or retrieval system, without permission in writing from the publishers.

Trademark notice: Product or corporate names may be trademarks or registered trademarks, and are used only for identification and explanation without intent to infringe.

British Library Cataloguing in Publication Data
A catalogue record for this book is available from the British Library

Library of Congress Cataloging in Publication Data
Sakwa, Richard.
Putin redux : power and contradiction in contemporary Russia / Richard Sakwa.
pages cm
Includes bibliographical references and index.
1. Russia (Federation)--Politics and government--21st century.
2. Post-communism--Russia (Federation) 3. Putin, Vladimir Vladimirovich, 1952- I. Title.
DK510.763.S246 2014
947.086'2--dc23
2013044517

ISBN: 978-0-415-63093-1 (hbk)
ISBN: 978-0-415-63097-9 (pbk)
ISBN: 978-1-315-78103-7 (ebk)

Typeset in Times New Roman
by Integra Software Services Pvt. Ltd.

Contents

Note on transliteration and translation		vi
Preface		vii
1	Introduction	1
2	The contradictions of Putinism	14
3	Crisis of modernisation	38
4	The impasse of power	61
5	On the eve	81
6	Putin's constitutional coup	111
7	Putin's return	134
8	Tightening the screws	159
9	The new traditionalism and regime reset	190
10	Conclusion: *Respice finem*	223
	Bibliography	232
	Index	245

Note on transliteration and translation

The transliteration system employed throughout this book is a modified version of British Standard, and is used in all cases except those where convention decrees otherwise. Thus the Russian letter 'ю' becomes 'yu', 'я' becomes 'ya', and at the beginning of names 'e' becomes 'ye' (i.e. Yevgeny rather than Evgeny). For the sake of reader-friendliness the '-ий' or '-ый' at the end of words is rendered simply as '-y' (i.e. Dmitry rather than Dmitrii); similarly, in forenames 'кs' has been rendered 'x' (i.e. Alexei rather than Aleksei). Diacritics representing the Russian hard and soft signs have been omitted in proper nouns.

Transliteration in bibliographical references will largely follow the more precise Library of Congress System (albeit with 'ya' for 'я' and 'yu' for 'ю'), and so the reader may at times notice variances between the spelling in the text and that found in the references.

All translations, unless otherwise indicated, are by the author.

Preface

This book builds on the two editions of my *Putin: Russia's Choice*, first published by Routledge in 2004 and with a much revised version in 2008. However, this is not a new edition of the earlier book but is an entirely new work. The focus now is on the dilemmas of power since 2008. There is a brief biographical sketch of Vladimir Putin and much analysis of his ideas and policies, but the focus is on the systemic contradictions that have created a blockage on modernisation and a stalemate in politics. The interregnum of Dmitry Medvedev's presidency from 2008 offered the promise of controlled liberalisation from above, but this strategy was derailed by the brutal announcement in September 2011 that Putin planned to return for a third term. The popular protests that followed the flawed parliamentary elections in December 2011 illustrated the waning power of the Putin project and the increasingly stark contradiction with its practices, but he nevertheless won the hard-fought presidential election in March of the following year, and formally returned to the Kremlin in May. Thereafter the screws were tightened, accompanied by a deterioration of relations with the West. However, with the end of the tandem, clarity at least was restored about who was in charge. This work assesses the achievements and failings of Putin's rule, but above all tries to make sense of contemporary developments.

I am once again most grateful to Craig Fowlie at Routledge for the support and encouragement he has given me in the preparation of this book. It is my pleasure to acknowledge the support of the British Academy for the Small Research Grant British (SG110035) 'Business Raiding in Contemporary Russia'. I am also happy to thank the Norwegian Institute of International Affairs (NUPI) and the Norwegian Research Council (project number 209365/H30) for their support within the framework of the project 'Modernizing the Russian North: Politics and Practice'. I much appreciate being an Honorary Senior Research Fellow at the Centre for Russian and East European Studies (CREES) at the University of Birmingham, which gives me access to Russian-language electronic materials. David Johnson's balanced and highly informative Russia List has been of immeasurable help in keeping up with facts and opinions on contemporary Russian matters. This work has greatly benefitted from conversations with my colleagues Philip Boobbyer and Adrian Pabst, as well as a host of fellow tillers of the Russian field too numerous to mention. I am, though, especially appreciative of discussions and substantive collaboration with Elena Chebankova, Piotr Dutkiewicz, Pavel Ivlev, Valentin Mikhailov, Andrew Monaghan, Vyacheslav Morozov, Nikolai Petrov, Cameron Ross, Sergei Yerofeev. My thanks for secretarial and other assistance go to the team in the department of Politics & International Relations, and in particular the School Administrative Manager Frances Pritchard, who together make the University of Kent such a congenial place in which to work. In trying to make sense of contemporary Russia for others, I have been forced to try to make sense of it for myself. As always, it has been like trying to hit a moving target, and the struggle for understanding continues. This is my modest contribution to what is undoubtedly a work in progress.

Richard Sakwa
Canterbury, October 2013

1 Introduction

An era in Russian history is now associated with the name of Vladimir Putin. Appointed prime minister in August 1999, he was designated acting president by the aged and infirm Boris Yeltsin, Russia's first president, just a few months later, on 31 December. Putin remains the dominant political figure in Russian politics to this day. However, neither he nor the country has stayed the same. Although there are profound continuities in Putin's leadership style, at least four different stages in his rule can be identified, coinciding with the classic cycle of leadership.

The first phase was a combination of continuity and remedial politics. In March 2000 Putin won the presidential election in a hard-fought ballot, and quickly set upon stamping his vision of politics on Russia. In policy terms Putin continued to implement Yeltsin's legacy, and in most ways more effectively. Crucial new Labour and Land Codes were adopted, tax collection was greatly improved by the introduction of a flat rate income tax of 13 per cent, and in general the economic liberals were in the ascendant. The new leader also distanced himself from the earlier period. Although Putin was careful not to attack Yeltsin personally, his politics was based on the idea that in the 1990s the Russian state lost the ability to manage affairs, the economy declined, and powerful special interests had emerged that threatened governance in its entirety. The era was presented as a new 'Time of Troubles' (*smutnoe vremya*), which takes an act of supreme concentration to overcome. Putin fostered a culture of trauma that reproduced in new forms the pathologies of the 1990s. He quickly clipped the wings of some of the more egregiously political of the so-called 'oligarchs' and established a new 'social contract' with them: as long as they stayed out of direct politics, they could get on with the business of making money. At the same time, he pushed back against what was widely perceived to be the excessive powers of the regional governors. In this way he bolstered his personal power, reinforced later by taking control of television, merging the two loyal parties, and the abolition of gubernatorial elections.

The latent powers of the Russian state, eclipsed by powerful oligarchs and governors in the 1990s, were re-activated. However, the only effective carrier of these powers was not the new forces unleashed by Russia's capitalist revolution, notably liberal political parties, an independent business class (the bourgeoisie) and an active civil society, representing the forces of democratic modernity, but the bedrock of the Soviet system, which had been overthrown with so much fanfare in 1991: the vast bureaucracy and the equally vast security apparatus (collectively known as the *siloviki*). From the first the Putin system was marked by the contrast between the declared goals of the administration, and the means by which its aspirations were implemented. Although in numerical terms the late Soviet bureaucracy may not have been so large in proportion to the size of the nation, it exercised a deep hold on the population. Regulate, control, stifle and, increasingly, extort became its mantra. Equally, Putin's accession to power reactivated deeper patterns of security service behaviour. In state organisations, ranging from banks, shipbuilding to the precious metals and stones reserve (Gokhran), there are endless accounts of how security officials began to exercise a type of secondary power, acting as the alleged emissaries of the regime while lining their own pockets. This provided fertile ground for corruption, while stifling the further development of a more competitive liberal economy.

The turning point that inaugurated the second phase of Putinite politics, a period of regime consolidation marked by intensified constraints, was the assault against the Yukos oil company and the arrest of its head, Mikhail Khodorkovsky, on 25 October 2003. Two logics of modernity collided. Khodorkovsky represented a more liberal and open style of politics and economic governance. Although the creation and development of Yukos in the 1990s was accompanied by the shortcomings and sharp practices typical of that era, nevertheless in the early 2000s the company was transformed and presented itself as the modern corporation that Russia needed to become a developed and diversified economy. Unfortunately, this programme became a sort of crusade, which was perceived to threaten once again the prerogatives of the state. The response of the statists and *siloviki* was not long in coming. The *silovik* faction, a core constituency in Putin's power base, reasserted the claimed prerogatives of the state over economic policy and political life as a whole. The result was a conflict in which the regime destroyed not only a political opponent but also the oil company. Yukos was broken up and mostly absorbed by the new 'national champion', Rosneft.[1]

In this period the gap between the regime and the state became increasingly apparent. The distinction between the two wings of the 'dual state', the constitutional state and the administrative regime, will be explored later in this book, and is central to our understanding of the contradictions of the Putin system.[2] In modern political theory the constitutional state is an entity that exists separate from any particular ruler, endures beyond the life span of a particular government, and is rooted in the public good. It is regulated by impartial norms of law and managed by a disinterested bureaucracy. In Russia this Weberian ideal was subverted by the administrative regime, which drew legitimacy from claiming to apply the principles of the constitutional state and authority from its representation of the common good, but in practice the polity and the state effectively became the property of the regime, and increasingly of the leader himself. When talking about strengthening the state, Putin in fact too often only reinforced the prerogative powers of the regime. In other words, a new form of a patrimonial regime was consolidated.

Instead of consolidating the rule of law, the authority of constitutional institutions such as parliament and the formal procedures of modern governance, regime practices predominated accompanied by the development of a whole range of para-constitutional bodies, such as the seven (later eight) federal districts, the State Council and the Civic Chamber. Putin never repudiated the formal framework of the constitution, and as we shall see a key part of his political identity was that he was serving the constitution, but the sphere of discretion (which exists in all political systems) became extraordinarily wide. This fostered the practice of legal populism, allowing the regime to avoid direct coercion. The law was used to advance policies that ran counter to the spirit of constitutionalism, thus eroding trust in its institutions. The legal system was subordinated to political authority and in certain cases, such as in the Yukos prosecutions, undermined the consolidation of independent courts and the rule of law in general. A system of 'legalistic nihilism' was established, in which the Soviet tradition of arbitrary 'telephone justice' was reinstated. People with influence and connections are immune from prosecution for even the most heinous criminal offences, whereas those who fall foul of the system are subject to prosecution.

Much of Putin's second term was devoted to ensuring the permanence of his power and to rendering the regime invulnerable to overthrow. Putin took advantage of the 1–3 September 2004 Beslan school hostage siege, organised by Chechen insurgents, to consolidate power. On 13 September Putin announced a range of measures, including the abolition of gubernatorial elections, many of which had at best a tangential relationship with the struggle against terrorism. I call this 'Putin's constitutional coup', the first of two such events (the second was the announcement of his return to the presidency on 24 September 2011). In that same autumn Russia was heavily engaged in supporting the regime's candidate, Viktor Yanukovich, in the hard-fought Ukrainian elections. Already in December 2003 the first of the post-Soviet 'colour revolutions' had taken place in Georgia, with the overthrow of Eduard Shevardnadze and the rise to power of Mikheil Saakashvili following a flawed election, the typical pattern of such events. In Ukraine the western-backed 'democratic' candidate, Viktor Yushchenko, finally won in an unprecedented third-round ballot, following a massive popular mobilisation in favour of free and fair elections. This 'orange' revolution was perceived as a warning to the Putin regime, and the response was a clamping down on independent political activity, onerous NGO regulations and the attempt to conquer the streets through the creation of loyal pro-regime youth movements.

In political economy, the Yukos affair inaugurated a period of active state intervention. It would be going too far to call this 'state capitalism', since there was little outright nationalisation, or even corporatism of the traditional kind where companies are bound to the state in social and investment policy.

The thrust of this period was 'deprivatisation', whereby independent companies were brought into a form of flexible but occasionally heavy-handed *dirigisme*. State corporations were established, notably the sprawling 'Russian Technologies' industrial empire that encompassed titanium production to car manufacturing. Political and economic power once again, as in the 1990s, converged but in a new way. The development of national champions, above all in the energy sector, was closely tied to elite interests, rendering them as much 'regime companies' as state entities, funding various pet projects of the system. Gazprom's long-established privileges were confirmed, while the state-owned Rosneft grew into a major international oil company on the back of expropriated Yukos assets. This was an era of social paternalism, with resources flowing into the social sphere. Whereas Putin's 2005 state-of-the-nation speech (*poslanie*) to the two houses of the Federal Assembly, drafted by his chief of staff Dmitry Medvedev, stressed democracy and liberalism, his 2006 *poslanie*, written by his new head of the presidential administration, Sergei Sobyanin, talked of a turning point in economic and welfare policy. The grant of generous 'maternity capital' to families for the birth of a second child was announced, which the mother could use for education, mortgage payments or pension savings after the child reached the age of three.

Putin was limited to two successive terms by the 1993 constitution. His *silovik* allies encouraged him to amend the constitution to remove term limits, as so many of the other post-Soviet states had done, to allow him to rule legally for an indefinite period. In practical terms this would have been possible, since the regime enjoyed constitutional majorities in both the State Duma (the lower house of the Federal Assembly) and the upper house, the Federation Council, as well as enjoying the support of the governors, most of whom had now been appointed in the new system. However, Putin insisted that he would remain loyal to the letter of the constitution. In an extraordinary manoeuvre, Putin engineered the election of his nominated successor, Medvedev, while he took on the post of prime minister. This brought to an end the 'classic' period of Putin's rule, which had moved from 'remedial' power accumulation into a more consolidated 'developmental' project. The remedial strategy had enjoyed widespread public support as some of the genuine abuses of the 1990s were mitigated, whereas the regime's consolidation accentuated concern about 'democratic backsliding', the suffocation of political pluralism and competitiveness. These two phases, the remedial and the developmental, comprise 'classical Putinism', in which the evolutionary direction of the system remained open.

In the third phase, between 2008 and 2012, Russia was governed by the 'tandem'. Medvedev was constrained by the terms of the deal, but from the first he showed signs of political independence and advanced a distinctive programme of his own. From condemnation of 'legal nihilism' to supporting what he called 'modernisation', including measures to ease the pressure on business, Medvedev shaped a policy that was not anti-Putinite but represented a modification of some of the key features of classic Putinism. Medvedev represented the Putin system at its most benign and progressive, although critics suggest also at its least coherent and competent. As a lawyer by profession, he was above all concerned with re-asserting the independence of the judiciary as part of a broader programme of strengthening the constitutional state against the arbitrariness of the administrative regime. While it is now customary to mock Medvedev's ineffectual style, in fact he represented a form of evolutionary development that could have retained the achievements of the remedial aspects of Putinism while pushing back against the excesses of the consolidation period. Just as Putin had transcended what he considered the limitations of Yeltsin's rule, so Medvedev, without condemning Putin the man, reflected the potential of the system to evolve by strengthening the institutions of the constitutional state, while clipping the wings of the administrative regime.

This was a normative but realistic possibility, and gained the support of a growing band of adherents who had been at the heart of the creation of classic Putinism, above all the economic liberals and even the democratic statists. In the end intra-systemic reform was stymied by the constraints of the tandem arrangements, which did not allow the reformist programme to take political form to challenge the power of the *siloviki* and other defenders of the administrative regime who aligned behind Putin. The gulf between exaggerated expectations and disappointment was in part fuelled by Medvedev's style, in which the anticipation of great reforms constantly collapsed into small actions, but also by the objective need to resolve some of the accumulating contradictions between liberal and conservative strategies. In the end, the swelling elite counter-movement to Medvedev's liberalising aspirations was provoked in no small part by concerns over the perceived geopolitical ambitions of the West in the wake of interventions in Iraq and Libya and the precipitate demonisation of Bashar al-Assad in Syria as the insurgency began there in spring 2011. The 'Arab Spring' of this period appeared to signal the continuation of 'orangism', reminiscent to the Putinites of the chaos unleashed by perestroika earlier. In the bowels of the administrative regime there was a swelling movement for Putin to return and reassert his authority.

Medvedev apparently anticipated being allowed a second run at the presidency, but the tide had turned against him. On 24 September 2011 the 'castling' (*rokirovka*) plan was announced to a shocked nation: Putin would return to the presidency, while Medvedev would become prime minister. The move in itself was not a surprise, since Putin had clearly been in permanent campaigning mode since assuming the premiership in 2008, with increasingly flamboyant (and ridiculed) publicity stunts. The intense negative reaction was provoked by two key factors: the claim that the deal had long been agreed (when in fact it had not, although of course it had been one of the most likely options); and the contempt for the Russian electorate and people that the move implied. Although couched in the appropriate constitutional language, everyone knew that in the era of 'managed democracy' the regime would get the result it wanted. Putin's return inaugurated the fourth phase of his leadership, and was indeed perceived to be a return (*redux*), a going backwards, confirmation of the power of an increasingly closed elite and a leadership insulated from the real demands, needs and aspirations of a changed society. In the event, the deeply flawed parliamentary election on 4 December 2011 was followed by the largest political protest movements of Putin's entire leadership. On 4 March 2012 Putin once again comfortably won the presidential election, but his support was clearly eroding.

The fourth phase is what I call 'developed Putinism', by analogy with the 'developed socialism' proclaimed during the mature phase of the Brezhnev era in the 1970s. The features of this developed phase will be the subject of the bulk of this book. The differences between the four stages should not obscure the elements of continuity, just as there are profound continuities between Yeltsin's regime of the 1990s and Putin's rule in the 2000s. Neither Yeltsin's nor Putin's system of rule was an autocracy, but both shared elements of authoritarianism in the management of political processes. Both sought to manage competing demands, with pressure for political participation and social welfare, to reverse the fragmentation of post-Soviet Eurasia, and to respond adequately to new security challenges. Nothing is black and white about the governance system, caught up in turbulent policy conflict over the most appropriate developmental path, the country's place in Eurasia and in energy markets, and in general the position that Russia should adopt in a world torn between rising powers and the defenders of the apparently triumphant western hegemonic system. As an aspirant power, Russia advanced 'multi-polarity' and defended the institutions of international governance, notably the United Nations system, as part of its struggle for recognition.

Putin's leadership remains the subject of intense and polarised debate. For many he remains the saviour of Russia. He presided over years of unprecedented growth, and even weathered the economic crisis from September 2008 with relatively little damage because of the counter-cyclical accumulation of reserves, which provided resources to support the banks and industry when the crisis struck. Sovereign debt fell from 51 per cent of GDP in 2000 to under 5 per cent in 2006 and is now around 3 per cent. In 2008 the sovereign wealth reserve (the Stabilisation Fund) was divided into two: the Reserve Fund (for a rainy day) and the National Welfare Fund, created for future generations as well as to plug the shortfall in the Pension Fund. The Reserve Fund allowed Russia to weather the global economic crisis without going cap in hand to external lenders. As in the West, the scale of support for banks and fragile enterprises was as controversial as it was enormous, with the Fund's holdings falling from an aggregate $125bn in 2008 to some $25bn in 2011, although by August 2013 it was back up to $85bn. This is textbook macro-economic management, pursued by none of the other major economies who find themselves embroiled in a sea of debt, accompanied by 'austerity' policies attacking the foundations of the welfare state. By 2013 the proportion falling below the poverty line in Russia had fallen from some 30 per cent in 2000 to 11 per cent.

Improvements in health care and welfare policies, accompanied by family support, ameliorated the predicted demographic crisis. In 2012 Russia for the first time in nearly two decades saw positive natural population growth, fostered by a range of pro-natalist policies. With a population of nearly 143 million, almost two million births are registered in Russia each year, and the birthrate reached the average European level and the infant mortality rate halved in ten years. Russia still faced the long-term consequences of the demographic catastrophe of the 1990s, with the number of women in the prime reproductive age (20–29) halving in the next decade, with a commensurate long-term decline in the labour force of 73 million in 2004, estimated to fall by seven million by 2020. In international affairs Putin is seen as having restored Russia's status as an independent player, defending its interests while avoiding becoming boxed into some sort of 'pariah' status. After a string of still-born integration efforts in its neighbourhood, moves towards the creation of the Eurasian Union by 2015 looked finally like a viable supranational project comparable to the European Union (EU). Russia allied with China in defence of the traditional postulates of state sovereignty and non-interventionism, while avoiding becoming the junior partner in what was becoming an increasingly unequal relationship. In short, the 2000s were the most successful decade in Russian history.

Putin's critics take a very different view. They consider him the deliberate executioner of Russian democracy, offering instead only the form while gutting political life of the competiveness, dynamism and pluralism that a great nation deserves. Putin's leadership is accused of being obsessed with power, and thus recreated a new Leviathan state to replace the one dismantled in 1991. The developmental rhetoric and rising living standards, declining poverty, a paternalist social security policy that prevented a radical restructuring of the economy and dreams of Eurasian integration are seen as ways of buying off the population with the windfall energy rents. Between 2000 and 2008 the oil price increased by 388 per cent. These rents allowed corrupt and self-serving elites to consolidate their power, using the language and forms of democracy to suppress dissent and pluralistic contestation. Expenditure on public service increased five-fold between 2002 and 2010, allowing the overall number of civil servants to rise by 44 per cent, with the federal bureaucracy alone increasing by 68 per cent between 2000 and 2009, revealing the trend towards the centralisation of power.

The undeveloped and predatory banking system encouraged the private sector to borrow abroad, and the external debt of banks and companies rose from 3 per cent in 2000 to over 30 per cent in 2008. Because of an insecure institutional environment there has been an unceasing flow of capital abroad throughout Russia's post-communist history, with over $380bn leaving between mid-2008 to the end of 2012. Capital controls had been liberalised in Putin's first term, culminating in the complete deregulation of capital accounts in 2006. Fear of government expropriation in the wake of the Yukos affair and the general insecurity of property rights and weak banking sector meant that by the end of the 2000s Russian corporations were using offshore locations not only to run their foreign financial operations but also their domestic business.[3] Capital flight is compounded by the lack of safe opportunities to invest at home, and has become a normal condition for Russia as it rid the country of liquidity that the economy could not digest. Fraudulent elections deprived the regime of the final vestiges of legitimacy as an authoritarian system took shape, defined as one lacking competitive politics, an active civil sphere and scourged by state oppression and violence. The chimera of post-Soviet integration was little more than a distraction from the very real challenges facing the long-term viability of a resource-based and undiversified economy. Anti-western rhetoric acted as a substitute for a genuine forward-looking programme, while Russia's 'cockiness' on the world stage reflected not a defence of traditional norms of international politics but the self-serving interests of an illegitimate ruling class. Authoritarian consolidation at home, from this perspective, was reflected in an aggressive and counter-productive foreign policy.

Neither of these views does justice to the complex reality.[4] Putin responded to some of the very real challenges facing Russia in a relatively competent and coherent manner. Thus his sharpest critics, who accuse the regime of failing to deliver the basics of effective governance, are off the mark. Even the various mega-projects, from the Sochi Winter Olympics in 2014 to the World Cup in 2018, although used to glean excess rents through construction costs, are something in which the country can take pride. There are undoubtedly elements of authoritarianism in all stages of Putinism, although implemented with punctilious regard for the black letter of the law although undermining the spirit of constitutionalism, but there remains an extraordinarily active public sphere critical of Putin and all his works. If Russia is an authoritarian system, it is not a very good one according to the classical precepts of what an authoritarian system should look like. However, the adaptability of the regime and its ability to provide public goods in a reasonably efficient and cost-effective manner is declining, and the country finds itself in a situation where modernisation is blocked and politics increasingly locked in stalemate. The features of the blockage and stalemate will be examined later and, together with the idea of the dual state, constitute the central arguments of this book.

The heart of the problem is a fairly simple one: the gulf between what we can call the 'Putin project' and the 'practices of Putinism'. The Putin project never received a sustained formulation by its progenitors, but developed by a process of endless accretion and adaptation. Typical of its paradoxical nature, the Putin system is consciously non-reflexive. It posits itself as a natural and non-political response to the challenges facing the country, with a pragmatic and technocratic approach to the resolution of problems. To that extent the Putin project, and the man at its head, was able to garner an astonishingly high degree of popular support over the years, and for good reason. Eschewing the extremes of left and right, the ultra-liberals and the virulent nationalists, the project defined itself as centrist and tried to create a political consensus drawing on all wings of the political spectrum. However, the practices of Putinism increasingly ran counter to the relatively benign aspirations of the project. For example, the broadly sensible reform of the party system soon led to the stultification of political competition and the dominance of the 'party of power', United Russia – even though it was certainly not a party in power. Instead, the administrative regime manipulated and micro-managed political processes, including electoral outcomes.

There was also a constant strain of disingenuousness, as when Putin argued that he was personally against the death penalty but was unable to achieve its formal abolition because of the intransigence of parliament. The argument may have washed up to 2003, but thereafter United Russia enjoyed a constitutional majority and Russia could easily have fulfilled its obligations assumed on joining the Council of Europe on 26 February 1996.[5] The stifling of mass media openness and the hermetic nature of the power system encouraged arbitrariness and corruption. The contradiction between the project and the practices became increasingly apparent. The Medvedev variant represented an attempt to return to the principles of the project by strengthening the constitutional state, but this was rudely terminated in September 2011. This is certainly how it was perceived at the time, and contributed to the explosion of popular anger after the flawed parliamentary election later that year. On his return to the presidency Putin tried to find new ways to perpetuate the classical features of the project, but he appeared mired in the practices of what increasingly looked like a tired re-run of developed socialism, including its conservative cultural policies.

Four points are clear. First, developments in the Putin era have been a function of the intense interaction of domestic processes and international dynamics, what transition studies call endogenous and exogenous factors. Russia is the world's largest country with the sixth largest population – the 2010 census identified 142.9 million inhabitants. According to the World Bank in 2013, in purchasing power parity (PPP) terms Russia is the world's fifth largest economy with $3.373trn, and in nominal GDP ratings compiled by the International Monetary Fund Russia ranks eighth at $2trn. The country ranked just behind Germany as Europe's biggest economy. However, the 2013 *Index of Economic Freedom* ranked Russia a lowly 139 out of 177 countries, although because of some effective reforms in the financial sector Russia jumped ten up to 101st place in the Fraser Institute's *Economic Freedom in the World* report, published in September 2013. State-owned companies account for just over half of Russia's economy, up from 38 per cent in 2006. Putin was in favour of the market, but he had less faith in market *forces*. He repeatedly condemned the Communists for their plans to turn back the clock by nationalising the means of production, but in his typically centrist style he was as much in favour of a managed market as he was of managed politics. He had long pushed for Russia's membership of the World Trade Organization (WTO), but when it finally came after 15 years of negotiations on 22 August 2012 his commitment to implanting its free market provisions had clearly waned. By that time Russia had entered what can be called a 'non-reform cycle', in which incremental changes substituted for a more radical overhaul of economic relations. However, pressure from below and elite fragmentation, accompanied by an alarming fall in the economic growth rate, forced reform back on to the agenda.

The fundamental point is that after the fall of communism Russia was by definition on a different track to the rest of the former Soviet bloc. The contradictions that led to '1989' (taken as the symbolic date for the collapse of the Soviet 'empire' in Eastern Europe) differed from those that precipitated 1991 (the combined dissolution of the communist system and the disintegration of the Soviet state). The 'meaning' of 1989 is very different from that of '1991', and many of the misperceptions and outright mistakes in analysing Russia and its future derive from the attempt to impose the logic of 1989, whereas Russia is in fact pursuing a different transition path to modernity based on the concerns of 1991 while at the same time trying to recover its status as a great power. The anti-communist revolutions of 1989 drew their inspiration and reference points from developments in the West, notably in recent years through the development of the European Union, whereas Russia had no such clear direction but only began to delineate its own path in the later Putin years.

Russia remains deeply integrated into global processes, being a permanent member of the United Nations' Security Council (UNSC), the G8 and the G20. The failure to establish a genuinely inclusive world order in the post-Cold War years has shaped developments. A type of 'cold peace' has been established in which the tropes of the Cold War are perpetuated, including a zero-sum approach whereby the achievements of the one side are considered a defeat for the other, accompanied by proxy conflicts throughout the post-Soviet space and elsewhere. This is accompanied by intense propaganda, denigrating the interventionism of the western hegemonic order on the one side while demonising Russia's alleged bullying of neighbouring states and disruptiveness on the world stage on the other. The result is the blockage on genuine dialogue (based on substantive respect for the political subjectivity of the interlocutor) that had been anticipated with the end of the Cold War. Even the idea of 'engagement' is ridiculed as little more than the traditional posture of the 'appeaser' and the 'fellow-traveller', if not reminiscent of what Lenin called 'useful idiots' (representatives of the western leftist intelligentsia who hailed the Bolshevik revolution). Russia was too often considered a 'spoiler', with its initiatives decried and its positions denigrated. A weak Russia was considered a danger, and a strong Russia a threat. The 'cold peace' could only be overcome by a fundamental shift in Russo-western relations towards more constructive and equal engagement.

This leads on to a second key point. Despite the prevalence of the ideology of 'globalisation' in the post-Cold War era, politics remains resolutely national, and in that context even the most cosmopolitan of Russia's liberals agree with the postulate that Russia's future has to be forged in Russia. For a number of post-communist countries, joining the western alliance system after the fall of the Berlin wall in late 1989 was the highest aspiration. In successive enlargements beginning in 1999 and again in 2004, the majority joined NATO, while in the two enlargements of 2004 and 2007 the EU extended its reach to the former Soviet Union, with the incorporation of the three Baltic states. For Russia there could be no such escape from the past: its future would be incommensurably temporal rather than spatial. In other words, for most of Central and Eastern Europe the future lay with the West; whereas for Russia there was no such easy option and it would have to define its future through a far more convoluted and complex process of national self-identification. All of this took place against fears for the territorial integrity of the state itself, with two wars in Chechnya and a persistent Islamic insurgency in the North Caucasus. More than this, with a repeated history of revolutions and state collapse, it is hardly surprising that the contemporary ruling elite is obsessed with security and integration. After all, within the lifetimes of all the main actors the high hopes of the perestroika period under the last Soviet leader, Mikhail Gorbachev, from 1985 precipitated not only the dissolution of the communist order but also the disintegration of the state in December 1991.

Third, objective concerns about keeping the country together and divisions in the international system are accompanied by reiterations of the fundamental debate about the appropriate 'modernisation' strategy for the country. During the period of accelerated industrialisation before the First World War Russia was the fastest growing economy in Europe, but the destructive impact of war, revolution and invasion has still not been overcome. Russia veered from the Soviet 'planned' system to a type of anarcho-capitalism in the 1990s, while in the 2000s Putin applied a *dirigiste* developmental strategy which, despite Medevedev's liberalisation and 'modernisation' rhetoric, remains to this day. Putinite political economy is a peculiar combination of high-minded advancement of state interests with the rather more venal concern of regime elites to benefit from the resources washing through the system (typically described as excess rents). The state acts as both regulator and player, creating a permissive environment for 'raiding' to become a mass phenomenon, stifling the development of small and medium business and depressing growth.

Finally, Russia faces the challenge of political self-identification. Putin repeatedly asserted that he was a 'democrat', but for him the term denotes less the free play of competitive interests but the maintenance of certain forms, however ritualistic, that allows the intervention of a force that stands outside of the democratic process itself. Such a system was already established in the 1990s, helping to discredit democracy when the notion became associated with the pursuit of ill-considered fiscal policy, loss of savings, mass immiseration and capitulation to the West. The formal carapace of a democratic political order was established with the adoption of the constitution in

December 1993, yet the 'habits of the heart' appropriate for a democratic system were far harder to establish. Yeltsin's re-election campaign in 1996 saw untold sums spent to boost what were minimal ratings at the beginning of the year and propelled him to victory in the second round in July of that year, and the media was openly partisan in its support. On 20 February 2012 Medvedev astonished a group of visitors by admitting that Yeltsin had not really won against his communist opponent, Gennady Zyuganov. It is astonishing to consider that not a single election in post-communist Russia can be considered free and fair. The shame is made all the worse when comparisons are drawn with developing countries (such as Kenya in 2013), with far lower levels of infrastructural development, that have been able to stage genuinely competitive and accurately counted elections.

Russia was a more pluralistic and open system in the 1990s, with Yeltsin remarkably tolerant of criticism while the communist-dominated parliament was the scene of intense debates, but Russia in those years was at best a flawed democracy. Putin's remedial strategy swiftly established a docile parliament dominated by his pedestal party, United Russia, created in 2001 through a merger of the Unity party, created in autumn 1999 to support Putin, and the Fatherland party of Moscow's mayor, Yuri Luzhkov. With 1.9 million members, including 74 of Russia's 83 regional governors, 63 per cent of the seats in regional legislatures and 315 out of 450 seats in the Duma in mid-2011, the party looked invincible. The Federation Council lost the critical edge it had in the 1990s, when on several occasions it withstood pressure from the Kremlin. Elections were still hard fought but the regime was able to bring the full weight of 'administrative resources' to ensure favourable outcomes, while the counting was the responsibility of the regime-friendly Central Electoral Commission (CEC). The judiciary and the Constitutional Court fell into line in support of the regime. This was accompanied by the positive social achievements noted above. The idea of democracy may not have been entirely rehabilitated, but in the period of developed Putinism it once again represented a path to the future. This was one of the most paradoxical legacies of Putin's rule. It took Putin's attack on the institutions of popular representation and adjudication to make Russians yearn once again for genuine democracy.

There were always limits to what the regime could get away with without repudiating its own self-identification as democratic. This allowed the institutions of the constitutional state to survive. There was no state of emergency, no mass imprisonment of the opposition, the internet and new social media remained largely free of government control, and the formalities of democratic politics were observed. Putin was not the 'bloody dictator' as caricatured by his opponents. Neither was he Russia's saviour and the wise 'national leader', as portrayed by his supporters. He has some substantial achievements to his credit, above all the creation of an integrated national market governed by a remarkably consistent and effective macroeconomic policy (which he may not have devised but which he endorsed); but there are also some significant failings, notably the lack of trust in autonomous political institutions and the interplay of political forces. Putin never lost his tutelary instincts for control, regulation and manual management. Some of his fears were justified, since Russian political society has never been known for its self-restraint while the nation remains fractured along ethnic, religious and regional lines. Yet, Russian history suggests that a gradual decompression after a period of emergency is preferable to allowing tensions to accumulate to the point that they explode in revolution. The Medvedev interregnum offered just such an evolutionary option, but Putin's return foreclosed that path and instead led to an intensification of all that was most negative in the classic period of his rule. It is far from clear whether an evolutionary opportunity to transcend the contradictions of the Putinite system will be available in the future.

Notes

1 Richard Sakwa, *Putin and the Oligarch: The Khodorkovsky - Yukos Affair* (London, I. B. Tauris, 2014).
2 For a full discussion, see Richard Sakwa, 'The Dual State in Russia', *Post-Soviet Affairs*, Vol. 26, No. 3, July–September 2010, pp. 185–206; and idem, *The Crisis of Russian Democracy: The Dual State, Factionalism and the Medvedev Succession* (Cambridge, Cambridge University Press, 2011).
3 Igor Logvinenko, 'The Dirty Truth about Russia's "Dirty" Money', *Moscow Times*, 10 October 2013.
4 For an overview of Putin's western critics, see Bruno S. Sergi, *Misinterpreting Modern Russia: Western Views of Putin and his Presidency* (London, Continuum, 2009).
5 Matthew Light and Nikolai Kovalev, 'Russia, the Death Penalty, and Europe: The Ambiguities of Influence', *Post-Soviet Affairs*, Vol. 29, No. 6, 2013, pp. 528–566.

2 The contradictions of Putinism

A whole period of Russian history has been stamped by Putin's preferences and character. He has effectively been in charge of the country's destiny since becoming prime minister in August 1999, followed in short order by the transfer of presidential power on 31 December and his formal assumption of the post in May 2000. His leadership is stamped by the fundamental paradox that such a strong character, with a vivid turn of phrase and strong communicative skills, remains so shadowy and, ultimately, formless. Sharply defined in detail, in aggregate the Putinite order remains protean and polymorphous. Putin's complex political identity is both powerful and contradictory, and is thus homologous to the country itself. Neither the country nor the man can be categorised in simple terms: are they pro or anti-western, for or against market forces, modernising or traditionalist? Ultimately, is Russia a democracy (however flawed) or did it revert under Putin to some new form of authoritarianism? For every answer there are numerous qualifications and caveats; no single answer can hope to capture the endless ambiguities of the man and the country.

Rise to the top

Russian politics is contradictory, and so too is Putin. His enemies characterise him through a number of stereotypes, above all drawing on his security service background. The image of 'Vlad the Impaler' has gained traction in the more lurid western media, presenting him in increasingly grotesque poses. In this model Putin has imposed a new yoke on Russia, stifling its democratic development and holding back the economy through his system of 'crony capitalism'. His friends see him as battling on behalf of a besieged Russia, fighting back the legions of internal malcontents, separatists and external foes while consistently enjoying the support of the majority of the people. There is, moreover, as a recent sympathetic study puts it, a 'propensity to judge Russia and Russians instead of trying to understand both'.[1] Putin was no doubt a 'democrat' in the sense that he reflected the basic aspirations of the mass of the people for much of the time, but his failure to trust that very same people to deliver the vote for him ultimately alienated even his supporters. In traducing the formal institutions, including elections through which popular preferences are typically expressed in a democracy, the Putinite system eroded its internal coherence.

I have described elsewhere Putin's background and spectacular rise to the top, as well as the main features of his rule in the first two terms of his presidency up to 2008.[2] The basic facts of his biography are well-known. Born as a late infant to a working class family in Leningrad on 7 October 1952, Putin grew up as a typical Soviet child. Following Joseph Stalin's death on 5 March 1953, the country began the long process of coming to terms with the savagery of his rule that is still not completed. Putin was too young to have been part of the ferment of the 1960s, when reform was in the air and numerous plans were advanced to render the Soviet economy more effective and the politics rather more open. The hopes of the *shestdesyatniki* (the people of the 1960s) were dashed with the Soviet invasion of Czechoslovakia in August 1968, putting an end to hopes of 'socialism with a human face'. Instead, the rule of Leonid Brezhnev, who had ousted Nikita Khrushchev in October 1964, entered a long period of decline, preparing the conditions for the fall of the Soviet Union in 1991. Brezhnev called this period 'developed socialism', but during perestroika the label of 'stagnation' (*zastoi*) described the falling economic growth rates, the stultification of intellectual and political life, and confrontation with the West. The détente of the early 1970s gave way to the second cold war after the Soviet invasion of Afghanistan in December 1979.

For Putin these were the golden years. Even as a youth he was attracted to work in the country's security organs, but was advised to study before applying. He entered the Law Faculty of Leningrad State University in 1970, and appears to have been a popular student, with a fine voice in singing the semi-dissident songs of the period, and good at recounting anecdotes. He took up martial arts and became sambo champion in the city. On graduating in 1975 he realised his ambition and entered service with the Committee of State Security (KGB). After ten years of routine work in Leningrad, in 1985 he and his family (by then he had married and had two daughters) spent five years in Dresden in the German Democratic Republic (GDR), where he worked his way up to become lieutenant-colonel. His duties in East Germany remain obscure, provoking much speculation, but in late 1989 he witnessed at first hand the dramatic collapse of the communist order in Eastern Europe. Moscow's paralysis in the face of the defection of its erstwhile allies, and the disintegration of the system for which so much had been sacrificed, haunts Putin to this day.

In early 1990 Putin returned to a Russia gripped by the final stages of perestroika, the last and greatest reform attempt launched by the last Soviet leader, Gorbachev. He left the KGB's active service and worked briefly in the international office of Leningrad State University before joining the staff of his former law professor, Anatoly Sobchak. In June 1991 Sobchak was elected city mayor, and Putin rose swiftly to become one of his closest advisors. In charge of foreign economic relations, Putin welcomed many foreign dignitaries to the city. He was appointed one of the deputy mayors, but all this collapsed in 1996 when Sobchak failed to be re-elected. The experience left Putin thoroughly distrustful of the unpredictability of the democratic process, and thereafter sought to ensure that electoral outcomes were aligned with his preferences.

After a brief period of enforced leisure, in late 1996 Putin was offered a job in the Kremlin through the efforts of his former St Petersburg colleague, Alexei Kudrin, later to be finance minister from 2000 to 2011. Once in Moscow Putin's rise was spectacular. Beginning as a senior official in the property department of the presidential administration, on 26 March 1997 he was appointed a deputy head of the Administration and head of the Main Control Directorate. Responsible for the audit of state agencies, Putin created an extensive analytical office, which gathered information on misconduct by state officials in government offices and the regions. Just over a year later, on 25 May 1998, he was appointed first deputy chief of staff responsible for relations with the regions. In this post Putin understood the degree to which the regions were engaged in a power grab, leading less to federalism than to 'segmented regionalism'. Putin learnt that 'the *vertikal*, the vertical chain of government, had been destroyed and that it had to be restored'.[3] From 15 July he headed the presidential commission drafting treaties on the division of responsibilities between the centre and the regions. It was experience gained at this time that prompted Putin to make the reform of regional relations the first priority of his presidency, notably by imposing a 'power vertical' as the backbone of his 'new federalism'.

Putin's administrative skills and loyalty were noticed by Yeltsin, and on 25 July 1998 he was appointed head of the Federal Security Service, the FSB (the new name for the KGB), becoming thereby minister of the agency in which he had once worked. Putin took up the post reluctantly: 'I can't say that I was overjoyed. I didn't want to step into the same river twice.'[4] Putin insisted that he returned to head the agency 'not as a colonel [of the reserves] but as a civilian', and thus no longer considered himself a professional *silovik*.[5] Less than a year later, on 29 March, he was given the additional post of secretary to the Security Council, making him one of the most powerful men in Russia. This was the period in which Yeltsin was desperately looking for a successor, who would not only ensure continuity in policy but who would also guarantee his security and that of his family. Putin's appointment as prime minister on 9 August was accompanied by clear statements by Yeltsin that he was considered heir-apparent, and this was confirmed on 31 December, when Yeltsin unexpectedly resigned and Putin took over as acting president. Elections on 26 March 2000 confirmed Putin as president for the mandated four years, and in March 2004 he was elected to a second term.

Putin's statecraft

The essence of successful contemporary statecraft is to leave the country happier, more prosperous and at ease with its neighbours. On this measure there is no consensus whether Putin was a 'good leader'.[6] In analysing Putin's statecraft observers veer between radical extremes of analysis. Putin at one moment is endowed with almost dictatorial powers, the great demiurge managing and deciding everything to the smallest detail; and at the same time, he is considered little more than the tool of a ruling class, who would ditch him if he came to threaten their interests or a better leader came along. The tension between power and powerlessness is a real one, and Putin's statecraft has traditionally sustained itself precisely by drawing on the power of this contradiction. Putin has the remarkable ability to portray himself as everything and nothing at the same time, galley slave and great helmsman.

The polymorphous nature of Putin's leadership is striking, and this was reflected in his ability to garner broad and in some respects incompatible support.[7] 'Sixty-one percent of Putin voters in 2000 believed Russia could combine democracy and a strong state and 69 per cent believed it could experience both democracy and economic growth'.[8] Putin's approval rating throughout his first two terms rarely dipped below 70 per cent. The 'Putin project' reflected the policy preferences of the population, with just under half supporting the continuation of reforms but with a stronger state role and popular welfare, while only 10 per cent called for the continuation of reforms with a decreased role for the state, and another 11 per cent supported the swift and decisive implementation of reform. Only 22 per cent favoured a return to the Soviet system.[9]

Putin's approach to politics was characterised by a number of features.[10] Anti-revolutionism was a theme stressed from the very first days of his leadership, reflecting no doubt the trauma of the fall of Soviet power that he witnessed at first hand in East Germany. He remained consistent in upholding the principle of constitutionally-endowed legitimacy and the ordered transfer of power, even if that entailed dealing with dictators and opposing democratisation movements. In his *poslanie* to the Federal Assembly on 3 April 2001 Putin noted that 'The past decade was a stormy time for Russia. It is no exaggeration to describe that time as revolutionary'. Against that background, the early years of the new century appeared calm in comparison. Although he insisted that the country should not be afraid of change, this should be justified by the situation. People's fears he noted were based on the logical chain: revolution was followed by counter-revolution, and 'reforms are followed by counter-reforms', accompanied typically by a witch-hunt against alleged 'culprits of a revolution carried too far'. Russia's historical experience was rich in such examples. But then Putin unexpectedly concluded: 'This cycle is over. There will be no more revolutions or counter-revolutions.'[11] This was an unconscious echo of Thermidoreans throughout the ages, who seek to repudiate the excesses of the revolution while enjoying the fruits of its achievements. Russia's revolution of the 1990s, of course, was of a distinctive type: seeking not to devise a new model but to graft an already functioning type of democratic capitalist system devised in the West on to Russia. It was, moreover, carried out largely 'from above', with the elements of popular mobilisation of the late

18 *The contradictions of Putinism*

1980s soon drying up and with a minimum of violence, the events of 1991 and 1993 excepted.[12]

A second key principle of Putin's leadership, following from the first, is his emphasis on legitimism. From the very first he stressed that he would not change the constitution and would abide by its stipulations. In technical terms he did just this, and his departure from the presidency in 2008 confirmed Putin as someone who ruled according to the letter of the law. Putin also appealed to the principle of legitimism in his relations with leaders in the Commonwealth of Independent States (CIS). This led him to support what in any lexicon are authoritarian leaders, such as Islam Karimov in Uzbekistan and Alexander Lukashenko in Belarus. Of course, legitimism here was reinforced by issues of geo-strategic advantage, but the principle was also applied in cases where Russia's national interests were less clear-cut. Putin's over-emphatic support for the succession of power from Leonid Kuchma to Yanukovych in Ukraine in late 2004 ignored the fact that the final winner, Yushchenko, had forged strong economic and political ties with Russia when prime minister earlier. Putin's aversion to revolutionary changes of power reinforced his conservative approach.[13] Opposition to the expansion of NATO to Ukraine and Georgia was considered resistance to an existential threat to Russia's fundamental security interests and not an attempt to limit the sovereignty of these countries. Equally, intervention in South Ossetia and Abkhazia in August 2008 from the Russian perspective was considered a defensive reaction to the Georgian attack.

The third feature is the one mentioned above, Thermidor. If we consider Putin's attempts to consolidate the state as a type of Thermidor, then it is indeed of a peculiar 'soft' sort, if anything a counter-reform rather than a counter-revolution. Rather than explicitly repudiating the revolutionary regime of the 1990s, Putin in fact was hand-picked as that regime's chosen instrument of succession. Complementing his remedial agenda, his aim was not to undo the work of the 1990s but to give it a firmer legal and economic basis. Above all, he sought to perpetuate and consolidate the institutions of the earlier period, with the 1993 constitution at its centre. Yet there are Thermidorian elements in Putin's rule, reflected in the rejection of the competitive politics of the earlier period. Above all, Thermidor signals the end of societal predominance and the attempt to insulate the state from direct social power. The nature of Putinite state restoration is certainly open to contrasting interpretations, but there is a clear tension between a strong state, which in the contemporary world entails the development of a ramified constitutional order, and the strengthening of the power system associated with a particular elite configuration in a regime interposed between the state and society. The latter is compatible with an appeal to the constitution in the form of a *Rechtsstaat* accompanied by exaggerated regime autonomy. Zakaria terms this an 'illiberal democracy',[14] Russian idiom at first called this 'managed democracy' and for a time 'sovereign democracy', while in the Singapore of Lee Kuan Yew and his successors it is known as 'trustee' democracy. The consolidation of the 'vertical' of regime power was accompanied by the loss of independence of the Duma, the Federation Council, the judiciary, and the undermining of the federal system, all of which contributed to a weakening of the division of powers and the establishment of a new system of patronage politics. Oligarchic capitalism gave way to neo-patrimonial bureaucratic capitalism with *dirigiste* overtones.

The fourth of Putin's paradoxes is his relationship to politics. We have noted the emphasis on pragmatism and a technocratic approach to problem solving, which provoked attempts to take the 'politics' (defined here as legally constrained competitive struggle over policy and power) out of politics. A consummate politician, Putin was nevertheless anti-political. He neutralised the irresponsible utopianism of the communist left while constraining the dangerous ambitions of the nationalist right. He retained the support of a large part of the population, the respect of important sections of the international community, and the loyalty of the bulk of the elite within the country. He drove through a reform agenda designed to turn Russia into a functioning market society. He also had a social agenda that raised living standards, ensured that wages were paid on time, and began to reorient welfare services towards more targeted needs, although he failed to push through some of the social reforms advocated by the liberals. When faced with mass public protest against the monetisation of social benefits in early 2005, he acted like any good politician: he made a concession here, found a scapegoat there; and in general he emerged relatively unscathed from the whole episode.

The 'teflon' character of his leadership was particularly visible following dramatic and catastrophic episodes such as the *Kursk* disaster in August 2000, the Dubrovka theatre siege in October 2002, and the Beslan school hostage crisis in September 2004. Although he managed to resolve the Chechen conflict, the price was a radical 'Chechenisation' that transferred power to native elites, allowing Ramzan Kadyrov from 2007 to consolidate an extraordinary sultanist form of personal power that effectively negated the writ of the Russian constitution. Putin's popularity endured through careful management, political dexterity and the ability to evoke trust by resonating with the people's aspirations and self-image.[15] In international affairs Putin gained much political mileage in the wake of 9/11, and he deftly avoided the pitfalls attending the second Iraq war. However, the plan to place elements of Missile Defence in Poland and the Czech Republic, announced in January 2007, represented a major threat to his vision of international relations, and his general sense that Russia's views were being discounted provoked his robust speech asserting Russia's interests in Munich in February 2007.[16] International tensions once again threatened to derail domestic development.

Putin's leadership was goal-oriented, focusing above all on state rehabilitation, while the quality of the political process was a secondary concern. The stress on outcomes fostered a negligent attitude to the finer arts of public debate, winning popular support for policies and engaging in the cut and thrust of election campaigns. The niceties of democratic politics were not his forte. On several occasions he noted his distaste for what he considered the populist politicking that accompanies electoral campaigns. His personal distaste for public politics encouraged him to focus on set-piece staged public events, notably the annual *poslanie*, question and answer sessions with the people, and speeches at public events. The 'malaise of antipolitics', to use Ghia Nodia's expression, is prevalent across the post-communist world, and Putin certainly shares this characteristic with Yeltsin. As Nodia puts it:

> The Communist regime parodied and discredited things political, such as political parties, ideologies, institutions, and the notion of a "public good" as such. The label of "falsity" firmly stuck to the public sphere, and politics was a priori considered a "dirty business", with the values of goodness and truth sought only in the private domain.[17]

Putin's antipolitics accentuated his pragmatic bent and attempt to insulate the regime from popular control. Putin is a state builder (although undermined as I argue throughout the book by the regime character of power) and mostly not a populist. When he felt it necessary, he adopted policies that threatened to damage his popularity, such as allying himself with American power after 9/11, including allowing an American military presence in Central Asia, traditionally Russia's 'back yard'. The demarcation of the long border with China was not something designed to win popularity at home, yet it was undoubtedly in Russia's interests finally to put an end to this long-running sore that in 1969 nearly led to war between the two 'fraternal' socialist states. He was a conviction politician, which occasionally provoked less than diplomatic outbursts and threatened to isolate him from popular concerns. Like Margaret Thatcher, he began to believe in his own infallibility.

The fifth feature, following on from the above, is Putin's instrumental view of politics, which shaped a whole set of practices. Putin reshaped the institutions of representative democracy, above all creating a manageable party system and supine legislatures. His 'antipolitics' lacked an ideological basis but operated at the level of technocratic functionality. While Putin was rhetorically committed to the development of democracy, he retained an instrumental view of its operation. His rhetoric espoused the 'public good', but the definition of the public weal remained outside of the political process and lacked a substantive sense of what the 'good life' should look like. Hence, however much activity his administrations engaged in, there was a permanent sense that short-term tactical gains trumped strategic direction. Putinite practices endowed his rule with an 'emergency' character, contesting with the routine application of constitutional norms. Most modern governments share this 'fire-fighting' character, but a system that retains a permanent liminal character, neither East nor West, neither a democracy nor a fully-fledged authoritarian system, neither fully emergency (unlike Egypt and some other countries, no formal 'state of emergency' was ever declared) nor dully routine, will lack solidity and ultimately be considered transitional. Putin's regime did not hesitate to use whatever administrative measures necessary to achieve the desired outcome. Putin's plans to restore normality to Chechnya, for example, were vitiated by the means chosen to implement them. Guardianship over the electoral process here and in Russia more broadly could not but weaken the legitimacy of the political system as a whole. Putin's administration had a developmental agenda, as long as this did not compromise the power of the regime.

Putin's instrumental view of politics gave rise to a sixth feature, which has been mentioned before: para-constitutionalism and its associated para-politics. Putin's commitment to legitimism did not stop him from creating a number of institutions that, while formally not subverting the constitution, are not based on the constitution. These include the presidential plenipotentiary in the seven (now eight) federal districts, the State Council duplicating the activities of the Federation Council, and the Public Chamber taking up aspects of the work properly the preserve of the State Duma. Para-constitutional institutions are accompanied by a range of para-political procedures, notably the use of 'administrative resources' in elections, frequent changes in the legislation regulating elections, changes to the way that the Federation Council is formed, and the abolition of competitive elections for regional governors until restored in 2012. None of these actions may technically have contravened the letter of the constitution, but they all eroded the spirit of constitutionalism. However many resources were poured into 'soft power' campaigns to improve Russia's image, they damaged the country's reputation. As long as the administrative regime was not brought back into legal and popular accountability, such abuses would continue and there would remain normative obstacles to Russia's recognition in world politics.

The seventh feature is Putin's emphasis on the leading role of the state in development. In France from the late 1950s this was known as *dirigisme*. In the post-communist transitional period, the 'dictatorship of the proletariat' envisaged by Marx as the period of extra-legal class dominance of the makers of the socialist revolution, in the 1990s gave way to the dictatorship of the executive designed to push through a modernisation process that would ultimately render that dictatorship, as it would for Marx, redundant. But as with Marx, no limiting time period was established, and in any case, the 'proletariat' and the 'executive' are to a degree abstractions, and the real subject of the dictatorship in both the Soviet Union and post-communist Russia was the bureaucracy. It was Putin's achievement not only to reconstitute the state, but also to endow it with a renewed legitimacy drawn from its developmental agenda. Modernisation is complemented by the idea that Russia has to act as an effective 'competition state', locked in struggle with other powers for economic and geopolitical advantage.

The notion of *dirigisme* in political affairs as a response to intense international competition was given political form by the leading exponent of the democratic statist faction in Russian politics, Vladislav Surkov, the first deputy head of the presidential administration responsible for the management of political affairs to December 2011. In a number of interviews and articles he talked of Russia's enemies trying 'to destroy Russia and fill its enormous expanses with numerous non-viable quasi-state formations. ... The main aim of the interventionists is the destruction of Russian statehood'.[18] In his speech to *Delovaya Rossiya* on 16 May 2005 he argued that the regime's aim was 'sovereign democracy': 'I often hear that democracy is more important than sovereignty. We do not agree with that. We think that both are needed. An independent state is worth fighting for.'[19] While the state's capacity to enforce rules remains limited, and the gulf between its claims to represent the universal interest of the public good and the empirical reality of self-seeking elites at the national and regional levels mired in corruption remains stark, Surkov sought to regenerate the legitimacy of state interests. In the end the stick was bent too far, and the functionality of pluralism, competing interest groups, partisan politics and open-ended debate was undermined. Rather than strengthening the constitutional state, the prerogatives of the administrative regime were intensified. Putin's developmental strategy was wary of political westernisation, and certainly of the influence of western agencies, and this lingering insularity of the Soviet type in turn fostered a residual spirit of the Cold War at home and abroad.

The eighth feature follows from the above, namely a tutelary model of political relationships. The Putin elite embodied a colonial image of state authority. Paternalism was deeply embedded in the operating code of the Soviet system, and the tendency to keep the population in a condition of political infantilism was perpetuated. Just as colonial regimes typically act *in loco parentis* over their subject populations, so, too, the tutelary nature of the Putin regime failed to foster the spirit of citizenship and political responsibility among the Russian population. Putin's state building was reminiscent of Jacobin holistic or integrative republicanism, deeply opposed to anything that could fragment the unity of the single people, and by the same token vital republicanism, based on the lively interplay of political forces and a distinct concept of 'the political', was eroded. The perpetuation, indeed intensification, of patrimonial features of governance exposed the failure of the Putin regime to embrace a more complex model of modernisation, when changes from above are rooted in engagement from below. Ironically, the fragmentation that Putin's administration so abhorred in society re-emerged at the level of the regime. A system of bureaucratic pluralism and fragmented elite structures at the state level, each with their system of patron–client relations, indicated that Russia had failed to establish an autonomous political sphere, and instead politics was riddled with factional conflicts rooted in the socio-economic order.[20] The patrimonial party-building endeavour associated with the development of United Russia is a case in point, where the absence of political autonomy rendered the party lifeless and subordinate to the regime.

Under Yeltsin in the 1990s, *vlast'* (the word typically used in Russia to describe the power system) took on an ever-stronger tutelary aspect, claiming the right to manage not only the sphere of policy – the usual job of governments – but also the exclusive right to manage political processes as a whole. This is what distinguishes a regime from a normal government. Fearing for the stability – indeed for the very existence of the state – Putin's statecraft intensified these features. It represented a powerful shift from representational to pacifying politics, from encouraging independent civic activism to controlling and regulating it, and in the process suffocated not only political pluralism but also eroded the sources of regime renewal. This was the system known as managed democracy. Popular inclusion in the Putin period was achieved but in an archaic manner reminiscent of Soviet practices. This was not modern civic participation of an active citizenry accompanied by the pluralistic representation of divergent interests. Instead, Putin's mutuality was top-down, mobilisational, and paternalistic, and vitiated by the internally hierarchical power system. Inclusion at the economic level was even more partial, with small businesses remaining at the mercy of the bureaucracy, while big business was incorporated as a subaltern partner of the regime. The modernisation agenda from above was not accompanied by the necessary modernisation from the middle, represented by a competitive party system, an entrepreneurial and independent business culture, and a vibrant public sphere.

The Putin puzzle

Putin's supporters compare him to Thatcher, two leaders who provoke polarised assessments. They came to power at times of national crisis, and 'Both leaders responded with energy, intelligence and integrity to the challenges facing them'.[21] Their critics are rather less complimentary, arguing that rather than uniting their respective countries, both ruled through division and conflict. Putin was the subject of numerous abusive epithets, including 'autocrat', 'despot' and the like. Putin's spokesman, Dmitry Peskov, observed the partisan character of these evaluations: 'Those who wanted to understand Putin have already done so, those who don't want to never will'.[22] Putin's political identity is intensely complex and is made of numerous facets. Putin identified himself as a corporate boss, the CEO of 'Russia PLC', once even harbouring the ambition to head Gazprom. He spent a large part of his career as a *silovik*, but he was far more than that. He was undoubtedly a hard-working patriot, and what I describe as the 'Putin project' won considerable support, but was vitiated by the administrative practices that excluded the freely-expressed political expression of popular preferences in favour of the tutelary state. He has also been seen as a 'godfather', the head of what we describe below as the 'deep state'. Typical of his contradictory character, he defended the extended welfare state inherited from the Soviet Union, but at the same time his economic policy was fundamentally neo-liberal.

Hill and Gaddy identify six dimensions to his character, which together shape contemporary Russian politics.[23] His self-image is as a galley slave toiling away for the good of Russia, but overarching that is his view of himself as the chief executive of Russia Inc, but paying little attention to the shareholders until, as Hill and Gaddy put it, the 'Stakeholders Revolt' took place from 2011. Putin the *statist* believes that the country in the late Soviet period and during the 'transition' in the 1990s became prey to disintegrative tendencies, and only the state could restore a modicum of coherence and direction to the polity. Putin the *history man* complements this feature, contextualising contemporary developments in the *longue durée* of Russian development. As a boy Putin was fascinated by history, and history books remain part of his reading to this day. On several occasions Putin took an active part in debates about appropriate textbooks and the treatment of contentious moments in Russia's past, above all the evaluation of the Stalin period. Putin the *survivalist* draws on the tough family background, enduring the 900-day siege of Leningrad, and then the street-fighting years of boyhood and youth in the mean streets of the city. Putin's reputation also managed to survive the early scandals when he worked in the St Petersburg mayor's office under Sobchak.

This aspect is reinforced by Putin's status as an *outsider*, who came to Moscow in 1996 as someone not linked to metropolitan networks. As an outsider Putin had less compunction later in attacking the Muscovite establishment. Despite the assault on Khodorkovsky and the Yukos oil company, Putin remains a *free-marketeer*, the fifth facet identified by Hill and Gaddy. Although there has been a shift back to greater state ownership and interventionism, this has not entailed the repudiation of market principles. Finally, there is Putin the *case officer*, the former security service official, the element in Putin's biography that Hill and Gaddy suggest is exaggerated in many accounts. Although of fundamental importance as part of a larger picture, it is not the whole picture.

Putin's political identity was clearly stamped by his security service experience, but the degree to which it is shaped by this remains a matter of considerable debate. For some he can be reduced to these formative years of his life, while Hill and Gaddy clearly demonstrate the importance of other aspects of his political personality. Putin clearly was not averse to drawing on the 'chekist' (security service) tradition that for so long was at the heart of the Soviet system. There was a brief period during Khrushchev's 'thaw' of the 1950s when the cruelties of the secret police, renamed the KGB in 1954, were exposed, but by 1967 and the appointment of Yuri Andropov to its head the service was rehabilitated. Rather than engaging in mass repression the KGB now focused on more technocratic forms of social control, accompanied by the selective persecution of dissidents and other perceived threats. A pattern was now established of the myth of a strong state served by a strong security service, accompanied by its obverse: attacks on the security apparatus betokened the weakening of the state in its entirety. This was certainly perceived to be the case in 1991, when the KGB was denigrated and soon after broken up as the state disintegrated. From the Putinite perspective, the story of the restoration of state power is also the story of restoring the security service as the sword of the regime. Like so much of the Putinite system, this has its roots in the 1990s. With the Russian state facing internal collapse and the threat of continued disintegration, notably in the Caucasus where the first Chechen war was raging, in 1995 Yeltsin began the rehabilitation of the security service. He reshaped what had become the Federal Counter-Intelligence Service (FSK) to create the FSB, and declared the Day of the Chekist a holiday, which as Julie Fedor notes was 'an unprecedented development: this marked the first time in history that the Russian state security apparatus had its own officially sanctioned professional holiday'.[24] In his speech marking the Chekist day in December 1997 Yeltsin praised the security service as 'genuine patriots' who 'worked for an Idea'.

This stream under Putin turned into a flood. Yet it would be a mistake to see Putin as little more than an 'operative in the Kremlin'. In his brief tenure at the head of the FSB in 1998–99 Putin subjected it to a ruthless purge, and his relatively lowly rank when he had left the active service in 1991 was considered an insult to its professional pride. Above all, the *leitmotif* of his leadership style is to maintain the maximum room for manoeuvre, and thus Putin sought to avoid becoming the instrument of the secret police. He certainly raised its status and privileges, and as we shall see the *siloviki* became one of the most powerful factions in his court, yet for the most part they were balanced by other groups. Security officials permeated the state apparatus, and were given various supernumerary tasks including the battle against organised crime and restoring order in Chechnya, and the 'raiding' activity by its officials was tolerated, and it was the *siloviki* who destroyed Yukos. However, on numerous issues the security faction did not get their way, above all in macroeconomic policy, and under Medvedev there was a pushback against their power and privileges, and their relative weight in the state apparatus declined. With a weakened Putin returned to the Kremlin in 2012, Putin was less able to manage factional conflict, and this provided an opportunity for the *siloviki* to exact their revenge through a range of repressive measures.

These six elements in his personal biography are also constitutive of the state itself in the Putin period. Hill and Gaddy end their analysis with a discussion of the protests from 2011. The attempt to manage the succession spectacularly misfired and provoked sustained resistance to the practices of 'Putinism', which overflowed into personal attacks and the slogan 'Russia without Putin'. The system remains vulnerable because of its focus on the leader; and this personalisation of power means that Putin ultimately becomes responsible for everything. The 'revolt of the stakeholders' revealed a system of rule collapsing under the weight of its own contradictions. Whether Putin could muster the political courage to develop a seventh persona and lead a movement of renewal, or become engulfed by the system he had created, was the fundamental question of his third presidential term. In other words, could Putin free himself of 'Putinism' to renew his leadership, or would he be destroyed by the very system that he had created?

Gleb Pavlovsky, the leading 'political technologist' (in British parlance 'spin doctor') of classical Putinism, had his Kremlin pass withdrawn in April 2011 because of his sharp critique of the ruling party and opposition to Putin's planned return. He now argued: 'Yes, I belong to the presidential team. Putin saved the country in the 2000s. He made his choice and turned down the third term of office. He cannot take it back now.'[25] Later he warned against excessive personalisation: 'We are discussing Putin too much. Putin is our zero, our empty place, a screen on which we project our wishes, our hatred, our love'. This was the argument that had greeted Putin in his early days, as a screen on which the nation projected its aspirations. In the intervening years the Kremlin had created a centralised system in only one respect: 'it is centralised in the dissemination and dispersal of symbols, pictures and memes'. There was certainly no centralised authoritative apparatus. Instead, Putin's system today 'is the tyranny of weakness. That does not mean that it cannot perpetrate terrible things, but only out of weakness and fear'. Pavlovsky considered Putin a misanthrope, and certainly not hedonistic like the Soviet Central Committee of old. For him, Putin 'is a very complex man', and indeed, 'He has become too complex for himself and in my opinion is not coping with himself. What makes him tick, that is the main secret that he will not reveal to anyone.'[26] We thus began with a puzzle and end with a mystery.

Six pillars of power

The rush to the market in the 1990s entailed a high degree of 'institutional nihilism', and this fostered what Medvedev in 2008 called 'legal nihilism'. It also transformed Russia in a historically unprecedented short period of time into a market economy, but one with certain distinctive features. Elite cohesion and collective action was achieved not primarily through the instrument of a ruling party, the classical route for a post-revolutionary settlement, but by the development of a distinctive administrative regime that reproduced some of the practices of the old party-state, creating a hybrid regime-state that applied many of the modes of governance of the old regime. Under Putin the regime-state quickly adapted itself to the task of extracting resources from a poorly-defended entrepreneurial class in the new market economy. The regime claimed to work for the good of the state, but the development of a whole network of side deals (which are not always identified as corrupt) eroded the legitimacy of the system as a whole.[27] Nevertheless, the liberal constitutional state remains constitutive of the polity, creating space for a critique of the regime and its practices.

The Putinite system represented a substantial restructuring of politics, but there were profound continuities with the 1990s. For example, from the very beginning political parties have played only a marginal role in structuring substantive decision-making, and instead powerful leaders and their associated elites are the key actors sponsoring political mobilisation. Yeltsin relied on changing coteries of supporters, in a system of factional balancing of which Putin later became the supreme exponent. From early on Yeltsin dispensed with the mass movement that swept him to power against Gorbachev, and instead politics became an elite affair. The assault against the intransigent and obdurate parliament, then called the Congress of People's Deputies, in September to October 1993 allowed Yeltsin to modify the draft constitution to enhance the powers of the president. The referendum to adopt the constitution and parliamentary election of December 1993 was deeply flawed, with widespread reports of ballot rigging accompanied by a lack of transparency, and this set the pattern for all subsequent Russian elections. The 'regime' model of governance, defined as a system in which the power system stands outside of the democratic procedures which formally legitimates its authority, became entrenched very early on.[28]

Putin built on the regime practices established by Yeltsin, but took a more systematic approach to the management of political processes. Very soon his system became known as 'managed democracy', although for a time in the mid-2000s it was adorned by the epithet of 'sovereign democracy', a term first used by the former editor of *Nezavisimaya gazeta*, Vitaly Tretyakov.[29] Surkov, as the regime's chief ideologist, later used the term to underpin Putinite rule with some sort of philosophical grounding. Putin from the first was impatient of such attempts, understanding that naming things is a form of constraint. The central feature of his leadership style was the struggle to ensure the maximum freedom of manoeuvre. Later the regime's pedestal party, United Russia, described itself as 'liberal conservative', but even this ideological formulation was not adopted by the regime as a whole. Putin would occasionally take up some thinker associated with a political model, such as Ivan Il'in or Petr Stolypin, but resisted all attempts to formalise his rule into some sort of ideologically consistent project. Drawing on the 'liberal conservatism' of the legal philosopher Boris Chicherin, the Stolypin tradition extolled the strong state combined with liberal policies. Stolypin's draconian suppression of the peasant uprisings following the 1905 revolution was tempered by his embrace of managed parliamentarianism thereafter.

Lacking grounding in philosophy, Putin did not feel the need to cast some philosophical anchor. His turn of mind was robustly pragmatic; yet pragmatism without a basis in some conceptual framework easily degenerates into opportunism or drift. Putin was, as Olga Kryshtanovskaya argues, both of the left and the right;[30] and this entailed a constant attempt to fill his 'centrism' with content. Asked what were his 'political guideposts', Putin classified himself as a 'pragmatist with a conservative perspective', while insisting that 'conservatism does not mean stagnation. Conservatism is based on traditional values, but at the same time it has one essential element, which is a goal for development'.[31] Putinism is characterised by policy moderation accompanied by power accumulation.

On coming to power the unruly regional leaders and oligarchs were quickly tamed, and the foundations of the system that lasts to this day were laid. The Putinite system rests on six main *pillars*. The first is the creation of a managed party-representative system, accompanied by endless engineering of the electoral system to maximise benefits to the regime and the subordination of parliament. It soon came to the point that no new laws could be adopted without the agreement of the presidential administration, and the rambunctious relationship characteristic of the 1990s was soon only a distant memory. The party law of September 2001 created the normative framework for fewer but bigger parties. Regional parties were effectively banned, and soon a mass cull took place that resulted in only seven parties being allowed to stand in the December 2007 Duma election. Only four were able to get over what was now a 7 per cent representation threshold, with United Russia enjoying a constitutional majority (over two-thirds of the seats in the 450-member assembly). The other parties became known as the 'systemic opposition' – the Communist Party of the Russian Federation (CPRF), the Liberal Democratic Party of Russia (LDPR), and Just Russia (*Spravedlivaya Rossiya*), established by the regime to represent the more welfare-minded part of the electorate. United Russia became the political wing of the administrative regime, and aggregated not concerns of the citizens of Russia but those of officialdom and special interests. It offered a path for career advancement within the regime, and thus replicated many of the functions of the Communist Party of the Soviet Union (CPSU). This was a point made by Viktor Chernmoyrdin, prime minister from December 1993 to March 1998, who noted that whatever the party, it always ended up reproducing the CPSU.

Although the CPRF and other parties remain formally independent, their 'oppositional' character is mostly formal. Just Russia drew on the hallowed European social democratic tradition for ideological sustenance, becoming a member of the Socialist International and advancing a coherent programme of systematic change. It retained the potential to defect from Putinite constraints and splitting the ruling elites by proposing greater autonomy for political life, and hence was 'managed' with particular attention. Putinite governance rests on various degrees of co-optation of all active social forces into the toils of the regime. This is not classic incorporation of the fascist type, and neither is it the 'transmission belt' politics of the Leninist sort. Instead, formal independence is maintained and no pacts are signed, but the acceptable limits are signalled by hints and signs, with the threat of coercion always held in reserve. This is government by semiotics, with a distinctive vocabulary of power which is seldom verbalised but which is understood by all key players. Those who step beyond the bounds (like Khodorkovsky) are punished, and thus the lesson is driven home to all. A system of rewards for loyalty ensured that classic Putinism could operate with the minimum of coercion to sustain a new type of political 'normality' to which all political actors, including the systemic parties, adapted. The country's failure to move from factions to parties, from informal understandings to formal institutions, means that the framework remains fluid and contingent, and practices overshadow procedures. In other words, the Russian political system is characterised by the law of informal rules, rather than the rule of law.

The 'systemic' parties exercised the self-restraint that is characteristic of the Putinite operative code, although of course exercising in full the right to bombast and bluster characteristic of parliamentary parties. The CPRF's residual leftism criticised the government's social and economic policies; but its nationalism encouraged an even harsher approach to the West, while endorsing moves to foster post-Soviet integration. The LDPR was little more than the creation of its charismatic leader Vladimir Zhirinovsky, pursuing a range of populist policies appealing to the marginalised and the poor in Russia's small towns, while voting loyally on most matters with the regime.

However, as the 2011–12 electoral cycle approach Just Russia showed signs of moving away from the Putinite consensus, demanding political reform and free elections. The regime had always been afraid that Just Russia could act as the focus for intra-systemic opposition. When the party registered electoral success in Stavropol region in 2007, it was subject to vicious attack and the Just Russia mayor of Stavropol city was forced into exile. The State Council meeting of 22 January 2010 was devoted to political reform, held in the wake of the scandalous 11 October 2009 regional elections where administrative manipulation, notably in the Moscow Duma ballot, had gone into over-drive. Sergei Mironov, chair of the Federation Council and leader of Just Russia, lamented the quality of political debate in Russia, which in his view was reminiscent of Soviet times. He said:

> To what extent does political life have to be suppressed and all bureaucrats turned into "yes" men, so that they can report total unanimity after 20 years of market reforms, albeit very controversial ones? And all this is happening in Moscow, a multimillion city with a huge social divide. Here we are again: total unanimity between the party and the people (a reference to the Soviet slogan).[32]

Mironov was a long-standing colleague of Putin's dating back to his work in the St Petersburg mayor's office; yet the system demanded his punishment for even an intimation of disloyalty. As we shall discuss below, in May 2011 Mironov was recalled from parliament by the St Petersburg legislative assembly, and stripped of his post as head of the Federation Council (in status the third in rank after the president and prime minister). He ceded the party leadership to Nikolai Levichev, although Mironov remained head of the parliamentary caucus. Just Russia's manifesto for the December 2011 parliamentary election demanded the direct election of governors, mayors and senators, the return of the 'against all' option, and simplified procedures for registering political parties. In short, the party called for a profound overhaul of the political system.

The failure of the liberal parties to enter parliament in December 2003 (amid suspicions that Yabloko's 5.7 per cent had been reduced to 4.3 per cent by official fiat) shifted the centre of political gravity to the conservative and reactionary end of the spectrum. Medvedev's attempts to revive a liberal party in 2011, in the form of Right Cause (the rump of the old Union of Right Forces, SPS) ended up, as we shall see, in a débâcle. The State Council meeting heard a whole raft of proposals for party and electoral reform, including reducing the minimum party membership from 50,000, removing the need to collect signatures to be registered to run in elections, while Levichev proposed transparent ballot boxes and video surveillance. All these measures were introduced following the mass protests following the 2011 election.

The second pillar was the careful management of social organisations. As noted, this was not state corporatism of the classical type, in which social organisations (such as trade unions) are brought into the governing system through the appointment of leaders sympathetic to the regime and their membership cajoled or bludgeoned into line. Instead, the Putinite system rested on a series of informal agreements, establishing expectations and the bounds of acceptable behaviour. The classic instance of this 'semiotic' type was the 'social contract' outlined between business and the state at a meeting on 28 July 2000: business was to keep out of politics in return for which there would be an effective moratorium on investigations into the 'black privatisations' of the 1990s. Business leaders could get on and make money as long as they accepted the new rules of the game. Khodorkovsky's defection from this framework unleashed the full power of the regime against him. At the same time, Putin encouraged the development of peak organisations to represent business: the Russian Union of Industrialists and Entrepreneurs (RUIE), formerly a lobby for the 'red directors', became the platform for big business; 'Delovaya Rossiya' ('Business Russia') represented medium and large 'neo-oligarchic' capital; while OPORA Rossii spoke for small and medium businesses. A 'consultative regime', to use Alexei Zudin's term, was created based on a system of collective representation.[33]

Third, following on from the previous point, Putinite political economy was based less on the extension of state ownership in the economy as on constraining business behaviour to align with regime objectives. The exile of the most political of the oligarchs, such as Boris Berezovsky, was greeted by many as an opportunity to reverse the rigged privatisations of the 1990s and to allow a real market to emerge. The outright expropriation of Yukos was the exception in the new model of state–business relations. The proportion of businesses in state hands did creep up to encompass half of the economy by 2011, but mass nationalisation was not on the agenda. Instead, a type of 'deprivatisation' operated that allowed the regime to pursue its goals through informal arrangements. In Putin's second term a number of state corporations were created, but they largely encompassed companies that were already in state hands. Putinite *dirigisme* sought to use the instruments of the market to achieve regime goals largely through market mechanisms. There was no return to planning of the French or South Korean sort, let alone of the Soviet type, although strategic planning was a constant refrain of Putin's statecraft. Under Medvedev there was an attempt to push back against even this limited sort of *dirigisme*, above all through clipping the wings of the state corporations. Putin's strategy of placing state officials on the boards of state companies was reversed by Medvedev in March 2011, giving ministers until 1 July to resign and others until 1 October to resign as directors. The 'clerks' were to be replaced by 'professionals who command respect'. By contrast, in preparation for his return Putin commissioned an extensive review of policy options and scenarios, which came out as *Strategy 2020* in March 2012.[34]

Fourth, Putin's first presidency is associated with a rollback of the powers of the regional authorities. Federal districts were created to ensure that state agencies were freed from gubernatorial tutelage, all bilateral treaties were allowed to lapse and no new ones were signed (with the exception of Tatarstan in 2006), and budgetary flows were concentrated in the Kremlin. This was designed to reverse the trend towards segmented regionalism, but failed to find an adequate new balanced form of federalism. Many of Putin's actions had been prefigured in the Yeltsin era, and the policy did not represent a simple attack on the powers of the regions but sought to find a new balance that would undermine separatism while creating a new regionalism.[35] In effect, Putin sought to forge a new 'federal contract' that was far from simply anti-region in content but tried to find a new balance between centralism and constitutional devolution. There was relatively little resistance since the new model of state-building reflected in part the preferences of regional elites.[36] In practice, the goal was pursued in the typically heavy-handed manner of the period, including the abolition of gubernatorial elections in December 2004 and the parachuting in of new leaders. Putin brought the governors into the new consensus, but some of the old guard (notably mayor Luzhkov of Moscow) defected at the earliest opportunity. From 2010 Luzhkov called for the restoration of elected governors, and more autonomy in general for the institutions of the constitutional state. The new regionalism reintegrated the national market and homogenised political and legal space, but it lacked the genuine constitutional vertical separation of powers that is the essence of federalism.

Fifth, from the first Putin paid considerable attention to ensuring that civil society would not be able to feed opposition to the regime. This activity was managed by the deputy head of the presidential administration responsible for political and social matters, Surkov. He was a genius at ensuring that NGOs, human rights organisations and social movements understood the limits of their freedom, without typically engaging in outright repression. In 2001 the regime organised a Civic Forum, attended by the main leaders of civic associations and human rights organisations, in an early attempt at shaping a co-operative relationship between the state and society. No new deal emerged from the meeting, but it signalled that the NGO sector would not be easily co-opted into the new order. Following the Orange Revolution in Ukraine in late 2004, the regulatory framework for NGOs was drastically intensified. Few were closed as a result, but their freedom of manoeuvre was greatly limited. The Yukos affair warned business not to support political parties without the regime's permission; and as the perceived threat from 'colour' revolutions pervaded the regime's consciousness, this proscription was applied to NGOs. The administration, moreover, created social movements of its own, notably the Nashi youth organisation. This was the crudest form of a 'war of manoeuvre', ensuring that the streets and squares remained under regime control, accompanied by the ability to mobilise a body of 'shock troops' against the enemy of the day. These ranged from the Estonian embassy after the moving of the Soviet war memorial, the Bronze Soldier, from the centre to the nearby Tallinn Military Cemetery in April 2007, to the harassment of British and American ambassadors at various points. Following Putin's return NGOs came under renewed attack, with the adoption of a law in November 2012 forcing those receiving funding from the West to register as 'foreign agents' (see below).

Finally, the Putin system was based on dominance over the mass media, above all television. The great majority of the Russian population rely on television for information about public affairs, although the urban middle class increasingly turns to the internet. Within weeks of his inauguration in May 2000, Putin had forced Vladimir Gusinsky, the owner of the NTV station, into exile, and the channel came under the control of the increasingly ramified media arm of Gazprom. Its political coverage was immediately tamed. Berezovsky was forced to give up his stake in the main television channel, ORT (later renamed simply Channel 1), and it soon became effectively the propaganda arm of the regime. The written press remained largely free, as did the internet until Putin's return in 2012, but this was balanced by the careful scripting of television news. Over 80 per cent of local TV and radio stations, as well as the print press, are controlled by the state, with some roubles (R)58bn spent on subsidies for the state media in 2011. Medvedev's proposal in mid-2011 to end this budgetary drain to promote greater openness aroused mixed feelings, especially in the regions where much of the media is subordinated to the regional authorities.[37] This is not to say that critical programmes disappeared entirely, but as always in the Putin system, the limits were not spelled out but they were known. In case anyone forgot, Surkov was always ready to remind them. When he moved out of the Kremlin in December 2011 to work in the government, the ideological work of the regime moved into the hands of Vyacheslav Volodin, who employed less subtle means to get the regime's message across.

Modalities of power

The operation of these pillars was far from uncontested, and indeed this was one of their central characteristics. Khodorkovsky called the whole complex of control mechanisms the *sistema*, a permanently flexible but always constraining system.[38] This is what I call in this book the 'administrative regime', and which in popular parlance is termed *vlast'*, the power system isolated and alienated from the people (*narod*), thus perpetuating in new forms a long historical tradition of a gulf between the state and society. Khodorkovsky talked about the interlocking networks of Russia's judicial and law enforcement networks:

You don't know a thing about the System until you find yourself in its claws. The System is in essence, a single enterprise, whose business is legalised violence. The enterprise is enormous, with a huge number of internal conflicts and clashing interests.[39]

The six pillars were buttressed by a number of *modalities*, a complex of practices that systematically undermined the autonomous operation of the constitutional state while endowing the regime with the utmost freedom of action. However, as Khodorkovsky observed and a point which I shall examine in the next chapter, the power system was torn by competing 'factional' concerns. Above all, there was always the potential for a counter-movement against the arbitrariness of the administrative regime based on the constitutional state. This could draw on elite divisions, defence of the legal autonomy of civil society and social mobilisation from below. Medvedev's rule was a premonition of this potential, which grew into a stream in the protest movement in 2011–12, but has yet to become a flood powerful enough to sweep away the abuses perpetrated by the administrative regime.

The fundamental modality was the strange interface between the regime and state. In an established liberal democracy a government is elected to rule, but there are numerous *ex ante* and *post facto* constraints. When these limits are inoperative or marginalised, then a government becomes a regime. In contemporary Russia this already occurred under Yeltsin, when the constitutional constraints were abused with impunity, as demonstrated in the way that the first Chechen war was launched in December 1994 and then pursued with a savagery that belied the fact that this was after all a conflict within a single state and not against some external enemy. It was seen once again in the presidential re-election campaign in 1996, when the spending limits were massively exceeded and media impartiality abused; and in general Yeltsin's supporters, who notably included the leading 'democrats' of the period, acted as if they were somehow exempted from the rules that they themselves had formulated. This was an early manifestation of the ideology of 'exceptionality' and *de facto* emergency powers that was taken to its logical conclusion under Putin. The regime claimed to be the guarantor of certain values and concerns that transcended the mere letter of the constitution; although these were pursued for the ostensible purpose of preserving the constitutional order. There was no official declaration of a state of emergency, but exceptionality operates as a milder version in which a regime does not repudiate a constitution but its practices run counter to the spirit of constitutionalism.

The logic of exceptionality generates endless contradictions and paradoxes. Nowhere were these sharper than in the realm of law. Putin came to power declaring the 'dictatorship of law', and in his early years he supported judicial reform and investment in the legal infrastructure, notably modernising courthouses, raising the wages of judges to render them less susceptible to bribes, and sponsoring laws to provide the normative basis for a capitalist democracy. Yet all of this came to be vitiated by the instrumental use of the courts in matters of political importance of the regime, as in the political trials associated with the Yukos affair. It would be easy to come to the conclusion that Putin was simply throwing chaff to confuse those opposed to what could be seen to be his 'real' aim – to create a one-man authoritarian regime. There is certainly evidence to support such a view, especially since so often Putin acted directly contrary to his avowed declarations (the gulf between the project and practices). Putin thereby threw his opponents off guard, and by sowing confusion was able to pursue what may well have been intended all along. Ultimately, this is too simplistic a view since Putin had various opportunities to consolidate his personal power but did not take them, as at the end of the two terms allowed him by the constitution. Instead of holding an 'extension plebiscite', which he would undoubtedly have won, he engaged in the complex mechanism of 'operation successor', which saw the most liberal of all possible contenders, Medvedev, come to power.

The necessary counterpart of exceptionality was depoliticisation. The logic of this is the standard technocratic argument that the administrators know best. It does not take much to convince the administrative elite that it would be irresponsible for them to allow various desirable public goods, such as political stability, national integrity and a balanced budget, to be threatened by the unpredictability of elections and a genuinely open political process. Equally, if something was right, then it was necessarily moral to fight for its achievements by all possible means. Necessity and rightness are both supra-political categories, generated by social realities as interpreted by technocratic rationality and the charismatic leader. This gave rise to the tutelary regime, in which citizens could not be trusted to make independent choices, and in which an ideology of *efficacy* substituted for classical modes of democratic *legitimacy*. Inevitably, social populism fills the gap created by depoliticisation. This provided justification for the regime to create an electoral bureaucracy that stood outside of the electoral process; and a policy-making process that effectively by-passed parliament and the representative system as a whole. In classical Leninist mode, the end justified the means; but as we know, in the end the Leninist system collapsed precisely because of the contradictions generated by such practices. Political institutions are gutted of meaning, elections become mere formal moments in the plebiscitary approval of the regime, public discourse is debased, and popular alienation ensues. Real power is concentrated in the hands of the small elite, while all the rest are simulacra.

Nevertheless, to leave things there would be reductionist. At some deep level Putin was not dissimulating in his protestations of loyalty to the constitution, and this sustained a semblance of balance in the dual state. Not only did he step down as stipulated at the end of his two terms in 2008 and his return in 2012 was validated, albeit crudely, by a hard-fought democratic process, but however much he developed administrative practices, the legitimacy of the power system remained deeply grounded in constitutional provisions. In formal terms Putin's exceptionality was not typically of the crude sort practiced by Yeltsin or by regimes elsewhere, such as Hosni Mubarak's in Egypt until his overthrow in February 2011 (where a state of emergency had been in almost continuous operation since 1967), but a more subtle form justified both by the logic of necessity and also by a certain logic of rightness. As long as the exceptionality of the regime could be justified by these two logics, then the Putin project was able to generate a degree of genuine popular support, however much it may have cut corners when it came to managing public affairs.

However, the bounds of toleration radically narrowed on the announcement of Putin's return in September 2011. At that point the interests of the Putinite power system appeared to take precedence over national development. Medvedev's tilt towards strengthening the constitutional state, modernisation, liberalism and international cooperation was sharply reversed. As far as Putin was concerned, nothing had changed and the logics of necessity and rightness still operated. For outsiders, it was the regime's defence of its privileges that now threatened national interests. Not only the opposition but the more future-oriented parts of society saw a growing gap between the constitutional state and the regime. The 'strange interface' between the two that Putin had been so brilliant at managing was now coming apart, allowing the regime to be identified as little more than a group of self-serving officials and their allies, headed by an increasingly embattled Putin clinging to power at all costs.

This generated an extraordinary 'war of legitimacies'. Putin insisted that his model of statecraft remained both necessary and right, and not just for regime preservation but also for the state in its entirety. His opponents insisted that not only the regime but the whole system had lost its legitimacy. If the constitutional state had not been able to constrain the arbitrariness of the regime for so long, if judges had not condemned the abuses of the electoral system and the naked manipulation of results, then what sort of a constitutional state was this. In other words, a dangerous elision had taken place on both sides. The Medvedev interregnum suggested a gradual diminution in the prerogatives of the regime to allow a strengthening of the constitutional state. Putin's return put an end not only to this gradualist perspective, but intensified the regime-like features of the power system. Putin's return, moreover, was accompanied by the failure of traditional Putinite mechanisms of political management, generating a series of political mistakes – defined here as actions that rather than bolstering the regime's and the leadership's goals, only served to undermine them. On the other side, disappointment with Medvedev's half-heartedness radicalised the system's opponents, with some increasingly ready now not only to attack the regime but also to bring down the system as a whole. This also was a categorical mistake, confusing regime and state, and serving only to allow the regime to claim that ultimately it was

36 The contradictions of Putinism

indeed the main defender of the interests of the constitutional state. Thus an administrative system that for so long had derived its legitimacy from a constitutional state while systematically undermining the functionality of formal institutions, could with some justification be portrayed as the defender of constitutionalism and the rule of law.

Notes

1 Peter Lavelle, 'Introduction', in Jon Hellevig and Alexandre Latsa (eds), *Putin's New Russia* (Washington, DC, Kontinent USA, 2012), p. 2.
2 Richard Sakwa, *Putin: Russia's Choice*, 2nd edn (London & New York, Routledge, 2008).
3 Vladimir Putin, *First Person: An Astonishingly Frank Self-Portrait by Russia's President Vladimir Putin*, with Nataliya Gevorkyan, Natalya Timakova, and Andrei Kolesnikov, translated by Catherine A. Fitzpatrick (London, Hutchinson, 2000), p. 129.
4 Putin, *First Person*, p. 130.
5 Putin, *First Person*, p. 133.
6 Richard Sakwa, 'Leadership, Governance and Statecraft in Russia', in Ludger Helms (ed.), *Poor Leadership and Bad Governance: Reassessing Presidents and Prime Ministers in North America, Europe and Japan* (Cheltenham, Edward Elgar, 2012), pp. 149–72.
7 For a good overview, see Allen C. Lynch, *Vladimir Putin and Russian Statecraft* (Washington, DC, Potomac Books, 2011); see also Angus Roxburgh, *The Strongman: Vladimir Putin and the Struggle for Russia* (London, I. B. Tauris, 2011).
8 Timothy J. Colton and Michael McFaul, *Popular Choice and Managed Democracy: The Russian Elections of 1999 and 2000* (Washington, DC, Brookings Institution Press, 2003), pp. 222–23.
9 Levada Centre poll, December 2005; http://www.levada.ru/press/2005122901.html.
10 This section draws from Richard Sakwa, 'Regime Change from Yeltsin to Putin: Normality, Normalcy or Normalisation?', in Cameron Ross (ed.), *Russian Politics under Putin* (Manchester, Manchester University Press, 2004), pp. 17–38.
11 RIA Novosti, 4 April 2001; http://en.rian.ru/rian/poslanie.cfm
12 Gordon M. Hahn, *Russia's Revolution from Above, 1985–2000: Reform, Transition, and Revolution in the Fall of the Soviet Communist Regime* (New Brunswick, NJ, Transaction Publishers, 2002); see also Michael McFaul, *Russia's Unfinished Revolution: Political Change from Gorbachev to Putin* (Ithaca and London, Cornell University Press, 2001).
13 As Putin put it, 'Of course, we should pay attention to, support and help democracies but, if we embark on the road of permanent revolutions, nothing good will come from this for these countries, and for these peoples. We will plunge all the post-Soviet space into a series of never-ending conflicts, which will have extremely serious consequences.', Vladimir Putin, 'This Year Was Not an Easy One', *International Affairs* (Moscow), Vol. 51, No. 1, January 2005, p. 2.
14 Fareed Zakaria, 'The Rise of Illiberal Democracy', *Foreign Affairs*, Vol. 76, No. 6 (November/December 1997), pp. 22–43; see also his *The Future of Freedom* (New York, W. W. Norton, 2003).
15 E. B. Shestopal, *Obrazy vlasti v post-sovetskoi Rossii* (Moscow, Aleteia, 2004), esp. Chapter 15.
16 http://president.kremlin.ru/text/appears/2007/02/118109.shtml.
17 Ghia Nodia, 'Putting the State Back Together in Post-Soviet Georgia', in Mark R. Beissinger and Crawford Young (eds), *Beyond State Crisis? Postcolonial Africa and*

Post-Soviet Eurasia in Comparative Perspective (Washington, DC, Woodrow Wilson Center Press, 2002), p. 435.
18 Vladislav Surkov, 'Putin ukreplyaet gosudarstvo, a ne sebya', interviewed by Elena Ovcharenko, *Komsomol'skaya Pravda*, 29 September 2004, p. 4.
19 Comments delivered to a closed meeting of the general council of the journal *Delovaya Rossiya* on 16 May 2005, publicized by Radio Liberty on 11 July 2005.
20 A feature identified already in the mid-1990s by Thomas Graham, 'Novyi rossiiskii rezhim', *Nezavisimaya gazeta*, 23 November 1995.
21 Martin Sieff, 'What Putin and Thatcher Have in Common', *Moscow Times*, 22 April 2013.
22 Anna Arutunyan, 'Will the Real Vladimir Putin Please Stand Up?', *Moscow News*, 10 May 2012.
23 Fiona Hill and Clifford Gaddy, *Mr. Putin: Operative in the Kremlin* (Washington, DC, Brookings Institution Press, 2013).
24 Julie Fedor, *Russia and the Cult of State Security: The Chekist Tradition, from Lenin to Putin* (London, Routledge, 2011), p. 124.
25 Yulia Taratuta, 'Nedeistvitelen', *Vedomosti*, 27 April 2011, p. 2.
26 Gleb Pavlovskii, 'Bol'she vsego Putin, po-moemu, opasaetsya stat' lishnim', *Novaya gazeta*, No. 121, 24 October 2012, pp. 12–15.
27 For a comparative analysis, see Dan Slater, *Ordering Power: Contentious Politics and Authoritarian Leviathans in Southeast Asia* (Cambridge, Cambridge University Press, 2010), pp. 10–11.
28 Richard Sakwa, 'The Regime System in Russia', *Contemporary Politics*, Vol. 3, No. 1, 1997, pp. 7–25.
29 Vitaly Tret'yakov, 'Suverennaya demokratiya', *Rossiiskaya gazeta*, 28 April 2005, p. 1.
30 Ol'ga Kryshtanovskaya, *Anatomiya rossiiskoi elity* (Moscow, Zakharov, 2005).
31 'Interview to Channel One and Associated Press News Agency', 4 September 2013, http://eng.kremlin.ru/news/5935.
32 BBC Monitoring, 'Russian President Speech at State Council Comes Under Fire', Rossiya 24, 22 January 2010; in *Johnson's Russia List* (henceforth *JRL*), 16/10, 2010.
33 A. Yu. Zudin, 'Rezhim V. Putina: Kontury novoi politicheskoi sistemy', *Obshchestvennye nauki i sovremennost'*, No. 2, 2003, pp. 67–83; see also ibid., 'Oligarchy as a Political Problem of Russian Postcommunism', *Russian Social Science Review*, Vol. 41, No. 6, November–December 2000, pp. 4–33; ibid., 'Neokorporativizm v Rossii', *Pro et Contra*, Vol. 6, No. 4, 2001, pp. 171–98.
34 Julian Cooper, *Reviewing Russian Strategic Planning: The Emergence of Strategy 2020* (Rome, NATO Defense College, 2012); Andrew Monaghan, 'Putin's Russia: Shaping a "Grand Strategy"?', *International Affairs*, Vol. 89, No. 5, 2013, pp. 1221–36.
35 Katherine E. Graney, *Of Khans and Kremlins: Tatarstan and the Future of Ethno-Federalism in Russia* (Lanham, Lexington Books, 2009).
36 J. Paul Goode, *The Decline of Regionalism in Putin's Russia: Boundary Issues* (London, Routledge, 2011).
37 Yan Gordeev, 'Kazennym SMI vse-taki pomogut vyzhit' *Nezavisimaya gazeta*, 21 July 2011, p. 1.
38 Note that there are equivalent terms applied in other countries. For example, in Iran there is the mix of democracy and ecclesiastical control known in Persian as the *nezam*, or 'System'. For how the 'system' in Iran works, see Michael Axworthy, *Revolutionary Iran: A History of the Islamic Republic* (London, Allen Lane, 2013).
39 Mikhail Khodorkovskii, 'Uzakonennoe nasilie', *Nezavisimaya gazeta*, 3 March 2010, p. 5. For a detailed study of how *sistema* works from a social-anthropological perspective, see Alena V. Ledeneva, *Can Russia Modernise? Sistema, Power Networks and Informal Governance* (Cambridge, Cambridge University Press, 2013).

3 Crisis of modernisation

Russia suffers from a political stalemate, and this is part of a broader developmental crisis. Russia appears to suffer from blocked modernisation, although its case is not as severe as that in evidence in North Africa and the Middle East up to the 'Arab Spring' of 2011. There is a stalemate between rent-seeking elites and profit-seeking groups. Few of the modernisation tasks facing Putin when he came to power in 2000 have been resolved. Indeed, it could be argued that the challenges facing the country after Stalin's death in 1953 still remain on the agenda. These include the country's assimilation into the international system and the international economy, the integration of the various national communities, the establishment of a set of authoritative and universal political institutions of the polity, the creation of an equal and free citizenry defended by an impartial and independent judiciary, the thriving of modern representative, participatory and legislative institutions, the development of a diverse and competitive modern economy, an inclusive and sustainable welfare state, and the attainment of standards of living matching those in advanced societies. Instead, certain patterns have become established, including the marginalisation of the autonomous participation of society in the management of public affairs, a continuing dependence on energy rents, lack of diversity and dynamism in the economy, above all in the small and medium sector, and the repeated failure to integrate into the international community as 'one of us'. In domestic affairs a 'regime' type entity (typically known as '*vlast*'') remains external to the operation of the constitutional order, while internationally Russia remains not so much a 'constitutive other' but something alien and indigestible.

Stalemate and development

The idea of schismogenesis (creation of division) was devised by the anthropologist Gregory Bateson in the 1930s to describe a condition where a society lives in a state of permanent conflict between various factions derived from the decomposition of an earlier order. The fragments are constituted by opposition to the others, entailing a constant struggle for position and power, but none is able to gain a hegemonic status. Such a condition can endure for a

Crisis of modernisation 39

prolonged and indefinite period.[1] Although the term was devised during fieldwork in Papua New Guinea, it powerfully describes the current state of Russian politics. An old order has decayed, spawning numerous contesting ideological stances, but none of the successor groupings can predominate. Groups based on material interest have inserted themselves into the very highest reaches of power, undermining regulatory and competitive transparency, effectively merging with the administrative regime. In conditions of modernity the impasse is typically resolved at the level of the state, imposing a single vision on the society and devising a method for the organised rotation of competing policy prescriptions.

In the Russian case, the polity itself was subject to factionalisation. The operative part, what we call administrative regime, was the site of permanent factional conflict, arbitrated by the supreme leader, Putin, who drew on the constitutional state to legitimise his arbitrating functions but was unable to transcend the logic of factional conflict by putting himself at the head of the constitutional state. In political terms, Putin devoted much effort to prevent the dual state becoming a condition of dual power, in which defectors from the regime ally with outsiders to build up alternative power structures. This would create a new dynamic in which the regime is challenged by a constituted opposition, rather than the various fragments that today make up the protest movement. The 2011–12 protests did have the effect of challenging Putin's role as supreme arbiter, eroding his support in the country and within the elite. The response was unequivocal. The regime sought to co-opt all the active elements in society that were willing to cooperate, suppressed its most resolute opponents, and convinced the rest to acquiesce through a range of populist and social protection measures (see Chapter 8). The state as such was unable to act as the focus of political and social integration.[2]

In economic terms an analogous condition holds, with the potential defectors subject to 'raiding' attack. The paradigmatic case was Khodorkovsky and Yukos, but all non-insider companies were vulnerable. For example, with Luzhkov's fall in September 2010 (described later in this book) the Bank of Moscow, which he had created but that had in due course become a successful national bank, was swiftly dismembered and its head, Andrei Borodin, exiled to London. There is an economic equivalent to the administrative regime, what can be called the economic regime. Oligarchic capitalism was crushed by elements of state capitalism. According to Shlapentokh and Arutunyan, the post-Soviet combination of private property and a market economy spawned feudal elements in society, preventing the creation of a democratic polity. Instead, a segmented social order emerged combining authoritarian, feudal and liberal forms of social organisation.[3] The destruction of independent oligarchs like Berezovsky, Gusinsky and Khodorkovsky allowed a number of 'state oligarchs', those who coordinated their actions with the Kremlin, to consolidate their positions. In other words, politicised non-economic forms of market relations co-exist with the logic of the free market. No society is

40 *Crisis of modernisation*

devoid of these, but as with the dual state, these non-market ties and relationships in the Putin era became systemic.

At the heart of the economic regime were a number of inside players in one way or another personally associated with Putin. They include Arkady Rotenberg, Putin's former judo partner and friend since childhood in St Petersburg, now a pipeline and construction billionaire, and Gennady Timchenko, the main owner of Gunvor, an oil trading company that rose to become the world's fourth biggest, in part by swallowing Yukos assets. They were part of Putin's inner circle of long-time associates, meeting every fortnight for a late evening game of ice hockey. As one perceptive report noted:

> Such social events link the state with some of the country's most powerful businessmen. For the president, managing such a situation is critical. Like a seventeenth-century tsar, Mr Putin needs to maintain a rough balance among various business clans, preventing them from fighting each other and posing a threat to his own ultimate authority. From this perspective, Putin's return to the presidency was in part an attempt to ensure infighting among the clans did not break out into open warfare and destabilise the country.[4]

The combination of a political and economic regime stymied both the development of the spirit of constitutionalism and distorted patterns of economic development. It also entailed high costs in terms of corruption, and made infrastructural development spectacularly expensive. The modernisation agenda advanced by Medvedev was an attempt to break out of this developmental impasse, and represented recognition of the fundamental challenges facing the country. This discussion took place at two levels: the very specific one of how to deal with the corruption spawned by the intermingling of the administrative and economic regimes; and the more general one about the sort of 'modernisation', and thus reforms, appropriate for a country such as Russia, with a long tradition of extended welfarism inherited from the Soviet Union and also with claims to some sort of 'economic sovereignty', to avoid becoming (as the neo-Soviets and traditionalists put it), a 'raw materials appendage' of the West or even worse, China.

The debate over the appropriate model of 'modernisation' reflects the lack of consensus on the form that Russia's redevelopment should take. For some the emphasis should be on technological development and competitiveness, with the focus on narrowly economic issues. There was an alternative school of thought which suggested that any top-down programme will be doomed to failure, just like so many of Russia's previous attempts at modernisation. For them, only the release of initiative from below will allow Russia to join the ranks of the dynamic societies with which it is associated as an 'emerging market', notably the other BRICS countries of Brazil, India, China and South Africa. For that, the administrative and economic regimes would have to be destroyed. In other words, the key to economic development lay in political change.

What sort of modernisation?

The leaders of the tandem advanced clearly distinct models of modernisation. Putin's was based on classical ideas of developmental modernisation. In the 2000s, and in particular following the expropriation of the Yukos oil company in 2003–4, President Vladimir Putin adopted elements of the *dirigiste* developmental state model – an authoritarian political regime, an active industrial policy, and elements of protectionism – whose features were so well-described by the political development school of the late 1960s.[5] The contradictions of applying a retrogressive developmental model to achieve advanced modernisation soon became apparent through relatively low underlying growth rates, if energy rents are stripped out, lack of advanced innovation and competitiveness, and social pathologies like corruption and raiding. By contrast his successor from 2008, Medvedev, adopted a modernisation programme (which in many ways is no more than a synonym for 'reform') that sought to build on the developmental achievements of the past, and thus his model focused more on competitiveness, innovation and political pluralism than his predecessor, and can thus be dubbed liberal modernisation. The first is a developmental model, whereas the second adopts a distinctive redevelopmental approach, based on more complex modes of state–society relations in what continues to be a transitional process.

Both models reflect the extraordinarily 'uneven and combined' nature of Russian development. The concept lies at the heart of Trotsky's analysis at the beginning of the twentieth century of the potential for revolution in Tsarist Russia, although he drew on a long tradition of theorising that rejected unilinear models of development based on a country going through necessary 'stages'. For exponents of this school, a country developed in interaction with more advanced economies, adopting elements and rejecting others, but allowing certain stages to be 'skipped'; but with the other countries also able to constrain development, what a whole range of thinkers at the time, notably J. H. Hobson and Rudolf Hilferding, and later Lenin, called 'imperialism'. Contemporary Russia is very much a syncretic economic order comparable to the late Tsarist period, with Moscow and some other cities firmly embedded in the world of globalisation, while rural areas and the 'mono-towns' (where life revolves around a single Soviet-area enterprise) are still firmly locked in Soviet mentalities and patterns of dependency. Deindustrialisation and capital flight are just two facets of this hybrid order, accompanied by strongly articulated core–periphery relations both within Russia and between Russia and the rest of the world. As we shall see later, this has given rise to the notion of many Russias, none of which is able to achieve hegemony over the others – another factor blocking 'modernisation' and exacerbating the political stalemate.

The Russian transformation has been accompanied by the sharp exacerbation in income inequalities while intensifying regional and developmental inequalities. Islands of advanced modernisation, notably in the energy, metallurgical and service sectors, coexist with depressed and technologically backward areas. This intense unevenness, with different parts of the country coexisting at fundamentally different levels of development, means that no single developmental strategy can encompass the diversity. What appears progressive in one area can be a step backwards in another. In other words, uneven and combined development means that developmental strategies also have to be combined. While liberal theory suggests that the state cannot be both a referee and a player, it is precisely this dual role that characterises *dirigiste* modernisation efforts from post-war Japan to South Korea and China today. It is unevenness that tempts the state to assume the developmental burden, but 'combination' means that for a large part of the economy this would be a regressive step. The international factor, notably provoked by military pressure and interactions with more advanced interlocutors, moreover, breaks open conceptualisations of modernisation as 'endogenous and unilinear'.[6] In the Russian context state management can play an important developmental role, but only in certain sectors. Classical economic theory, moreover, would suggest that this has to be done within the framework of a regulatory regime to which it is itself subject. Otherwise, traditional patterns of arbitrariness are reproduced, and modernisation gives way to stagnation. In other words, modernisation is as much a political project as it is an economic one.

At a certain point the paths divide and a decision has to be taken about what is the subject of the modernising process: the state or business. In South Korea and elsewhere this moment was called the transition to democracy, when the state withdrew to permit the freer operation of market *forces*, and allowed itself to be buffeted not only by these forces but also placed at the mercy of the fickleness of the electoral process and international markets. China is approaching this point (or so critics of the present regime suggest), while Russia remains locked in an extended moment of transition, giving rise to a dual state and economy and a stalemated political order. Two regulatory regimes in the political and economic sphere coexist, which in short-hand we can label the democratic and the *dirigiste*, allowing neither free rein and the inherent ordering principles of both are stymied. At any given time it cannot be predicted which order will predominate.

The combination of the two provides the Russian regime with a certain short-term managerial capacity. Putin was a master at balancing the forces and factions generated as a result of this dualism, so as to allow none to gain a permanent advantage in more than one sphere at any one time. This permanent balancing act continued into the period of tandem rule, with Putin remaining faction manager in his role as prime minister. He permanently balanced the factions, which themselves were generated by the conflict between the two orders and came to represent facets of the two. However, the logic of the tandem situation forced him to become the leader of a particular

Crisis of modernisation 43

faction as well, something that he could withstand when he enjoyed all the powers of the presidency. The presidency in Russia is designed to ensure that the incumbent can withstand factional capture. This parallel institutional design entails numerous deficits in term of democratic accountability and responsiveness, yet formally provides for executive leadership to drive through the strategy of post-communist and post-industrial modernisation. This is not the developmental state of old, since Russia is engaged in the singular process of re-development. At the same time, given the clash of orders, the presidency is locked into a permanent balancing game to retain its autonomy.

Thus the fundamental question is what sort of modernisation is in play in any given historical situation, and what relationship this has with 'the international'. The Soviet Union's attempts to 'catch up and overtake' the West reinserted the western model at the heart of Soviet ambitions, even though in political terms the two systems were antagonistic.[7] In the post-communist era the traditional form of this antagonism has disappeared, but a new logic of competition is inherent in a competitive state system in conditions of 'cold peace'. This is overlain by the tendency to reduce democracy to an ideology, associated in particular with the ambitions of the dominant hegemonic constellation, and thus weakening its inherently polymorphous character. Despite the nostrums of post-communist democratic fundamentalism, it is clear that there is no such thing as democracy in the abstract, only democracies: specific instances of self-managing societies, nowadays generalised at the level of the state but with numerous examples of social self-organisation able to balance heteronomy with the generation of unity through some sort of isomorphic political process.[8]

A re-developmental state will be inherently contradictory, especially when it claims to be a great power. Democracy is less a reflection of the organic evolution of society but part of a transformative process in which democracy seeks to create the conditions for its own existence. In this context liberal modernisation can be ascribed to the neo-modernisation paradigm. Instead of a straightforward appeal to technical modernisation and emulation, Medvedev's engagement with the civilisation of modernity provided a unique framework for the development of a sustainable Russian form of modernity. This was reflected in his speech on 3 March 2011 in St Petersburg celebrating the 150th anniversary of the abolition of serfdom by Alexander II in 1861. Medvedev outlined five principles of what we can call Russian neo-modernisation:

> First, we cannot postpone freedom until later and we should not fear the free person, who may in one way or another use their freedom inappropriately. This leads to a dead-end. Second, political and social reforms must be well-considered, rational, gradual, but unwavering. Third, now and in the future, intolerance and extremism, and its extreme manifestation terrorism, are the enemies of free development. ... Fourth, we should remember that the state is not the ultimate goal but an instrument of development. Only through society's inclusion in the development process

can a positive effect be achieved. Fifth, we should not forget that a nation is a living organism, and not a machine for the reproduction of dominant ideas. The country cannot be held by a tightening of the screws. Excessively harsh orders usually do not lead to the triumph of the good, or in contemporary parlance, to victory over corruption but to its increased prevalence; not to systemic development and improved quality of administration, but to the degradation of governance. Thus we must give society the chance for self-development.

He concluded with the slogan of his presidential campaign in 2008: 'Most importantly, in the last 150 years we have come to understand that freedom is better than unfreedom'.[9]

Despite the clearly delineated programme, Medvedev was unable to forge a genuine coalition for modernisation, and thus his rhetoric tended to hang in the air, rather than helping to forge a political movement in support of his ideas. Putin remained firmly in control of what in Soviet days was called the *apparat*, the combination of the bureaucracy and the security apparatus, and thus Medvedev governed effectively by sufferance of the Putinite regime, and lacked the resources to create his own. His modest personality became the subject of intense denigration, especially by the intelligentsia.

Social development and political change

A study by Renaissance Capital covering 150 countries found that democracy is fragile when per capita income is below $6,000, but becomes much stronger when it reaches $10,000, with countries tending to experience instability in the mid-range, such as Tunisia whose per capita income was $8,300 in 2009, while China also has now entered this zone, while Brazil ($9,352) and Turkey ($9,910) are edging close to the $10,000 level.[10] Democracy once established becomes consolidated, although far from indestructible, in the richer countries. However, in all of this Russia is an exception. With a per capita GDP of $18,570 in purchasing power parity terms Russia was clearly in the top range of middle income economies, only 15 per cent lower than Poland's, equal to Croatia's, and 30 per cent higher than Turkey's. In 2013 the World Bank and the IMF upgraded Russia as an upper middle income economy, ranked 72nd in the world, with a gross national income per capita of $12,700, above the $12,616 threshold of an upper-middle-income economy. Yet the country has at best a weak democracy, and at worst a deep-rooted authoritarianism.

No study examining the relationship between economic development and democratisation has suggested an automatic determinative relationship, yet the anomalous case of Russia does need explaining. In part, the answer undoubtedly lies in the country's troubled history, with the Soviet experience still shaping structures and practices, and the 'chaos' of the 1990s still weighing heavily on public consciousness. The Putinite reshaping of the political system in the 2000s allowed the consolidation of the administrative regime accompanied by the luxuriant growth of para-constitutional institutions and para-political practices, factionalism and corruption. At the same time, it delivered important public goods based on a hard-won 'stability' that was far from automatic and certainly fragile. Given the relatively benign international environment and the flood of natural resource rents the country could have done better; but with a separatist insurgency in the Caucasus, oligarch capitalism, regional segmentation and a fragmented society with a hybrid ruling class, it could certainly have done far worse.

In his re-election campaign in early 2012 Putin argued that there should be a shift from the remedial, but it remained unclear what precisely Putin understood by his 'development' model. Putin stressed the more discerning role for the middle classes in politics. The sentiment was echoed by Igor Shuvalov at the time when he argued that the protests were a sign of 'Russia's irreversible political transformation' and 'would not be stifled', arguing that 'When per capita GDP approaches $15,000, a country crosses a certain line, it begins to perceive itself differently, and the political system becomes more flexible'. He argued that the momentum for reform was becoming almost unstoppable, and argued 'Our task now is to transform tension into stability', praising 'civilised' protest as an 'extremely positive factor'.[11] There is no generally-agreed definition of the middle class, but it typically denotes a social group that shares certain educational, professional, income and lifestyle characteristics, including ownership of property (although not always all four together). The political characteristics of this class are too often imputed rather than analysed, with the suggestion that they would tend towards more liberal policies. This depends on the political conjuncture, since all sorts of trade-offs are possible and the middle class has a long tradition of turning to authoritarianism in times of crisis. There is no shortage of examples of the middle class opposing universal and political inclusion to protect its class position. In the Putin era this took the form of a 'social contract' in which stability, security and personal freedoms were guaranteed in exchange for a tutelary political environment.

Estimates of the size of the Russian middle class range between 10 and 25 per cent. According to Tatyana Maleva, the director of the Institute for Social Analysis and Forecasting, the Russian middle class is no longer an instrument for political change. It has stopped growing in size, and its composition has changed as more state officials, public sector managers, security officials and state company employees have entered the middle class, while entrepreneurs and the intelligentsia have declined as a proportion. For the newcomers, stability is a higher value than freedom and they tend to uphold conservative values.[12] Without a catalysing event such as fraudulent elections, this class was unlikely to mobilise spontaneously. In addition, the high level of inequality tended to squeeze out the middle class. According to the Global Wealth Report, in October 2012 1 per cent of the wealthiest people in Russia owned 71 per cent of personal assets, double the rate of the United States, and four times as much as in Japan. Ninety-six billionaires own 30 per cent of all personal assets in Russia, 15 times the world average.[13] An astonishing 35 per cent of household wealth was owned by just 110 people. According to the federal statistics service Rosstat, the Gini index, which measures the concentration of incomes and social stratification, rose from 0.29 in 1991, 0.395 in 2000 to 0.42 in 2012.[14] Incomes had grown rapidly in the Putin years, but so had inequality. In sociological terms, there was no middle class in Russia, just a growing section of the urban population aspiring to live as a western middle class. Olga Kryshtanovskaya argued that 'We have a middle class that exists in a type of vacuum: We do not have a lower class; we do not have an upper class. There is only a middle class and a vacuum around it'.[15] Typically, little was said about the changing nature of the Russian working class, including its differentiation according to the ownership structure of the plants and sector in which it worked.

Nevertheless, a new consumer class has emerged in Russia, analysed by Valery Panyushkin. He asks whether the anti-communist revolution was about pluralism or democracy at all, when it may simply have represented a 'revolution of the consumers'. The low quality of democracy in the Yeltsin years was accompanied by the low quality of consumer goods, and in response the Confederation of Consumer Societies (CCS) was created to defend the rights of consumers. The Putin years finally saw Russia become a consumer society, with unparalleled access and affordability of domestic and imported goods in the vast new shopping malls created in all big conurbations. At the time of his return in 2012 Russia was Europe's second largest consumer market, and it was estimated that it would overtake Germany within five years. Panyushkin is explicit in drawing the analogy: just as consumers fought to ensure quality and reliability in the consumer sphere, so as citizens they shifted their attention to another arena where they were being mercilessly cheated – politics. Alexander Auzan, the economist who was the guiding figure of CCS, noted in an interview with Panyushkin at the end of the book: 'A consumer revolution is a necessary condition for a democratic revolution', although he recognised that it was not a sufficient condition.[16] Auzan noted the various examples of citizen self-assertion, such as the blue bucket movement, mocking the officials who flashed their blue lights (*migalki*) and forced ordinary drivers off the road. Equally, when citizens realised how much tax they were paying (the 13 per cent flat rate income tax is supplemented by social taxes that typically amount to half people's salaries), they would start demanding improvements in services. As Auzan put it, 'Consumerism desacralises everything, including the state'.[17] It is also about individualism, although certainly not precluding collective action in defence of rights. Consumer pluralism, as in the motorists' movement, does not operate in a vacuum, and by highlighting official abuses fosters political pluralism and a sense of citizenship responsibility. Russia moved from communism to consumerism without an intervening stage of democracy; but ultimately consumerism can act as the seedbed of democracy.

The Putin years witnessed a conservative turn in popular attitudes. All polls suggest that young people shifted towards more conservative orientations.

Putin's paternalistic regime based its legitimacy on a range of symbolic values, including respect for Russia's many pasts (including the Soviet period), statist patriotism, and self-assertion abroad. Classical Putinism largely left personal affairs to the individual, but in his third term the tutelary regime demanded a higher degree of personal conformity and sought to reshape the whole system of 'bio-politics', the relationship between the self and society (and not just the political regime). The condemnation of multiculturalism, same sex marriage, single sex adoptions, the propagation of lesbian, gay, bisexual and transgender (LGBT) life styles, and 'slavish' westernism were the foundations of a new conservatism.

According to one study, the proportion of the population that could be defined as 'modern' inexorably fell from 2004, to reach only 20 per cent in 2009, and even among young people the importance attached to individual freedom fell in that period from 37 to 27 per cent, while the proportion of 'traditionalists', positively evaluating the values advanced by the Soviet regime, rose from 29 to 39 per cent. In 2007 nearly half (47 per cent) of Russians declared themselves in favour of the earlier values, with another 33 per cent in the middle. Thus the study declared, 'The reforms were conducted, but new modernised values were not adopted'.[18] By contrast, other studies reveal a strong commitment to democracy. According to the study 'Democracy: Development of the Russian Model', 78 per cent of Russia's citizens believed that the country needed democracy.[19] Thus the developmental modernisers underestimate the democratic potential in society.[20]

The stalemate between potential and achievement, aspirations and reality, provoked a growing emigration of professional and skilled workers. In the new brain drain, some 1.25 million Russians, 'mainly business men and representatives of the middle class', left the country between 2008 and 2011, a number greater even than those who left after the collapse of the Soviet Union in 1991, although only 145,000 of these left the country to settle permanently abroad.[21] The total number of entrepreneurs also remained stable, if not actually fell. The number of individual entrepreneurs dropped from 4.61 to 4.11 million in 2010, with most of the half million not only leaving business but Russia as well. The 'nightmaring' of business continued, and those who refused to enter into 'exclusive' relationships with the authorities saw no choice but to leave. As Yana Yakovleva, the head of 'Business Solidarity', noted, to avoid 'criminal cases to order', the only option was to leave. One study suggests that the latest wave of emigration saw some four million Russians settle in the EU and the United States, a disproportionate number of whom were highly qualified and with higher education.[22] The main cause was often attributed to a sense of a 'lack of a future' within Russia, prey to a predatory bureaucracy and hamstrung by a self-seeking officialdom. If in the 1990s there was at least a sense of light at the end of the tunnel, now there was light all around but only darkness ahead, hence the lack of confidence to invest in the country. As Yakovleva put it, investors did so not 'because of' but 'despite': 'You feel that you anger bureaucrats (*chinovniki*) by the mere fact of your existence: with innumerable absurd certificates, and permits, total corruption, this is the acid, toxic environment which suppresses any desire to invent or innovate.'[23] Skilled professionals felt safer abroad. At its root, the protest movement from 2011 was about the active part of the population no longer being willing to endure government abuse and humiliation.

How many Russias?

One of the symptoms of the crisis of modernisation in contemporary Russia is the attempt to map the various constituencies, none of which has been able to become hegemonic. The political geographer Natalya Zubarevich famously identifies four Russias. The 'first Russia' is the big cities, where the population quickly adapted to consumer behaviour. It was here that the middle-class 'angry urbanites' are concentrated, fearing years of Putinite stagnation and blocked social mobility. The 'second Russia' comprises the medium-sized industrial towns, and even where the plants had closed in the post-Soviet years, the spirit of the communities remains associated with the past. These towns have a large proportion of *byudzhetniki*, dependent on state wages and transfers. Some 25 per cent of the Russian population lives here, 10 per cent of whom live in the 'mono-towns', dominated by a single major plant. Here the struggle for survival is central and there is little concern with the 'middle class' issues that predominate in the first Russia, something that the authorities played on in trying to turn the two against each other. The third Russia is the enormous periphery in small towns and villages, who make up some 38 per cent of the total population. They survive 'from the land' and associated activities, and are far from politics. Their protest potential is minimal, even if a crisis held back their wages and pensions. And finally, the fourth Russia is composed of the North Caucasian republics and south Siberia (Tyva, Altai), making up some 6 per cent of the population, where clan, religious and other conflicts shape the local environment, and national politics are only important as long as the subsidies keep coming.[24]

This schema has been much criticised, with all sorts of other political geographies proposed (for example, the singling out of Moscow and St Petersburg as a separate category), yet it provides a vivid insight into the dynamics of Russia's internal 'geopolitics'. It highlights that Russia's political space is not homogenous, as described in the section on uneven and combined development, and that the imposition of westernising liberal ideas has to reckon with the enormous diversity of Russia's political cultures. The conflict between these various non-hegemonic Russias is one of the determining features of Russia's present stalemate. Those who saw the protest movement of 2011/12 as the prelude to a period of revolutionary change were way off the mark, but equally, they revealed profound social and political tensions. A study by the Institute of Sociology and the Friedrich Ebert Foundation examined 'what Russians dream about' and stressed the incomplete nature of Russian state building: 'The process of building in Russia a modern nation state, a political nation, uniting citizens around generally agreed values interests and institutions, is far from complete, and society remains atomised and divided.' Stability remained the central political value for 64 per cent of the population, and apart from the first Russia, the others remained in 'political hibernation.'[25]

The study replicates my threefold model of a liberal, traditionalist and centrist Russia, discussed in the next chapter. Russia is divided into three 'parallel worlds', less tied to geography than Zubarevich's categorisation. The first comprises carriers of the values of the contemporary megapolis, the middle class not reliant on the state for support, and who see the country as part of the larger western (and in the first instance European) civilisation, oriented towards the liberalisation of political and economic life. The group is dubbed the 'new Russian sub-ethnos', comprising some 25 per cent of the population. The second group is the traditionalist periphery, focused on customary horizontal links and values, concentrated in the 'national' regions. This group is some 10–12 per cent of the population. The third group is by far the largest, over half the population, and is characterised as 'intermediate'. It lauds traditionalist values and conditions, requiring economic and social support from the state, but it has lost the social links customary for traditionalist groups and is focused on the values of a mass consumer society. It has little potential for political mobilisation. It is effectively 'quasi-traditionalist', and thus its leftism (political neo-Sovietism) is superficial. Thus liberals, like Anatoly Chubais and Mikhail Khodorkovsky, who argue (in Vladimir Milov's words) that 'a temporary move to the left in economic policy is the price we have to pay for the country's democratisation' are mistaken.[26]

Powerlessness and corruption

Those who study contemporary Russia have a constant sense that they are barking up the wrong tree in looking at institutions and the policy process, and that just beyond the horizon there is a 'third state', termed by some the 'deep state', a power beyond power, a force rooted in a non-political network of relations. In this world informality becomes the determining institution. The economic crisis from 2008 'morphed into something more profound and fundamental – the sustainability of Russia's current governance model and its preferred longer-term modernisation paradigm'.[27] Reflecting the division between liberal modernisers and statist developmentalists, Herd argues that those who argue that 'the *sine qua non* of sustainable modernization in Russia is political liberalization' are pitted against those in favour of 'conservative modernization', a more gradualist and organic path.[28] Even Herd questions whether 'such contestation highlight a genuine and deep-seated, fundamental and strategic division over Russia's future pathway at the very top of Russia's governance structure, or is it a mirage, sound and fury signifying nothing?'.[29] Monaghan argues that the tension between the two strategies should not be exaggerated: 'despite what has become orthodoxy, there are no major gaps

50   *Crisis of modernisation*

between the political agendas of Medvedev and Putin'.[30] The diarchical structure of the tandem, in his view, gave way to the emergence of 'the Team', which basically agreed on the main principles of foreign and domestic policy, and which in 2011–12 struggled to preserve its status. The approaches of the two leading figures, despite some different nuances, 'may be more complementary than assumed'.[31] A collective leadership of around a dozen people transcended the alleged divisions within the tandem; with no substantial alternatives to them.

The much-vaunted *vertikal* was not so much one of power as of mutual obligations:

> The meaning of the vertical of power, however, has evolved to the extent that some see it more as a networked group mechanism to eliminate the negative effects of mistakes and crises for the authorities themselves – a version of a 'circle of shared responsibility' (*krugovaya poruka*).[32]

This applies at all levels but above all at the top, where officials are forced to give an appearance not only of reliability but also of loyalty. Vladislav Inozemtsev describes the *vertical* as follows:

> At every level of the hierarchy a certain degree of bribery and clientelist parochialism is not only tolerated but presupposed in exchange for unconditional loyalty and a part of the take for one's superiors. ... The weak pay tribute up, the strong provide protection down.[33]

We thus have a power system without power, and the system is little more than a series of ad hoc mutual protection arrangements.

The top-down system thus lacks dynamism, mired in the corrupt pathologies of its social base. This prompted Medvedev to complain:

> Whatever the president does not coordinate, nobody else bothers to coordinate either. It's bad. It means that we have an obsolete and wholly inadequate control system that ought to be replaced (with something better). When all signals have to come from the Kremlin alone, it plainly shows the system to be unviable and in need of being attuned.[34]

The point was stressed by Monaghan, when he argued that 'If the vertical of power is about the fulfilment of the leadership's instructions and goals, it has become apparent that it does not function'.[35] The reasons were numerous, but include 'bureaucratic rivalries and blurred lines of responsibility between institutions and ministries, including the White House and the Kremlin, widespread (even systematic) corruption, incompetence and a bureaucracy so unwieldy that exactly where instructions fail is unclear'.[36] Fears of the destructive effects of a new perestroika prompted the caution with which political reform was conducted. However, technocratic economic reform on its own could not weaken the systemic corruption that undermined the investment climate in the country. Predatory officialdom stifled the development of small and medium business and exposed businesses to 'raids' of various sorts, ranging from sanitary inspectors to business rivals who enlisted the support of officialdom in their attack.

In its 2008 Corruption Perception Index, which measures the perception of public corruption, Transparency International (TI) placed Russia in joint 147th place with Bangladesh, Kenya and Syria, its worst position in eight years.[37] Not surprisingly, Medvedev in June 2008 warned that:

> It [corruption] is a very painful and difficult problem for our country. ... Corruption as a systemic challenge, as a threat to national security, as a problem which leads to a lack of faith among citizens in the ability of government to bring order and protect them.[38]

A head of state could hardly make a more devastating comment. Medvedev made the fight against corruption one of the key planks of his policy, but admitted that only limited headway had been made. On 31 July 2008 his national anti-corruption plan was adopted with three key elements: updating legislation, specific anti-corruption measures to prevent officials taking bribes, and the involvement of civil society in the struggle. Little headway was made. The TI rankings for 2010 placed Russia jointly at 154 (out of 178) with such countries as Cambodia, the Central African Republic and Tajikistan, while China was placed at 78 on the list.[39] By 2012 there had been some improvement, with Russia now ranked 133 out of 176 placing it just above Azerbaijan, Nigeria and Pakistan, but below Armenia, and Mali.[40] In TI's *Global Corruption Barometer 2013* Russia was one of the countries in which respondents thought that corruption had increased (p. 9), over 80 per cent considered that personal contacts were important to get things done in the public sector (p. 14), and Russia was one of only seven countries in which citizens considered public officials and civil servants to be the most corrupt members of society, a view held by 92 per cent of respondents (p. 17).[41]

The size of bribes appears to have increased, and whole sectors such as healthcare, education, housing and communal services were plagued by corruption. There are great variations in the estimates of the corrupt proportion of Russian GDP, with official Rosstat figures suggesting between 3.5 and 7 per cent, most independent experts arguing that it amounts to about a quarter, while a World Bank report put the figure at an astonishing 48 per cent. There was a change in the nature of corruption. If in the 1990s businesses had to pay criminal groups to provide a *krysha* (literally, 'roof', i.e. protection), in Putin's Russia this 'protective' function was performed by officials, above all from the FSB and the Ministry of Internal Affairs (MVD).[42] On the everyday level, the system of 'blat' (pull, or connections) was woven into the fabric of social relations, even when the shortages that had given birth to the system no longer existed. The Soviet adage 'Blat vyshe Sovnarkoma' ('Pull is higher than the Council of People's Commissars') still had currency. Was this corruption or forms of social adaptation?

Putin's leadership has been accompanied by persistent rumours about his personal venality. No sooner was he installed as assistant to Sobchak in St Petersburg in 1990 than the food for materials export programme mired him in scandal that is difficult to untangle to this day. There is endless speculation of his personal wealth, kept in off-shore accounts. Various reports suggested that in the 2000s he indulged in the building of personal palaces. Although ostensibly owned, and certainly funded, by the state, these were ostentatious and unnecessary expenditures in the best of circumstances. One of these was a magnificent property on the Black Sea, known as 'project South', covering 4,000 square meters and built by construction teams of the presidential guards service.[43] Sergei Kolesnikov, a St Petersburg banker who had been involved in its construction in the mid-2000s, argues that with roads and services, the total cost was in the region of a billion dollars. Becoming a whistleblower, he fled to Turkey and then the United States in early 2011. He noted that 'if you could show the whole truth to the whole country, about this palace and all these machinations, Putin would be gone in two weeks'.[44]

In March 2011 the former prime minister Mikhail Kasyanov, former deputy premier Boris Nemtsov, and the independent politicians Vladimir Ryzhkov and Vladimir Milov issued a report alleging that corruption had worsened under Putin. Citing data from the Indem think tank, they argued that corruption in Russia had increased tenfold between 2001 and 2005 to well over $300bn, or a quarter of Russia's GDP. Despite Medvedev devoting his leadership to the struggle, he admitted that $35bn of government funds were stolen in state contracts in 2010 alone. The report described how a small group of Putin's friends, many of them grouped around the Ozero dacha collective, had enriched themselves in the 2000s. In 1996 Putin and seven neighbours in a gated community near St Petersburg formed a management company called 'Ozero' ('Lake') to manage their plots of land. Five Ozero members have since then done exceptionally well. The small Rossiya Bank, controlled by Yuri Kovalchuk and Nikolai Shamalov (two co-founders of Ozero) from 2004 grew many-fold through gaining assets from Gazprom, notably the Sogaz insurance company and the Lider company managing the Gazprom and Gazpromdom pension fund. It also gained control of Gazprombank, among whose assets were Gazprom Media, NTV and TNT. The whistleblower who had worked for Shamalov, Kolesnikov, as noted, revealed details about the cost of building the enormous Italian-style palace on the Black Sea, allegedly for Putin's use.[45]

Equally, the oil trader Timchenko gained most of Yukos's trading assets, allowing his Gunvor International company to trade at least a third of Russian oil exports, allegedly buying oil from state oil companies at preferential rates. Putin's friends the brothers Arkady and Boris Rotenberg, his judo sparring partners, controlled no fewer than 11 distilleries within the Rosspirtprom system, including the Kristall plant. Vladimir Yakunin was also a member of the Ozero collective and went on to head Russian Railways and to support many important social projects, including the World Public Forum and its 'Dialogue of Civilisations'. The report was unsparing in its description of the luxury items enjoyed by Putin and Medvedev, with five yachts and launches at their disposal, the use of 26 properties of luxury real estate, and expensive watches.[46] An updated study ironically contrasted Putin's image of himself as a galley salve and his alleged wealth.[47] A study called 'Corporation Russia' argues that the destruction of Khodorkovsky's Yukos empire following his arrest in October 2003 'at a stroke destroyed an alternative centre of power', removed the sponsor of the political opposition, and removed the last barrier to the *siloviki* seizing control over the country's natural resources.[48]

Putin's preferences increasingly set the tone for the era, with parliament and other institutions seeking to gain his approval through 'anticipatory obedience'. Putin gained a greater degree of discretionary authority, although the 'power vertikal' remained more of an aspiration than an achievement. The polity would remain strong as long as Putin's personal preferences and those of the elite coincided, and in particular where leaderism and rentierism were compatible (raising the intriguing question of what would happen if they ever diverged). The various mega-projects of Putin's Russia were intimately bound up with Putin personally, but were also a means of extracting rents. The cost of the Sochi Winter Olympics rose inexorably from the original budget of $12bn to over $50bn. In part the massive cost over-run was attributable to the genuine physical problems with building infrastructure in the Imerets Lowlands, above all a deep silt layer that made foundations expensive. Although much initially had been made of private investment in Olympic sites, above all from the oligarchs Oleg Deripaska and Vladimir Potanin, in the event 96 per cent of capital investment came from the state budget. The role of the Rotenberg brothers, Boris and Arkady – Putin's childhood friends – in Olympic construction projects was particularly controversial, winning 15 per cent of all the funds allocated for the games. Their company built the Dzhugba–Sochi gas pipeline and the Kurortny Avenue bypass, key infrastructure projects, for allegedly inflated prices.[49] Putin's longtime Petersburg associate Dmitry Kozak was charged with ensuring readiness for the opening on 7 February 2014, and in the end he delivered.

One of the most popular placards in the protests following the flawed 4 December 2011 Duma elections was 'Putin is a thief', and as many noted, Putin in his direct line of 16 December 2010 had argued, a propos Khodorkovsky, that 'A thief should sit in jail'. One of the factors propelling Putin to return to the presidency was clearly elite fear that a change of government would entail a change of regime, with the normal 'revolutionary justice' and elite expropriations to follow. Garry Kasparov, the former world chess champion and now a fiery opposition leader, noted the powerful internal divisions within the elite, stressing that the Kremlin 'did not have the stomach for severe repression'. He argued that if Putin were to lose power a minority of the elite, perhaps up to 20 per cent, would lose everything and possibly face trial, whereas the other 80 per cent would swiftly make their peace with the new government:

54 *Crisis of modernisation*

If it comes to a choice between hanging on to political power or hanging on to at least some of their Swiss bank accounts, Mr Kasparov is betting that 80 per cent of the elite will be prepared to do a deal.[50]

Material presented in the *New Times* of 31 October 2011 called 'Russia, Inc: How Putin and Co. Divided up the Country', suggested that Putin and his entourage controlled between 10 to 15 per cent of GDP through insider deals. Many of Putin's friends became millionaires, if not billionaires by leveraging Kremlin connections.[51] The most effective way to insure against prosecution was to stay in power. Alexei Navalny, the anti-corruption campaigner and one of the most effective leaders of the protest movement against Putin's return, declared that one of the first acts he would do as leader would be to free Khodorkovsky and establish an independent tribunal to investigate the corruption allegations against Putin's associates. Navalny first came to prominence in late 2010 for his investigations into corruption in state-run corporations and by loyalist MPs. The Yukos case saw at least $45bn expropriated and distributed to state-favoured companies, notably Rosneft. The list of Kremlin-aligned companies includes Gazprom, Transneft, Gunvor, Russian Technologies, VTB, National Media Group, the various enterprises owned by the Rotenberg brothers, Bank Rossiya, the arms trader Rosoboronexport and dozens more.[52] The experience of the Arab spring saw old dictators fleeing for their lives or put on trial, if not summarily shot, and their property redistributed.

The head of the Audit Chamber responsible for monitoring probity in the management of public funds, Sergei Stepashin, himself became embroiled in a scandal. In a report compiled by Marina Litvinovich and five co-authors called 'The Power of Families: The Government, Part 1', filed on the web site Election2012.ru on 22 April 2011, the family affairs of 18 senior officials, including Stepashin, were examined.[53] The report argued that the families and friends 'are controlling cash flows that go from the state budget to private, mainly offshore, coffers'. The report suggested that Stepashin's family benefited from activities associated with the work of the Audit Chamber, noting in particular the acquisition of Bank of Moscow by VTB, where Stepashin's wife Tamara is a senior vice president. Stepashin's son Viktor allegedly received shares in some Cyprus-based companies affiliated with the East Line group, the owners of Domodedovo airport, at a time in 2011 after the Audit Chamber opened an investigation into East Line. It was also reported that a long-time associate of Tamara Stepashina, the head of Moscow Metrostroi Vladimir Kogan, in 2010 had a business dispute with Dmitry Gaev, the former head of the Moscow Metro, who was sacked in February 2011 and was under investigation following an investigation by the Audit Chamber. The report concluded that 'We are basically dealing with some 50 families of top officials and businessmen who have not just taken control over oil and other natural resources, but also organised financial flows to go into their families' collective pocket'.

The allegations were drawn from open sources but denied by the Audit Chamber.[54]

The scale is disputed, but the head of the National Anti-Corruption Committee Kirill Kabanov estimated the corruption market at about $300bn. Petty venality and bribe taking made up only a small proportion, with the bulk derived from illicit distribution of budgetary funds, state property and natural resources. The elite became accustomed to 'rentierism', and its appetite had become so voracious as to threaten the political system. The third state eroded both legs of the dual state. Following his return to the Kremlin Putin was forced to 'betray' some of his own, notably the minister of defence Anatoly Serdyukov, for the sake of political stability and to respond to public concerns, in part stimulated by Navalny's anti-corruption campaign waged on his RosPil website, but this was a selective response. On 6 November 2012 Serdyukov was sacked and an investigation was launched into Oboronservis, a company that he headed which had allegedly sold R95.5m of property, land and shares at below market rates to temporary shell companies, with the profits assumedly funnelled back to the beneficiaries and their families. Serdyukov's affair with Yevgeniya Vasileva, the head of the defence ministry's department of property matters, at whose apartment Serdyukov was found at the time of her arrest and from which over three million roubles, antiques, valuables and documents relating to the case were found. Serdyukov was beleaguered on all sides, being in conflict with his predecessor, Sergei Ivanov, whom he had pushed out of a post in 2007, the head of the Russian Technologies Group, Sergei Chemezov, and finally with his father-in-law, Viktor Zubkov, because of his affair.

His sacking revealed the 'war between the Kremlin towers', the factional struggle hidden behind the regime's mask of unity. A year later, however, Serdyukov had still not been brought to trial, demonstrating Putin's reluctance to 'give up' one of his own. Factional conflict in the Putin system meant that, with rare exceptions such as Khodorkovsky, one set of elites could not destroy another. This also entailed maintaining the contradiction: elite venality undermined the legitimacy of the system as a whole, but there could be no genuine sustained anti-corruption campaign as long as the beneficiaries of the Putin system remained in power. Russia ratified the UN Convention against Corruption in 2006, but it refused to ratify Article 20, which introduced the concept of 'illicit acquisition of personal wealth'.[55] Putin's attack on corruption was limited and instrumental, and certainly did not betoken a systematic attempt to eradicate it from public life. In fact, Putin assumed a remarkably cavalier attitude to the question, arguing that corruption was a Russian tradition. In his December 2012 news conference (see below) Putin noted that Peter the Great had suggested that corrupt officials should be either sent to Siberia or executed, to which his prosecutor general responded 'But then who will be left, Your Majesty? We are all thieves.'

The authoritarian social contract and rentierism

There was a time until not so long ago that the first question asked of a political system was about its social base. This approach could lead to simplistic reductionism, whereby agency, the role of leadership and choices were denigrated in favour of what was often simplistic determinism. Nevertheless, the question is still a fundamental one. In the Russian case, as in so many post-Soviet states, the 'upper bourgeoisie' has effectively merged with the governing system, the administrative regime. The business class after the Yukos affair aligned its concerns with the preferences of the regime. This certainly did not preclude conflicts, notably during the economic downturn from mid-2008, and over specific issues, as when Tyumen Oil Company (TNK)-British Petroleum (BP) was able to block a tie-in between Rosneft and BP to exploit Arctic and other reserves. The heads of state corporations and state-owned businesses and the private sector became part of a single neo-corporatist compact. This was 'light touch' corporatism, adapted to the competitive rules of the international neo-liberal order (globalisation), with coordination achieved through a system of understandings and informal relations.

The Putinite social contract was a complex phenomenon, with differentiated deals with most politically salient sections of the society. Pensioners received sustained increases in their allowances, the budgetary sector saw wages rise and paid regularly (teachers did particularly well), the liberal intelligentsia could travel freely and enjoy the internet, while loyal state oligarchs could make their billions and transfer funds abroad, and even a large section of the bourgeoisie could buy property on the Adriatic and other desirable coasts. This was a rent-based system of what in the Middle East was called 'petrolism': 'Rents are incomes which are not balanced by labor and capital, and are thus at the free disposal of the recipients.'[56] The concept of a political rentier state is contested, but at its heart is the distribution of unearned wealth.[57] The Putin system displayed two of its key features. The first is the creation of distributional coalitions, often based on wasteful capital projects that provide a mechanism to funnel resources into the beneficiaries of this form of crony capitalism. Rentier states do not limit their largesse to elite groups, but also ensure that rents are distributed more broadly. This leads to the second feature, namely depoliticisation accompanied by the etiolation of political institutions, as their strategic functions are rendered redundant by the direct management of resources. Putin's state in its best years was an enclave of petroland, insulated from political pressures at home and more assertive abroad. For Gaddy and Ickes, this was a system in which natural resource rents were redistributed by the closed elite.[58] Instead of the generation of profit through competitive markets, the country was run through the feudal appropriation of unearned income. Putin was at the heart of the distributive system, but also became its servant since his own power ultimately came to depend on its perpetuation.

The crisis of rentierism occurs when the system based on guaranteed wages and rising living standards breaks down as government spending increases and cannot be compensated by rising taxes revenues from the neglected non-resource sector. Equally, society is politicised by certain signal events. So-called 'colour revolutions' have typically been provoked by attempts by incumbent regimes to steal elections. In the Russian case, the egregiously provocative 'castling' move of September 2011 followed by deeply flawed elections sent thousands onto the streets. The regime was greatly weakened, facing a degree of elite fragmentation and popular mobilisation, and sought to recoup its position through a dual process of tightening the screws and political concessions. Historical experience suggests that this only postpones the inevitable day of reckoning. In the Middle East authoritarian regimes that had appeared stable for decades collapsed one after the other, accompanied on occasion by judicious western intervention. As the Iranian revolution against the Shah in 1979 amply demonstrates, those that make the revolution do not necessarily inherit power: a lesson that many conservatives in Russia remember as the lesson of February 1917.

Modernisation in the Russian context means the break-up of the rentier system, the 'limited access order' and its precarious stability, in favour of an 'open access order'.[59] This was in effect at the heart of Medvedev's modernisation agenda, and demonstrates that although powerful structural factors are at work, at the systemic level leadership makes a big difference. The shortcomings of Medvedev's leadership style were compounded by the constraints of the tandem form of rule, but the contradictions of the dual state were exposed and a programme for strengthening constitutionalism outlined. The incentives for this type of democratisation are high. The EU is just over the horizon, and while the prospects for membership are negligible at present, a democratised Russia would gain immediate benefits. The temptations of a 'pivot' to the East also beckon, reinforced by the fact that geopolitics and domestic politics are not aligned. It is in the forks of this contradiction that the Putinite state was forged. Rentierism represents a powerful structural impediment to change, but leadership (political agency) retains its autonomy and with the appropriate political will could challenge the 'third power', especially if reinforced by pressure from below. Popular mobilisation against electoral fraud from December 2011 suggested that this force had finally arrived.

Notes

1 Gregory Bateson, 'Culture Contact and Schismogenesis', *Man*, Vol. 35, December 1935, pp. 178–83; in *Steps to an Ecology of Mind* (Chandler, 1972; new edition Chicago, University of Chicago Press, 1980).
2 Pekka Sutela, *The Political Economy of Putin's Russia* (London, Routledge, 2012).
3 Vladimir Shlapentokh and Anna Arutunyan, *Freedom, Repression, and Private Property in Russia* (Cambridge, Cambridge University Press, 2013).

58 *Crisis of modernisation*

4 Catherine Belton and Charles Glover, 'Vladimir Putin has Traditionally Balanced Factions, but Tensions are Rising', *Financial Times*, 31 May 2012.
5 Landmark publications of this approach include David Apter's *The Politics of Modernization* (Chicago, University of Chicago Press, 1965) and his *Some Conceptual Approaches to the Study of Modernization* (Englewood Cliffs, NJ, Prentice-Hall, 1968); and Samuel Huntington's *Political Order in Changing Societies* (New Haven, CT, Yale University Press, 1968). For a later critique, see M. Cowen and R. Shenton, 'The Invention of Development', in J. Crush (ed.), *The Power of Development* (London, Routledge, 1995).
6 For a restatement of the use of the concept, see Justin Rosenberg, 'Basic Problems in the Theory of Uneven and Combined Development. Part II: Unevenness and Political Multiplicity', *Cambridge Review of International Affairs*, Vol. 23, No. 1, March 2011, p. 168.
7 This is the argument advanced by Immanuel Wallerstein in his world-system theory.
8 John Keane, *The Life and Death of Democracy* (New York, Simon & Schuster, 2009). See also John Dunn, *Setting the People Free: The Story of Democracy* (New York, Atlantic Books, 2006).
9 'Dmitrii Medvedev vystupil na konferentsii "Velikie reform i modernizatsii Rossii"', 3 March 2011, http://news.kremlin.ru/transcripts/10506.
10 Ol'ga Kuvshinova, 'Tsena demokratii', *Vedomosti*, 23 June 2011, p. 1.
11 Speaking to the Gaidar Forum, 'First Deputy PM Justifies Public Protests', RIA Novosti, 18 January 2012; http://en.rian.ru/russia/20120118/170829320.html.
12 In Georgii Osipov, 'Konservy srednego klassa', Gazeta.ru, 23 May 2013; http://www.gazeta.ru/comments/2013/05/23.
13 Reported by Yevgeny Primakov, 'Perception of Russia in the World', Valdai Discussion Club, 29 April 2013.
14 'Russia Among World Leaders in Terms of Income Inequality', *Itar-Tass*, 10 October 2013.
15 Interview with Olga Kryshtanovskaya, 19 July 2013; http://russia-direct.org/
16 Valerii Panyushkin, *Vosstanie potrebitelei* (Moscow, Astrel', 2012), p. 249.
17 Ibid., p. 254.
18 Yevgeniya Albats and Andrei Kolesnikov, 'Homo Postsoveticus', *New Times*, 9 February 2009, pp. 4–5, with data on p. 4 drawn from research by Natalya Tikhonova at the Higher School of Economics, and the quotation on p. 5.
19 The survey was conducted by the company Bashkirova and Partners. The five main components of democracy support (in descending order) were as follows: equality of citizens before the law (63 per cent); freedom of speech, religion, and movement (36 per cent); the duty of the state to take into account the opinions and interest of each person (35 per cent); the right to elect and change the government (32 per cent); the government's accountability to citizens (29 per cent). Reported by Igor Bunin, 'Contemporary Russia: The Return of Politics', Politkom.ru, 9 April 2009; in *JRL*, 72/15, 2009.
20 Ellen Carnaghan, *Out of Order: Russian Political Values in an Imperfect World* (University Park, PA, Pennsylvania State University Press, 2007).
21 'About 145,000 Russians Left the Country for Good in Past Three Years', RIA Novosti, 20 September 2011.
22 Paul Goble, 'Window on Eurasia: Middle Class "Fleeing" Russia, Moscow Experts Say', *JRL*, 93/4, 2011.
23 Natalya Alyarinskaya, Dmitrii Dokuchaev with Irina Zavidonova, 'Ot"ezd s otyagchayushchimi obstoyatel'stvami: Srednii klass bezhit iz Rossii', *New Times*, No. 17, 23 May 2011.
24 N. Zubarevich, 'Chetyre Rossii', *Vedomosti*, 30 December 2011.
25 M. K. Gorshkov, R. Krumm, N. E. Tikhonova (eds), *O chëm mechtayut rossiyane: Ideal i real'nost'* (Moscow, Ves' mir, 2013), p. 79.

26 Ibid., pp. 80–81.
27 Graeme P. Herd, *Russia's Strategic Choice: Conservative or Democratic Modernization?* Geneva Centre for Security Policy (GCSP) Policy Paper No. 2, May 2010, p. 2; www.gcsp.ch.
28 Ibid., pp. 2–3.
29 Ibid., p. 4.
30 Andrew Monaghan, *The Russian* Vertikal*: The Tandem, Power and the Elections*, Chatham House, Russia and Eurasia Programme REP2011/01, June 2011, p. 2.
31 Ibid., p. 6.
32 Ibid., p. 11.
33 Quoted by Monaghan, *The Russian* Vertikal, p. 12, from V. Inozemtsev, 'Neo-Feudalism Explained', *The American Interest*, March–April 2011; www.the-american-interest.com.
34 Medvedev, cited by Brian Whitmore, 'The Powerless Vertical', RFE/RL, *Russia Report*, 10 June 2011.
35 Monaghan, *The Russian* Vertikal, p. 9.
36 Ibid., p. 10.
37 http://www.transparency.org/news_room/in_focus/2008/cpi2008/cpi_2008_table.
38 Aydar Buribayev, 'Russian Corruption at 8-Year Peak', *Moscow Times*, 23 September 2008.
39 http://www.transparency.org/policy_research/surveys_indices/cpi/2010/results.
40 Transparency International, *Corruption Perceptions Index 2010* and *2012*; www.transparency.org; http://cpi.transparency.org/cpi2012/results/.
41 http://www.transparency.org/gcb2013.
42 Alexandra Kalinina, 'Corruption in Russia as a Business', *Institute of Modern Russia* (henceforth *IMR*), 29 January 2013.
43 George H. Wittman, 'Putin's Personal Piggy Banks', *The American Spectator*, 16 December 2011; http://spectator.org/archives/2011/12/16/putins-personal-piggy-banks.
44 Scott Shane, 'From Success at Putin's Side to Exposing Corruption', *New York Times*, 4 February 2012; Catherine Belton, 'A Realm Fit for a Tsar', *Financial Times*, 1 December 2011.
45 Evgeniya Albats, Ol'ga Osipova and Ol'ga Beshlei, 'Parallel'naya real'nost'', *New Times*, No. 15, pp. 4–11.
46 Vladimir Milov, Vladimir Ryzhkov, O. Shorina (eds), *Putin: Korruptsiya – nezavisimy ekspertny doklad* (Moscow, Partiiya Narodnoi Svobody, 2011).
47 Boris Nemtsov and Leonid Martynyuk, *Zhizn'raba na galerakh (dvortsy, yakhty, avtomobili, samolety i drugie aksessuary)* (Moscow, 2012); www.putin-itogi.ru.
48 Evgeniya Albats and Anatolii Ermolin, 'Korporatsiya "Rossiya"', *New Times*, No. 36, 31 October 2011, pp. 4–12.
49 Boris Nemtsov and Leonid Martynyuk, *Winter Olympics in the Sub-Tropics: Corruption and Abuse in Sochi* (Moscow, 2013).
50 Chrystia Freeland, 'Battle Raging at Heart of Russian Elite', *New York Times*, 19 January 2012.
51 For early studies, see Stanislav Belkovskii and V. Golyshev, *Biznes Vladimira Putina* (Ekaterinburg, Ul'tra.Kul'tura, 2006); and Stanislav Belkovskii, *Imperiya Vladimira Putina* (Moscow, Algoritm, 2008).
52 This list is drawn from Michael Bohm, 'Why Putin Will Never, Ever Give Up Power', *Moscow Times*, 20 January 2012.
53 Marina Litvinovich, *Vlast' semei: 20 klanov, kontroliruyushchikh ekonomiku Rossii* (Moscow, Eksmo, 2012).
54 Natalya Krainova, 'Audit Chamber Lashes Out at Activist', *Moscow Times*, 28 April 2011.
55 Tatiana Stanovaya, 'Putin's Corruption Trap', *IMR*, 16 April 2013.

56 Martin Beck and Simone Hüser, *Political Change in the Middle East: An Attempt to Analyze the 'Arab Spring'*, Hamburg, German Institute of Global and Area Studies (GIGA), Working Papers No. 203, August 2012, p. 8.
57 Hazem Beblawi and Giacomo Luciani, *The Rentier State* (London, Croom Helm, 1987).
58 Clifford G. Gaddy and Barry W. Ickes, 'Russia after the Global Financial Crisis', *Eurasian Geography and Economics*, Vol. 51, No. 3, 2010, pp. 281–311.
59 Douglas C. North, Joseph Wallis and Barry R. Weingast, *Violence and Social Orders: A Conceptual Framework for Interpreting Recorded Human History* (Cambridge, Cambridge University Press, 2009).

4 The impasse of power

One of the great conundrums of our time is why it has been so hard to establish the rudiments of a working democratic system in Russia. After all, in the late perestroika period the first relatively free elections, for the Soviet parliament in spring 1989 and for the Russian legislature in spring 1990, were greeted with enormous popular enthusiasm, and up to half a million people gathered in the great demonstrations in Moscow in 1991. What could be called the Soviet middle class, the great mass of officials, professionals and creative intelligentsia, supported Boris Yeltsin's struggle against the Soviet system to perpetuate itself. In the end, little could be done to prevent the dissolution of the Soviet order, squeezed by Gorbachev's reforms from above, Yeltsin's attack from the middle, and pressured by mass mobilisation from below. In Russia there was rather less enthusiasm for the disintegration of the Soviet Union, although on the whole accepted as a brute necessity. The experience of the 1990s turned this Soviet middle class against the democracy as it was practised at the time, and thus welcomed Putin in the 2000s. He offered what they needed: wages to be paid on time, the pushback against national disintegration, and above all the restoration of a sense of coherence and purpose to the state in domestic and foreign affairs.

But Putin's leadership is not only contradictory but also paradoxical. A paradox is defined as a self-contradiction that conflicts with preconceived notions of what is reasonable, possible or true, but which is essentially well-founded. Putin's leadership is paradoxical in two senses: it is self-contradictory in its internal characteristics, in which the developmental and constitutionalist rhetoric is balanced by more tawdry practices; but also in the way that it is received and interpreted, as both dynamic and regressive. The quality of ambiguity is thus inherent in Putin's leadership, in domestic affairs as much as in foreign policy. A system that declared as its goal the restoration of the authority of the state and the rule of law proceeded to undermine both through the selective and occasionally vindictive application of justice while strengthening a system of *vlast'* based on the normative foundations of constitutionalism but on traditionalist 'understandings' (*ponyatie*) and patrimonial forms of loyalty. In this chapter I argue that Russian politics finds itself in an impasse caused by four stalemates, in which contrasting principles of order and contending visions of the polity collide.

The dual state: constitutional state vs administrative regime

The first is the clash of two political orders, the forms of order associated with the constitutional state and the neo-patrimonial features of the administrative regime. As noted, in the dual system in Russia the formal procedures of the *constitutional state*, together with the political practices of public competition between parties and other representatives of society, is balanced by the shadowy and opaque structures of the *administrative regime*, populated by various factions and operating according to the practices of Byzantine court politics and mafia dons. In the Yukos affair from 2003 the administrative regime flexed its muscles, but still a rough parity remains between the two systems, and thus Russia today finds itself in a deeply entrenched stalemate. The tension between the two systems is the characteristic feature of Russian politics today. This is more than a hybrid system but one in which there is a continuing struggle between the two orders to shape the future of the country.

The typical panoply of democratic institutions has been created within the framework of the constitutional order, but a parallel system has emerged that claims certain prerogatives that transcend the rules and constraints of the constitutional state. This 'prerogative state', or as we call it, the administrative regime (*Verwaltungsstaat*), represents a distinctive case of 'domain democracy', where the rules applied to the rest of society do not apply to itself.[1] The duality in Russia is even more pronounced than even, for example, in Turkey, where journalists are regularly imprisoned, parties closed down by the order of dependent courts, and major restrictions imposed on various communities, notably the Kurds.[2] Elements of this duality are present in most countries, but in Russia the combination constitutes a distinctive order of its own. The two types of rule interact on a daily basis, leaving observers to clutch at every small sign as evidence of the predominance of one or the other. The apogee of systemic stalemate was reached in the tensions apparent in the tandem form of rule in the final period of Medvedev's presidency, as it became clear that Putin, as prime minister, was considering whether to assume the presidency in 2012, as allowed by the constitution.

Treisman argues that the present power system in Russia is far more comparable to mature capitalist democracies than we like to think.[3] In this light, there are many who argue that government in Russia is no more of a 'regime' than in countries where there have been long-entrenched ruling parties. This certainly has been Putin's argument, made at various sessions of the Valdai Club. In post-war Japan the Liberal Democratic Party ruled uninterrupted for 40 years and remains predominant, while in Sweden the Social Democrats ruled for 84 years, from 1917 to 1991. However, the difference is that in these countries elections were held relatively autonomously. The advantages of incumbency were undoubtedly exploited, but the courts were not suborned, the media remained relatively diverse and there were no artificial impediments to organising opposition parties.

From the time Putin came to power in 2000, the regime took on an ever stronger tutelary character, claiming the right to manage not only the sphere of policy, the usual job of governments, but also the exclusive right to manage political processes as a whole. This is what distinguishes a 'regime' from a normal 'government'. Fearing for the stability, and indeed for the very existence, of the state, Putin's regime represented a powerful shift from mobilisational to pacificatory politics; from responsiveness to independent civic activism to controlling and regulating it; and in the process suffocating not only political pluralism but also eroding the sources of regime renewal. This was the system known as 'managed democracy'. Popular inclusion in the Putin period did take place, but in an archaic manner reminiscent of Soviet practices. This was not modern civic participation of an active citizenry accompanied by the pluralistic representation of divergent interests. Inclusion at the economic level was partial, with small businesses remaining at the mercy of the bureaucracy, while big business was incorporated as a subaltern partner of the regime. The modernisation agenda from above was not accompanied by the necessary modernisation from the middle, represented by a competitive party system, an entrepreneurial and independent business culture, and a vibrant public sphere.

Russian politics is characterised by the dominance of a powerful yet diffuse administrative regime, recognising its subordination to the normative state on the one side and its formal accountability to the institutions of mass representative democracy on the other. However, it is not effectively constrained by either, hence the 'regime' character of the dominant power system. It is also for this reason that it would be an exaggeration to suggest that a full-blown 'prerogative state' has emerged in Russia, ruling through emergency decrees and sustained repression (which would have to hold to allow Russia to be characterised as a full-blown authoritarian state; hence Russia is often dubbed as 'soft authoritarian'). Instead, we have an 'administrative regime' as the protagonist of the normative state. There is no prerogative state as such in Russia, constituted through formal but extra-constitutional decrees or laws, but instead there is informal behaviour by an administrative regime that fulfils some of the functions of the prerogative state but that has no independent legal or institutional status of its own. The presidency maintains a Bonapartist type of independence by playing off the one against the other, while keeping a foot in both camps.

The administrative regime is both a network of social relations, in which political and economic power are entwined in a shifting landscape of factional politics, but it also functions as an actor in the political process. In that sense, Russians use the term *vlast'* (literally, power) rather than *gosudarstvo* (the state) to describe the authorities. Regime, or *vlast'*, has a passive element, acting as an arena of intra-bureaucratic contestation (since the social basis of the administrative regime overwhelmingly lies in Russia's burgeoning bureaucracy); but it also has agency features, allowing active purposive behaviour. The secret of Putin's power to a degree lay in his ability to draw on the resources of both systems, but in the end ran the danger of negating the functionality of both. The notion of undifferentiated *vlast'* draws on the long Russian tradition suggesting a gulf between the state and society, the classic idea of two Russias: one in which the insulated and distant power system rules, while the people get on with their own affairs and try to minimise the depredations of *vlast'*.

Two types of domination, or rule, identified by Max Weber as 'patrimonial' and 'legal-rational', generate two distinctive political orders, which in turn have given rise to the dual state. The neo-patrimonial elements generate systemic insecurity about which rule will apply at any particular time and thus actors have recourse to a range of informal behaviours to reduce risk, but this only generates further systemic insecurity and undermines the consolidation of the formal constitutional rule-bound political order. The arbitrary application of rules, and constant changes to the regulatory framework governing the conduct of elections and party development, gives a very short time horizon to individuals and to the behaviour of organisations. This has not yet been trumped by the emergence of a system-forming party with a longer time frame. Formal and informal rules operate at the same time, reproducing dualism at all levels and allowing actors to operate elements of either, but undermining the inherent internal logic of both. Actors devise numerous strategies to overcome insecurity, above all by operating in a 'dual' way: by employing both the formal and informal arenas. This reproduces systematic insecurity, and reinforces the insecurity that is endemic to the operation of the system as a whole. The combination of legal-rational behaviour and patrimonial forms of domination is typical for neo-patrimonial systems, but the application of the model of the dual state to describe this behaviour gives substance to a more dynamic model, identifying the process itself (which is the advantage of theories of neo-patrimonialism) as well as to the contradictory nature of this form of rule, and thus identifies the dynamics of resistance to that rule.

The constitutional state is based pre-eminently on the formal order of institutions, and thus its practices are unlike the factionalised politics of the administrative regime. Its adherents are found in legal-constitutional structures, among the liberal intelligentsia and those who have advanced into the elite up the electoral ladder. The latter route for independent politicians up to 2012 was increasingly blocked by the suffocating regulations imposed on the electoral process by the administrative regime. By definition, the defenders of constitutionalism and the rule of law appeal to openness and due process, although that does not preclude some factional fighting of their own. The goal of universal law has been proclaimed by all leaders since Gorbachev, and both Putin and Medvedev, with their legal background, have proclaimed the supremacy of law (*gospodstvo zakona*), although the achievement falls far short of the ambition. Post-communist Russia has been in a permanent state of exception, exercised not through constitutional provisions of some sort defining a state of emergency (as in Mubarak's Egypt) but through an informal and undeclared derogation from constitutional principles. This is exercised by the administrative regime, which in the long-term undermines the viability of constitutionalism as a whole. Elsewhere, notably in Malaysia and Singapore, regimes of exception have been unable to return to a condition of constitutional normality, but the problems associated with exceptional rule have been mitigated by the delivery of significant public goods, notably security and economic growth. In classic terms, the Putinite system pursued rational economic and social policies, but its duality meant that there was no coherent institutional framework to ensure that policies are pursued with the appropriate consistency or coherence while avoiding the pathologies of the 'third state'. Paradoxically, the chronic short-termism that blights much of governance in the West because of the imperatives of the electoral cycle was avoided in Russia because of the managed nature of elections, but the imperative of regime survival introduced its own logic of incoherence.

In Russia the state of exception has not become the norm and coexists with the routine exercise of law, and thus the situation remains liminal and open-ended. From early on there were misgivings that it was the regime that was being consolidated rather than the state being strengthened. These were far from mutually exclusive processes, but when the law was used against the regime's perceived opponents, notably Khodorkovsky, the electoral process engineered in an increasingly brazen manner to ensure regime perpetuation, and elites aligned with the power system became not only super-rich but also super-arrogant, then the well of support began to dry up. A new 'middle class' emerged, in part created by the stability and economic growth of the Putin period, which was less willing to put up with an unaccountable regime. At that point, from 2011 onwards, the country entered a new period when the regime could no longer so easily argue that its own survival was synonymous with the national interest. It became increasingly embarrassing for the urban professional classes that a country with the world's fifth largest economy, and with per capita income approaching $20,000p.a., could not even organise relatively free and fair elections. The fundamental demand was for the strengthening of the constitutional state: the rule of law and independent courts; an autonomous civil society and with it independent NGOs; a public sphere free of regime manipulations and crude propaganda campaigns against its opponents and the West; and above all a pluralistic and competitive political sphere, with parliament acting as a check against the executive authorities. However, there was no shortage of supporters for Putin's neo-authoritarianism, believing that the West was indeed engaged in an attempt to subvert the Russian political order to put in place someone who would be more amenable to western concerns. In other words, as so often in Russia, geopolitical contestation and constitutional consolidation came into fateful contradiction.

The contrast between an administrative and a constitutional state thus provides the key to interpreting developments in post-communist Russia. The fundamental legitimacy of the regime is derived from being embedded in a constitutional order to which it constantly proclaims its allegiance. The interaction between the constitutional (legal-rational) and administrative (neo-patrimonial) state in Russia has become the defining feature of the current political order. This dynamic tension precludes assigning Russia simply to the camp of authoritarian states in an essentialist manner, but it also means that Russia's democracy is flawed, above all because of abuses in the rule of law and the lack of political competition conducted on a level playing field. It is for this reason that the 2011–12 electoral cycle was accompanied by demands, including from leading ministers, for the elections to be held in a free and fair manner. Although the rule of law in Russia remains fragile and is susceptible to manipulation by the political authorities, no fully-fledged prerogative state has emerged either. Neither, however, has a fully-fledged rule of law state, and thus Russia remains trapped in the stalemated grey area between an administrative and a genuine constitutional state.

Socio-economic stalemate

The second stalemate is rooted in the socio-economic level, some of which has been discussed earlier and thus here I will simply outline the fundamental issue. Two great class forces are locked in stalemate in contemporary Russia. The first is the neo-Soviet bureaucracy: a great mass of officialdom entrenched in the ministries, the security apparatus and the military. Pensioners, the bedrock of Putin's support, also keep the CPRF alive. This represents a type of 'sociological communism', analogous to what Paul Preston has called 'sociological Francoism' in post-authoritarian Spain.[4] This is balanced by the emergence of sociological liberalism. New social forces created by the transition to the market now demand political freedom, the rule of law and secure property rights. In the early years of Russian post-communism, the liberal forces lacked defined social support and thus remained an idealist project relying on the state to achieve their goals of economic and political transformation. The protest movement from late 2011 signalled the emergence of social groups and a nascent bourgeoisie on which the liberal project could be grounded.

Various rent-seeking groups took advantage of the impasse, notably parts of the security apparatus and state-affiliated economic elites, and thus the idea of 'partial reform equilibrium' (when further reforms are blocked prematurely) – an idea advanced by Joel S. Hellman in the late 1990s – still has some traction. Hellman, a leading analyst of the Russian economy, argued that the early economic winners block measures that would complete the transition to a market economy.[5] Khodorkovsky's challenge in 2003 to the regime's proclaimed role as manager of modernization revealed a new force in the land – an independent bourgeoisie. At the same time, the challenge was interpreted as a throwback to the era of oligarch power in the mid-1990s. In truth, Khodorkovsky looked backwards to the 1990s in seeking to use economic power to manage the financial and tax environment in which business operated, but he also looked forwards to a more pluralistic political order and an active citizenry. The Yukos affair set back the advance of the new order by nearly a decade, allowing the administrative regime to consolidate its economic power and ability to undermine the constitutional state. This system was challenged by the mass demonstrations during the 2011–12 electoral cycle, which indicated the emergence of a politically conscious middle class, confident in its economic achievements and now demanding free and equal inclusion in the political order.

Numerous studies have noted the correlation between economic development and political democratization, but Russia remains an exception to this general rule.[6] With a per capita income of an upper-income country, Russia can be classified as a rich country, yet it has at best a weak democracy. It appears to be caught in the classic 'middle-income trap', in which the politics need to be sorted out before the country can achieve sustained economic growth. The great majority of countries that were classified as middle income in 1960 remained so in 2008; only a handful became high-income economies by that year.[7] Countries engaged in catch-up growth appear to hit an invisible ceiling. There are only a few breakout states, such as Japan and Korea, while some 90 countries failed to reach middle-income status. Even the Chinese model of state-driven industrialization is running out of steam.[8] The usual recipe to break out of the trap is increased productivity through innovation, and for this the political conditions have to be right, above all a competitive political system.

Russia appears to have hit the economic middle-income ceiling. In political terms, for at least a decade it has languished in some sort of democratic backwater. No studies examining the relationship between economic development and democratization suggest an automatic determinative relationship between economic growth and political change, yet the anomalous case of Russia demands further explanation. In part, the answer undoubtedly lies in the country's troubled history, with the Soviet experience still shaping structures and practices of contemporary Russia (above all, the undigested legacy of the past, a huge bureaucratic apparatus and an overweening security apparatus), and the chaos of the 1990s weighs heavily on public consciousness. The flood of natural resource rents in the 2000s is also an important factor, allowing the regime to insulate itself from genuine political accountability. With its cup running over, the regime was freed from reliance on parliamentary-sanctioned tax revenues and could buy support from state employees, pensioners and others by raising wages and public benefits.

The Putinite reshaping of the political system in the 2000s allowed consolidation of the administrative regime accompanied by the luxuriant growth of corruption. As we shall see, it also provided a social basis for renewed political struggles and popular mobilisation.

The third state: reality vs appearance

I have already alluded to the tenebrous third reality in contemporary Russian politics, and here I will argue that these deeper processes inhibit not only rational policy making but above all contribute to the impasse in constitutional development. The gulf between the visible part of politics and various subterranean processes became apparent very early on in Yeltsin's rule. The 'democratic' revolution of 1991 was quickly captured by the Yeltsin group, which, despite its reformist achievements pushed through by the economic liberals, soon became transformed into 'the family', with all of its mafia 'deep state' implications. The first incarnation of the *siloviki*, the Alexander Korzhakov, Mikhail Barsukov and Oleg Soskovets group, provoked the first Chechen war in December 1994, but was effectively defeated by the counter-move of the liberals led by Chubais in 1996; but the same Chubais sponsored Putin's move to Moscow in 1996 and helped smooth the ascent of the 'enlightened securocrats' later in the decade. The degradation of the constitutional state continued as representatives of *vlast'* became in certain respects the power of *avtoritety*, the godfathers in the mafia tradition.

Thus the administrative regime and the constitutional state are joined by what in Italy is called the 'deep state'. This is a subterranean nexus of bureaucratic power, the security services and various types of criminal organisations. In Russia this dense network of corrupt relationships is variously called 'the mafiya' or some similar designation. This third state reaches into the very heart of government and is characterised by two types of corruption. The *venal* sort is focused on classic bribe taking and bribe giving, transferred for services that should be free but which take on a pecuniary character in a system in which elements of degradation erode ordinary transactions. The scale of this of course is unknown, but is reflected in Transparency International's Corruption Perception Index. There is a second form which I call *meta-corruption*, when the autonomy of the political system is eroded and administration is placed at the service of criminal and inappropriate activities, undermining the independence of the courts and the impartial management of social processes.

The concept of the 'deep state' is applied in several contexts. It has been used in Italy to describe the interaction of state officials, security agencies and organised crime, and was particularly prominent at the time of political stress in the 1970s.[9] Several incidents of that time still remain unexplained, notably the death of Aldo Mori, prime minister from 1963 to 1968 and then again from 1974 to 1976, who was kidnapped by the Red Brigades on 16 March 1978 and killed after 55 days of captivity precisely at the time when he was reciprocating the Communist Party of Italy's idea of a 'historic compromise' to create a 'national solidarity' government (opposed by the United States). The bombing of Bologna railway station on 2 August 1980 killed 85 people amid persistent rumours of Italian secret service involvement.[10]

But it is in Turkey that the idea of a deep state has the most profound impact, and the most pertinent comparisons with Russia. Following the military coup of 1980, the 1981 constitution reserved a privileged place for the military as the defender of the Kemalist secular, nationalist, militarist and semi-isolationist (in the sense of keeping out of wars, although Turkey joined NATO in 1952) political order. This tutelary element is reminiscent of Putin's representation of the functions of his regime in defending political order by transcending the spirit of the constitution. In Turkey, the military was empowered to intervene to defend the constitution, and thus by definition became supra-constitutional. The relevant clauses were abolished by the government of Recep Tayyip Erdoğan in the early 2000s as it pursued its ambition to join the European Union. Hailed as a progressive measure by Turkey's allies, paradoxically the removal of a balance against the Justice and Development Party (AKP) after its crushing electoral victory (winning 52 per cent of the popular vote in the 2012 election) opened the door to majoritarian populism and accelerated Islamisation.[11] The 'Putinisation' of the Turkish regime became a matter of popular discussion following the harsh crackdown on the wave of protest catalysed by plans to redevelop Taksim Square, including the destruction of Gezi Park, from May 2013.

In Russia enormous resources are devoted to maintaining the security apparatus. The country spends some $60bn a year, about 3 per cent of GDP, on the security services, and roughly the same amount in addition on regular military forces. A core Putinite practice is the allocation of resources to groups who would normally be disadvantaged in a market economy – state employees, pensioners, and in the case under discussion, the security apparatus. The overblown security apparatus generates interests of its own, with department piled upon section, each of which fights for its own perpetuation, its slice of the budgetary pie, and to advance its vision of the world. But does this constitute a deep state? Was there some force in Russia that could over-ride elections, the government, the administration and impose its will, by force if necessary. In Egypt the deep state was based on a 'power triangle' between the military (above all the army), the security services (the police and security policy under the control of the interior ministry), and the political authorities. The coup of 3 July 2013 showed the power of this deep state, which overthrew the legally-elected president who took office in June 2012, Mohamed Morsi, and thereafter ruled as a junta, reinstating Mubarak's secret police, gunning down oppositionists, and imposing the emergency rule of the Mubarak years. Putin and his associates constantly warn against popular democratic revolutions ending up like this, and with some justice. In the Soviet Union and in Russia the regular military has long resisted becoming politicised, especially after the bitter experience of 1991 and 1993 when they were drawn into political battles, but the MVD and other security agencies have in effect armies of their own who could act as the praetorian guard.

In short, it would be an exaggeration to argue that Russia has a 'deep state' as defined above, but the powerful security-economic nexus acts as part of the blockage on modernisation. In the context of a dual state a regime has emerged that can trump the stipulations of the constitution, but which remains constrained by the constitutional framework. Its subversions of legality remain illegitimate as defined by the system itself, and there has been no legal invocation of emergency rule. Instead, there is a system of meta-corruption, in which the agents of the state are heavily implicated. The security forces have a special role, but even their illicit political and economic activities are balanced by other features of the complex organism that is the Russian power system. Unable to act as a state within the state, they have operated as a sub-faction within the regime. A powerful description of the rise and operation of various security force factions is provided by Felshtinsky and Pribylovsky, including the way that the Korzhakov faction provoked the first Chechen war. Putin was appointed head of the FSB on 25 July 1998 to reform the body and not simply as their emissary in the power system.[12] In other words, even in their sensationalist account a political level remains outside the deep state, which retains decisional autonomy. This is also reflected in the excellent account of the 'new nobility' by Soldatov and Borogan, in which they note that:

> Putin opened the door to many dozens of security service agents to move up in the main institutions of the country, perhaps hoping that they would prove a vanguard of stability and order. But once they had tasted the benefits, agents began to struggle amongst themselves for the spoils.[13]

There is no unity of purpose in Russia's third state, and instead a mix of venal and meta-corruption erodes the quality of government at all levels.

This has not prevented a great flood of literature describing how 'the secret police control all the centres of the economy, security and social life'. The quotation comes from Francesca Mereu's addition to the genre, *My Friend Putin*, published in Italian in June 2011. The book contains a foreword by the well-known journalist and politician Paolo Guzzanti, who chaired the parliamentary commission into the so-called Mitrokhin case, examining KGB activities in Italy between 2002 and 2006. Guzzanti was a close friend of Berlusconi's but broke with him over the latter's continued commitment to Putin, whom he called 'friend Vladimir', from which the book draws its title. Like Masha Gessen's book of the same genre, the basic idea is that Putin was the spearhead of a group of former security officials who took control of Russia. For Gessen, Putin came to power with a conscious plan to install some sort of dictatorship, and leaves out any complicating details such as policy conflicts over the economy or external relations, and assumes some sort of perfect state of governability.[14] Mereu sees Putin more as a figurehead for the group, talking in terms of 'Putin's project'. He came to power as the representative of 'the family', the Yeltsinite group desperate to manage the succession in 1999–2000 to preserve the status quo under a new leader.

According to Mereu, the oligarchs headed by Berezovsky offered Putin a deal whereby he would occupy the presidency while they would continue to rule from behind the throne. Putin allegedly agreed to the deal unreservedly. The bombings of the apartment blocks in September 1999 and the second Chechen war were then organised by the KGB in support of Putin's election. Once in power, the KGB then turned its hand to exploiting vulnerable entrepreneurs, closing down media diversity, killing enemies such as Alexander Litvinenko and Anna Politkovskaya, and thriving in conditions of high oil prices. A *rentier* class consolidated its power, disposing of the country's wealth to its personal advantage. An appendix argues that Berlusconi adopted and imitated from Putin such features as the personality cult, stifling of media freedom and attacks on the independence of the judiciary, and not the other way round. Putinism thus represented a new international style of governance.[15] Unlike in the Soviet years, there was no need for total media control, and thus websites and newspapers were largely left alone. As Derk Sauer, the head of Sanoma Independent Media which own 60 per cent of the Russian magazine market, argues, Putin modelled himself not on Brezhnev but on Berlusconi: 'It's not for nothing that they are such good friends. They understand that if you control the main TV stations and make propaganda there, you'll go far.' This led to the paradoxical outcome that 'there's complete press freedom for the informed but none for the uninformed'.[16]

A no less lurid account comes from Edward Lucas, an editor at *The Economist*. As in his earlier book, *The New Cold War*, which never quite decided whether it sought to avert or to provoke a new conflict,[17] Lucas leads the charge for the prosecution: Russia is a 'pirate state', mired in corruption and venality, with up to half of the country's budget of £140bn siphoned off illegally; ruled by a 'criminal conspiracy' of Soviet-era security officials in which organised crime and big business collude and merge; and above all, exploiting the naïveté of the West, these spies take advantage of open societies to steal commercial and diplomatic information. Not much is left to the imagination, with the book describing the role of the FSB and Putin-associated networks interchangeably, using the terms 'spookdom', 'officialdom' and 'gangsterdom'.[18] This is a genre of populist scare-mongering that has a long pedigree in Britain, already focused on Russia in the 1830s because of the brutal suppression of the Polish uprising of 1830–31, and which provoked Britain's first catastrophic invasion of Afghanistan in 1839.[19] This style of targeted xenophobia also shaped Britain's intervention in the Crimean War (1853–56); it was for a time directed against Germany in the run-up to the First World War (by which time Russia was an ally, to the latter's disastrous cost); before turning once again against Russia in the Cold War and after. The use of emotive terms, simplified narratives which make little attempt to explain the motives and concerns of the other party, and preying on alleged domestic vulnerabilities to whip up a new crusade, all come from the playlist of imperial mentalities.

Medvedev's reform of the militia in 2010 demonstrated concern that the abuses of the third state were beginning to threaten governance in its entirety. Rather than fighting criminality, there was much evidence that militia personnel were heavily engaged in various criminal activities, including extortion and various scams, the most notorious of which is the Hermitage Capital Affair (see below). As a report in *The Economist* noted, 'Police violence is not new in Russia, but a recent wave of publicity is. A simple explanation is that police lawlessness has exhausted people's patience and that pent-up anger has finally burst into newspapers, websites and even state television.'[20] Medvedev fired Moscow's police chief and launched a reform of the interior ministry (MVD). Police numbers were slashed by 20 per cent and central control was reasserted over regional police forces. There were new requirements on police conduct during searches and other operations, and all police personnel were re-certified to root out corruption and incompetence. The Soviet-style name 'militia' was rebranded with the western style 'police'. Thousands of police were fired as part of the re-attestation of all serving officers, but the efficacy of the reform was questioned. Taken in isolation and without a reform of the state, police reform would not be able to change the fundamental relationship in which:

> The main function of law-enforcement agencies in Russia is not to protect the public from crime and corruption, but to shield the bureaucracy, including themselves, from the public. To ensure loyalty the system allows police and security services to make money from their licence for violence. [One of the most common was] raiding businesses for competitors.[21]

Khodorkovsky wrote that 'the police, prosecution and prison services are component parts of an industry whose business is legitimised violence and which uses people as raw material'. More disturbingly, under Putin traditional antagonisms were overcome and the MVD fell under the influence of the FSB. As the lawyer and independent scholar Vladimir Pastukhov put it, 'The FSB can dabble in any business it likes, but relies on the police to do the footwork. Serious police reform is therefore impossible if the masters are left alone'.[22] In another study he argues that Putin did not eliminate arbitrariness but gave it 'a more or less organised character'.[23] The securo-judicial apparatus remained a powerful instrument of regime power, but it was as factionalised as the rest of the system. Despite Medvedev's calls for reform, the law enforcement agencies remained a law unto themselves. On 1 January 2011 the Investigative Committee was removed from the jurisdiction of the General Prosecutor's Office (GPO) to become the free-standing Russian Investigative Committee (RIC) answerable directly to the president. The head of the GPO, Yuri Chaika, was furious at this drastic reduction in his power, but this was just one of the inter-departmental conflicts plaguing the Putin system of Byzantine politics. Headed by the pugnacious Mikhail Bastrykin, who became one of the most powerful and independent figures in Putin's power elite, RIC was involved in the prosecution of some high-profile individuals, including Sergei Storchak and Sergei Magnitsky. Bastrykin stressed that one of RIC's main tasks was to fight corruption.[24]

Putin came to power in 2000 promising to root politics in the normative power of the constitution, but instead the neo-patrimonial order brought all institutions and political processes under the tutelage of the administrative regime. The power system is susceptible to weaknesses of its own, above all fragmentation and elite factionalism. Putin's reconstitution of the state shifted the basis of presidential hegemony away from dependence on oligarchic or other forces. However, the failure to move away from 'manual control' of political processes prevented a more self-regulating system from emerging, and instead the mechanical approach created a system that showed signs of brittleness and a lack of adaptive resources. Above all, the dualism identified earlier was in danger of degenerating into a triple system in which the merger of power and property jeopardised the viability of the economy as a whole.[25] There is more going on than meets the eye, with venal corruption in danger of metastising into meta-corruption and degeneration of the whole system.

Contesting epistemes

At least three epistemes, to use a Foucauldian term to denote justified true beliefs, are locked in conflict. The first is *political liberalism*, drawing on the democratization agenda within the framework of the project of '1989', with its representations of normality, 'the return to Europe', standards of civilization defined by western norms. Economic liberals are at the core of this trend, but not all sympathise with its political precepts. The liberal 'revolutionaries' of the 1990s were happy to rely on the power of the state to drive through the transition to capitalist democracy. Putin himself is mostly an exemplary economic liberal, pursuing neo-classical macroeconomic strategies of a sound currency, balanced budgets and international economic integration, although he also favours the relatively active role of the state in economic management.

The political liberal episteme is often accompanied by the iconoclastic denunciation of backward Russia, with neo-Trotskyite appeals to sacrifice Russia on the altar of the world capitalist revolution, so that a new and more acceptable version of the country can emerge out of the bonfire of traditionalism. The standard charge against the liberal episteme is that it lacks a sense of history and place; Russia emerges as a subject-less entity, with its thousand-year history denigrated and its location on the great North European–Eurasian plain, with all of the attendant threats, downplayed. The liberal paradigm tends to see itself as part of a 'little and weak' European Russia, overshadowed by a 'very big' Asiatic Russia, and thus perceives itself to be a permanently embattled minority. Even Putin began his reign as a committed Europeanist, and gradually shifted to more Eurasian, if not 'Asiatic', perspectives, in both the geographical and political senses.[26] But for the radical wing of the political liberals, Putin was little more than a 'bloodthirsty despot', and hence an illegitimate ruler to be overthrown. For these radical liberal 'Leninists', Russia's history is a burden and its geopolitical assertions are dangerous. The search for a 'usable past' – a version of history that could give legitimacy to the new political order – was doomed, from this perspective, to reproduce the pathologies of the past. The radical liberal episteme is burdened by a partial sense of history and geography, and on the geopolitical level it has no basis to critique, let alone challenge, the broader structures of the contemporary international system.

The liberals are associated with the 'chaotic 1990s', and since the 2000s have not been able to define an attractive political programme, although their ideas, above all in the economic sphere, remain hegemonic within the polity. The Medvedev interregnum allowed a specific variation of the liberal paradigm to prosper, a faction that can be called the *civiliki*. In contrast to the *siloviki*, they favoured a more open and competitive domestic political environment and were more ready to embrace the West's representation of itself as benign and progressive. The fundamental dilemma for Russian liberals and *civiliki* is that in open and free elections it is unlikely that they would win more than 10 per cent of the popular vote. Their influence in politics and culture greatly exceeded their social base, and hence they were forced to accommodate themselves to the exigencies of regime politics. However, at the moment of regime rupture, the crisis accompanying Putin's return in 2011–12, the urban intelligentsia and professional classes, the liberals' natural constituency, and the so-called 'Russian middle class' catalysed the protest movement and thereafter continued to press for free and fair elections.

The liberal view is challenged by a *neo-traditionalist* episteme – the word 'traditionalist' is intended to encompass the broadness of the phenomenon, while the 'neo' denotes that all adapt to new circumstances. The category includes monarchists appealing to the imperial era, arguing that some sort of return to the moral world of the pre-revolutionary epoch could contribute to the resurrection of Russia. There are also groups with neo-Soviet tendencies, including dyed-in-the-wool Stalinists seeking his political rehabilitation, socialists of various stripes, and those with an affective nostalgia for the comforts and certainties of the Brezhnev years. Contemporary Russian nationalism, based on ideas of national integrity and a separate developmental path, is a core part of the traditionalist episteme. The Russian Orthodox Church expresses some of the most profound beliefs of the traditionalist episteme, although also responding to the challenge of renewal.[27] These two epistemes appeared prominently even within the protest movement after the parliamentary elections in December 2011, and in part explain the difficulties in establishing a common platform. The liberals espoused a return to constitutional norms and the establishment of pluralist competitive elections, whereas the traditionalists assumed a more radical inflexion, pursuing nationalist themes and neo-Soviet aspirations. The partnership between church and regime was intensified, to the point that many feared that the country was once again being 'clericalised'.

The idea of neo-traditionalism was applied to the Soviet Union in its final manifestation.[28] It draws on historical experience and civilisational complex, founded on a cultural matrix. This cannot be simply counter-posed to modernity, since neo-traditionalism is increasingly becoming a political inflection of modernity. Neither is it anti-modern; that is, repudiating achievements in science and technology or even the spirit of critical enquiry, which is the essence of modernity (although some aspects of course are obscurantist). Neo-traditionalism represents a critique of neo-liberal capitalism, anti-statism and anti-communitarianism, and sustains the conservative cultural turn that is an essential part of Putin's return. The demand is for a more pluralistic understanding of traditionalism (as well as of modernity) based on the idea that modernisation is heterogeneous. The late Putinite form of neo-traditionalism for the first time presented itself as a cultural and ideological project. Its critics feared that it fostered some of the most obscurantist aspects of Russia's history and oppressive forms of social management.

Defending restrictions imposed on the Russian LGBT community, Sergei Markov, one of the most eloquent exponents of the new traditionalism, argued that Russia, recently emerged from 'the communist period and failed attempt to build a utopian society', 'is rediscovering Russian Orthodox principles along with other traditional spiritual values that will bolster society and protect it against the turbulent present and uncertain future'. He condemned the idea that 'Russia is somehow more backward than the West', which he insisted was 'a typical error based on the linear understanding of progress that dominated in the 19th and 20th centuries'. In his view Russia was pioneering a new concept based on the 'zoning of public space', with LGBT minorities free to pursue their lifestyles, 'but only within private zones'.[29] Classical Putinism in his view had been predicated on a passive population, but the authorities were now 'transforming the political system based on the serious challenges it faces'. The growth in social activism was wider than political protest and the growth in opposition, and the main challenge for the authorities was to channel this civil activity 'to avoid triggering unpredictable political developments such as those that occurred during former Soviet leader Mikhail Gorbachev's fateful era'. Hence it was necessary to reduce the dependence of NGOs on foreign funding, to strengthen 'the moral fibre of society', and to ensure that 'the protest movement stays within the limits of the law' by tightly regulating political rallies.[30]

A number of patriotic think tanks were established to give substance to the neo-traditionalist offensive.[31] The Izborsky Club, founded in Pskov on 8 September 2012, propounded themes such as the need to preserve Russia's 'national and spiritual identity', which were echoed in Putin's speeches, such as in his *poslanie* of December 2012 and the Valdai speech in September 2013, as well as giving some ideological depth to his Eurasian aspirations. The Club explicitly sought to provide an intellectual alternative to liberalism, and thus to underpin the new more conservative brand of Putinism. Bringing together some two dozen conservatives and nationalists and with a radical desecularising agenda, the group was led by the veteran editor of *Zavtra*, Alexander Prokhanov, long the beacon of the neo-Soviet *revanche*. Others involved included the partisan of Eurasianism, Alexander Dugin, Mikhail Delyagin and other critics of liberalism, and they did not hesitate to draw on the thinking of 'new right' thinkers such as Alain de Benoist to press home the attack. The appointment of Vladimir Medinsky, who attended the Club's second session in October 2012, as culture minister was a clear sign of the growing reach of this tendency. A surprising member of the Izborsky Club was Sergei Kurginyan, who had long criticised Dugin for his apparent neo-fascist inclinations. Kurginyan had been active in the late Soviet years as a critic of Gorbachev's reforms and later as a partisan of the reconstitution of the Soviet Union. As part of the counter-movement to the liberal mobilisation following Putin's return, Kurginyan established the Anti-Orange Committee, bringing together the virulently anti-western television commentators Mikhail Leontiev and Maksim Shevchenko, together with the neo-Stalinist publisher Nikolai Starikov and Prokhanov. At the extreme end of the new right mobilisation was the Florian Geyer Conceptual Club, founded in September 2011 by the well-known anti-western Islamist Geidar Dzemal. The name is drawn from one of the leaders of the German Peasants' War of the sixteenth century, but it was also the nickname of the Third Reich's 8th SS Cavalry Division.[32]

Between these two epistemes is a third: the *centrist* ideology originally espoused by Putin, but which in his third term became hollowed out. The centrist line was substantiated by opinion poll evidence. The 'what Russians dream about' study found little support for either the American system or the liberal European model as the ideal organisational model for society, and instead stressed 'social justice, equal rights for all and a strong state that takes care of its citizens'. This ideal of a strong, socially-orientated, law-based state approximated to the 'illiberal democracy' of Bismarck's late nineteenth-century Germany. The great majority, 71 per cent, supported a larger role of the state in the economy and social sphere, including the nationalisation of the main enterprises and strategic sectors, and 57 per cent supported a 'strong leftist state' in which the government played a major role, including planning and distribution. The ideal was the combination of social and legal justice. Although some 28 per cent of Russians were broadly liberals, no social group expressed preference for the western political or socio-economic model. Equally, only 19 per cent favoured regime change, with this group found concentrated not in the 'creative classes' but in the blue-collar workers of Moscow and the big cities, alienated by pervasive inequality, the lack of social justice, official abuse and rampant corruption.[33] Thus Putin's model of a strong state and *dirigisme* was rooted in popular preferences, although the lack of social and legal justice provided plenty of scope for critique, as did the lack of opportunity for ordinary people to fulfil their potential in the stifling tutelary system. There was also a potential well of opposition in the social classes considered the bedrock of Putinism. The blockage on upward social mobility represented a clear danger to the system.

Putin had always instinctively been a conservative, but in his third term this became more clearly articulated. The classic Putinists were well aware of the danger posed by the militancy of some sections of the traditionalist wing (above all radical Russian nationalists), but the developed Putinite system was forced to draw on the authority of the Russian Orthodox Church and other traditionalist forces to bolster its shaken authority. Equally, the centrists had no consistent economic policy of their own and thus pursued broadly liberal macroeconomic strategies tempered by the needs of the distributional coalitions and rent consumers on which the regime was based. The centrists also appealed to national development strategies but failed to enunciate a consistent vision or strategy of how this could be applied. The renewed programme of Eurasian integration sought to re-energise the centrist perspective by providing it with an economic base and a political perspective, but this was in danger once again of succumbing to the anti-European and *Sonderweg* (special path) illusions of the original Eurasianists of the 1920s and earlier. From the very beginning of his leadership Putin stressed that Russia must pursue its *own* path towards modernity and democracy, but he has not claimed that this path is *special*, in the sense that Russia represents an alternative modernity.[34] Russia's uniqueness was accentuated on his return, to give substance and legitimacy to the move, but Putin rarely imbued his actions with metaphysical purport but now he talked of Russia not as a 'project' but as destiny.[35] He was and remained a pragmatic power-maximising politician, and it was this that prompted some of the more radical Sonderwegers, like those in the Izborsky Club, to develop an agenda of their own. Putinite centrism was eroded from the left and right, and paradoxically as we shall see even from the centre as Medvedev sought to expound an ideology of progressive conservatism opposed to the Izborsky-style special-pathers and reactionaries.

In foreign policy, the centrist regime pursued a policy of neo-revisionism: fearful of becoming the centre of a balancing coalition against the West, it was equally unable to integrate into the West's institutional and normative framework.[36] Above all, in political terms, Putinite centrism espoused a technocratic managerial ethos, whose inevitable concomitant was depoliticisation. In the classic period this allowed Putin's leadership to insulate itself from the excessive influence of privileged oligarchs, regional bosses and other special interests. However, by the time of Putin's return to the presidency in 2012, this insulation claim was far less credible, especially when the regime itself was perceived to have become a special interest of its own, no longer governing in the national interest.

Beyond the impasse

The centrist episteme provided movement and strategic direction in the early 2000s, buoyed by windfall energy rents, but by 2012 the public perceived that it had become both exhausted and corrupted. Thus Russia suffers from a stalemate operating at several levels: the administrative regime undermining the institutionalisation of the constitutional state, the new 'creative' class stymied by the neo-Soviet officialdom, the third state corrupting social relationships, and the liberal episteme countered by various traditionalist ideas. Centrism was able to feed on these contradictions to sustain a certain developmental dynamic of its own, but in the end it was unable to transcend these deeply entrenched blockages. Attempts to appeal to the rule of law and state strengthening were vitiated by the application of 'telephone law' (as in Khodorkovsky's two convictions, which led to him being sentenced to a long prison term in what were undoubtedly political trials) and the personalization of power accompanied by the systemic failure to allow the institutions of the constitutional state to work in the way envisaged by the spirit of the constitution.

The political stalemate was part of the broader developmental crisis, in which the entrepreneurial class inspired by the liberal episteme was stymied and persecuted by officialdom and corrupt security and judicial agencies, giving rise to the mass phenomenon of raiding, attacks by corrupt officials and business leaders to seize the property of rivals.[37] By the time Putin re-entered the Kremlin in 2012, Russia was suffering all of the classical symptoms of blocked modernisation and its associated political impasse. Its case may not have been as severe as those in several North African and Middle Eastern states leading up to the Arab Spring in 2011, yet there were enough commonalities – above all in the practices of political exclusion and depoliticized centrism – to make the comparison valid. In broad terms, the stalemate between rent-seeking elites and profit-seeking groups was characteristic of both regions.[38] In Russia, the stalemate was sustained by the broader sociological realities of balanced class forces accompanied by the middle income trap, reinforced by two major epistemic communities unable to gain hegemony, allowing a centrist ideology to triumph until wounded by the events of 2011–12. This is not equilibrium of the sort described by neoclassical economics, but rather a stalemate.

The rest of this book is about how the impasse worked out in practice, and I will return to the question of the possible paths to break the stalemate in the final chapters. The stalemate could be broken by sociological developments, notably the consolidation of a politically conscious and liberally-minded middle class, or it could be transcended through some sort of political crisis and breakdown of the old regime or the assembly of a neo-traditional patriotic consensus. The Medvedev presidency opened up the possibility of a gradual liberalisation of the regime. This would have allowed the constitutional state gradually to expand its sphere, above all by asserting the independence of the courts and limiting the arbitrariness of the administrative regime, but it was perceived as weak and incoherent, and above all unable to defend Russia's national interests and foreign policy concerns. Putin's return put an end to that evolutionary option, and raised the spectre of a violent breakdown. Developed Putinism proceeded to reshape the country's developmental trajectory based on more conservative values, Eurasian integration, a turn to the East and a reshaped polity.

Notes

1. Cf. Wolfgang Merkel, 'Embedded and Defective Democracies', *Democratisation*, Vol. 11, No. 5, December 2004, pp. 33–58.
2. For an examination of some of the factors provoking such a situation, see Lauren McLaren and Burak Cop, 'The Failure of Democracy in Turkey: A Comparative Analysis', *Government and Opposition*, Vol. 46, No. 4, October 2011, pp. 485–516.
3. Daniel Treisman, *The Return: Russia's Journey from Gorbachev to Medvedev* (London, Simon & Schuster, 2011).
4. Paul Preston, *The Spanish Holocaust: Inquisition and Extermination in Twentieth-Century Spain* (London, HarperPress, 2012).
5. Joel S. Hellman, 'Winners Take All: The Politics of Partial Reform in Postcommunist Transitions', *World Politics*, Vol. 50, No. 2, 1998, pp. 203–34.
6. For a classic statement, see Seymour Martin Lipset, 'Some Social Requisites of Democracy', *American Political Science Review*, Vol. 53, No. 1, 1959, pp. 69–105.
7. "The Middle-Income Trap," *Economist Online*, March 27, 2012. For a more detailed comparative analysis, see Harpaul A. Kohli and Natasha Mukherjee, 'Potential Costs to Asia of the Middle Income Trap', *Global Journal of Emerging Market Economies*, Vol. 3, No. 3, September 2011, pp. 291–311.
8. Data drawn from a joint report by the World Bank and the Development Research Centre of the State Council, PRC: *China 2030: Building a Modern, Harmonious, and Creative High Income Society* (Washington, DC, The World Bank, 2012).
9. See J. Patrice McSherry, *Predatory States: Operation Condor and Covert War in Latin America* (Boulder, CO, Rowman & Littlefield, 2005), pp. 43–45.
10. For a popular account, see Tobias Jones, *The Dark Heart of Italy* (London, Faber & Faber, 2007).
11. The persecution of the Ergenekon secularist and nationalist 'Kemalist' organisation (allegedly part of the deep state) by then had already led to the imprisonment of some 500 officials and officers, including members of the High Command, while in separate prosecutions the same number of journalists had been detained. This far outweighs anything that Putin had done by that stage, although there are potent comparisons in terms of regime type.
12. Yurii Felshtinsky and Vladimir Pribylovsky, *The Age of Assassins: The Rise and Rise of Vladmir Putin* (London, Gibson Square, 2008), pp. 87–92.
13. Andrei Soldatov and Irina Borogan, *The New Nobility: The Restoration of Russia's Security State and the Enduring Legacy of the KGB* (New York, Public Affairs, 2010), p. 241.
14. Masha Gessen, *The Man Without a Face: The Unlikely Rise of Vladimir Putin* (New York, Riverhead Books, 2012).
15. Francesca Mereu, *L'amico Putin: L'invenzione della dittatura democratic* (Reggio Emilia, Aliberti Editore, 2011). For a summary, see 'Friend Putin: The Invention of the Democratic Dictatorship' prepared by Valdai Club staff, http:// valdaiclub.com/books_italian/43640.
16. Simon Kuper, 'What Putin Learnt from Berlusconi', *Financial Times*, 31 May 2013.
17. Edward Lucas, *The New Cold War: How the Kremlin Menaces both Russia and the West* (London, Bloomsbury, 2008).
18. Edward Lucas, *Deception: Spies, Lies and How Russia Dupes the West* (London, Bloomsbury, 2012).

19 J. H. Gleason, *The Genesis of Russophobia in Great Britain: A Study of the Interaction of Policy and Opinion* (Cambridge, Cambridge University Press, 1950).
20 'Police Brutality in Russia: Cope for Hire', *The Economist*, 18 March 2010; http://www.economist.com/node/15731344/print.
21 Op. cit.
22 Ibid.
23 Vladimir Pastukhov, 'Legenda No 1917', *Novaya gazeta*, 22 August 2013. For an extended analysis, see Vladimir Pastukhov, *Restavratsiya vmesto reformatsii: Dvadtsat' let, kotorye potryasli Rossiyu* (Moscow, OGI, 2012).
24 Boris Yamshanov and Viktor Vasenin, 'Neposredstvennaya zhizn': Predlozheniya ot Bastrykina – sozdat' edinyi sledstevnnyi komitet I vvesti otchety o raskhodakh chinovnikov', *Rossiiskaya gazeta*, 7 September 2010.
25 For a typical analysis along these lines, see Maksim Kalashnikov, *Putin inkorporeited: Kak Putinu obustroit' Rossiyu* (Moscow, Algoritm/Eksmo, 2013).
26 For an excellent analysis, see Alexander Yanov, 'Putin and the "Russian Idea"', *IMR*, 1 July 2013.
27 See for example Sergei Chaplin, *Tserkov' v postsovetskoi Rossii: Vozrozhdenie, kachestvo very, dialog s obshchestvom* (Moscow, Arefa, 2013).
28 For example, the chapter 'Neotraditionalism', in Ken Jowitt, *New World Disorder: The Leninist Extinction* (Berkeley, University of California Press, 1992), pp. 121–58.
29 Sergei Markov, 'Russia Should Create Private Zones for LGBT', *Moscow Times*, 6 February 2013.
30 Sergei Markov, 'The Myths of Putin's Political Repression', *Moscow Times*, 11 July 2013a.
31 Marlène Laruelle, *Inside and Around the Kremlin's Black Box: The New Nationalist Think Tanks in Russia* (Institute for Security & Development Policy, Stockholm Paper, October 2009).
32 Andreas Umland, 'New Extreme Right-Wing Intellectual Circles in Russia: The Anti-Orange Committee, the Izborsk Club and the Florian Geyer Club', *Russian Analytical Digest*, No. 135, 5 August 2013, pp. 2–6.
33 Gorshkov *et al.*, *O chëm mechtayut rossiyane*, pp. 54–84.
34 Cf. Andreas Umland, 'The Claim of Russian Distinctiveness as Justification for Putin's Neo-Authoritarian Regime', *Russian Politics and Law*, Vol. 50, No. 5, September–October 2012, pp. 3–6.
35 'Meeting of the Valdai International Discussion Club', 19 September 2013; http://eng.kremlin.ru/news/6007.
36 Richard Sakwa, 'The Cold Peace: Russo-Western Relations as a Mimetic Cold War,' *Cambridge Review of International Affairs*, Vol. 26, No. 1, 2013, pp. 203–24.
37 Ledeneva, *Can Russia Modernise?* pp. 179–210.
38 Douglas C. North, Joseph Wallis and Barry R. Weingast, *Violence and Social Orders: A Conceptual Framework for Interpreting Recorded Human History* (Cambridge: Cambridge University Press, 2009).

5 On the eve

Successive Russian elections only deferred the time when a substantive choice between governments was presented to the public. The electoral process has been captured by the administrative regime, and although formally conducted according to the rules of the constitutional state, has been used to legitimise the tutelage of the regime. In the run-up to the 2011–12 electoral cycle the country found itself facing the distinctly unpleasant fact that in the end it was not the people who would decide the elections but one man, Russia's former president and from 2008 prime minister, Vladimir Putin. Putin was undoubtedly a strong leader in terms of efficacy and ability to manage the fractious Russian elites, but he fell prey to the patrimonial curse common in developing countries: the sense of indispensability, accompanied by shades of the infallibility syndrome.

Putin's patrimonialism arose out of mixed motives: a desire to defend the property settlement of his era, the political privileges of the regime, as well as a sense of responsibility for the country. However, when this degenerated into neo-patrimonial reflexes of personalised rule, the opportunistic exploitation of the institutions of the constitutional state, and a sense of lordship over the fate of the country, then strengths became weaknesses, and positive leadership qualities inexorably deteriorated into hubristic challenges to the normal life cycle of political leadership, accompanied by the degradation of governance in its entirety. Wise leaders (or at least those who are remembered as such) know when to leave in time, and thus allow institutionalised succession mechanisms to operate. The Chinese learnt from the Soviet experience and now have a well-tried mechanism of leadership rotation, whereas Russia has not learned the lessons from its own history. Despite repeated changes to the institutional framework, Russia remains a leader-dominated political order. There has been a consistent failure to transfer the legitimacy vested in charismatic personalities to institutions.

What did Medvedev do?

Although elected president in a legal ballot and enjoying enormous powers according to the 1993 constitution, Medvedev found himself trapped in a tandem form of rule in which the former president enjoyed enormous authority derived from his popularity and achievements. Putin as prime minister kept himself in the public eye, and although observing the constitutional niceties – above all in allowing Medvedev pre-eminence in foreign affairs, it was clear that Putin had no intention of relinquishing a controlling grasp on policy. Medvedev lacked an autonomous power base and a personnel cadre of his own, and in any case accepted the core principles of the 'Putin project'. However, Medvedev sought to temper some of the practices, and in the end was able to carve out a distinct political identity and establish himself as a symbol of the more liberal potential in Russian politics. This came out clearly in his address to the State Council meeting devoted to the development of Russia's political system on 22 January 2010:

> Our task is to ensure that the principles of political management are appropriate for the ideological and cultural multiplicity of society. Politics should become more intelligent, more flexible, more contemporary, but in practice, unfortunately, we frequently encounter other approaches, when the growing complexity of social processes is attempted to be managed through primitive, and I would even go so far as to say stupid, administrative measures.[1]

At the end of the session Putin rose unexpectedly to defend the system that he had created over the last decade. He warned that while adjustments were undoubtedly needed, changes should be introduced carefully to avoid the 'Ukrainisation' of the political system or a reversion to despotism. He stressed that 'Any efficient political system has an inherent degree of conservatism. It shouldn't be shaky like a jelly that shakes at every touch.'[2]

The common charge against Medvedev is that he was loud in his rhetoric but achieved very little. There is substance to this, since undoubtedly there was a mismatch between what he promised, or at least implied, and actual achievements. However, he posited a different social ontology to what had preceded his presidency; but since this ontology was rooted in the system shaped by his predecessor, it was caught in a logical trap which prevented a radical breakthrough. Although the list of initiatives launched by Medvedev is impressive – including elements of political liberalisation, police, prison and sentencing reform, mitigating pre-trial detention for business crimes, judicial, prosecutorial, investigative and anti-corruption changes, and greater freedom of association – none were carried through to any sort of logical completion. In part this was because of his inherently cautious approach, with the experience of the chaos and disintegration of the perestroika years acting as a salutary warning of what could happen if liberalisation was too radical and speedy. He launched the most comprehensive and effective military reform in autumn 2008 following the inadequacies revealed by the Russo-Georgian war earlier that year. He allowed the release of the Yukos lawyer Svetlana Bakhmina in April 2009. Many of his initiatives are commonly mocked, amounting to little more than reducing the number of time zones from eleven to nine, the controversial introduction of the Single State Examination to higher education institutions, which opened the door to extensive corruption, the law on state purchases, which turned even the most simple of operations into a bureaucratic nightmare, the abolition of vehicle inspections, and the reckless widening of Moscow city's borders. There is also a deeply personal facet to the attacks, with Medvedev portrayed as little more than a good-natured receptionist. This is not only unfair but also irrelevant, since if the substantive initiatives had been allowed to work autonomously then the country could have begun to move beyond its traditional leader-fixation.

Above all, a new ideology of reform was developed which abandoned the postulates of 'sovereign democracy' and instead advanced a range of ideas based on 'humanism', restraints on the use of the coercive power of the state, attempts to strengthen the rule of law and a softening of the harsh regulations constraining the opposition and civil society associations.[3] This approach could not overcome some of the fundamental structural impediments to a sustained renewal of the system. For example, although Medvedev sought to mitigate the harsh economic environment, he was unable seriously to restrain the prerogatives of the officialdom that continued to 'nightmare' business. As Pavlovsky put it, 'We have had quite sensible government in the last ten years, but we have a totally unacceptable structure to that power'.[4] The mutually-constraining tandem format allowed neither Putin nor Medvedev scope for the full expression of their approaches. Nevertheless, Medvedev quickly outgrew the 'empty shirt role', as an article in *Der Spiegel* put it: 'He has pushed through laws that free private companies from some harassment and, in his three years in office, he has replaced more governors than Putin did in eight', but 'Medvedev has not launched a revolution against Putin'.[5] This was always unlikely, since the two came out of the same camp, yet as long as systemic dualism remained, there was scope for innovation and a rebalancing of the system.

This was reflected in Medvedev's programmatic article 'Russia, Forward!', published in both Russian and English on a liberal website (Gazeta.ru) in September 2009.[6] Although the form was original, the style resembled Putin's lengthy question and answer sessions with domestic and foreign media. Both allowed the leader to communicate in a relatively free format while at the same time retaining control of the agenda. Both were thus another type of para-political behaviour. The article reflected Medvedev's view that continued political drift was no longer an option, but it also suggested uncertainty over what was to be done. The article was presented as a discussion document for the president's annual state of the nation address to the Federal Assembly (*poslanie*), but the harshly critical tone went beyond what would be acceptable on such a formal occasion.[7] Couched in the form of a historical analysis, Medvedev characterised Russian social life as a semi-Soviet social order, 'one that unfortunately combines all the shortcomings of the Soviet system and all the difficulties of contemporary life'.[8] Underlying the article was the view that the rent-extraction model of Russian political economy was unsustainable in the long run. The fundamental question was whether Russia, with its 'primitive economy' and 'chronic corruption', has a future? Medvedev attacked not Putin but the system that Putin represented, an ambivalence that blunted his message.

The article listed a devastating series of Russian problems, and although the socio-economic remedies were vague, when it came to politics his ideas were 'revolutionary'. First, Medvedev argued that the country was economically backward and distorted by dependence on extractive industries. Second, 'As in the majority of democratic countries, parliamentary parties will take the lead in political struggle, periodically taking turns in power. Parties and coalitions will form the federal and regional executive authorities (and not vice versa), propose candidates for head of state, regional leaders and local government'. In short, Medvedev proposed an end to the quasi-dynastic succession of power. He had long been a critic of the concept of 'sovereign democracy', and he now suggested a way to move beyond its manipulative practices. Third, corruption had been one of Medvedev's bugbears, and here he once again condemned the phenomenon. It would require a wholly impartial and independent judiciary to achieve a breakthrough, yet as the endless cases of judges working closely with business 'raiders' demonstrated, little progress was made in the Medvedev years. Fourth, Medvedev condemned the 'paternalist mindset' prevalent in Russian society, but although he was right to identify passivity and dependency, this perhaps was less of a cultural trait than a natural response to the overbearing administrative and economic regimes. Successive revolutions in the twentieth century demonstrated that the Russian people were quite capable of trying to take control of their own destiny, although the outcome certainly did not match expectations. Given the predatory context, the most desirable career for young people shifted from business to administration, indicating a return to a 'quasi-Soviet social contract'.[9]

Medvedev sought to break away from such neo-Soviet attitudes, viewing innovation, democracy and freedom as the responsibility of the individual; but he recognised that entrenched interests stymied popular initiative. With businesses under attack from bureaucrats, it was safer to join the latter. Who would act as the modernising force, however, was not clear: the state or private enterprise? More broadly, it was all very well blaming the elite for having driven Russia up a dead end, but that same elite retained its full powers and it would take an act of political courage from above or a revolution from below to remove its grasp on power. Medvedev rejected the latter, but that only placed a greater weight of expectation on changes from above. As Furman notes, 'Medvedev was condemning the system which he led'.[10] The absence of a social subject of modernisation was a weakness noted by Khodorkovsky in his commentary on the article, insisting that 'it takes a whole stratum, a real modernising class, to achieve genuine modernisation', and he outlined a 'Generation M' that could achieve this.[11] Medvedev's reform programme failed to devise a process of modernisation from the middle, mobilising not a centrist political coalition (that was Putin's constituency) but social forces that could provide substance to the space between the two pillars of the dual state, and thus to establish a dynamic to transcend the division.

In a speech to the modernisation commission in Magnitogorsk on 30 March 2011 Medvedev effectively delivered a presidential campaign address. He outlined ten measures to improve the business climate, including the removal of government ministers from the boards of directors of state companies, the reduction of the influence of state-owned companies on the investment climate, and the privatisation of large stakes over the next three years. He argued that 'We have to eliminate the practice where government officials, I mean those responsible for regulating rules in individual sectors, are board members at companies which operate in a competitive environment.'[12] Board seats would thus have to be vacated by deputy prime minister Igor Sechin (Rosneft, Inter RAO), finance minister Kudrin (bank VTB), Viktor Zubkov (Rosagroleasing), Sergei Ivanov (the state holding United Aircraft Corporation and Rusnano) and transport minister Igor Levitin (Aeroflot) and energy minister Sergei Shmatko (RusHydro, FSK, Transneft and Gazprom). Seventeen companies were due to lose their government ministers by 1 July, with the remaining officials in state-owned or controlled companies to leave by 1 October. In other words, Medvedev was calling for the dismantlement of what passed for state capitalism in Russia. Business was to be separated from politics. It also indicated that instead of open political competition, the struggle between bureaucratic factions was intensifying as the election approached.

The tension between Medvedev's liberal modernisation strategy and Putin's more tutelary developmental path was becoming apparent. Medvedev rebuked Putin's comments on the Libya campaign, even though Russia's abstention on 17 March 2011 on the UN vote on resolution 1973 to impose a no-fly zone was agreed by the Russian Security Council with Putin's apparent approval. Speaking to workers at a missile factory on 21 March, Putin argued that the UN resolution was 'defective': 'If we look at what is written there, it becomes obvious that it allows everybody to take any action against a sovereign state. And it reminds me of a medieval call for a crusade – when countries call on each other to go out and liberate something.' He went on to note that 'I am worried more about the ease with which decisions are being made to use force in international affairs nowadays'. In response, on the same TV channel, Medvedev argued 'Everything that is happening in Libya is a result of the Libyan leadership's absolutely intolerable behaviour and the crimes that they have committed against their own people. There are different views about what is happening but I believe we should be extremely careful in our assessments. In no way is it acceptable to use expressions which essentially lead to a clash of civilisations, such as "crusade" and so forth'.[13] The recriminations deepened later, with Medvedev accused of having given the West a blank cheque to intervene and ultimately to overthrow Muammar Gaddafy's regime and to kill him in barbaric circumstances on 20 October. The Libyan precedent shaped much of Russia's thinking on Syria later.

At the Fifteenth St Petersburg Economic Forum on 17 June 2011 Medvedev nevertheless set out his goals. He insisted that

> Modernisation is the only way to address the many issues before us, and this is why we have set the course of modernising our national economy, outlined our technology development priorities for the coming years, and set the goal of turning Moscow into one of the world's major financial centres.

The fruits of this, he admitted, were small, 'but they are there'. He went on to declare unequivocally:

> I want to state loud and clear here that we are not building state capitalism. Yes, there was a point in our development when we increased the state's share in the economy, but this was an unavoidable step and in many ways necessary in order to stabilise the situation after the chaos of the 1990s, and re-establish basic order. That avenue has exhausted its potential now. ... This economic model jeopardises the country's future. It is not my choice. My choice is different. Private business and private investment should dominate in the Russian economy. The state must protect the choice and assets of those who consciously decide to risk their money and reputation.

He outlined a number of measures, including fulfilment of the Magnitogorsk objectives, and he now stressed that there was a timetable for the privatisation of a swathe of large companies. His programme also included reform of the federal system:

> It is not possible in the modern world to run a country from one single place, all the more so when we're talking about a country like Russia. In fact, we have already gone through the kind of system when everything operates only on the Kremlin's signal, and I know from my own experience that this kind of system is not viable and has always been adjusted to suit the particular individual. We therefore need to change it. I will soon set up a special high-level working group to draft proposals on decentralising powers between the different levels of power, above all in favour of the municipal authorities. This will include proposed adjustments to the tax system and principles for relations between the budgets at the different levels too.

He also stressed that reform of the judicial system would continue and the struggle against corruption would be intensified.[14]

Medvedev pushed forward his agenda of greater judicial independence and transparency. On 30 June 2011 the Constitutional Court protected whistleblowers by upholding the right of civil servants and bureaucrats to criticise state institutions, while Medvedev recommended that courts publish all appeals, a measure designed to limit 'telephone law'. The Supreme Court also placed limits on the 'anti-extremism' legislation by distinguishing between criticism and incitement.[15] Meeting with judges, Medvedev insisted that 'the investment climate has changed in recent years', but admitted:

> Despite the improvement in our legislation, despite the simplification of tax regimes and strengthening the safeguards to protect property rights, the amount of litigation has not decreased. ... According to the Arbitration Court, the number of bankruptcy cases has increased 1,700% in the past two years.[16]

Medvedev repeatedly spoke in support of freedom of expression and saluted the advances of the internet. He encouraged the development of e-government to allow people to access state services online. In keeping with the Electronic Russia programme, by 2009 all Russian schools had gained internet access, and over 20,000 post offices were equipped with online terminals. Medvedev was a keen blogger and Twitter user, and on several occasions noted that he would go online to gain independent news.[17] He repeatedly blocked attempts to limit the media, the internet and free speech. For example, he vetoed a bill, passed by the Duma on first reading in April 2008, which would have placed limits on the internet.[18] The Russian internet remained a relatively open forum, with none of the technical filtering or controls practised, for example, in China. The new electronic media was hailed as facilitating the development of civil society and democratisation, if not an instrument for regime change.[19] In practice, in Russia its political effects were limited.[20] Indeed, there is much talk of 'networked authoritarianism', whereby governments can use the internet as an instrument of censorship, surveillance and propaganda.[21] Morozov's polemic against 'cyber-utopians' seeks to expose the 'information myth', the idea that exposed to the pleasures of capitalist life, people would revolt against authoritarian regimes. Drawing on the experience, inter alia, of East Germany and his native Belarus, Morozov argues that populations have become quiescent, and he describes how the electronic media tranquilises the Russian people and distracts them from the consolidation of what he calls neo-Stalinism.[22]

At the heart of Medvedev's rhetoric was a different concept of reform. It became clear that he came to view Putin's stability as a recipe for stagnation. At the same time, Medvedev was the alter ego of the Putin who had driven the country into an impasse, and needed a Medvedev to offer the prospect of an evolutionary passage out of the dead end. However, Putin kept a tight rein on Medvedev's freedom of action but went along with Medvedev's order for senior state officials to relinquish their directorial posts on the boards of state companies and other initiatives. Even where there were evident disagreements, as over Khodorkovsky and Libya, these were not enough to tear the tandem apart. Putin scrupulously observed the proprieties, fearing to give Medvedev and his backers cause to renege on their side of the bargain and run against Putin.

Luzhkov's dismissal

The run-up to the election saw increasing signs of elite disarray. The dismissal of Luzhkov on 28 September 2010 was preceded by a 'black propaganda' campaign against him, including savagely defamatory documentaries about him and his wife, Elena Baturina, beginning with a harshly critical documentary on 10 September 2010. For several weeks the Russian public sphere buzzed with rumours about his imminent dismissal, yet to the end Luzhkov insisted that he was not going to resign. At the World Public Forum in Yaroslavl on 10 September he cut a lonely and isolated figure. At that time the Kremlin-friendly media ran a series of programmes criticising his 18-year reign as Moscow's mayor, raising questions about his lavish estate outside the city in Kaluga region (where he became one of Russia's leading bee keepers), as well as the sources of wealth for his wife, Baturina, whose property business thrived to make her reputedly the world's third richest woman. In 2008 Forbes declared her Russia's richest woman with $4.2bn, but the economic crisis from that year reduced that sum by at least three-quarters.

On 21 September Luzhkov celebrated his 74th birthday amidst withering criticism of his failure to return from holiday in time to deal with the peat-bog fires and smog that afflicted Moscow for much of August. It was clear that his relationship with Medvedev had broken down entirely. In his two years in office the president had gradually been removing the 'untouchables', the long-serving heads of regions such as Mintimir Shaimiev in Tatarstan in March 2010, Murtaza Rakhimov in Bashkortostan in July 2010 and, most recently, Kirsan Ilyumzhinov in Kalmykia. Luzhkov was one of the last of the old guard to go. In most cases the change of leader was accompanied by property redistribution, unless the old governor went quietly. Medvedev's policy of removing regional leaders after three terms and accelerated rotation of governors saw one-third changed during his presidency.

Born in Moscow in 1936, Luzhkov began his working life in the chemical industry and joined the Communist Party in 1968. In 1977 he became a deputy in the Moscow City Council (Mossovet), and acted as vice-mayor to the ineffectual Gavriil Popov before taking over as mayor in June 1992. Luzhkov was a classic *krepkii khozyaistvennik* (strong manager), transforming the city from the drab, run-down Soviet capital into a well-run international metropolis. His methods may have been questionable, and he has often been compared to mayor Richard J. Daly in Chicago, but his achievements are undoubted. His project to rebuild the Cathedral of Christ the Saviour (the original was blown up in 1934) is typical in its grandiose sweep and opaque sources of financing, yet the outcome stands in its dazzling glory opposite the Kremlin and has become the main cathedral for the Russian Orthodox Church. His scant respect for Moscow's architectural heritage was often criticised, including the destruction of some 50 monuments and 700 historic buildings, yet large parts of the old city were renovated under his leadership. Many of the enormous construction projects were undertaken by his wife's company, Inteko. The city's budget grew to over 1 trillion roubles ($32.8 billion) and accounted for nearly a quarter of the national economy.

During Putin's presidency between 2000 and 2008 there had been sporadic attempts to unseat Luzhkov, but none had come to anything. There was no love lost between the two men (although no open hostility either), since Luzhkov had been one of the main movers behind an attempt by regional elites to take over the presidency in 1999, when Yeltsin came to the end of his two terms. Luzhkov had created the Fatherland (*Otechestvo*) party in late 1998, and in 1999 he joined with other insurgent regional leaders in All Russia (*Vsya Rossiya*) to create the Fatherland–All Russia (OVR) alliance, and together they nominated Yevgeny Primakov as their candidate for the presidency. Instead, Yeltsin gave Putin a clear run for the presidency, and Luzhkov returned to the Moscow mayoralty to lick his wounds. In 2001 Luzhkov joined Putin's Unity party, which absorbed Fatherland, but it was clear that his heart was not in it, even though he became a co-chair of the Supreme Council of what became United Russia in December 2003. Luzhkov never became the national politician at the level he craved, but on the way he made some powerful enemies who finally brought him down.

Luzhkov had long been a beacon of relative independence in a system that had gradually been transformed into a 'power vertical'. Although Luzhkov was one of the founder members of United Russia, he retained a robust independence. Luzhkov had never been averse to policy entrepreneurship of his own, notably in supporting alleged Russian national interests in the Crimea. He also took a robust line against unsanctioned demonstrations, and was famous for his refusal to allow gay pride marches in the city. He was outspoken in calling for the reinstatement of direct gubernatorial elections, which already at that time provoked a sharp riposte from Medvedev, who on 15 September 2009 asserted that there would be no return to gubernatorial elections in Russia for 'a hundred years'. With his populist touch, symbolised by his trademark flat cap, Luzhkov was repeatedly re-elected (in 1996, 1999 and 2003) with huge majorities. However, with the abolition of gubernatorial elections in 2004 his tenure became dependent on the goodwill of the authorities. He was reappointed for a fifth term by Putin in 2007 (due to expire in July 2011), since Luzhkov had regularly been able to deliver the vote for United Russia. Nevertheless, Medvedev had clearly decided that the time was ripe for a change of leadership.

Luzhkov was persistently criticised for Moscow's mounting traffic problems. In July 2010 poorly planned repairs to the main road to Sheremetevo airport led to six-hour delays. Luzhkov's star was further dimmed by his advocacy of the environmentally-damaging route of the new Moscow–St Petersburg highway through the Khimki forest. The two leaders publicly clashed over this project, with Medvedev, bowing to popular pressure, on 26 August imposing a moratorium on construction while Luzhkov insisted that the original route would be built. It appears also that Putin had been dismayed by the decision to halt work on the highway, especially since it was being built by his long-time associate, Arkady Rotenberg. Luzhkov criticised Medvedev's administration, arguing that 'the Russian government needs to recover its true authority and meaning'.[23] The mayor noted a 'difficult atmosphere' in the country, evoking on 17 September 2010 a sharp response by Medvedev: 'If my colleagues are not pleased, they have an opportunity to draw their own conclusions'. 'Officials should either participate in improving public institutions or move into opposition.'[24] Medvedev's patience with Luzhkov was clearly exhausted. His credibility was on the line, and on 28 September he sacked his rival. Medvedev's decree 'dismissing' (not the usual 'discharging') Luzhkov, issued while on a trip to China, stated a 'loss of confidence' in the veteran leader. This is the only time that Medvedev used this formulation in sacking someone, and threatened that he would do so again if necessary: a warning to his opponents not to over-step the mark. There was time to appoint a successor who could prepare for the parliamentary elections in December 2011 and the presidential contest in March 2012. Medvedev insisted that 'I will decide who will lead Moscow';[25] while Putin insisted that he would influence the decision: 'I hope I will have a chance to express my opinion'.[26]

Putin's role in all of this is unclear. Luzhkov already on 26 September had sent a letter (received only two days later) demonstratively leaving United Russia, stating that they 'did not provide any support and did not want to sort things out and stop the flow of lies and slander', even though he was a member of the party's ruling council.[27] Luzhkov complained of being abandoned by the party. Putin was the party's leader, even though he was not formally a member. Commenting on the dismissal, Putin stated that 'Yuri Luzhkov has done a great deal for the development of Moscow, and to some extent he is a symbolic figure in modern Russia'. As for the successor, 'Of course, we will think it over and talk some more'.[28] It is unusual for such public splits to take place in Russia's ruling elite. Luzhkov was able to drive a wedge in the ruling tandem of Medvedev and Putin and their respective supporters. Luzhkov insisted that the reason for his dismissal was simple: 'The answer to your question [why he had been sacked] is very simple: the 2012 presidential elections are ahead. The authorities need Moscow to support the Kremlin-proposed candidate', and he added that the authorities would need 'a person from their circle as the mayor'.[29]

Luzhkov continued to insist that he would remain: 'I will not quit politics. I will fight for the election of the [Moscow] mayor and governors.'[30] Such a show of political independence is against all the rules, and risked turning him into another martyr of the opposition, with the whole weight of political retribution brought down on him, including the use of the judicial system. His offence had not been the accumulation of great wealth or corruption, but his persistent insistence on political and policy independence. Investigations into his business affairs soon began. Indeed, economic issues were a key factor in his dismissal, signalling a redistribution of property in Moscow. The Bank of Moscow was taken over by the giant Kremlin-friendly VTB financial conglomerate. Although Medvedev asserted his authority, Luzhkov's messy exit from the mayoralty was far from an unmitigated triumph for him. The struggle for his successor, moreover, reflected the balance of power in the tandem and in the elite as a whole. Vladimir Resin, the city's first deputy mayor, was appointed interim mayor, but at 74 was not a long-term candidate. The fact that a replacement was not waiting in the wings suggests that in the end Luzhkov's dismissal was rushed through.

On 15 October Sergei Sobyanin was nominated mayor by Medvedev, with the latter stressing the need to resolve social problems and traffic jams.[31] Sobyanin, a former communist youth leader and then a welder in his native Khanty-Mansiisk, went on to become governor of oil-rich Tyumen region, where he had registered no great successes and indeed had been renowned for his harsh control of the media. As a member of the Federation Council in 2000, Sobyanin had helped Putin sack Yuri Skuratov, Russia's general prosecutor, on behalf of Yeltsin. He had also been one of the first governors to back Putin's call for the abolition of direct elections for governors in late 2004. In 2005 he entered the Kremlin to replace Medvedev as head of the presidential administration, led Medvedev's presidential campaign in 2008, before moving over with Putin to the White House to become a deputy prime minister.

Sobyanin was neither a *silovik* nor an avowed moderniser, and although recognised as a Putin associate, he was clearly a compromise appointment. He was also someone with no track record of achievement, and this rather anodyne figure, more of a back-room bureaucrat than a public politician, was now to represent Europe's largest city. Above all, his task was to ease Putin's return to power, and indeed, his appointment was taken as yet another sign that Putin was preparing the ground for his return to the presidency in 2012.[32] Although Sobyanin was appointed with the avowed aim of cracking down on corruption, his tenure would be far from untainted. In particular, his wife Irina owned a road construction business called Ira Bordyur.[33] The company was given the contract to provide the new paving stones to replace tarmac pavements. Although not aligned with any of the factions, Sobyanin was known to be sympathetic to the state-oriented business oligarchs who thrived under Putin. According to the political analyst Kirill Rogov, Sobyanin's task was not only to deliver the vote in the 2011–12 elections, but 'a large part of his work will be redistributing business away from what remains of Luzhkov's vast financial machine': 'Most important are the city's financial flows, which are mainly generated from control over real estate. ... It is impossible to run the city if you don't control them.'[34] Sobyanin had effectively managed the presidential administration in the turbulent transition in 2007–8, and now his job was to deliver the vote for the ruling party in the parliamentary election of December 2011 and to deliver the Moscow vote for Putin in the presidential election in 2012.

Luzhkov did not go quietly. In a closed lecture to students at the Russian State Trade and Economic University on 21 October 2010, Luzhov stated that he had always taken a 'critical attitude' towards United Russia, even though he had been a founding member. 'I often told party chairman Boris Gryzlov that we don't have discussions', referring to Gryzlov's famous aphorism that 'parliament is no place for discussion'. 'We are always taking orders from the administration', Luzhkov went on, calling the party a Kremlin 'servant' (again, a reference to Lenin's view of the anti-Bolshevik parties), and he condemned the Kremlin's 'dictatorial' power to dismiss governors.[35] In another interview at that time Luzhkov asked 'What does a change in the mayor's status have to do with the change in the status of the Bank [of Moscow]. His response to the rhetorical question was none: 'I see no reasons other than perhaps another opportunity for revenge against the mayor who had organised this bank.'[36] Any hopes that Putin would retain his relative neutrality in the affair were dissipated during his 'direct line' question and answer session on 16 December 2010. Asked whether the new mayor was being too harsh, Putin replied that Sobyanin 'is not being harsh. He's putting things right'.[37]

Luzhkov's ouster was the first time that a major governor had been dismissed in such brutal circumstances. His fall was expected to be followed by legal recriminations. The editor of *Nezavisimaya gazeta*, Konstantin Remchukov, drew a parallel with Putin's persecution of Khodorkovsky, which confirmed Putin 'as the all-powerful leader of Russia'; and Medvedev's persecution of Luzhkov was seen as possibly having the same effect for his successor. However, the circumstances were very different, with Luzhkov part of the ruling elite, and his persecution by Medvedev threatening to destabilise the ruling group, especially with only a little more than a year to go before the elections. Clearly Putin had been informed of the dismissal in advance, although he remained formally neutral throughout.[38] As the storm clouds gathered over Luzhkov's fate, Baturina stressed just how vulnerable people were in Russia. In an interview with the *New Times*, she noted that 'There is something else that worries me in the Khodorkovsky case. I am put on my guard not by justice itself, but by the selective manner in which it is applied. It is this that poses a much greater danger in actual fact'.[39] Yulia Latynina warned that 'It is scary to think what is going to happen to the huge empire that Luzhkov's wife, Yelena Baturina, has built since Putin came to power'. She stressed that:

> The Luzhkov scandal is a classic Putin-orchestrated setup and intrigue. Luzhkov and Medvedev devoured each other in public while Putin emerged unscathed and stronger than ever. Don't believe for a second

analysts who claim that Luzhkov's firing is a victory for Medvedev – that he was able to come out of Putin's shadow and make a very bold, risky and independent decision for the first time. I assure you, Medvedev couldn't have made this kind of decision without Putin's approval. ... It is difficult to predict what will happen with Luzhkov, but one thing is already clear: Medvedev will not serve a second term as president. If he did have such ambitions, the scandal over Luzhkov has squashed them completely.[40]

These sentiments were shared by Mikhail Delyagin, the director of the Institute of Globalisation Studies in Moscow. As he notes: 'The replacement of senior Bank of Moscow executives was fairly predictable after the high-profile sacking of Moscow Mayor Yury Luzhkov. That's the way "oligarchic capitalism" works; key companies were bound to have their executives replaced, at the very least'. He also stressed other regularities:

The way it was done wasn't far out of the ordinary either: a criminal investigation combined with an aggressive PR campaign. Any sensible businessman should have seen the writing on the wall and given up, unless they wanted to end behind bars like Mikhail Khodorkovsky or, worse still, Sergei Magnitsky. There's nothing new about the practice of selling a business at a ridiculous discount to obscure but clearly influential buyers.

He warned that there was no danger of 'a revival of corporate raiding', because 'it had never died out in the first place'. He went on to note the unusual features of VTB's takeover of the Bank of Moscow, especially since the structures of the two banks were almost identical, with many of their branches next door to each other.[41] Factional conflict remained fragmented and opaque, but as Medvedev's rule entered its final straight there was an increasingly delineated contrast between those rooting for Putin's return, including the *siloviki* and conservative statists, and a 'modernising' group of increasingly assertive intra-systemic reformers. Instability within the ruling elite became increasingly apparent.

The dual campaign

In the only substantive amendment since the constitution's adoption in December 1993, in December 2008 the presidential term was extended to six years (up from four), while the parliamentary term was extended to five years (up from four). The new leader would thus enjoy an extended period without having to face the electorate. Succession issues and the strategy for the long-term modernisation of the country placed the tandem under increasing strain. Medvedev advanced a number of initiatives that ran counter to the logic of the Putinite system. This did not necessarily provoke conflict, since Putin shared most of Medvedev's goals. The difference lay in the speed and manner in which these goals were to be achieved. Both agreed on the need to restore state power, but whereas for Putin this entailed the strengthening of the administrative capacity of the regime, Medvedev favoured the strengthening of state power through liberalisation and the effective application of the infrastructural power of the constitutional state. It would be a mistake to see Putin as the leader of a 'conservative' bloc intent on preserving the existing system, and Medvedev as a radical reformer. The two shared too much, and in practice agreed on basic principles. In certain respects Medvedevism can be seen as an experimental form of Putinism, an attempt to devise new forms of governance without breaking with the essential postulates of Putinism. Nevertheless, tensions in their respective approaches became increasingly evident.

Putin was the brilliant faction manager, keeping all wings off-balance but giving each enough to ensure their loyalty, whereas Medvedev appealed to the normative values of the institutional order. In other words, Medvedev's strength lay in transcending the logic of factional struggle by strengthening existing political institutions, more open and honest elections, independent courts and a free public sphere. Medvedev also appealed to the deep-seated aspirations of 'society' (*obshchestevennost'*, which includes the intelligentsia, professionals, and the civic-minded part of the middle class) for an end to the stultifying and manipulative (and corruptive) governance techniques of the old regime. The Putinites, of course, countered by arguing that the people were not yet ready for such an open pluralistic process, and that they would still vote for anyone Putin suggested, including himself. His elite supporters were well aware that as soon as Putin left office he and his team would become vulnerable to reprisals from myriad opponents. Up to September 2011 the Medvedev camp sought to shape the discourse to demonstrate why it would be wrong for Putin to try to return to the presidency, and why it would be right for Medvedev to stay in the Kremlin. Putin allegedly was tired, lacked a positive agenda, and represented a narrow self-aggrandizing part of the elite. Another factor often adduced was that the West would prefer not to see him back at the helm. The US vice president Joe Biden, at a meeting with Putin in March 2011, made this clear, although 'this advice from the Americans is a sufficient reason in itself to do just the opposite'.[42] A further argument was that Putin's return would mean the restoration of a previous order, a sense of regress rather than progress, and thus a lack of invigoration.

There was growing pressure for political change amid clear signs of intra-regime dissatisfaction with stultifying political managerialism. Luzhkov, as we have seen, provided a trenchant critique of United Russia. Equally Kudrin, one of the St Petersburg group in the Russian government, called for free and fair elections. He worked with Putin in the St Petersburg city administration in the early 1990s and then moved on to a governmental job in Moscow. It was Kudrin who nominated Putin for a post in the presidential administration in 1996, when Putin became unemployed following the break-up of Sobchak's administration in the city. Kudrin therefore was one of those who set Putin on his dizzying career path in Moscow, which culminated in his assuming the presidency on 31 December 1999. Kudrin maintained a resolutely non-partisan approach for the next decade as finance minister, although he occasionally came into conflict with United Russia. This changed as the elections approached. This was a clear sign that the old system of 'managed democracy', administered by Surkov, was breaking up. Even core members of the Putin team, notably Mironov as well as Kudrin, understood that the decade-long style of 'manual management' had exhausted its potential.

This was reflected in Kudrin's critical statements at the Krasnoyarsk Economic Forum on 18 February 2011. Referring to the forthcoming Duma campaign, he declared that 'society should perceive these elections as a review of the work of the authorities', and for this they had to be 'fair and honest, so that all leading forces are represented in these elections'. In addition to his criticism that economic policy was too populist and unable to deliver simultaneously on social promises, increased expenditure on defence, and modernisation of infrastructure and industry, Kudrin argued that the formation of a new post-crisis model of development required free and fair elections:

> It is of paramount importance for society to understand that these elections are a test, a free and fair test of all leading political forces. It alone will provide the mandate necessary for the reforms. Unless the people's trust is won, we cannot hope to succeed.[43]

He repeated this invocation when addressing the RUIE on 21 April 2011, when he spoke of the necessity of political competition and insisted on a government formed by political parties. Noting the experience of advanced countries, where economic strategies are adopted at elections, Kudrin argued that 'It is through elections that people choose the political party and the government that will execute this strategy.' He insisted that political competition was 'a necessary element of any society and any economy'. Since the economy depends on businesses, the state should make life easier for business.[44] Medvedev sought controlled liberalisation, but the pressure for change from even within the elite was beginning to out-run what he could deliver. Discontent was building on several fronts, which exploded into view after 4 December.

The succession operation took two forms. There was the open campaign, in which parties honed their programmes and prepared their candidate lists for the official contest. However, there was a more decisive subterranean struggle for the presidential succession. It was clear that Medvedev, as well as an active part of his entourage, were fighting for a second term; and at the same time the Putinite faction now wished to retake the reins of power. With an extended presidential term, the stakes could not be higher. There is much evidence that the final decision on who would run in 2012 was decided quite late. Putin ensured that the option was kept open, and for this reason he kept himself in the public eye with a series of PR events, many of which were staged in an increasingly ridiculous manner. There is no doubt that the Putin elite, and in particular those who had enriched themselves during his leadership, pushed for him to return. Yet a section of the elite had misgivings, understanding the dangers that the lack of leadership rotation entailed. Even Putin's friend Andrei Kostin, the head of VTB, argued later that Putin should resign after his renewed six-year term.[45] This was a clear indication that the technocratic part of the elite feared stagnation.

As with the 2007–8 ballot, the period before these elections was accompanied by a series of crises, démarches and declarations. These were accentuated by the unrolling of the 'Arab Spring', and above all the conflict in Libya. The events in North Africa and the continuing bloodshed in Syria acted as the backdrop to debates in Russia over the viability of the 'Putinite stability', accompanied by comparisons between the repressive authoritarianism of Hosni Mubarak in Egypt and the stifling of public politics in Russia. In the end the Libyan intervention provoked one of the sharpest public disagreements between Putin and Medvedev, not only because of Russia's UNSC abstention but the way that its spirit was in Putin's view flagrantly transgressed to overthrow Gaddafy, hence the public reprimand by Medvedev for calling Nato's campaign a 'crusade'. From the Putinite point of view, this was a mistake not to be repeated, and in February 2012 Russia (with China) vetoed an Arab League sponsored resolution that could in the end have been interpreted to mandate a similar intervention in Syria.

Party moves

Putin devised a number of stratagems in the campaign. Chief among them was the creation of the Russian Popular Front (RPF) in May 2011, as an alternative means to allow members an avenue for career advancement outside of the formal party membership in UR.[46] The work of the Agency of Strategic Initiatives, another of Putin's ideas, was also in this spirit, to provide a 'social lift' for ambitious individuals.[47] The RPF and other initiatives were classic 'Putin gambits', since UR had fallen so sharply in public esteem. It was known at this time as 'the party of thieves and swindlers', a term popularised by the anti-corruption blogger Navalny and which had entered the popular lexicon. The creation of the RPF gave Putin freedom of manoeuvre, but by the same token it continued his classic para-political strategies that undermined the formalisation of political contestation.

The exhaustion of the old political mechanism was reflected in the stultified political scene, dominated by stale parties and leaders. Not a single genuinely new party had been registered since the minimum size of a party was raised from the 10,000 set in 2001 to 50,000 in 2006 (subsequently reduced to 45,000 in 2009). In addition to the four parties represented in the Duma (UR, CPRF, Just Russia and the LDPR), there were three non-parliamentary parties. Right Cause (*Pravoe Delo*) was founded in 2008 as a result of the merger of the Union of Right Forces (SPS), the Democratic Party of Russia, and civic Force (*Grazhdanskaya Sila*). Yabloko was one of the oldest parties in Russia, but after the 2003 elections no longer had a fraction in the Duma. The other was Patriots of Russia. According to Duverger's law, a proportional system should encourage the fragmentation of the party system, but instead of a myriad of smaller parties, the concomitant tightening of legislation reduced the number from over 50 in 2001 to just seven by 2009.

On 22 June 2011 the Ministry of Justice turned down the application from the Party of People's Freedom (Parnas) to register as a political party. The group was jointly led by the veteran 'democrats', the former prime minister Mikhail Kasyanov, Nemtsov, the head of the deregistered Republican Party Vladimir Ryzhkov, and a former deputy energy minister Vladimir Milov. The decision was based on possibly flawed data for just 79 individuals out of over 46,000 party members, a thousand over the minimum legal threshold. The party was also accused of lacking the required mechanism for rotating the leadership, whereas in fact there were clear provisions for this. Third, the ministry argued that Parnas had inadequate procedures for appointing executive positions in the centre and regions, whereas Parnas had copied word for word the provisions on this from the statutes of United Russia. In its judgement disqualifying Parnas the ministry quoted the law concerning NGOs rather than the law on parties, demonstrating according to Ryzhkov 'not only the incompetence of the ministry, but underscores the completely arbitrary nature of the campaign against the party', as part of the larger 'campaign to destroy independent opposition parties'.[48] The use of clumsy pretexts to deny Parnas registration delegitimised the outcome of the Duma elections even before they had taken place, and aroused a storm of protest abroad.[49] Instead of facing the competition head on in a free election, which the authorities would undoubtedly have won, they preferred to exclude them from the race altogether. This exercise of anachronistic control mechanisms only reinforced the impression that the regime itself was becoming obsolete.

The leadership of Right Cause was originally comprised of Boris Titov, former head of the Delovaya Rossiya business association, Leonid Gozman, a close associate of Chubais, and the well-known journalist Georgi Bovt. This proved an ineffective arrangement, with Gozman and Bovt in the end openly supporting Medvedev for a second term, while Titov migrated to the Putin camp. With United Russia supporting Putin, Medvedev was looking to find an institutional base of support. The political managers in the Kremlin had a clear agenda in trying to revive the party's fortunes. With support for United Russia and the political leadership declining, and the obviously debilitated condition of the political system, the plan was to ensure that a 'liberal' party was elected to the Duma in December 2011. Medvedev hoped to have independent parliamentary support for his candidature and his programme. Medvedev promised a free and fair electoral contest, and reminded his listeners that he had introduced a bill into parliament reducing the electoral threshold from 7 to 5 per cent, to be applied to the 2016 elections, and stressed that government should be decentralised: 'We have an over-centralised nation ... we have about one thousand federal structures, and naturally, they are all trying to keep busy'.[50]

In June 2011 Right Cause was furnished with a new leader. Various names had been mentioned, including finance minister Kudrin, who was offered the post but refused, as did first deputy prime minister Igor Shuvalov. None of these political heavyweights could be persuaded to sacrifice themselves for Right Cause. In the end the billionaire industrialist Mikhail Prokhorov took up the poisoned chalice, becoming leader on 25 June 2011. Prokhorov was head of the powerful Onexim industrial and banking group, with the resources to finance the party's electoral campaign. Still only 46 years old, according to Forbes he was Russia's third richest man with an estimated fortune of $18 billion derived from his earlier stake in Norilsk Nickel. Prokhorov was installed as the sole leader of the party in a manoeuvre apparently engineered by Alexander Voloshin (the former presidential chief of staff who resigned in October 2003 over Khodorkovsky's arrest). Prokhorov had already gained notoriety because of a number of scandals, including issues associated with his holiday home in Courcheval in France. Prokhorov's charisma it was thought would rub off on Right Cause. Thus clearly a deal had been struck: Prokhorov would invest his time and money in the party, and in return he would be guaranteed a seat in the next Duma for himself and in all likelihood up to 50 seats for the party as well. As long as he did not criticise the tandem and the system and took some Kremlin favourites onto his party list, then he could cut a political career for himself. The pact, however, soon fell apart in a spectacular manner.

Prokhorov's leadership was quickly endorsed by Medvedev, meeting him the day after his election, and approved some of his suggestions such as the return of elected mayors to Moscow and St Petersburg. Prokhorov sought to broaden the party's base by engaging in a populist strategy to shift the perception that Right Cause was a party of business to one in which it was seen as defending the Russian middle class. The party thus positioned itself on the centre right, a niche already occupied by United Russia. Prokhorov turned out not to be the man the Kremlin needed. Both sides miscalculated. Prokhorov was found wanting as a political leader in a number of respects. First, as a manager he treated Right Cause as little more than a branch of an industrial enterprise, scorning the old generation of party cadres. Many from the old SPS had spent a decade fighting for the party in the regions and at the centre, and they now found newcomers parachuted in who showed nothing but contempt for the old guard. A group of Ukrainian 'political technologists' once again demonstrated the same skills that had been applied in support of Viktor Yanukovich in autumn 2004. Prokhorov's dictatorial style was at odds with the liberal principles espoused by the party, and soon alienated regional leaders and top officials. Second, the initial election platform issued by Prokhorov was an inadequate document, released in haste and consisting of little more than populist banalities with an emerging nationalistic edge. Prokhorov espoused a vague centrism that failed to identify any fundamental political identity: 'I care nothing for capitalism or socialism. I care for the people. Addressing the problems people are facing is our main priority.'[51]

Prokhorov's style was more suited to a corporate takeover than leading a democratic party, and had little impact on public sentiments, with opinion polls showing consistently around 2 per cent. Third, Prokhorov began to shift the policy terrain on which Right Cause stood towards a more aggressive nationalism and neo-liberal fundamentalism, bewildering the traditional liberal electorate and alienating those who sought a more 'compassionate' social face to the party that had been advanced by SPS in its final days. Prokhorov began to poach traditional United Russia voters accompanied by criticism of the government, even though he was at pains to stress that he was not an opposition figure. Fourth, and most fundamentally, Prokhorov overestimated his freedom of manoeuvre from the authorities. This sin was compounded by his brusque refusal to explain the logic of his actions, not only to his own colleagues but also to those who had promoted him.

This provoked the crisis of September 2011. The formal reason for the clash was Prokhorov's intention to include Yevgeny Roizman, the leader of the Ekaterinburg-based 'City Without Drugs' fund, on Right Cause's candidate list for the elections. The Kremlin had long declared that those with a criminal past were not to be nominated for the Duma, and thus Roizman had been dropped from Just Russia's election list in 2007. Surkov demanded that Roizman, who as a young man spent two years in a penal colony after he was convicted in 1981 for theft, swindling and possession of a firearm, be dropped. Surkov reportedly issued an ultimatum: 'Either him or you'.[52] Prokhorov refused, citing his public commitment to Roizman on which he felt he could not renege. Instead of taking the nuclear option and dismissing Prokhorov, Roizman could simply have been voted down at the party congress, but by then the Kremlin's patience had been exhausted. On the first day of the Right Cause party conference on 14 September Prokhorov's opponents, apparently at the behest of the Kremlin, seized control of the party. By a vote of 75 to nil with two abstentions, Prokhorov was dismissed as party leader. The putsch against Prokhorov was led by Vladimir Bogdanov, who had won 1.3 per cent of the ballot in his 2008 presidential run, which represented fewer votes than the two million alleged supporters who had signed up to support his nomination. The co-conspirator was the lawyer Andrei Dunaev, the head of the Moscow party organisation. They had been incited to oust Prokhorov by Surkov, working through his deputy responsible for party management, Radi Khabirov.

The mutiny provoked Prokhorov to leave the party, but he did not go quietly. 'I personally call on those who back me to leave that puppet Kremlin party', Prokhorov told his supporters at a hastily convened breakaway party conference at the Russian Academy of Sciences. On 15 September Prokhorov resigned and launched a tirade against Surkov, but was careful not to criticise either Medvedev or Putin: 'We have a puppeteer in the country, who long ago privatised the political system and who for a long time has disinformed the leadership of the country about what is happening in the political system, who pressures the media, places people [in the media] and tries to manipulate public opinion.' In return, as if to prove Prokhorov's point, he not only disappeared from the television screens and joined the category of non-persons, like Nemtsov, Kasyanov and others who had fallen foul of the Kremlin, but also became the object of character assassination. In the event, the mass demonstrations against electoral fraud rescued Prokhorov's political career and he was kept as a reserve. He was allowed to run in the presidential ballot in March 2012, as part of the plan to split the opposition and to endow the whole exercise with legitimacy. Prokhorov's dramatic rise and fall as leader of Right Cause illustrates not only the debilitated condition of right-wing parties in Russia, but also more profoundly the character of the political system as a whole. Prokhorov had been selected by the Kremlin, yet barely three months later he was unceremoniously jettisoned and cast into the political wilderness.

Medvedev had demonstratively supported Prokhorov, but a few months later he was thoroughly disappointed. United Russia, moreover, had always opposed this threat to its own hegemonic position, and this turned to concern when Prokhorov sought to attract United Russia's electorate. By jettisoning Prokhorov now, Medvedev consolidated his support in United Russia and reinforced his position in the party and allowed him to go on to head its candidate list in the December election. However, Medvedev's options were now circumscribed and the system as a whole had been discredited. The Prokhorov affair represented a political debacle of the first order for the Kremlin. Its competence in managing political matters was brought into question. The speed with which the whole Prokhorov initiative unravelled could only reflect badly on Medvedev. If Right Cause was indeed little more than a Kremlin project, then a new leader should have been put in place far earlier, and only after considerably more vetting. The high-handedness with which Surkov managed political affairs now rebounded. Russian political life was not quite so malleable as he liked to believe; and his competence in managing the process was shown to have been exaggerated. Once the mechanisms of political management were revealed, they were rendered vulnerable. The whole affair was a classic case of hubris, and the collapse of the Right Cause project threatened the Kremlin's plans for the election as a whole.

Another sign of growing intra-elite fragmentation was Mironov's partial defection. The creation of Just Russia (Spravedlivaya Rossiya) before the 2007–8 election, headed by Mironov, the speaker of the Federation Council, was intended to provide a second leg to the official party system, this time covering the centre left flank. From the first the creation of a second regime-sponsored party created a divisive dynamic, especially when Mironov started to criticise United Russia's record. Just Russia was reined in and its victorious candidates in regional elections persecuted, although the party was allowed to pass the representation threshold in 2007. At the State Council meeting in January 2010 devoted to political reform Mironov argued that reform was about more than technology but 'Modernisation is always about political, social and cultural changes'. He condemned those regions where the ruling party officially won nigh-on a 100 per cent of the vote, and warned that 'people already no longer believe such results', and he presciently warned that this could happen in national, including presidential, elections.[53] In an interview with the veteran broadcaster Vladimir Pozner on 1 February 2010 Mironov disagreed with Putin's anti-crisis plans, and noted that 'contradictions arise since Putin now heads United Russia', which is 'in opposition to us' and whose ideology was unacceptable because of its 'doubtful conservatism'.[54] Mironov became an increasingly radical critic of the regime. Concerns that Just Russia could once again challenge United Russia and split the elite led to Mironov's rapid fall from grace. In formal terms he was the third most important person in the political hierarchy, yet when his fall came, it was swift and merciless. In early 2011 he came under increasing pressure, and in May was summarily dismissed as chair of the upper house and removed as senator from the St Petersburg legislature. Like Luzhkov's dismissal as mayor of Moscow in September 2010, past loyal service to the regime counted as nothing when the political conjuncture changed. Just Russia took the demotion of its leader calmly, with Mironov reverting to become the party's fraction leader in parliament while Levichev became the official party leader.

Just Russia devised a programme distinct from that of United Russia, and some of its MPs were active in exposing corruption and the shortcomings of the regime. In the months before the parliamentary election Just Russia put forward a substantive programme that offered an alternative vision of development. In his speech to the St Petersburg Legislative Assembly shortly before his recall the previously obedient Mironov gave a highly critical account of the situation in the government and the country. As Nikolai Zlobin noted, one wonders why he was not so honest when in power: 'It certainly raises the question of the immanent dualism or the hypocrisy of political consciousness of Russia's ruling class and certain of its representatives.'[55] Later that year, using the Valdai Club as his tribune, in rousing tones on 10 November he called for 'the liquidation of the political monopoly of one party', for the immediate return of gubernatorial and mayoral elections, as well as the abolition of so-called city managers, the direct election of the Federation Council, the easy registration of political parties, changes in the electoral law to return the 'against all' category, and above all a 'law on opposition', which would guarantee the rights of parliament and minority factions in it. Such actions would help return the political pluralism that had been suffocated over the last decade. It was precisely this programme that was announced in response to the protests following the parliamentary election.

Mironov showed acute awareness of the dangers arising from the stalemated political situation in the country. He is a classic case of the former insider going into semi-opposition. Given the constraints of Russian politics, there are clear bounds to what is allowed (for example, no personal condemnation of the leadership). Just Russia represented another attempt to give expression to social democratic ideas in Russia, of the sort long advocated by Mikhail Khodorkovsky and Mikhail Gorbachev. The very existence of Just Russia, although originally founded as yet another 'project party', reflected the potential for intra-systemic renewal. The dualism of the political system once again reflected the Soviet phenomenon of *Les hommes double*;[56] and just as in the communist period, this reached up to the very highest echelons of power. In part this was based on distrust in the people, hence the conservatives (*okhraniteli*) appealed to the non-political rationality embedded in classical notions of developmental modernisation, accompanied by elections without choice and a strait-jacketed public sphere. However, the very condition of conducting an election in which the elite itself began to reflect the dualism that characterised the system inevitably reintroduced an element of competitive politics. The regime of normalisation gave way to a more competitive normality.

Medvedev on the edge

The final phase of Medvedev's presidency was a nail-biting period of hints and whispers about whether he would run for a second term. In an interview with Chinese television on 12 April 2011 he stated: 'I do not exclude that I will run for a second term. The decision will be taken in the not-too-distant future, since as you say, less than a year remains.' Commenting on this, the journalist Dmitry Kamyshev noted that if Putin did decide to return to the Kremlin, what would he tell the population: 'How to explain why a fully successful president, under whom Russia won the war with Georgia, overcame the consequences of the global economic crisis, undertook the reset with the United States, and even turned the militia into the police, was refused the right to ballot for a second term'? Would he then have to 'confess that he made a mistake in advancing an inappropriate successor in 2007 and apologise'? And would Medvedev say that 'The idea of modernisation was mistaken and Russia will only be saved by enlightened conservatism', represented by Putin, or even that 'I was a bad president'?[57]

Medvedev lifted the curtain on how Russia was really ruled, including the powerlessness of the allegedly all-powerful presidency. The system was over-centralised, with inadequate control over the bureaucracy, endless inter-agency conflicts and weak accountability. The so-called power *vertikal*, in the sense of a machine that would unswervingly carry out the Kremlin's instructions, was exposed as a myth. The various components of the system lived their own existence on the horizontal plane, providing the system with flexibility but at the price of coherence. The dual state and the penumbra of the third state generated systemic anarchy in the Russian polity. In response, Medvedev in effect launched a 'perestroika 2.0', a programme of reform to move 'beyond autocratic reforms and incomplete perestroikas'. In Gordon Hahn's view, the tradition of reforms and revolutions from above needed to give way to a 'Regime transformation that involves society, including elements of opposition', allowing 'free and fair elections while one is still popular'.[58] For the more conservative Putin supporters, Medvedev's reforms represented the danger of another reform that would spiral out of control, just as

Gorbachev's perestroika between 1985 and 1991 was accompanied by a destructive dynamic. Hence the analogy between Medvedev's reforms and perestroika was not well-chosen, yet it was clear that the country needed change. The demand for 'stability' had been the bedrock of the Putin system, yet the system of 'manual control' had exhausted its potential and become a hindrance to effective governance accompanied by the proliferation of extra-constitutional centres of influence in the country. The security of property rights had not improved and corporate raiding flourished, discouraging foreign direct investment.[59]

On 26 July 2011 Putin announced that United Russia would hold its annual congress on 23–24 September, where its presidential candidate would finally be announced. This unleashed a frenzy of speculation and criticism as the elite hedged between the two main candidates. Putin stepped up what had already long been an unofficial campaign, criss-crossing the country and promising higher wages, pensions and benefits. Putin had long been in a permanent campaigning mode, keeping himself in the forefront of popular attention by various stunts – such as bare-chested horse-riding, a car trip across the Russian Far East, or discovering putatively long-hidden amphorae on the sea bed. Putin was clearly upset by Medvedev's attempts to gain independence, and he was reputedly disturbed 'by the fact that Medvedev had failed to secure broad support within the political establishment, business elites, and electorate in general'. Putin's supporters insisted that he enjoyed far greater support across the country, and that Medvedev overestimated his weight within the system.[60] Putin effectively presented the choice as between him and chaos, and thus squeezed out the Medvedev option.

To give substance to Medvedev's aspirations, beyond his much-lampooned image as a 'Twitter liberal', his associates began to develop a programme for a second term. The Institute of Contemporary Development (Insor) was established by Medvedev in 2006 to generate ideas for his forthcoming presidency. Headed by Igor Yurgens, the body became the headquarters for Medvedev's undeclared campaign. Already its 2010 report *Twenty-first Century Russia: Model of a Desired Future* had been the subject of fierce criticism by the regime's defenders, and in particular the report's postulate that the social contract between society and the authorities was in jeopardy.[61] In March 2011 INSOR published a strategic analysis called *Attaining the Future: Strategy 2020*. Its two key arguments were that the country needed modernisation of its institutions and economy, and that this could only be achieved through changing its political structures. It argued that the Russian state was in crisis, with the country divided up into petty principalities at all levels, and that only a 'reset of democracy' could avert the impending economic collapse and disintegration of the country. The political system established by Putin was to be dismantled through a reduction in the representation threshold to 5 per cent, allowing parties to form alliances, the return to gubernatorial elections, removal of the informal ban on independent sponsorship of political parties, and abolition of TV censorship.[62] Although the report understood that many of the country's problems were rooted in society and not in the government, political reform was seen as the way to deal with both. The report was to serve as Medvedev's electoral programme, although it had not been explicitly commissioned by the president.

In what became the 'war of the think tanks', the Centre for Strategic Research (CSR) took a rather different tack. Headed initially by German Gref and Elvira Nabiullina in Putin's early years to give strategic direction to his leadership, the CSR was now headed by Mikhail Dmitriev. After a period of quiescence, its report of March 2011 recommended the postponement of the presidential election to June 2012, but above all issued a warning that in the event proved highly prescient: 'If we assume that the elections of 2011–12 take place in the planned manner, whatever the outcome they will deal a very serious blow to the legitimacy of the authorities as a consequence of the fact of obvious political manipulation.' The report considered Medvedev unelectable, but also argued that Putin had lost the shine of youth and freshness, and thus in effect argued for a third candidate. Polls showed that the electorate was tiring of both Putin and Medvedev, and above all the endless game of cat and mouse about which of the two would become the next president.[63] It was unlikely that Dmitriev had any of the existing party leaders in mind, and his closeness to Anatoly Chubais was well-known. The report reflected growing fears in the elite that neither of the tandem duo could successfully and legitimately run the country. Medvedev's pusillanimity meant that he had failed to develop as an independent leader, while Putin's charisma was dissipating.

The under the carpet struggle for the official nomination was criticised by two of Medvedev's strongest supporters, Yurgens and the economist Yevgeny Gontmakher, key figures in Insor. They criticised the tandem's idea that 'When the time comes, we will sit down and decide'. They warned that the continuation of the policy of 'stability' advocated by the other member of the tandem 'has become a synonym not even for stagnation (we went through that stage in the pre-crisis 2000s) but rather for obvious deterioration in all areas of Russian life'. They noted that the 'Simple fact of the current president deciding not to continue his mandate will cause a major crisis in the country'. They urged Medvedev to 'cross his personal Rubicon, turning directly to society with a call to undertake together the difficult job of pulling the country out of the swamp we have all fallen into', and this should immediately take the form or creating 'mechanisms for partnership between the government and society'.[64] In effect, a second Medvedev presidency would be in a position to repudiate Putin and his mode of governance.

Putin or Medvedev?

Medvedev startled a meeting of the top management of 27 leading state and private companies on 11 July 2011 when he stated that in recent years the country had followed Putin's path, and Medvedev had outlined his plans in speeches in Magnitogorsk and St Petersburg: it was now up to business to decide which path they would follow. As one delegate put it, 'The president clearly and politely gave us to understand that it is time for business to decide who it wants to see as the next president'.[65] These manoeuvrings took place against the background of an overall loss of confidence in both Putin and Medvedev, accompanied by growing demands for a new leader. The tandem presided over corruption and a general sense of stagnation with a declining confidence in the future. Although Russia was climbing out of the global economic crisis with around 4 per cent growth per annum, this was considerably less than its BRIC partners. The Russian middle class was growing in weight and confidence. The number of people earning $20,000 in Moscow and environs was rising rapidly. The population boom of the 1980s was reaching its most productive period (aged 30–40), strengthening the ranks of a Europeanised middle class. In this group there was a growing readiness to protest against corruption and to defend their interests (especially as car owners). They had a defined set of values, although contradictory: 'the demand for a law-governed state; the refusal to tolerate corruption; a lack of confidence in the authorities; sympathy for the needy; a pro-Europe orientation; and moderate nationalism'.[66]

The elite began to line up behind the two candidates, and outsiders also made their preferences clear. For example, the former Soviet president, Gorbachev, warned that Putin's return would damage the country. Speaking at the thirteenth session of the Russian-German 'St Petersburg Dialogue' in Hannover, he argued that 'The Petersburg project in Russia is over. It has run its course'. He noted that 'If you try to do everything in the country without taking people into account, while imitating democracy, this will lead to a situation like in Africa where leaders sit and rule for 20–30 years'. He thus concluded: 'It would be better if Putin chose not to seek a return to the Kremlin'.[67] In his speech at the forum on 19 July 2011 Medvedev returned to his familiar themes, stressing the need to narrow the gap between laws and their enforcement (that is, between the letter and the spirit of law), the reduction of state interference in the media (he even mooted the idea of creating an independent public television network), the burden of state regulation on NGOs ('at a certain point we simply over-tightened the screws'), and the problem of excessive bureaucracy in general.[68] Pavlovsky commented on the speech as 'a long-winded preamble': 'The president listed genuine problems ... The question is then: who is going to resolve them and improve the situation?'. The speech once again appeared to be part of a polemic with an unstated interlocutor, presumed to be Putin, but never mentioned by name. The endless repetition of problems with no clear method for their resolution would hasten the day, according to Pavlovsky, when 'people will stop taking Medvedev's statements seriously'.[69]

The 2011–12 electoral cycle proceeded in a way already tried and tested in previous cycles in the 2000s, namely in a plebiscitary manner, although attended with the typical duality whereby the open campaign was accompanied by hidden factional conflict. However, in conditions of tandem rule where the diarchy came to represent two increasingly delineated contrasting programmes, the open campaign itself had two facets. Medvedev represented evolutionary liberal change, whereas Putin symbolised a more forceful model of managed modernisation. Both agreed on development, but took different approaches to how this should be achieved. Concern over mutual survival had kept the tandem intact, but the conventional limits on intra-regime contestation were now being transgressed. What began as yet another managed process conducted according to the time-honoured procedures of a 'normalised' system became genuinely normal – defined as a relatively unpredictable and open contest.

Just Russia had been weakened by Mironov's downfall and dismissal as head of the Federation Council, depriving it of administrative and political support. It increasingly looked as if Just Russia would not cross the 7 per cent representation threshold in December. This would leave just three parties represented in parliament: United Russia, 'the party of thieves and crooks' to use the term popularised by Navalny; the CPRF, a tired yet relatively independent political force under its dour veteran leader, Zyuganov, with very few ideas on how to transform Russia into a dynamic and modern society; and the LDPR under the fading star of Zhirinovsky, posing as an independent party yet acutely sensing the limits of its own autonomy. Such a Duma would hardly be able to lead Medvedev's modernisation agenda; hence his attempts to bring in new blood in the form of the liberal Right Cause. Attempts by the Party of People's Freedom (Parnas) to register had been blocked, leaving them outside the terrain of electoral competition. Right Cause's implosion left only the stoutly independent Yabloko in the field. Grigory Yavlinsky was back on active duty to lead the party list in the Duma elections, yet the party was unmanageable and thus considered unsuitable by the Kremlin.

The fundamental truth was that the selection of Russia's next president was basically in Putin's hands – a fact which was humiliating for those of a more liberal persuasion who pinned their hopes on Medvedev. In early September 2011 Yurgens and his Insor colleagues urged Medvedev to run for a second term. Putin retained the loyalty of the mighty administrative machine, whereas Medvedev had no cadre of loyal staff. Very few ministers and top officials owed their advancement to Medvedev, and even though there had been a significant turnover of governors, there was no loyal regional group. In addition, Medvedev alienated large sections of the elite by driving through (however contradictorily and inadequately) a series of anti-corruption measures, and in general he tried to rein in the powers of the 'sovereign bureaucracy'. The latter looked back to the good old Putin days, and looked forward to the restoration of their privileges after 2012. There was a strong lobby who argued that Russia did not need further democratisation, even if they agreed that democracy in Russia was far from perfect.[70]

The creation of the Popular Front and the other stratagems of the regime amounted to a 'mechanism to keep the current elite firmly in control with the appearance of a more democratic system', called by him 'managed pluralism', all designed to keep what Monaghan called 'the Team' in power, a system that Whitmore argued was 'the Deep State'. Brian Whitmore argues that this was all designed to 'make sure that the appearance of democracy doesn't turn into the real thing'.[71] The fate of the country was being decided by intra-elite squabbles, reflecting the blocked modernisation and political impasse. The sense of alienation provoked the large-scale emigration of professionals, with 'middle class' emigration at the time estimated to be running at about 300,000 people a year, a haemorrhage of skills that no country can sustain. The nation's future was in effect being lost. The poor investment climate and all the other problems which Medvedev decried were symptoms of the crisis of a political system that had reached the limits of its potential. Putin had stabilised the country and established a developmental trajectory based on bureaucratic management. This delivered certain remedial achievements but lacked an adequate developmental dynamic. This ultimately was the central issue of the 2011–12 election.

There are numerous reasons why a second term for Medvedev made sense. First, the popularity ratings of the tandem were beginning to fall, suggesting a growing popular alienation with the existing system. Second, Medvedev represented a phased liberalisation of the Putinite system while retaining its achievements. Fear that Medvedev would allow the destructive genie of uncontrolled reform out of the bottle was the stock response of the Putinites, but perhaps even worse was the possibility that he would successfully devise a programme that would lighten the stifling hand of the bureaucratic management of the public sphere and the manipulative supervision of public contestation. A second term Medvedev would be liberated from the political constraints under which he laboured during his first term. This was countered by a powerful swell of opinion that Putin should return to the presidency, a view shared even by some liberals. His supporters argued that a third term Putin would be a different man, one who would be able to lead an 'authoritarian modernisation' programme to overcome the entrenched resistance of special interest groups. From this perspective, Medvedev lacked the political authority to lead such a programme. However, the idea of 'iron liberalism' of the Peter Stolypin sort (who was advanced as Putin's hero at this time) repudiated precisely the need to remove the manual management of the polity and the economy to allow autonomous free play within the constraints of the constitution. It is precisely this top-down managerial logic that Putin's critics argued needed to be transcended.

Notes

1 'Stenograficheskii otchët o zasedanii Gosudarstvennogo soveta po voprosam razvitiya politicheskoi sistemy Rossii', 22 January 2010; http://www.kremlin.ru/transcripts/6693.

2 'State Council Discussion Useful but No Start to Political Reform', Itar-Tass, 25 January 2010.
 3 Il'ya Barabanov, 'Kreml' rabotaet nad novoi ideologicheskoi doktrinoi', *New Times*, No. 34, 28 September 2009, pp. 8–11.
 4 Gleb Pavlovskii in discussion with Andrei Piontkovskii, 'Chto oznachayut novye slova i ponyatiya, kotorye v poslednee vremya proiznosyat president i ego okruzhenie', *New Times*, No. 34, 28 September 2009, pp. 12–15, at p. 13.
 5 Matthias Schepp, 'The Shadow Boxers: Putin and Medvedev Eye the Kremlin – and Each Other', *Der Spiegel*, 18 July 2011; *JRL*, 129/9, 2011.
 6 Dmitrii Medvedev, 'Rossiya, vpered!', 10 September 2009; http://www.gazeta.ru/comments/2009/09/10_a_3258568.shtml.
 7 Something that Medvedev himself admitted in his meeting with the Valdai Club, when he argued that 'The actual Address is of course a much more conservative document', 'Beginning of Meeting with Valdai International Club Participants', 15 September 2009, http://eng.kremlin.ru/speeches/2009/09/15/1647_type82914-type84779_221667.shtml
 8 *Ibid.*
 9 Andrei Kortunov, 'The New Russia', Kennan Institute, event summary, 5 February 2009; *JRL*, 71/10, 2008.
10 Dmitrii Furman, 'Respublikanets na trone', *Nezavisimaya gazeta*, 9 November 2009, p. 9.
11 Mikhail Khodorkovskii, 'Modernizatsiya: Pokolenie M', *Vedomosti*, 21 October 2009, p. 4. Medvedev's press secretary Natalya Timakova revealed that Medvedev read the article as he prepared his annual address.
12 'Top Russian Energy Officials Likely to leave Company Boards', RIA Novosti, 31 March 2011.
13 Transcribed in *European Neighbourhood Watch*, Issue 69, March 2011, p. 6.
14 'Dmitry Medvedev Spoke at the St Petersburg International Economic Forum: The President Gave an Assessment of the Current State of Russia's Economy and Outlined the Main Modernisation Priorities', 17 June 2011, http://eng.kremlin.ru/news/2411.
15 Gordon M. Hahn, 'Medvedev Makes More Progress on Judicial Reform', *Russia: Other Points of View*, 22 July 2011.
16 'Meeting with Regional, Municipal and District Judges', 26 July 2011; Kremlin.ru.
17 Dmitry Yagodin, 'Blog Medvedev: Aiming for Public Consent', *Europe-Asia Studies*, Vol. 64, No. 8, October 2012, pp. 1415–34.
18 Floriana Fossato and John Lloyd with Alexander Verkhovsky, *The Web that Failed: How Opposition Politics and Independent Initiatives are Failing on the Internet in Russia* (Oxford, Reuters Institute for the Study of Journalism, 2008), p. 15.
19 Leon Aron, 'Nyetizdat: How the Internet Is Building Civil Society in Russia', *Russian Outlook*, American Enterprise Institute, Spring 2011.
20 Sarah Oates, *Revolution Stalled: The Political Limits of the Internet in the Post-Soviet Sphere* (Oxford, Oxford University Press, 2012).
21 Rebecca Mackinnon, 'China's "Networked Authoritarianism"', *Journal of Democracy*, Vol. 22, No. 2, April 2011, pp. 32–46.
22 Evgeny Morozov, *The Net Delusion: How Not to Liberate the World* (London, Allen Lane, 2011).
23 *Rossiiskaya gazeta*, 6 September 2010.
24 Andrew Osborn, 'Medvedev and Putin at Odds over Moscow Mayor', *Telegraph.co.uk*, 12 September 2010.
25 'Sacked by the Kremlin after 18 Years in Power, the Moscow Mayor "Who Let His Wife Make Billions"', Mail Online; http://www.dailymail.co.uk.
26 BBC News, 'Moscow Mayor Yuri Luzhkov Sacked by President Medvedev', 28 September 2010; www.bbb.co.uk.

On the eve 109

27 'Dismissed Moscow Mayor Luzhkov Leaves United Russia (Update 1), RIA Novosti, 28 September 2010; Alexandra Odynova, 'Luzhkov Fired Over "Loss of Confidence"', *Moscow Times*, 29 September 2010.
28 Vladimir Putin, 'Comments During a Visit to Komi Republic', 28 September 2010; http://premier.gov.ru/eng/visits/ru/12326/events/12336.
29 'Luzhkov Links Dismissal to 2012 Presidential Election', RIA Novosti, 7 October 2010.
30 'Defiant Ex-mayor Plans to Stay in Politics', RIA Novosti, 12 October 2010.
31 'Sergei Sobyanin's Candidacy for the Position of Moscow Mayor will be Presented to the Moscow City Duma', 15 October 2010; http://eng.kremlin.ru/news/1146.
32 Andrew Osborn, 'Putin Eyes Presidency as Loyalist Appointed Moscow's Mayor', Telegraph.co.uk, 21 October 2010a.
33 Alexandra Odynova, 'Mayor Sobyanin to Court Investors', *Moscow Times*, 18 October 2010a.
34 Gregory Feifer, 'Nominee for Moscow Mayor Set to Impose Kremlin Control', *Moscow Times*, 20 October 2010.
35 Alexander Bratersky, 'Luzhkov Goes On Attack in Closed Lecture', *Moscow Times*, 22 October 2010.
36 Svetlana Petrova, 'Andrei Borodin, vozmozhno, sobral blokpaket aktsii Banka Moskvy', *Vedomosti*, 25 October 2010.
37 'A Conversation with Vladimir Putin', 16 December 2010, http://premier.gov.ru/eng/events/news/13427/
38 Confirmed by Natalia Timakova, Medvedev's spokesperson, Charles Clover, 'Medevedev Gains Strength from Power Show', *Financial Times*, 28 September 2010.
39 Evgeniya Albats, 'Ne ponimayu, pochemu rukovoditeli strany delayut vid, chto nichego ne proiskhodit', *The New Times*, 20 September 2010; http://newtimes.ru/articles/print/27723.
40 Yulia Latynina, 'Putin Divides and Rules', *Moscow Times*, 29 September 2010.
41 Mikhail Delyagin, 'The Fight for Control of Bank of Moscow: Isolated Incident or Resurgence of Corporate Raiding?', RIA Novosti, 29 April 2011.
42 Mikhail Rostovskii, 'Neizbezhnost' Putina', *Moskovskii komsomolets*, 15 July 2011, p. 1.
43 Brian Whitmore, 'Kudrin vs. United Russia', RFE/RL, Russia Report, 21 February 2011a.
44 Aleksandra Samarina, 'Aleksei Kudrin uporstvuet v "erese"', *Nezavisimaya gazeta*, 22 April 2011, p. 3.
45 Andrei Kostin, 'Za chestnye vybory Vladimira Putina', *Kommersant*, 13 February 2012.
46 Valerii Smirnov, *Front Putina: Protiv kogo?* (Moscow, Algoritm, 2011).
47 Putin was explicit about this motivation in answering a question, 'V khode poseshcheniya OAO "Magnitogorskii metallurgicheskii kombinat" V. V. Putin pobosedoval s rabotnikami predpriyatiya', 15 July 2001; http://premier.gov.ru/visits/ru/15901/events/15900/.
48 Vladimir Ryzhkov, 'Konovalov's Ministry of Manipulation', *Moscow Times*, 19 July 2011.
49 For example, by the European Parliament in a resolution of 7 July 2011, '"Real Obstacles to Political Pluralism" in Russian Duma Elections', in which MEPs condemned 'cumbersome registration procedures' for political parties, which do not comply with the ECHR and demonstrate 'that there are still real obstacles to political pluralism in Russia', http://www.europarl.europa.eu/en/pressroom/content/20110706IPR23549/html/Real-obstacles-to-political-pluralism-in-Russian-Duma-elections.
50 Meeting with the leaders of the parliamentary parties on 12 July 2011, 'Vstrecha s rukovoditelyami politicheskikh partii, predstavlennykh v Gosudarstvennoi Dume',

http://www.kremlin.ru/transcripts/11912. The idea that was reported informally, Liliya Biryukova, 'Vyiti iz zastoya', *Vedomosti*, 13 July 2011, p. 2.
51 Aleksandra Samarina and Yan Gordeev, 'Politdistrofiya posle partiinkh kanikul', *Nezavisimaya gazeta*, 22 July 2011, p. 1.
52 Eugene Ivanov, 'Knocked Off the Right Cause', *Russia Beyond the Headlines*, 19 September 2011; www.rbth.ru
53 'Stenograficheskii otchët', http://www.kremlin.ru/transcripts/6693.
54 'Parliament Speaker Could Be Dismissed Over Anti-Putin Remarks', www.russia-today.com, 3 February 2010.
55 Nikolai Zlobin, 'Sergei Mironov and the Inter-Party Competition', *Snob*, 24 May 2011; http://www.snob.ru/selected/entry/36001.
56 Alexandre Dimov, *Les hommes doubles: la vie quotidienne en Union Soviétique* (Paris, Éditions J.-C. Lattès, 1980).
57 Dmitry Kamyshev, 'Proekt "Nu, pogodi!"', *Kommersant-Vlast'*, No. 15, 18 April 2011, pp. 24–26, at p. 25.
58 Gordon Hahn, 'Reform Lessons for Perestroika 2.0', *Russia: Other Points of View*, 21 August 2011a.
59 Nikolai Zlobin, 'Otvet Medvedeva', *Vedomosti*, 17 May 2011a, p. 4.
60 Aleksandra Samarina and Roza Tsvetkova, 'Rasstroistvo tandema', *Nezavisimaya gazeta*, 28 July 2011, p. 1.
61 Insor, *Rossiya XXI veka: Obraz zhelaemogo zavtra* (Moscow, Ekon-Inform, 2010).
62 Insor, *Attaining the Future: Strategy 2020. Synopsis* (Moscow, Ekon-Inform, 2011).
63 Centre for Strategic Research, Sergei Balanovskii and Mikhail Dmitriev, *Politicheskii krizis v Rossii i vozmozhnye mekhanizmy ego razvitiya* (Moscow, 2011).
64 Igor Yurgens and Yevgeny Gontmakher, 'Razvilka-2012: Medvedevu pora pereiti Rubikon', *Vedomosti*, 27 July 2011, p. 4.
65 Andy Potts, 'Medvedev in Surprise Plea to Russian Business', *Moscow News*, 13 July 2011.
66 Mikhail Dmitriyev, 'Vse nachnetsya posle vyborov', *Vedomosti*, 11 July 2011, p. 4.
67 Ilya Arkhipov and Scott Rose, 'Gorbachev Warns of Danger from Putin Return', Bloomberg, 19 July 2011.
68 'Rossiisko-germanskii Forum obshchestvennosti "Peterburgskii dialog"', 19 July 2011; http://www.kremlin.ru/transcripts/12017.
69 Aleksandra Samarina, 'Medvedev iz Germanii dal signal otechestvennomu elektoratu', *Nezavisimaya gazeta*, 20 July 2011.
70 This was the import of a report presented to UR's liberal-conservative 4 November Club by the Public Planning Institute (InOP), a riposte to INSOR's calls for further democratisation. Vera Kholmogorova, 'Ne nado ottepeli', *Vedomosti*, 10 June 2009.
71 Brian Whitmore, 'Putin's Plan', RFE/RL, *Russia Report*, 19 July 2011b.

6 Putin's constitutional coup

Putin was barred from standing after two consecutive terms, but the constitution allowed him to return for a third (and even a fourth) term after a break. There was only one problem in 2011. It had become increasingly clear that the alleged 'placeholder' since 2008, incumbent president Medvedev, wanted another crack at the job. The stakes, moreover, had now been raised with the lengthened presidential term. The various factions intervened behind the scenes as they sought to secure their positions, but a sign of the increasingly normal character of Russian politics was that public contestation increasingly came to the fore and eclipsed para-political intrigues. The political challenge facing Russia was whether the manual management of the administrative regime could be suppressed enough to allow the procedures of the constitutional state to operate to allow a relatively free and fair contest. If open competitive elections could be held, then this boded well for the longer-term consolidation of the rule of law, procedural regularity in political processes, and the strengthening of the constitutional state in general.

Failure to do so risked not only discrediting the results but threatened a more profound delegitimation of the regime in it is entirety. The modernisation challenge remained as sharp as ever: to move from the remedial agenda that was the heart of the Putinite stability in his first two terms towards a more complex developmental strategy. The politics of the perceived remedial challenge – to overcome the alleged chaos of the 1990s and the threats to the viability of the state and governance – were very different from those appropriate to complex modernisation. While the one involved the consolidation of power and institutions, the other required greater freedom to unleash the energy of the people, the resources of entrepreneurs and the fulfilment of the free and unfettered expression of universal and equal citizenship rights. The efficacy of the tutelary regime in politics and a heavy-handed programme of managed modernisation in the economy were increasingly questioned. Thus the political and economic challenges were effectively one and the same: to establish an environment where investors felt safe from the predations of officialdom, and where initiative and talent could flourish in all spheres.

The September coup

September often proves to be a decisive turning point in Russian politics. In September 2004 Putin launched his first 'constitutional coup' in the wake of the Beslan school siege of 1–3 September 2004. The 1,300 hostages were held for three days without food or water, and ended in a botched rescue operation; overall, 334 people were killed, including 186 children. In its wake, on 13 September Putin announced a raft of measures intended to enhance the security of the country.[1] Putin spoke of the attempts of the terrorists to achieve 'the disintegration of the country, the break-up of the state and the collapse of Russia'. The very existence of the state was in question. Of the seven proposed measures, however, only one – the establishment of a special federal commission on the North Caucasus – was directly connected with the problems of which Beslan was a symptom. At least five of the other measures appeared to represent a sharp escalation in the strengthening of the 'presidential vertical': the appointment of governors; 100 per cent proportional representation in parliamentary elections (between 1993 and 2003 parliaments were elected under a mixed system, with 225 deputies elected from single-member districts and 225 from nationwide party lists); the creation of a public chamber; the establishment of Khrushchevite voluntary patrols to maintain public order; and the formation of a 'crisis management system' to conduct the war against terror. The final measure, the re-establishment of a ministry responsible for issues of regional and ethnic policy, turned the wheel full circle to the early 1990s.

The idea of a 'constitutional coup' is derived from the events of 1958 in France – the radical shift from the parliamentary Fourth Republic to the semi-presidential Fifth Republic, still in operation today. Charles de Gaulle rammed through a series of measures, legitimated later by a referendum, which significantly strengthened the powers of the presidency. François Mitterrand later argued that the new system represented a permanent threat to the constitutional order, although not formally transgressing the bounds of that order.[2] Russia's strongly presidential system falls into that category. By exercising the sovereignty of being able to decide on the exception, the regime subverted the constitutional state from within. The Beslan measures accentuated the para-constitutional features of the Russian system. Typically, they were not so much anti-constitutional as para-constitutional, strengthening the administrative regime at the expense of the constitutional state. In the event, they did not strengthen the system of executive power or render the working of government more efficacious. Para-constitutionalism is a strategy of the regime rather than of the defenders of the impartial and predictable workings of the constitutional state. By devising a series of measures that were intended as a response to a particular crisis, they accentuated the scope and intensity of that crisis.

Putin now engineered a second constitutional coup, an extraordinary coup de main that would have fateful long-term consequences. At the United

Russia congress on 24 September 2011 Medvedev announced that Putin would seek the presidential nomination, which was duly granted by the 10,000-strong obeisant congress. The hopes of those who had wanted Medvedev to serve a second term were dashed. Instead, at Putin's suggestion Medvedev was placed at the head of United Russia's electoral list for the December elections. He was thus foisted with responsibility for the electoral fortunes of a party from which he had so demonstratively distanced himself. To sweeten the pill, Putin declared that he would nominate Medvedev to 'form a new, effective, young and vigorous administrative team. I am sure that he will head the government of the Russian Federation to continue our work to modernise all aspects of our life'.[3] Putin stressed that 'we [with Medvedev] have long since reached an agreement on what we will be doing in the future'; a sentiment that was reiterated by Medvedev in his speech: 'What we agreed [with Putin] is a deeply thought-through decision. And even more, we already discussed this scenario when we first formed a friendly alliance.'[4] If this was indeed the case, then the four years of Medvedev's presidency were no more than a farce, a simulacrum of leadership.

However, the demonstrative emphasis that both leaders placed on the planned nature of Putin's return suggests that in fact the decision was rather more spontaneous. Medvedev's presidency from the first had been attended by speculation about who would be nominated for the presidency. When the decision was finally announced few were surprised, yet the decision was not entirely foreordained. With his return Putin effectively nullified the four years of Medvedev's presidency. Medvedev was personally humiliated, since clearly he was not to be trusted with another term, and the accompanying rhetoric – that the two had from the first decided on this 'castling' move – was an insult to the rest of the country. The manner in which the operation was conducted was messy and counter-productive, and far from guaranteeing a smooth transition.

The 24 September 2011 events will go down in Russian history, like the Beslan initiatives earlier, as another Putin démarche that consolidated his grip on the Russian polity. With presidential terms now extended to six years, the prospect now opened up of Putin being at Russia's helm for another 12 years. This represented a constitutional coup of the first order. Without infringing a single line of the constitution, Putin consolidated an extraordinary hold on power. It was constitutional because everything was done according to the book, without recourse to a referendum or plebiscite to change term limits. But it also represented a type of coup, because of the exclusive character of the system. This was a quiet coup, without bloodshed or armed bodies of men, but its effect was to eviscerate the institutions of the constitutional state to consolidate an increasingly personalistic political regime.

Kudrin was clearly shocked by the 'castling' manoeuvre. He harboured ambitions to become prime minister himself, and now he saw that the post would be taken up by his rival, Medvedev. He made clear his disapproval. Speaking at a conference in New York, he announced that he would not serve in a Medvedev cabinet. He also criticised Medvedev's plan to allocate enormous resources for the modernisation of the armed forces. Back in Moscow, on 27 September Medvedev, at an extended cabinet meeting, publicly requested Kudrin's resignation in a humiliating televised grilling. Kudrin insisted that he would have to consult with the prime minister, and Putin (who was absent from the meeting) soon afterwards felt forced to give his consent to the dismissal of his long-time colleague. However, Putin insisted that Kudrin remain a member of his team and that a worthy role would be found for him. Commenting on Kudrin in his question and answer session on 15 December Putin stressed 'As you know, Alexei Kudrin never left my team. He is my long-time compañero, and I would even say that he is my friend'.[5] Medvedev's public and humiliating confrontation forced Kudrin to resign his post as finance minister and his other responsibilities, but Medvedev was exposed as vindictive, petty and spiteful.

The Putinite elite feared Medvedev's return to the presidency for six years. The tandem had proved an effective mechanism to blunt his reformist aspirations and to constrain political change, but if re-elected Medvedev would be off the leash and in a position to challenge entrenched interests. Tensions within the regime took the form of fissures between the Kremlin and the White House, and Putin's return was intended to control intra-regime factional conflict while blunting the gathering reform momentum. The 'Medvedev narrative' of a new perestroika and 'capitulation' to the militaristic West was seen as an aberration, and instead a counter discourse of Eurasian integration, cultural resistance to western decadence, and political sovereignty sought hegemony in shaping Russia's future. Pressure from Putin's entourage and elites threatened by promised reforms propelled Putin back to the Kremlin. This version of events was effectively admitted by Putin in interviews after the fateful events of 24 September. Putin's return was always the cardinal option, but it had not been long decided. Medvedev wanted a second term, and this would have allowed a smooth and safe exit for Putin and his associates, but they were not yet ready to leave.

There remain conflicting versions about when the final decision was taken. Both Putin and Medvedev backed away from the bald assertions made on 24 September that the decision had been part of the plan all along. If that was indeed the case, then the Russian people had been deliberately misled when Medvedev insisted that the decision would be taken in the light of circumstances. Thus Putin's return may well have been foreordained, but it appears that no one had told Medvedev. He, and certainly a group of influential liberal supporters, had begun to vest hopes in his return as a way of strengthening the constitutional state, and averting the wholesale personalisation of politics. Not only were these hopes dashed, but if the swap had been planned from the start then proponents of the view that Medvedev's return would allow greater scope for democratic political evolution looked silly and naïve. If Medvedev did indeed act as no more than a placeholder, then he played this role in an exemplary manner. At the Yaroslavl Forum on

10 September Medvedev enunciated the alternative vision, and no one denied his capacity for hard work. At the 11 November meeting with the Valdai Club, Putin asserted that if Medvedev had not carried out his presidential duties in an appropriate manner then he would never have been nominated for the premier's office from May 2012.

Putin's 'return', of course, is a misnomer, since he had never gone anywhere. As prime minister Putin continued to rule as a member of the 'tandem'. Those who had talked of a possible 'schism' between the two wings of the tandem were clearly wrong, since the two worked effectively as a team. Indeed, on certain issues Medvedev was more of a hard liner than Putin, notably in foreign affairs and in personnel matters. Medvedev had a wider political spectrum than Putin: stretching further to the conservative side, but also, significantly, with a more liberal domestic aspect. Thus Medvedev repeatedly blocked attempts to impose political controls over the internet – not surprisingly, as an all-tweeting all-blogging president. Medvedev did some of the dirty work in anticipation of Putin's return, notably the removal of 'heavy-weight' governors, some of whom had been in power since the fall of communism (notably Luzhkov in Moscow and Shaimiev in Tatarstan). In conditions of economic crisis he had stalled on the implementation of substantive social changes, notably welfare reforms that would have shifted the burden on to individuals.

Medvedev's initiatives in the political sphere were limited, although as we have argued earlier, certainly far from nugatory. However, in identifying problems but then delaying the implementation of change (for example, the reduction of the 7 per cent representation threshold in parliamentary elections to 5 per cent to take effect only in the next Duma election in 2016), he discredited belief in intra-systemic change in its entirety. Similarly, the idea of modernisation was reduced to little more than the creation in November 2009 of the Skolkovo Innovation Centre near Moscow. This was a classic case of modernisation from above. Although in setting standards it could act as a beacon for the rest of the country, but it sucked out much need venture capital and state investment in research and development from the rest of the sector. Some attempts were made to ease the administrative burden on business, and to reduce the scourge of unjustifiably lengthy pre-trial detention, but after four years at the helm the situation had barely improved. Despite the launching of investigations into the death of Sergei Magnitsky in jail on 16 November 2010, his persecutors mostly remained at large, and in some cases given state honours. Khodorkovsky and Lebedev, moreover, remained in correctional camps, despite much talk of an amnesty.

Putin's return to the presidency was the defining event of the era. Russia really did become Putin's, with his increasingly conservative views shaping the country's destiny. Putin's return negated the four years of liberalising and modernising rhetoric under Medvedev. On the other hand, his return broke the log-jam on decision-making of the tandem years; the ambiguity was over and it was now clear who was boss. Nevertheless, even for those who had predicted Putin's return, the brutal manner in which it was achieved and its far-reaching significance still came as something of a shock. Yet, it may be asked why the events of 24 September are so important. After all, it was not as if anything really unexpected happened. The person who had dominated Russian politics since 2000 planned to return to the Kremlin, from which he had been involuntarily exiled because of his unwillingness to join the ranks of plebiscitary dictators elsewhere by changing the constitution.

The political scientist Alexander Morozov later identified precisely what was at stake. Noting that protest movements traditionally address a number of real political subjects:

> But in new, weak democracies an implacable societal law operates: when the head of state completely destroys the political subjectivity of all political institutions, a catastrophe occurs shortly afterwards. This is precisely what Vladimir Putin did on 24 September 2011. Even before that date the autonomy of the RF's political institutions – parliament, courts, government, parties, the media and so on – were relatively weak. But on 24 September 2011 Putin turned the tumbler upside down, after which the whole political system operated according to a different functional regime. Not only the classical institutions but also the informal ones lost their relative autonomy.[6]

After 24 September, in his view, there were no longer the 'towers of the Kremlin', no tandem, nor the 'demonic Surkov', responsible for everything. Now, like in so many 'bad regimes' in the third world, all responsibility shifted to Putin. The security apparatus after that point was no longer defending the state, but protecting Putin personally. Protesters could no longer appeal to some impartial institution, but to the only force in the land that still retained its autonomous political subjectivity – Putin. This was not all, because by the same token the country was now ineluctably headed for a political crisis. With little immediate prospect of the institutions of the constitutional state regaining their political subjectivity, sooner or later the one-man system of rule would collapse. This is why I call the events of 24 September a coup.

Parliamentary election

The law on elections had been amended 60 times since 2002, and was intended to deliver the appropriate results, yet as the 4 December 2011 parliamentary elections approached there was a high degree of contingency and unexpectedness. There were clear signs of a 'pre-crisis' situation in the country. One of the manifestations of this was the so-called 'booing revolution'. In early November at a concert of the legendary rock band Mashina Vremeni (Time Machine) in Kemerovo it was announced that the event had been sponsored by United Russia. The announcer had to stop in mid-sentence since the wave of booing was so loud and persistent. A fortnight later at a Chelyabinsk ice hockey game the captain of the local team 'Traktor' skated on to the ice and began a speech in favour of United Russia, but he was forced to retreat to the bench when the boos became too loud. The booing revolution peaked when Putin on 20 November attended a Moscow stadium for a mixed martial arts fight between Russian Fyodor Emilianenko and American Jeff Monson. The Russian won, and when Putin climbed into the ring to praise him as a 'real Russian knight' some 20,000 shouted 'go away' accompanied by booing. In all cases the authorities came up with barely credible explanations of the events. This was not the liberal intelligentsia making itself heard, but the great mass of Russian blue-collar workers. Putin failed to turn up to two previously announced events later in the week. Pavlovsky at this time noted:

> I fail to understand [Putin] any more. ... He is losing contact with reality. ... In the past he was a team player; he wasn't so narcissistic, and didn't consider himself to be a genius. ... He seems to believe that his great success over the past 10 years means that he understands Russia and the world better than anybody else.[7]

Putin addressed a sympathetic rally with some 11,000 United Russia supporters on 27 November, but this was not real engagement with the country. The party had lost 10 per cent in its rating since September, falling to around 50 per cent support. To compensate, the whole gamut of mechanisms were activated to bolster the pro-regime vote. Students, the military, patients in hospital and schools were all mobilised to get the vote out, and governors were threatened with sanctions if they failed to deliver. Participation was not so much in support of United Russia but part of the 'contract' with the regime. In return for their vote and passivity thereafter, the regime promised rising living standards and to keep out of their private lives.[8] United Russia had clearly become a liability for Putin, hence the creation of the People's Front in May 2011. Medvedev led United Russia's parliamentary campaign, even though he had never associated himself with this 'party of power', and indeed had condemned its bureaucratic and corrupt practices. Medvedev fought a rather lacklustre campaign that saw United Russia slide in the ratings, accompanied by a general fall in the support for both Putin and Medvedev.

Even before the ballot the field had been skewed in favour of the authorities, with Parnas refused registration on an unconvincing pretext. The poll itself was marred by widespread irregularities, extensively reported on the internet, including the liberal use of absentee voter certificates (AVCs). Nevertheless, even the official result saw United Russia lose its constitutional majority, but it remained by far the single largest party in the new Duma (see Table 6.1). On a turnout of 60.1 per cent (a 3 per cent fall on 2007 but up 5 per cent on 2003) United Russia received 49.3 per cent of the vote, which gave it 238 out of 450 parliamentary seats, down from the constitutional majority of 315 it enjoyed in the previous convocation. The CPRF was the beneficiary of

Table 6.1 State Duma election of 4 December 2011

	Name of party	Percentage vote	Votes (mln)	Seats
1	United Russia (UR)	49.32	32.38	238
2	Communist Party of the Russian Federation (CPRF)	19.19	12.59	92
3	Just Russia (JR)	13.24	8.69	64
4	Liberal Democratic Party of Russia (LDPR)	11.67	7.66	56
	Sub-total	**93.42**	**61.32**	**450**
	Seven per cent representation threshold			
5	Yabloko	3.43	2.25	-
6	Patriots of Russia	0.97	0.64	-
7	Right Cause	0.60	0.39	-
	Sub-total	**5.0**	**3.28**	-
	TOTAL	**98.42**	**64.60**	**450**
	Number of registered voters	109,237,780		
	Number of valid votes	64,623,062		
	Number of spoilt ballots	1,033,464		
	Turnout	65,656,526 (60.1%)		

Source: Central Electoral Commission: http://www.cikrf.ru/banners/duma_2011/itogi/result.html.

a large protest vote, winning 19.2 per cent of the ballot. The biggest surprise of the election was the 13.2 per cent received by Just Russia, a party initially formed at the behest of the Kremlin but which had gradually consolidated its reputation as an emerging independent social democratic party. The Liberal Democratic Party just exceeded the 7 per cent representation threshold. Yabloko once again failed to enter the Duma, but its 3.4 per cent represented a great improvement on its performance four years earlier. Yabloko insisted that much of its vote in its Moscow and St Petersburg heartlands had been stolen, and throughout the country there were numerous cases of ballot stuffing and other fraudulent practices. The anomalous variation in the vote between and even within regions is attributed to different levels of falsification, with some 15 million extra votes allegedly transferred to United Russia. Although United Russia came top everywhere, its vote varied from 29 per cent in Yaroslavl to 99.5 per cent in Chechnya, and in general the party fell below 35 per cent in 15 regions.[9]

On 18 January 2012 the GPO sent an interim report to Medvedev stating that some 3,000 violations of the electoral law had been uncovered. Administrative proceedings had been launched against about 100 people, and there had been two criminal prosecutions. The opposition insisted, in the words of the Yabloko leader, Sergei Mitrokhin, that this was but 'a drop in the ocean'.[10] The OSCE report summarised the issues. Although technically well-conducted, 'the quality of the process deteriorated considerably during the count, which was characterized by frequent procedural violations and instances of apparent manipulation, including several serious indications of ballot box stuffing'.[11] The denial by the justice ministry of registration to a number of parties reduced the choices available to voters, there was unequal treatment of the contestants by the election administration, 'the distinction between the state and the governing party was frequently blurred by state and local officials taking advantage of their office or position to advance the chances of one party over the others', and media coverage was skewed, while 'coverage of all monitored national broadcasters except one channel favoured the governing party'.[12] The Parliamentary Assembly of the Council of Europe (PACE) came to similar conclusions, arguing that 'Any election needs an impartial referee and, to this day, this is clearly missing in the Russian Federation. A structural change is needed in the short time in order to promote citizens' trust in the election results'. In other words, the Central Electoral Commission needed to be reformed to make it impartial. The report went on to note, however, that the results demonstrated that 'voting can make a difference'.[13]

Estimates suggest that the declared result deviated by about 15.3m votes from the real result, up from the 14.8m in 2008 and 13.9m in 2007. These data need to be increased by the number of voters in special categories, including the abuse of AVCs, a perennial source of complaint, which meant that in December 2011 some 25.1m votes were subject to 'electoral anomalies'. The divergence thereafter decreased, and the 2012 presidential ballot according to these calculations deviated by 'only' 11m.[14] The large-scale vote-monitoring drive in both the parliamentary and presidential elections sought to compensate for the evident partiality of those whose legal duty it was to ensure an accurate and fair vote. Above all, a wave of protest against flawed elections inaugurated a period when the costs of electoral manipulation began to outweigh perceived benefits.

Protest and counter-protest

Popular tolerance of administrative interference in elections reached breaking point. Society had matured, in part as a result of the long Putinite stability, and a new class had emerged demanding its citizenship rights. Sometimes described as a 'middle class', such a designation is misleading since many of the students and young people involved could hardly be described as such either in income or status terms. Another term current at the time was to assign the protests to the 'creative class', those not tied to the bureaucracy or some other 'service' class. Surkov called them 'angry urbanites', and unexpectedly indicated a degree of sympathy with their aims. The protest movement has naturally been at the centre of analysis, because of its scale, degree of coordination and substantive political challenge to the Putinite order, but it was not unprecedented.

Protest and civil activism was nothing new in the Putin era. The monetisation of social benefits had provoked a wave of protest in early 2005, with a large number of pensioners and others from the 'dependent' classes taking to the streets across the country. In the wake of the economic crisis from 2008, street meetings peaked in 2009 as demonstrators across the country protested against social and economic problems. In January 2010 up to 12,000 protesters in Kaliningrad called on Prime Minister Putin to resign in an outburst of anger. The immediate spark was a planned increase in the regional transport tax, but this demonstration and some smaller ones elsewhere signalled growing frustration.[15] At the time of the wildfires in summer 2010 large numbers of volunteers made up for the deficiencies of the authorities. At that time the 'blue buckets' movement mocked officials who sped by with their blue lamps flashing, while ordinary motorists remained locked in worsening traffic jams. Already motorists had mobilised against the ban on the importation of second-hand right-hand drive cars, notably in Vladivostok in December 2007, and the persecution of motorists in collision with official motorcades.

Already on 5 December 2011 an unexpectedly large number of protesters, up to 10,000, gathered on Chistoprudny Boulevard in Moscow to condemn fraud in the parliamentary ballot. The protests thereafter gathered pace, with the first of the large demonstrations taking place on 10 December in Bolotnaya Square with some 80,000 participating, and with the second on 24 December on Sakharov Prospekt bringing together some 100,000. The demonstrators condemned the practices of 'managed democracy', watched over by a large but passive police presence. It was clear that the authorities had decided on concessions rather than coercion. This was reflected in the package of political reforms, including the easier registration of political parties and the restoration of elections for regional governors, announced by Medvedev in his *poslanie* on 22 December (see below). A third large demonstration was again held in Bolotnaya Square on 4 February, despite the freezing temperatures.

At the Sakharov Prospekt demonstration two days after Medvedev's speech, a wide spectrum of oppositionists addressed the crowd. The main slogan was 'Russia without Putin', while the placard with the words 'Putin is a thief' were prevalent, accompanied by a range of striking and witty posters. Kudrin had long been calling for free and fair elections, and now he joined the tribune on 24 December to call for a re-run of the 4 December poll. While Kudrin may have been ambivalent about attacks on his friend, he endorsed the demand for a re-run of the elections and the dismissal of CEC's head, Vladimir Churov. Kudrin called on the demonstrators 'to organise a platform for dialogue', including with the authorities. 'Otherwise it is revolution, and we will lose the chance that is before us today – peaceful transformation and the trust that is necessary for a new ruling power to be created.' He also noted that steps had already been taken to create a new party, to consolidate the liberalising reforms. There were clear signs of intra-elite splits. Democratisation theory tells us that this is precisely the most dangerous time for an old regime, and the moment when a democratic breakthrough becomes possible.

The protest movement brought together an eclectic mix of concerns. Although liberal issues were prominent, a large contingent of the demonstrators was made up of nationalists protesting against Putin's apparent lack of concern for the Russian ethnic majority. The authorities failed to establish an effective system to manage labour migration from Central Asia and the Caucasus, prompting the idea that Russia would be better off without the North Caucasus, and that Tajiks and others should be chased out of the big cities. Russia is the world's second largest recipient of immigrants, after the United States, with, according to the Federal Migration Service, some ten million legal and an estimated three million illegal immigrants. The majority come from the former Soviet republics of Kyrgyzstan, Tajikistan, Uzbekistan, Ukraine and Moldova to work as cheap labour in the construction and service industries. The immigrant community as a whole is severely exploited, with two-thirds, according to a 2010 estimate, earning between $300–$600 a month in Moscow, one of the most expensive cities in the world. What is left flows out in the form of remittances, where such transfers constitute half of Tajikistan's GDP and a third of Kyrgyzstan's. Some $20bn leaves Russia annually in this way. Polls suggest that an overwhelming 85 per cent support a strict visa regime with Central Asia and the South Caucasian republics, and stricter monitoring of the registration rules for Russian citizens from the North Caucasus.

The demonstration on 4 February in Bolotnaya Square assembled no more than 60,000, and revealed the divisions in the protest movement. The whole spectrum of the anti-systemic opposition was on view, divided not only ideologically but also generationally. The old guard democrats, such as Nemtsov and Rzykhov, were over-shadowed by the new militants, such as Navalny and the coordinator of Left Front, Sergei Udaltsov. They in turn were over-shadowed by a counter-rally on Poklonnaya Hill, which served as a warning that once Russia mobilised, the liberals would find themselves in a minority. Only a few liberals were ready to recognise that ultimately Putin was a compromise figure, and held at bay the real power of Russian *revanchism*. His ability to maintain a balance in policy positions as well as a consensus among Russian elites reinforced the arguments of his supporters that there was no positive alternative to his leadership. With the Medvedev option discredited and the autonomous development of political parties stymied, the argument became self-reinforcing.

According to Levada Centre surveys, the protest movement was overwhelmingly young and middle class. Of those who marched on 24 December 2011, 62 per cent had university degrees or higher, a quarter were aged below 25 and over half were under 40; almost half were professionals, and almost a quarter were either managers or owned a business; while 12 per cent were college students, the third largest group. The overwhelming majority, some

70 per cent, considered themselves 'democrats' or liberals', while a plurality supported Yabloko, the 'party of the intelligentsia'. Alexei Levinson of the Levada Centre argued that it was misleading to emphasise the movement's middle-class character. Research by the Centre found that although plenty of middle-class people participated, there were also many poor people, pensioners and students. He condemned the class approach to the question, warning the regime of attempts to mobilise the working class from the provinces (notably, the Urals) against the metropolitan demonstrators – a tactic that Ceaușescu had tried in Bucharest in December 1989 when he brought in the miners, but it was his final act. Levinson insisted that 'It was not the middle class who protested. Society as a whole sent out its heralds to say that they wished to live differently.'[16]

There are two major interpretations of the protest movement. The first is the liberal one, arguing that they reflected dissatisfaction with the general sense of stagnation and the need for political reform. From this perspective, the flawed ballot of 4 December was the catalyst that brought the simmering dissatisfaction with the Putinite system of regime rule to the boil. Medvedev had long advocated reform, but had been stymied at every turn by those arguing that there was no need for change, and as we shall see he now used the opportunity to introduce a range of changes to the political system. The second view is the conservative one, arguing that the existing system was perfectly viable, and that Medvedev's flirtation with political reform had emboldened the ungrateful section of the population, sponsored by the West. For the conservatives, political reform would lead to another perestroika, and threaten once again Russia's hard fought stability and sovereignty. Classic Putinism contained both the liberal and the conservative interpretations, but once back in power it would be hard to restore the equilibrium.

The protest movement threatened the factional balance that Putin had so assiduously maintained. All the factions were torn by internal tensions, but broadly we have identified a division between the *siloviki* and the *civiliki*. For the former, a strong and independent Russia in global affairs was the priority, and at home a centralised and authoritative political system with a strong dose of state management in the economy. They also favoured the minimum of public accountability, to allow their various nefarious schemes to prosper. On the other side, the *civiliki* had gathered around Medvedev's modernisation agenda designed to create a more liberal economy, integrated with the West, and with functioning democratic institutions and the rule of law. The popular movement, despite its divisions, broadly supported the latter programme, hence the immediate de facto alliance between the *civiliki* and the civil protesters. Putin's balancing role was in danger of becoming redundant, something that Putin could not accept. The leading *civiliki* were dispersed, with Surkov exiled from the Kremlin and Kudrin out of office, while the *siloviki* regrouped. The sophisticated Sergei Naryshkin was sent to manage the Duma, Igor Sechin went into the business world, and Sergei Ivanov was brought in to manage the presidential administration.

The rise in real incomes in 2011 had been a mere 0.8 per cent, and although the economy had returned to growth (at around 4 per cent, far higher than most of its European competitors) after the recession, this was still below that of the BRIC countries. Studies at this time revealed that 38 per cent of Russians had little hope for their future, a sense of failure that was marked in small towns with a population under 20,000.[17] There had also been institutional decay, with a degradation of some of the institutions of modernity, such as the courts, the security and police apparatus, and the educational system. Property rights had become less secure, while the instruments of democratic governance had been hollowed out. Putin's leadership sought to depoliticise governance and to render it the preserve of a special elite vouchsafed with a privileged relationship to deciding what was in Russia's national interest. The protest movement precisely challenged this postulate and demanded the re-establishment of a political process which would at once be more pluralistic and competitive. In other words, the fundamental demand was for the return of politics. Putin's pragmatic centrism precisely sought to counter the logic of competitive pluralism in favour of his distinctive brand of tutelary patrimonialism. The question now became not whether Putin would return, but whether he could preserve his classic mode of rule.

The counter-demonstration on 4 February on Poklonnaya Hill gathered at least 140,000, possibly double the number protesting against the regime. The Kremlin sought to demonstrate that in sheer numerical terms, more supported the regime than opposed it. However, United Russia was barely mentioned and instead the official sponsors of the rally were the Union of Afghan Veterans, the Pensioners' Union, the Congress of Russian Communities, and the Patriots of Russia party. The rally's theme was not direct support for Putin but condemnation of 'the Orange threat'. The theatre director and militantly anti-American Sergei Kurginyan headed the list of speakers, accompanied by the virulent anti-liberals Alexander Dugin (the 'Russian Heidegger') and Prokhanov, the editor of the far-right/left patriotic paper *Zavtra*. Dugin was the leading exponent of neo-Eurasianism and an associate of the French New Right. Although there were undoubtedly regime enthusiasts at the rally, there were numerous reports of 500-rouble payments for attendance, accompanied by a range of implied sanctions for students and other dependent groups if they failed to attend. This, however, was not the main lesson of the event, which grew to be far bigger than the organisers had anticipated. The rally was not so much pro-Putin as anti-liberal and anti-West, and revealed a great well of Russian *revanchism* that was bigger than Putin, and indeed served as a warning that the Russian nativist movement could overwhelm the whole structure of power so laboriously built up by him. For this strand of traditionalism, Putin was at best the lesser evil, constraining the excesses of the neo-liberals with their craven westernism and geopolitical capitulationism.

The protest movement lacked a clear leader or programme. The 'systemic' parties, those that were allowed to participate in the formal political process, played little part in organising the demonstrations. Of the seven parties that participated in the parliamentary elections, Just Russia garnered a healthy vote but continued to swing between systemic and more radical action. It was potentially in a position to constitute itself as a genuine opposition, but in the end succumbed to regime pressure. The sudden mass mobilisation brought a new generation of activists to the fore. The 1990s generation of professional politicians, such as Ryzhkov, Nemtsov and Kasyanov, had spent the wilderness years after the liberal failure to enter the Duma in 2003 in organising various movements and had kept the flame of opposition alive. Their latest venture had been 'Strategy 31', holding unsanctioned meetings on the final day of months with 31 days, to defend Article 31 of the constitution: 'Citizens of the Russian Federation have the right to assemble peacefully without weapons and to hold meetings, rallies and demonstrations, processions and pickets.' Now a new generation of non-systemic leaders came to the fore.

Foremost among them was Navalny, who made himself a hero with vivid speeches and a view of Russian politics that combined radical political liberalism with nationalist obscurantism. Navalny had used various web projects, notably RosPil from 2010 and RosYama from 2011, to expose the corrupt activities of state officials and bureaucrats.[18] As one of the most effective leaders of the protest movement, he came to epitomise the angry 'urban middle class'. On Putin first coming to power Navalny had joined the Yabloko party, but soon came to criticise Yavlinsky's domineering style and the failure to mount a successful campaign in the 2003 elections. He remained deputy head of Yabloko's Moscow branch and between 2005 and 2007 worked with the Democratic Alternative!' (DA!) group. Participation in the nationalist Russian March on 4 November 2006 exposed his adoption of a more patriotic stance. Navalny's participation in the marches, held in November of each year as a replacement for celebration of the Bolshevik Revolution, was accompanied by a critique of official policy in the Caucasus. Like the LDPR, he favoured Russia becoming a unitary state and considered federalism unnecessary and an impediment to national development. Navalny sought an enhanced role for cities accompanied by the abolition of the ethno-federal republics and autonomies to create a 'national state', instead of a federal or multinational one.[19] While he certainly had a point, given the arbitrariness of many regional borders and the emergence of 'ethnocratic' republics, in political terms any attempt to abolish Russia's ethno-federal system would almost certainly provoke the disintegration of the country.

In 2007 Navalny was expelled from Yabloko, ostensibly because of his attempt to seize power, but his 'nationalist' leanings at the same time were condemned, and in particular his slogan 'stop feeding the Caucasus'. In that year he was one of the founders of the Nation patriotic movement, which later became the core of a coalition of right wing groups called collectively the Russian National Movement, which disbanded in 2011. One of the central concerns was labour migration from Central Asia, an issue that gained salience as the Russian population aged. Each year the indigenous labour force shrinks by one million. In 2009 Navalny served as an adviser to the liberal governor of Kirov (Vyatka) region, Nikita Belykh, and became implicated in an economic venture that would, as we shall see, have grave long-term consequences on his political career.

The third level of leadership comprised the 'elite opposition'. They were not 'defectors' in the classical sense, but reflected deep misgivings within the regime. Kudrin was pre-eminent among them, seeking to act as a conduit between the regime and the people. Even before the September 2011 events it was clear that Kudrin was becoming an independent politician, and he now shed his grey technocratic profile. For ten years Kudrin had managed the nation's finances with an iron hand, refusing to allow the mass disbursement of the windfall energy rents. Instead, he was the architect of the counter-cyclical accumulation of the money in various sovereign wealth funds. This provided the country with the resources to weather the economic crisis from mid-2008, providing liquidity for troubled banks and enterprises without driving the country into debt. Not surprisingly, in 2010 Kudrin was named 'banker of the year' by Forbes. He also aroused the hostility of those of a populist disposition who wanted to see energy wealth invested in infrastructure and society. Kudrin was one of the core members of the Putin team, and even after his dismissal Putin went out of his way to stress his continuing friendship with the fallen minister. However, Kudrin was not a street politician, and his speech at the Sakharov Prospekt demonstration on 24 December was received with a mix of boos and cheers. He sought to position himself as a mediator between the government and the protesters, and had credibility with both although in the end no formal 'roundtable' dialogue was held. Kudrin did not defect from the regime, but his stance exposed clear divisions within the elite.

In April 2012 Kudrin established the Civic Initiatives Committee to channel ideas on resolving political and economic problems into the system, while drawing on the newly-mobilised professional classes. He explicitly refused to create a party, and instead used the Committee in a variety of ways, including specialist expertise and offering to act as the core of election monitoring once the independent monitoring NGO, Golos, fell foul of the new 'foreign agents' legislation. Although Kudrin was a strong advocate of economic 'reform', it was not clear what specific measures he advocated, other than raising the pension age (currently 55 for women and 60 for men), strict controls on government expenditure, more investment in infrastructure, and to 'stop distributing social benefits with a watering can'. On politics, though, he was unequivocal: 'Russia needs free elections'; not simply a rerun of the parliamentary elections, advocated by the opposition, but a thorough review of the normative framework to ensure the fairness of future ballots.[20] Prokhorov also rode the protest wave and later created the Civil Platform party, but remained constrained by the systemic constraints on genuine political pluralism. Overall, the popular movement sought to strengthen the constitutional state and reduce the administrative interference of the regime, but with a fundamental division of views about the capacity of the Russian constitutional order for reform and renewal, accompanied by clear signs of intra-elite fragmentation. Democratisation theory tells us that this is precisely the most dangerous moment for an old regime, and the moment when a democratic breakthrough becomes possible.

Putin's response

The protest movement was far from representing a 'Russian Spring', let alone a 'snow revolution', although it was sometimes seen as a continuation of the events in North Africa. Putin's Russia was not a consolidated authoritarian regime of the likes of Egypt, where there had been some 30 years of repression in the framework of a state of emergency. Instead, the election revealed the contradictions of the Russian dual state. Hesitant to embrace full-blooded authoritarianism, the regime was forced to make concessions through the liberalisation of the political system and the strengthening of the impartial institutions of the constitutional state, notably free, fair and transparent elections.

Just four days after the vote, as popular revulsion against the manipulations gathered force and the mass arrest of demonstrators, Putin typically insisted that the turbulence was the result of outside forces, notably the American foreign minister Hillary Clinton: 'From the outset the secretary of state said that [the elections] were not honest and not fair, but she had not yet even received the material from the observers. She set the tone for some actors in our country and gave them a signal. They heard the signal and with the support of the US State Department set to work.' He went on to note that 'We are the largest nuclear power, and our partners have certain concerns and shake us so that we don't forget who is the master of this planet, so that we remain obedient and feel that they have leverage to influence us within our own country.'[21] He warned that those who 'dance to the tune of a foreign state' would be held to account. His minions heard Putin's signal, unleashing a vicious anti-American campaign that soon targeted NGOs funded by western agencies, and provoked the nasty harassment of the new American ambassador, Michael McFaul, who as one of his first acts met with civil society activists in an event long planned by his predecessor.[22]

Putin had never really bought into the 'reset' in Russo-American relations, considering the US an unscrupulous and untrustworthy actor with whom it was impossible to have a mutually advantageous relationship. Specific deals could be done, but there could be no serious prospect of a 'partnership'. The relapse of the relationship into the anachronistic nuclear disarmament agenda, which gave rise to the New Start treaty in 2010, demonstrated the shallow foundations of the relationship. Bitter experience, including the establishment of the Eastern Partnership (EaP) in May 2009, seems to have led him to much the same view of the European Union. Worse, hardliners in his entourage nurtured similar suspicions about Medvedev, who they argued had mismanaged affairs and encouraged the protesters. Once back in the Kremlin, elements in Putin's administration waged a cold war against their own prime minister; organising leaks, investigations and smears that paralysed the work of the cabinet.

In his question and answer 'direct line' session on 15 December Putin was laconically contemptuous of the protesters who had gathered on Bolotnaya Square on 10 December with white ribbons on their lapels, the symbol of the desire for free and fair elections. 'To be honest, when I saw on TV what some people had attached to their chests – it's not very polite, but I'll say it anyway – I thought it was an anti-AIDS campaign. I thought they had stuck, excuse me, condoms on themselves.' He appeared to be tolerant of those who 'reject me in principle, in general one should treat all our citizens with respect'. However, he condemned others: 'There are of course people who hold a Russian passport but act in the interests of a foreign state and are paid foreign money, and we will try to reach these people as well, though this is often futile or impossible. What can one say in this respect? At the end of the day, all you can say is, "Come to me, Bandar-logs". I've loved Rudyard Kipling since childhood.' The reference to protesters as 'Bandar-logs' (a term used in Kipling's *The Jungle Book* to describe 'monkey-people' – in Hindi 'Bandar' means monkeys and 'log' means people – who chatter and fight among themselves, parroting phrases that they do not understand) provoked widespread revulsion. He insisted that the election reflected the balance of political forces in the country, and noted that 'the opposition will always claim that they were dishonest, always. And this happens everywhere, in all countries'. However, he did acknowledge the need to ensure that the forthcoming presidential should be seen to be fair, and for that he proposed installing web cameras at all the 90,000 plus polling stations.

He was pressed further by Alexei Venediktov, the chief editor at the Ekho Moskvy radio station:

> You are talking about the opposition, but trust me there was more to it than just an opposition rally on Bolotnaya Square. You are now responding to the opposition but what are you going to say to the new disgruntled, the new offended who believe that their votes had been stolen? What are you going to do about the elections that they don't trust? They are going to stage legally another rally on December 24. They had demands and requests; they were looking for justice, which is also very important.

To which Putin responded: 'I have already made my point clear. I said that different kinds of people gathered there, and I was pleased to see fresh, healthy, intelligent and energetic faces of the people who were actively expressing their views. I can say it again that if this is the result of the Putin regime, then I'm truly pleased that we have such people in our country now.'

Putin took credit for having created the conditions in which an active civil society had been born. He vigorously defended his record, and took the opportunity to say 'a few words about stability, and the fact that this word is acquiring a sort of negative connotation. Stability does not imply that we are standing idle and marking time. Stability implies sustained development. This is my idea of stability'.[23]

The test would be the presidential election. Putin promised the installation of webcams in all 93,000 polling stations, and that the ballot boxes themselves would be made of clear plastic. Surkov was transferred out of the Kremlin and into the government, and thus the *éminence grise* of sovereign democracy lost power. Surkov applied enormous resources to ensure that the streets remained in the Kremlin's hand, above all through the creation of Nashi and other youth organisations, and he had not only palpably failed in that task, but was suspected of harbouring sympathies for the protesters. Kudrin's stance allowed a negotiated exit from the crisis, building on the concessions from the authorities while seeking to convince the 'non-systemic' opposition to adopt an evolutionary strategy for change. For some this represented a 'crack in the wall',[24] and undoubtedly the coordinating centre governing the various elements making up the regime had weakened. Surkov personified the Kremlin system of manual management, and it was far from clear that his successor would be able to restore it.

Anger at the flawed Duma election was compounded by the pre-selection of the presidential candidates and the view that the leading contender, Putin, had been the architect of the falsifications. Andrei Zubov gave voice to the view that the new parliament lacked the legal basis of popular election to be able to adopt laws with the force of normative acts. He noted the creation of 'an enormous hole in the juridical field' by what he called the falsification and the protests against this falsification, 'which threatened to swallow the legal basis of Russian statehood and push our society towards the chaos of institutional lawlessness'. The people had awoken, and now any unpopular action by the illegitimate Duma could be refused by society, leading to political chaos and violence. Zubov trawled the constitution to find legal ways for the Sixth Duma to be declared dissolved and some provisional arrangements to operate until new parliamentary and postponed presidential elections could be held.[25] The whole Putin system, from this perspective, was in crisis.

Medvedev's counter-coup

Paradoxically, instead of becoming a 'lame duck' after September 2011, Medvedev's leadership was galvanised. In his final months as president Medvedev sought to establish an irreversible agenda of political reform that would seal his legacy as a political moderniser. Bolstered by a popular movement pushing for changes of the sort that he had long advocated, Medvedev could now advance a radical and systematic programme of political reform. Some of Medvedev's proposals for political reform had been prepared long before the protest marches but had been blocked.[26] Medvedev now hoped to create a dynamic that would be difficult to reverse. Putin was no longer the sole real source of political authority, and the latent conflict between Medvedev and Putin became more obvious. During the presidential campaign Putin was forced, because of the double movement of intra-elite splits and popular pressure, to adopt more of a Medvedian course.

In his *poslanie* on 22 December Medvedev began by recognising that 'we treat any criticism of state institutions and individual officials with the utmost attention and respect', but he stressed that 'attempts to manipulate Russian citizens, to mislead them and incite social discord are unacceptable ... Russia needs democracy, not chaos'. He argued that the 'political system's modernisation has made it more efficient', asserting that 'we have improved the quality of popular representation and stimulated the development of political competition'. He proposed, in light of 'the new stage of the nation's development' and in support of initiatives advanced by Putin, 'a comprehensive reform of our political system'. The measures included:

i) The return to direct regional elections for the heads of Russian constituent entities.
ii) The introduction of a simplified procedure for the registration of political parties. Medvedev suggested that it should require an application signed by at least 500 people representing no less than half the regions.
iii) The abolition of the requirement to collect signatures for elections to the State Duma and regional legislatures.
iv) A change in the system of elections to the State Duma. 'I consider it expedient for strengthening the links between the deputies and the electorate to introduce proportional representation of 225 districts. This measure will allow each region to have a direct representative in parliament. Now, unfortunately, as everybody knows, some constituent entities of the Russian Federation do not have a single deputy elected by local residents.' The idea had been mooted by Putin in his question and answer session on 15 December 2011, but the substance of Medvedev's proposal was unclear.
v) A reduction in the number of voter signatures needed to participate in the presidential elections to 300,000, and for candidates from non-parliamentary parties to 100,000.
vi) He also suggested changing the procedure for forming the central and regional election commissions. 'We should have broader representation by political parties in the election commissions. The parties must have the right to recall their representatives in the commissions before term, if necessary.'
vii) He also announced that laws on decentralisation would be submitted to the State Duma to allow the redistribution of 'powers and budgetary resources in a way that favours our regions and municipalities'.[27]

Other measures included: the right of winning parties in regional legislatures to submit their nominations for governorships; an annual report delivered by the government to the Duma; parliamentary parties gained the right to equal coverage of their activities on state media; a new procedure was introduced to form the Council of the Federation whereby only those who had won federal, state or municipal elections could stand; and the electoral threshold in State Duma elections was reduced to 5 per cent (but only starting from 2016).

The direct election of governors was the most radical of the package of reforms. As we have seen, gubernatorial elections had been abolished in December 2004 following the Beslan crisis, shifting the primary loyalty of governors to the central authorities and not their constituents. The bill sent to the Duma on 23 January 2012 allowed registered political parties to nominate candidates following consultations with the president, although these would not be quite the 'presidential filter' that Putin had proposed in his direct line session on 15 December. Even after consultations parties could nominate whom they liked. Candidates who were not nominated by parties would have to collect a certain number of signatures, as specified by the regional legislature. A 'municipal filter' was introduced based on the French model, requiring the endorsement of a certain proportion of local legislators. The president retained the power to sack governors for corruption, failure to perform their duties or what was called a 'conflict of interests'. There would also be the option of popular recall through a referendum organised by the local parliament. A sacked governor had the right of appeal to the Supreme Court. The new system came into operation in May 2012, but governors remained in office until their existing term expired.[28] They were to be elected for five-year terms, with political parties having the right to nominate candidates. Putin was clearly uncomfortable by the weakening of the provision for a 'presidential filter' on candidates, but this was never going to apply for independent candidates but only those nominated by parties. Even some governors voiced concern that the return of the old system would stimulate 'separatism'.[29] At the same time, Just Russia and the former speaker of the Federation Council introduced a law to the Duma for the restoration of direct elections to the upper house.[30]

A crucial part of the package of reforms was the simplification of procedures to register political parties. Hitherto a party had to have 45,000 members, 50 per cent of Russia's regions had to have at least 450 members in them and the other 50 per cent had to have no fewer than 200 members. The new law stipulated that a party must have at least 500 members and represent not less than 50 per cent of the regions (in theory, ten members per region). The law also abolished the need for non-parliamentary parties to collect at least 150,000 signatures in their support. Another bill reduced the number of signatures required to participate in elections for non-parliamentary and independent candidates. Following the judgment of the European Court of Human Rights in April 2011 that the dissolution of Ryzhkov's Republican

Party had been illegal, contravening Article 11 of the European Convention on Human Rights (ECHR) on the right to freedom of assembly and association, it was up to the Russian Supreme Court to rule on its restoration. The decision was postponed until January 2012, and soon after the Justice Ministry announced that the party would be registered, returning the party's status to that of May 2007 when the decision had been taken to deny it formal status. In June 2012 the restored party merged with the Party of People's Freedom to create RPR-Parnas. At precisely the same time the registration rules on forming parties were greatly relaxed.

In his 22 December speech Medvedev proposed introducing proportional representation in the 225 districts 'to improve communication between deputies and the electorate', complaining that some regions lacked a single representative in parliament. The electoral system was reformed through the introduction of a modified constituency system, with the whole country dived into 250 roughly equal electoral regions. The package of reforms was criticised for its lack of a coherent or systemic character, and instead various ad hoc measures were introduced.[31] It had never been entirely clear why gubernatorial elections had been abolished in the first place. The ostensible reason – to enhance the fight against terror – was obviously inadequate, and now their restoration lacked a broader review of how federalism should work in Russia. The Putin system added layer upon layer of para-constitutional accretions, and it was not clear what role, for example, the State Council or the Public Chamber would have in a system in which certain institutions of the constitutional state were being reinvigorated.

On 22 December Surkov, in his last interview as first deputy head of the presidential administration, argued that 'political changes are not coming; they have arrived. The system has already changed'. The parliamentary election, the Bolotnaya Square demonstration, the internet debate, Putin's question and answer session and Medvedev's state of the nation speech had changed the country, and now 'all that is required is to give these changes juridical form', notably for the easier registration of parties, direct gubernatorial elections and more transparent elections. Asked about the 'orange revolution' aspect of the demonstrations, he argued that 'There are some who wish to convert protest into a colour revolution', but he stressed:

> the absolute reality and naturalness of protest. The best part of our society, or more accurately its most productive part, demand respect. People are saying that we exist, we are significant, we are the people. We should not high-handedly dismiss their views. ... To grant the sensible demands of the active part of society is not a forced manoeuvre by the authorities but their obligation and constitutional duty.

As for his 'conservatism', Surkov asked 'and what are we preserving? Who wants to defend corruption and injustice? Who wants to defend a dumb and stupid system?' The 'moral high ground' that the authorities had enjoyed for

132 *Putin's constitutional coup*

so long had to be regained, and he hoped that 'the street would quieten down and the reforms take place'.[32]

Notes

1 http://president.kremlin.ru/appears/2004/09/13/1514_type63374type63378_76651.shtml.
2 Thomas M. Nichols, *The Russian Presidency: Society and Politics in the Second Russian Republic* (Basingstoke, Macmillan, 2000), p. 2.
3 V. V. Putin, 'S"ezd partii "Edinaya Rossiya": Predsedatel' Pravitels'stva Rossiiskoi Federatsii V. V. Putin prinyal uchastie v XII s"ezde vserossiiskoi politicheskoi partii "Edinaya Rossiya"', 24 September 2011, http://www.premier.gov.ru/events/news/16552/print/.
4 D. A. Medvedev, 'S"ezd partii "Edinaya Rossiya": Glava gosudarstva prinyal predlozhenie vozglavit' spisok "Edinoi Rossii" na vyborakh v Gosudarstvennuyu Dumu 4 Dekabrya 2011 goda', 24 September 2011, http://kremlin.ru/transcripts/12802.
5 'Stenogramma programmy "Razgovor s Vladimirom Putinym. Prodolzhenie"', 15 December 2011, http://premier.gov.ru/events/news/17409/index.html.
6 Alexander Morozov, 'Izuchaya fotografiyu: Chto sluchilos' s rezhimom putina?', Radio Ekho Moskvy, 25 July 2013; http://echo.msk.ru/blog/morozov_a/1122606-echo/.
7 Fred Weir, 'Putin's Next Marquee Event: Russia's Presidency', *Christian Science Monitor*, 29 November 2011.
8 Grigorii Golosov, 'Russia's Silent Election Campaign', 29 November 2011, www.opendemocracy.net.
9 For a concise analysis, see Arkady Lyubarev, 'An Evaluation of the Results of the Duma Elections', *Russian Analytical Digest*, No. 108, 6 February 2012, pp. 2–5.
10 'Observers Unhappy About Russian Prosecutors' Report on Election Fraud', RIA Novosti, 18 January 2012.
11 OSCE, *Elections to the State Duma, 4 December 2011: OSCE/ODIHR Election Observation Mission Final Report* (Warsaw, 12 January 2012), p. 1.
12 Ibid., p. 2.
13 PACE, *Observation of the Parliamentary Elections in the Russian Federation (4 December 2011)*, Doc. 12833 (Strasbourg, 23 January 2012), p. 11.
14 Alexander Kynev, presentation at the University of Dundee, 30 June 2013.
15 Alexandra Odynova, 'Thousands Decry Putin as Public Anger Swells', *Moscow Times*, 1 February 2010b.
16 Aleksei Levinson, 'Eto ne srednii klass – eto vse', *Vedomosti*, 21 February 2012.
17 Research by Nataliya Zubarevich, reported by Nadezhda Petrova, 'Stagnation Produces Political Change', *Russia Beyond the Headlines*, 15 February 2012; www.rbth.ru.
18 For details, see Konstantin Voronkov, *Aleksei Navalnyi: Groza zhulikov i vorov* (Moscow, Eksmo, 2012).
19 'Aleksei naval'nyi: Byt' luchshim oppozitsionnym politikom v Rossii – eto ochen' prosto"', *GQ*, June 2013; www.gq.ru/magazine.
20 'Former Russian Finance Minister Alexei Kudrin: "We have to Take Chance with More Democracy"', 23 January 2013; http://www.spiegel.de/international/world/interview-with-putin-ally-alexei-kudrin-on-democracy-in-russia-a-878873.html.
21 'Russia PM Vladimir Putin Accuses US Over Poll Protests', BBC News, 8 December 2011, and various other media reports.
22 Putin later defended this, arguing 'I can hardly imagine the Ambassador of the Russian Federation to the US actively working with members of the "Occupy Wall

Street Movement"', 'Interview to Channel One and Associated Press News Agency', 4 September 2013, http://eng.kremlin.ru/news/5935.
23 'Stenogramma programmy "Razgovor s Vladimirom Putinym. Prodolzhenie"', 15 December 2011, http://premier.gov.ru/events/news/17409/index.html.
24 Vladimir Gel'man, 'Cracks in the Wall: Challenges to Electoral Authoritarianism in Russia', *Problems of Post-Communism*, Vol. 60, No. 2, March–April 2013, pp. 3–10.
25 Andrei Zubov, 'Vykhod iz krizisa legitimnosti', *Vedomosti*, 22 December 2011.
26 Stated by Kudrin in an interview with Vladimir Pozner, Channel 1, 23 January 2012.
27 Dmitrii Medvedev, 'Poslanie Prezidenta Federal'nomu Sobraniyu', 22 December 2011a, http://news.kremlin.ru/news/14088/print.
28 'Medvedev Submits Bill to Reinstate Governor Elections', RIA Novosti, 16 January 2012; http://en.rian.ru/russia/20120116/170780108.html.
29 For example, Sakhalin Oblast governor Aleksander Khoroshavin, Editorial, 'Toska po vertikali', *Nezavisimaya gazeta*, 13 February 2012, p. 2.
30 Ivan Rodin, Mironov predlozhil vernut'sya v 1993 god', *Nezavisimaya gazeta*, 13 February 2012, p. 3.
31 Nikolai Zlobin, 'Bessistemnaya vlast'', *Vedomosti*, 30 January 2012.
32 Elena Shishkunova, 'Vladislav Surkov: "Sistema uzhe izmenilas"', *Izvestiya*, 22 December 2011.

7 Putin's return

Putin's hopes for a smooth succession were disappointed. The plan announced on 24 September 2011 provoked a neuralgic reaction across society. The staged process immediately came off the rails amidst popular revulsion at the cynical way in which the 'castling' move was announced and planned. Medvedev had harboured hopes for a second term, and his frustration was evident at the congress and later, even though in his characteristic manner he subordinated himself to the decision, but kept his options open. The parliamentary election on 4 December and its aftermath revealed flaws in the Putinite system that had long been evident. The lack of an ordered mechanism for leadership change and policy innovation meant that firefighting successive crises became the standard mode of government. The Putin consensus began to disintegrate at all three levels: elite, societal and administrative. In response, through a supreme effort Putin won the presidential election of 4 March 2012 in the first round, but there was no return to the easy successes of the classic period of his rule.

Putin's bind

This was Putin's fourth presidential campaign, but the first in which he faced a real challenge to his authority. The election turned into a plebiscite on him personally, as well as on the system that he had built. The last time Russia had faced such a choice was in the 1996 presidential election, in which Yeltsin had snatched a victory by demonising his opponents, warning of the existential threat to the state if the Communists won, and by wilfully abusing media impartiality and flouting limits on campaign expenditure. Putin had dismal memories of elections that had to go into a second round. In 1996 not only did Yeltsin have to manoeuvre between the two rounds, but in the mayoral elections held in St Petersburg that May Putin's mentor, Sobchak, lost in the second round. The whole stability system since 2000 was built on Putin's high ratings, and without this cement the regime was vulnerable. His key task was not only to win the election in the first round, but above all to demonstrate that his return was 'dictated by objective necessity'.[1]

Putin galvanised his campaign in the attempt to win a convincing first-round victory. He was clearly shocked by the scale of the animus against him, and now sought to win over public opinion. Putin was forced to change his master narrative. As late as in his 15 December 'direct line' session he had arrogantly dismissed the protesters as 'Bandar-logs', and crudely dismissed the white ribbon movement. Putin's view that the protest movement was little more than a foreign-supported intervention was as alienating as it was unconvincing. It required enormous effort for Putin to recover lost ground and to change the paradigm of his thinking. For a ruling class to embrace such a change requires a new understanding of the challenges facing them and an awareness of their own vulnerability. Revolutions occur when ruling regimes fail to make the required cognitive and policy changes, as they failed to do before 1789 and 1917, or indeed before the great recession from 2008. Business as usual would no longer do.

The intra-elite splits intensified in the period between the parliamentary and presidential elections. Mironov announced that if elected president he would leave office early, but only after carrying out far-reaching political reforms. Speaking on 12 January, he informed reporters that he and Zyuganov had received a proposal from the socialist Left Front for one of them to become a 'transitional president' in the event one won the presidency. The idea was for the interim leader to carry out 'comprehensive reform of the election law' and then step down in March 2013. Mironov said that he would be willing to stand down, but he would need two years to complete the necessary reforms.[2] This indicates the sort of possibilities that were being discussed at the time, with a sense that the Putinite system was crumbling and an era of change had begun.

The field initially included three independents – the billionaire Prokhorov, who had recovered after his bruising experience as the Right Cause leader, the veteran liberal Yavlinsky, and the governor of Irkutsk region, Dmitry Mezentsev. Mezentsev was a former colleague of Putin's from St Petersburg and was on the list as a 'technical' candidate, to ensure that the ballot was valid in the unlikely event of all the other candidates stepping down, thus annulling the election. The three collected the necessary two million signatures by the deadline of 25 January, whereas the 'three Duma elders' (as Prokhorov called them), Just Russia's Mironov, the Communist leader Zyuganov, and the LDPR's Zhirinovsky were not required to collect signatures but were directly nominated by their parties since they had representation in parliament. In the event too many of the two million signatures collected by Yavlinsky and Mezentsev were declared invalid by the CEC, and the two were disqualified from running – with Prokhorov's participation guaranteed, Mezentsev's candidature had clearly become redundant. The time allowed to collect the signatures was ridiculously short, and mistakes inevitably crept in. Yavlinsky's exclusion undermined the election's credibility, leaving only Prokhorov as the standard bearer for the liberals. In addition to Putin, the candidate list included the veterans Zyuganov,

Zhirinovsky as well as the newly-radicalised Mironov and the rightist Prokhorov.

On 24 January Prokhorov announced that he would consider appointing former finance minister Kudrin or the fallen oligarch Khodorkovsky as his prime minister, and he also repeated his offer that he would be willing to serve as prime minister if Putin won re-election.[3] Prokhorov's decision to run reflected the divided state of the elite. When asked whether he had received a 'green light' from the Kremlin, he insisted that any light would have to come from the elite as a whole, insisting that the elite was far from monolithic: 'The Kremlin is not like one person or two people, there are wings, liberal wings and conservative wings. It's an ongoing fight between them. This is the nature of Russia right now, that even within the parties, within the government, in the Kremlin, we have these wings. So it is a fight between the liberal and the conservative wings.' In his rather fanciful view, the liberals were gaining the ascendancy.[4] Prokhorov fought the election as the champion of the liberals, but he was careful not to overstep the mark of tolerated critique.[5] His candidature split the critical vote, drawing support away from Mironov at the head of the buoyant Just Russia after its successes in the parliamentary ballot, and allowed the Putinite system to experiment with another variant on how to perpetuate itself.

The opposition now focused on ensuring a second round run-off, which Putin could conceivably lose. A first round win required 50 per cent plus one vote, which Putin was unlikely to achieve given his sliding poll ratings. By December 2011 his support was down to 36 per cent. The same poll found that 41 per cent believed that the country was moving in the wrong direction, while 38 per cent approved of the strategic line, the first time in many years that the critics enjoyed a majority. However, the work of both Medvedev and Putin received strong endorsement.[6] Given the sense of crisis and mobilisation, the prime minister and president set themselves the goal of legitimising the presidential elections by ensuring a relatively free contest. However, habits of electoral manipulation died hard, as demonstrated by the refusal to register Yavlinsky. The danger for Putin was that in the run-off (scheduled for 18 March) the protest vote would mobilise behind an alternative candidate. It was assumed that this alternative would conduct political reforms and then resign to force pre-term presidential elections. The regime was caught in a bind: any attempt to commit industrial-scale fraud would delegitimise Putin's victory and risk serious mobilisation in the country, as witnessed after the flawed parliamentary election; but leaving matters to fate risked humiliation if not defeat for Putin if he failed to win in the first round.

Putin was criticised on three main counts. First, that he had become out of touch with the realities of the new Russia that he had himself in part created. Rising standards of living and political stability provoked new demands for greater political and media freedom and recognition of the dignity and rights of a new generation of mature and responsible citizens. One can understand Putin feeling that people were ungrateful for what he had achieved for them, but that only confirmed his patrimonial view that he was master of the country's fate. Second, Putin appeared to have nothing to say about the problems of corruption, abuse of office by officialdom, and the relatively poor investment climate in the country. It was all very well for him to talk about his genuine achievements in the past, but they had been accompanied by negative features that the population was clearly no longer willing to tolerate. Third, Putin appeared to lack a positive vision of the future. His critique of the West for its failings and double standards were mostly accurate, but politically futile. The prospect of a decade more of 'Putinism' filled the liberal and active part of society with dread.

Doubts thus emerged about whether Putin would be able to win in the first round of the presidential poll on 4 March. In the run-off to be held a fortnight later the opposition would unite behind a single candidate. The major challenge was for the regime to widen the base of its own legitimacy. For much of the Putin period this rested on the twin pillars of Putin's personal popularity and a package based on 'stability' – economic growth without structural reform, the taming of over-mighty subjects and secessionist movements, and constrained political competition accompanied by personal freedoms. This was also a period marked by the consolidation of power and property accompanied by the decay of an independent judiciary and the consolidation of a 'sovereign bureaucracy'. Paradoxically, 'Almost by definition, the regime is unstable'.[7]

Crisis and reform

Any illusions that Putin may have had that his return to the Kremlin would be hailed as the return of the rightful Tsar were swiftly smashed. The castling arrangement aroused misgivings even within the elite, as evidenced by Kudrin's refusal to serve in a Medvedev cabinet and his departure from office. The booing at various sports events illustrated that the taboo on showing mass public hostility to Putin was broken. As became clear after the parliamentary elections, part of the rising middle class was no longer prepared to remain passive consumers of 'managed democracy'. The Putin spell was broken, accompanied by a sense that he was increasingly out of touch with the concerns of voters.

Putin was forced back on the defensive and challenged to rethink his strategy. This undoubtedly represented a major trauma for him, since Putin was a man who always liked to remain loyal to his own theories; but as a man of supreme pragmatism, it was not beyond him to adapt to new circumstances. The series of mass protests in Moscow and some other towns clearly demonstrated that after over a decade Putin's charisma was losing its sheen. His clumsy dismissal of the protest movement in the 'direct line' session on 15 December only antagonised his critics while failing to win over his potential supporters. Nevertheless, his four years as premier provided him with enormous experience and awareness of the need for compromise. His whole persona was based on the readiness to come out fighting when forced into a corner, and he demonstrated this trait now. Equally, the regime was not going to give in easily, and although it was ready to undertake some reforms, it was not ready to give up its privileged political status. In other words, some of the excesses of the administrative regime would be tempered, but it was not yet ready to dissolve itself entirely into the constitutional state.

The plan for a Eurasian Union outlined in a newspaper article soon after the castling announcement was the centrepiece of Putin's strategy for his new term, reflecting the turn away from the West and a new focus on achieving the long-held plans to reintegrate voluntarily parts of the former Soviet Union. On 4 October Putin issued a major programmatic article in *Izvestiya* outlining the plan to create a Eurasian Union. Putin emphasised the success of the Customs Union with Belarus and Kazakhstan, which was completed on 1 July 2011, and the imminent creation on 1 January 2012 of the Single Economic Area with the three countries encompassing 165 million consumers, standardised legislation and the free movement of capital, services and labour. Putin outlined plans for the enlargement of this project to encompass Kyrgyzstan and Tajikistan and its evolution into a Eurasian Economic Union and eventually a Eurasian Union. Putin insisted that the integrative dynamic in the Commonwealth of Independent States (CIS) was prompted in part by the challenge of the global economic crisis but also reflected the needs and traditions of the region. This was Putin's big idea for his third term. Later, the American secretary of state Hillary Clinton at an OSCE foreign ministers' meeting in Dublin, on 6 December 2012 condemned Russia's alleged attempt to 're-sovietise' countries that had emerged from the ruins of the USSR: 'We know what the goal is and we are trying to figure out ways to slow down or prevent it', an astonishing statement by any measure.[8]

With the Duma elections out of the way, Putin started to build a new team. Surkov, the first deputy head of the presidential administration and the architect of 'sovereign democracy', was moved out of the Kremlin and made a deputy minister responsible for a vague portfolio encompassing 'modernisation'. His replacement on 27 December was Volodin, the former deputy chair of United Russia (2007–10) and since October 2010 a deputy prime minister in charge of running the government apparatus. His appointment clearly signalled a new style. Volodin has the reputation of a no-nonsense result-driven individual, with a far more formalistic and bureaucratic approach lacking the gothic political imagination characteristic of Surkov. Volodin had been responsible since May 2011 for organising the Russian Popular Front, a broad network of affiliated organisations intended to have a broader appeal than United Russia, a party that was seen as no longer a reliable vehicle for delivering the vote and entrenching the power of the regime. Responding to the new challenges, the emollient head of the presidential administration, Naryshkin, was sent to manage the unruly newly-elected State Duma, in which United Russia no longer enjoyed a constitutional majority, and he was replaced as chief of staff by Putin's long-time confidant, Sergei Ivanov.

Putin galvanised his campaign. He broadly accepted the package of political reforms outlined by Medvedev, including easier registration for political parties, more competitive elections and the return of gubernatorial elections, although ultimately accustomed tutelary practices remained. A government-commissioned expert report published in March, *Strategy 2020*, outlined the fundamental socio-economic problems facing the country and a new model of growth. Bringing together ten experts from across the political spectrum under the leadership of the respected economist Vladimir Mau, the document suggested measures to improve the business and investment climate, outlining three scenarios, and ended with a section on 'an effective state', including measures to improve the civil service and the working of regional and municipal government, but steered away from demanding greater security of property rights and political accountability.[9] This was a moderate programme for strengthening the constitutional state as it affected the socio-economic sphere, but following the election it fell into the same black hole as so many strategic plans earlier.

Putin's programme

Above all, Putin began to outline some of his ideas for the future. This took the form initially of his first formal written platform, a text he worked on over the New Year. Published on a special website (www.putin2012.ru) on 11 January 2012, the programme combined 'personal vision' with a set of economic and political proposals. The text drew on earlier material drafted by the Putin-affiliated think-tank, the Institute for Social, Economic and Political Research, headed by Nikolai Fedorov, the former justice minister and then governor of Chuvashia. The draft programme reviewed the past decade and forthcoming challenges, 'our values', social and citizenship issues, the economy, 'effective power controlled by the people', and 'a strong Russia in a complex world'. At its heart was the idea of gradualism, although recognising the dangers: 'A recurrent problem of Russian history has been the desire of elites to achieve sudden change, a revolution rather than sustained development. Meanwhile, both Russian and global experience demonstrates how harmful these sudden historical jolts can be. ... This is balanced by a different trend, a diametrically opposed challenge – in the form of a certain inclination to inertia, dependency, the lack of competitiveness by elites and high levels of corruption'.

The text was moderate in its assertions and democratic in spirit. It stressed popular accountability by the authorities, reliable protection for individuals from official arbitrariness, while stressing the important role for the middle class: 'The middle classes are people who can choose a policy and whose high standard of education allows them to take a discriminating attitude to candidates rather than "voting with their hearts". In short, the middle class have begun shaping their real demands in the various fields'. He categorised some 20–30 per cent of the population as middle class. On foreign affairs, he warned that 'international co-operation is a two-way street', stressing that the rules of the game in international politics and economics 'cannot be decided behind Russia's back'. However, while eminently reasonable, the document lacked detail or any immediate practical steps. The programme was rather abstract and could not wrest the political initiative from the protesters and intra-elite dissidents. It did not seem to take into account the fundamental demands of the protesters for the restoration of genuinely competitive politics, and not just the ability to 'choose a policy'. However, in praising the civic competence of the growing middle class as opposed to those who 'voted with their hearts', Putin clearly delineated a fundamental political choice facing the regime, but was careful not to align himself unequivocally with one or another approach, and thus remained true to his proclivity to portray himself above the fray. Most of the sentiments could equally have been drafted by Medvedev, and indeed much of the text reflected classical Medvedevite themes – raising once again the question of quite why Putin had decided that his nominated successor in 2008 was not to be trusted with a second term.

Soon after, Putin published another programmatic article in *Izvestiya* and on his website on 16 January entitled 'Russia is Concentrating: Challenges that We Must Meet'.[10] The title referred to foreign minister Prince Alexander Gorchakov, who used the phrase as Russia recuperated from defeat in the Crimean War to represent a period of spiritual renewal. Thus Gorchakov joined the pantheon of Putin's heroes, among whom latterly Stolypin had figured prominently. Putin once again echoed Medvedevite themes, expressed notably in the 'Forward Russia!' article of September 2009, although accompanied by swipes at unnamed enemies. Putin welcomed popular demands for democracy and improved living standards, and even suggested that the protests could be considered a measure of the success of his leadership. The basic theme was the need to shift from a programme of restoration to one of development. All the prerequisites for progress, he argued, were now in place. He asserted that he was the only one who could guide Russia between the twin dangers of stagnation and instability. There was no mention of electoral fraud, capital flight or how to deal with systemic corruption, and thus did not adequately address the issue of why he considered himself the best person to treat Russia's problems. Nevertheless, the text represented a thoughtful attempt to defend the political and economic system that he had created. The kernel of a programme was at last beginning to emerge, based on the maturation of a middle class with demands for economic progress and political dignity. This was a typically Putinite 'economistic' reading of political change: first the economic conditions must mature, and then democracy could be granted.

The ideas were developed in a series of follow-up articles, with the first, focusing on the 'national question', published in *Nezavisimaya gazeta* on 23 January.[11] He stressed that Russia had never been either a mono-ethnic state or an American-style 'melting pot', but had developed as 'a multinational state, in which different ethnic groups have had to mingle, interact and connect with each other'. In this he stressed the central role of the Russian people and Russian culture, which in his view acted as 'the glue that binds together this unique civilisation'. He added his voice to the warnings that had sounded throughout his presidency: 'I am convinced that the attempts to preach the idea of a "national" or mono-ethnic Russian state contradict our thousand-year history. Moreover, this is a short-cut to destroying the Russian people and Russian statehood, and for that matter any viable, sovereign statehood on the planet.' Although not mentioning Navalny by name, he condemned such slogans as 'stop feeding the Caucasus', which could lead to similar slogans such as 'stop feeding Siberia, the Far East, or the Moscow region': 'This sort of slogan was used by those who drew the Soviet Union to collapse.' He called for a policy based on civic patriotism and the creation of a special agency to take responsibility for 'ethnic development, inter-ethnic accord and interaction'. In addition he stressed the need to develop 'a democratic, multi-party system', but one in which the ban imposed in 2011 on the creation of regional parties would be maintained, since in his view this was 'a direct path to separatism'.

His article contained a number of controversial propositions. He asserted that the Russian language was 'the fundamental basis of the unity of the country', an idea that would be challenged by the defenders of the use of native languages in Tatarstan and elsewhere. He also called for a single national history textbook that would highlight 'the uninterrupted path of Russian history and the interconnection of its various stages', so that all citizens would 'know the genuine history of the country's peoples and the ingathering of Russian lands into a single powerful multinational state'. Again, those nations 'ingathered' into the expansive Muscovite state would look at things differently. Putin also supported the work of the country's 989 national-cultural associations, a distinctive hybrid form with few powers but feared to be a way of under-cutting the ethno-federal units. The article confused the fight against 'newcomers', migrants who are not citizens of Russia, with patterns of internal labour migration. He argued that the 'multicultural' project, which questions the idea of integration through assimilation, had failed in Europe, and although he talked of the concept of a 'polyethnic civilisation' as opposed to a multicultural one, his strategy to develop a collective Russian identity through educational and other means failed to address fundamental questions of justice and equality. In keeping with his view of Russia as a nation in formation, Putin argued that the various major sports events due to be held in Russia, including the Winter Olympics in 2014, would help unite the Russian people into one. Others questioned the enormous resources diverted to fund these mega-events. In sum, the attempt to forge a Russian nation, rather than a union of diverse peoples, was fraught with danger. In the end, the new nationality policy drafted in 2013, intended to replace the one in force since 1996, was careful not to exacerbate the fears of

Russia's many people. It retreated from the idea current among Russian nationalists that ethnic Russians were the 'state-forming' nation in the polity.

On 30 January in an article in *Vedomosti* he turned his attention to economic matters. Putin adopted a Medvedevian stance in calling for diversification, technological modernisation and a reform of state expenditure and improvements in the business climate, while condemning corruption and excessive state interference. He set ambitious targets for increases in high-tech production and improvements in real average wages. He defended himself against accusations of state capitalism, insisting that in certain sectors the state had to take the lead where private capital would not go. The state corporations in 2007–8 had helped rationalise state-owned assets, but he admitted that they had not become globally competitive and it was time for them to be reviewed. He acknowledged that Russia's bloated bureaucracy deterred investors, and noted that Kazakhstan was placed 47th in the World Bank's *Ease of Doing Business* index, whereas Russia languished in 120th place. He argued that 'Over the last few years, on President Medvedev's initiative, we have launched a whole series of reforms aimed at improving the business climate, but there have not yet been any noticeable improvements', and he condemned 'the lack of transparency and accountability to society in the work of state representatives', which he condemned as 'systemic corruption'. The planned privatisations, he argued, were designed to improve efficiency rather than to raise money. He stressed the need for balanced budgets and in a nod to the protesters called for greater transparency in government tenders. He announced that Gazprom would sell off its media holding Gazprom Media, which owns the NTV channel, and he revealed that one of the crucial reasons for the attack on Khodorkovsky's Yukos oil company was its plan to sell a significant stake to foreigners.[12] Addressing the VTB Bank's investment forum at this time, Putin argued that 'Our strategy aims to gradually reduce the state's direct involvement in the economy. Therefore we will gradually (please note the word "gradually") withdraw from the capital of state corporations'.[13]

The text published on 6 February in *Kommersant* was the most directly political, dealing with 'Democracy and the Quality of the State'.[14] If there is a single word to describe Putin's political philosophy, it is 'statism'. Already in his academic work of the 1990s he had extolled the importance of the state in managing the country's energy resources, and in the 2000s he had applied a *dirigiste* model of economic development. This steered a course between the outright nationalisation of leading manufacturing and industrial sectors and the radical liberalism of the 1990s. Putin's policy was effectively 'deprivatisation': there was some change in ownership structures, but on the whole an active industrial policy employed a range of methods to ensure that the whole sector fell in with the government's priorities. This included corporate social responsibility à la Russe, with wages paid on time, various welfare benefits and a reluctance to shed staff. This may not have been good for productivity, but this neo-Soviet paternalism was directed towards ensuring social peace.

In his article Putin began as he meant to go on: 'Society cannot have sustainable development without a viable state; and conversely, genuine democracy is an indispensable condition for building a state that serves the interests of society'. He argued that 'Genuine democracy cannot be produced overnight', and it could not be copied by reproducing someone else's model – the key features of what had earlier been described as 'sovereign democracy'. He once again condemned the practices of the 1990s, arguing that the introduction of democracy 'almost immediately resulted in stopping the necessary economic reforms, and a little later those forms themselves were taken over by local and Moscow-based oligarchic elites, who shamelessly used the state for their private interests and pocketed the wealth that belonged to the people'. Instead, 'what we got in the 1990s with the supposed coming of democracy was not a modern state. What we got was turf wars between various clans and lots of semi-feudal fiefdoms' (Putin had in mind the regional 'barons'). The fear of renewed state capture was the driving force behind the attack on Yukos, while regional segmentation motivated the abolition of gubernatorial elections in December 2004. The 1990s were a period that combined 'both anarchy and oligarchy', accompanied by the lack of 'responsible statesmanship'. In his self-image Putin was precisely that responsible statesman who 'genuinely cared about the common good' (as he described the small band of responsible officials in the 1990s).

Now, he argued, society had undergone a 'difficult maturation process', with the emergence of a middle class who had 'gone beyond the small universe of building their own prosperity', and while noting that 'political competition is the heartbeat of democracy', he argued that 'today, the quality of our state does not match civil society's readiness to participate in it'. Coming from a man who had spent the previous decade tightening the screws on political competition, this could appear to represent a Lenin-like last minute conversion to a cause that he had spent so long undermining. Facing the intractable problem of a burgeoning bureaucracy and the stultification of political life in the young Soviet republic, Lenin in his article of 2 March 1923 'Better Fewer, but Better' called for a cultural revolution in which the political authorities would be overseen by the Workers and Peasants Inspection (Rabkrin), a non-party body, increased education for the workers, and the reduction of the government 'to the utmost everything that is not absolutely essential in it', but all this should be done through small, cautious steps. The reduced government should concern itself with electrification, heavy industry and education. This was his last substantive work before his death in January 1924. Up to that time Lenin had argued that the working class and society in general could not be trusted to manage its own affairs; and this substitution of a ruling regime for popular management was a neo-Leninist trope at the heart of Putin's statecraft in the 2000s. Facing the shock of a public no longer willing to be infantilised politically, Lenin sought to find a new formula for managing public affairs. It was too late for Lenin as his health collapsed, but Putin, ninety years later, was in a position to fulfil the promise of Lenin's last thoughts.

Putin endorsed the political reforms outlined by Medvedev earlier, although he could not resist repeating his classical anti-political mantras: 'I strongly believe that we do not need the circus of various candidates competing with each other to give more and more unrealistic promises. We don't need a situation where all that is left of democracy is a façade ... where real politics is reduced to shady deals and decisions made behind the scenes but never discussed with voters.' His analysis of the pathologies of contemporary democracy would be familiar to many in the West. As so often, his analysis of the problem was acute, but he fell short when suggesting remedies. Few would disagree with his insistence that 'In addition to providing a legitimate government, our political system should guarantee that people see it as fair even when they are in a minority'. To achieve this he proposed new mechanisms of involvement, including greater access to information and some sort of 'internet democracy', with mandatory review by parliament of initiatives that collected 100,000 or more signatures on the internet. Above all, he returned to Alexander Solzhenitsyn's view that democracy in Russia would have to be built on the foundations of local government, which in Putin's words was 'the school of democracy'. This was to be accompanied by a new emphasis on federalism, now that the 'blatant separatism' of the earlier period had been defeated. The direct election of governors was being reintroduced, and there would be some further merging of regions, but Putin insisted that 'neither centralism nor decentralisation should be followed blindly as a fetish'.

In closing, Putin insisted that 'the link between power and property' should be broken, accompanied by 'clear limits on government involvement in the economy'. He was sceptical about much of the anti-corruption rhetoric, insisting that 'All talk of corruption is banal' and that it could not be fought by repressive measures since the problem was 'much more profound': 'it comes from the lack of transparency and accountability of government agencies to society', and thus the fight against 'systemic corruption' required not only the separation of power and property 'but executive power and the system of checks on it'. Parliamentary hearings should become more effective (a practice that Putin had undermined earlier). Nevertheless, he was undoubtedly right to warn that 'Primitive decisions, like a call for mass repression, are not the solution. Those who warn of rampant corruption and demand retribution fail to comprehend that in a corrupt environment, repression could also become subject to corruption'. Instead, he offered 'systemic solutions', which included reform of the court system, encompassing the creation of administrative courts to hear complaints against officials. All of this was sensible, but underestimated the threat that abuses to power and corruption posed to stability and the degree to which the regime itself was responsible for the pathologies he condemned.

The next in the series on 13 February dealt with Russia's social development in an article called 'Building Justice: A Social Policy for Russia'. Putin gave flesh to the idea of Russia as a welfare state, and stressed the need for adequate professional mobility based on an effective educational system. He warned of the dangers arising from American levels of social inequality, the need for an active demographic policy, and a reform of the pension, welfare, education, healthcare and housing systems. He pledged to double the average salaries of lecturers, teachers, doctors and cultural workers, representing a redistribution of some 1.5 per cent of GDP. The country needed a 'smart' migration policy, including a planned programme for compatriots and skilled workers to move into the country, to ensure that Russia did not turn into a 'geopolitical void'.[15] As Kudrin pointed out, Putin's new spending commitments would have to be at the expense of something else: 'I would support some of Putin's measures if the source of financing were named.'[16] Putin's article provoked some harshly critical commentary. An editorial in *Vedomosti* the following day noted that one of Putin's sub-heads 'protecting the people' was drawn from Ivan Shuvalov, a counsellor to Empress Elizabeth in the 1740s–60s and a noted patron of the arts, on whom Solzhenitsyn had drawn to argue that quality of life was as important as foreign policy achievements. The article acidly noted that even in the 'fat' Putin years of an oil-fed bounty Russia had fallen in the UN Human Development Index (using data on per capita GDP by purchasing power parity, life expectancy, access to health care and education, access to modern technologies and the like) from 63rd place in 2001 (out of 177) to 66th place in 201 (out of 187).[17]

The article on 18 February dealt with 'Being Strong: National Security Guarantees for Russia', published in the official government paper, *Rossiiskaya gazeta*.[18] Putin discussed Russia's defence capability, strengthening the army and the navy, the shift to the brigade form of military organisation, the country's nuclear missile capacity, and reviving a high-technology defence industry. Putin endorsed the military reform programme launched in 2008, although noting some of the mistakes in its implementation, but stressed the greatly enhanced combat readiness of Russia's armed forces because of the improved professional training of officers, contract forces and drafted soldiers. The goal was to create a more compact, stronger, better-armed, mobile and professional army. Putin stressed the central role of the nuclear deterrence forces and outlined plans for their modernisation. Indeed, he set out an ambitious re-armament programme:

> In the coming decade, Russian armed forces will be provided with over 400 modern land and sea-based inter-continental ballistic missiles, 8 strategic ballistic missile submarines, about 20 multi-purpose submarines, over 50 surface warships, around 100 military spacecraft, over 600 modern aircraft including fifth generation fighter jets, more than 1,000 helicopters, 28 regimental kits of S-400 air defence systems, 38 battalion kits of Vityaz missile systems, 10 brigade kits of Iskander-M missile systems, over 2,300 modern tanks, about 2,000 self-propelled artillery systems and vehicles, and more than 17,000 military vehicles.

Table 7.1 Top ten countries for military spending (2012) (billions $)

USA	682.5	Japan	59.3
China	166.1	Saudi Arabia	56.7
Russia	90.7	India	46.1
UK	60.8	Germany	45.8
France	58.9	Brazil	33.1

Source: SIPRI Database on Military Expenditure; www.sipri.org.

The Russian military budget had already doubled between 2006 and 2009 to $50bn, and it was planned to increase it to $128bn a year on average between 2014 and 2020, or about 3.2–3.7 per cent of GDP, bringing Russia up to the US level as a proportion of GDP, although far below America's annual defence budget of over $600bn (see Table 7.1). It was over this issue that Kudrin resigned in September 2011. Putin clearly sought to seize the historic opportunity for Russia to re-arm, and was no longer interested in reducing its nuclear arsenal, a force that guaranteed Russia's security and seat at the top table of great powers. Putin outlined the problems in the defence industry, and indeed devoted a third of the article to the issue of its modernisation, as well as the problem of corruption, which 'in the sphere of national security amounts to no less than high treason'. Putin's return was thus accompanied by a massive programme of military rearmament designed to ensure that Russia would remain a great power, which in Putin's view was the only guarantee of the country's sovereignty.

The seventh and final document, 'Russia in a Changing World', was published in the newly-revived Russian-language version of *Moscow News* on 27 February 2012.[19] The article gave a broad overview of the challenges facing Russian international politics as Putin returned to the presidency. The tone was cooperative but asserted Russia's sovereignty and autonomy in world affairs. 'Russia is part of the greater world. We do not wish to and cannot isolate ourselves from it. However, we intend to be consistent in proceeding from our own interests and goals rather than decisions dictated by someone else. Russia will continue to conduct an independent foreign policy'.[20] He insisted that global security could only be achieved by working with Russia rather 'than by attempts to push it into the background, weaken its geopolitical position or compromise its defences'. He conducted a brisk *tour d'horizon* of the challenges facing Russia, with comments on the Arab Spring and the role of the United Nations, condemning the 'itch for military intervention' by certain powers, analysed the problem of nuclear proliferation and Iran, and stressed that all major political and border issues with China had been resolved. He then moved on to stress the importance of Europe: 'Russia is an inalienable and organic part of Greater Europe and European civilisation. Our citizens think of themselves as Europeans', and on this basis Putin called for the creation of a 'common economic and human space from the Atlantic to the Pacific Ocean', including the long-standing Russian demand for visa-free travel and condemnation of the EU's 'Third Energy Package', which required the unbundling of production, transport and downstream activities. As for the US, the key sticking point was once again plans to install a missile defence system in Europe, accompanied by America's propensity to engage in 'political engineering'. He ended on a conciliatory note and reminded his readers that Russia had much to contribute to the equitable management of world affairs.

The various campaign materials were reminiscent of the style of Putin's original 'Millennium Manifesto', published on the eve of his assumption of the presidency in the last days of 1999.[21] The Manifesto had been marked by acute analysis, ambitious goals, but also by a realistic appreciation of the genuine problems facing Russia. Putin's analysis then was credible and refreshing, but over a decade later substantive results were required. The new cycle of articles cumulatively presented a devastating critique of the system that Putin had himself built, including 'systemic corruption' and a poor business environment. The obvious question is why Putin had not dealt with these issues earlier, especially when enjoying the income from the commodity boom of the early years of the century. Putin's remedy now lacked a sustained dimension of institutional reform, and tended to rely on some cosmetic changes accompanied by increased expenditure. The articles lacked detailed plans for reform. His repeated trope about the failures of the 1990s, while in the main accurate although a partial account of those years, failed to examine the deeper structural flaws of the Russian economy and society reaching back into the Soviet years, and the problem of the resurrection of neo-Soviet forms of political management. The stress on *dirigisme* in the economy was accompanied by a paternalist approach on welfare issues – probably preferable to the *laissez-faire* approach of the 1990s but unsustainable in the long-run. Clearly Putin was trying to win over vulnerable social groups and the entire budget sector as part of his election campaign, but his programme lacked a sense of systemic renewal. The old model was being reproduced, and neglected to bring on board the new active citizenry and creative classes as joint creators of the future. The articles displayed a strange sort of myopia, with proposals to remedy problems that Putin himself had created (as with the limited powers of parliamentary investigations, which had been imposed on parliament by the regime itself).

These articles and a busy round of meetings with key groups (some of which are discussed below) represented attempts by Putin to rally 'the Putin majority', that had begun to dissipate. His permanent campaigning over the previous years had been an attempt to keep this majority intact while he temporarily occupied the prime minister's office. His articles sought to consolidate the great mass of public officials and dependent population to his cause, if not to Putin personally. Thus the situation of the 1990s was restored when Yeltsin's personal popularity was desperately low, yet a plurality supported the regime. This is why Putin insisted that a second round would destabilise the situation, since power shared would be power destroyed, the essence of his political philosophy. Equally, he held the incipient pluralism within the tandem as responsible for the protests. Even his own core supporters, including governors, began to separate the fate of the power system and Putin's own career. This was a situation that he had not faced in all his years in power.

The presidential election

The campaign demonstrated the rebirth of competitive politics in Russia. Facing a real political challenge, Putin sought to engage the newly-awakened public in genuine political debate. It also showed Putin in a new light as a political campaigner, but the stress of his exertions was clear. This was in evidence in his rather bad-tempered exchanges with media representatives on 18 January. He accused the oligarchs of fuelling a 'negative' attitude to business, noting that they had profited from the 'unfair' sale of state assets in the 1990s and squandered the proceeds on buying foreign sports teams and the like, which provoked those negative reactions. One of those who best fitted that characterisation was Prokhorov. He also took issue with Venediktov, asserting that Ekho Moskvy served the interests of 'foreign' countries: he had in mind what he felt was the anti-Russian bias of coverage of the Russo-Georgian war in 2008. He asked Venediktov 'I see that you are upset with me, I see it in your face. Why? I have no hard feelings against you when you pour bucketfuls of excrement all over me from morning till night'.[22] The political instability provoked yet another flood of net capital outflow in 2011, totalling $84.2bn, including $37.8bn in the last three months alone. Russia's international currency and gold reserves continued to fall, reaching $497bn in mid-January from their recent peak of $528bn in June 2011.[23] This certainly gave the regime a cushion against economic shocks, but the trend was worrying.

Putin was unused to engaging in public politics to ensure his position. Andrei Illarionov, Putin's former economic advisor, even suggested that Putin would be tempted to impose some sort of junta (along the lines of that attempted in August 1991), but this was far-fetched.[24] Instead, with the alienation of the liberals and the discrediting of Medvedev's programme of controlled political liberalisation, Putin fell back on to his core support, above all the security establishment. In January 2012 police and military salaries were raised, accompanied by the massive growth in military expenditure in a ten-year plan costing some 19tn roubles ($614.5bn) that made Russian defence spending one of the highest in the world as a proportion of GDP. The country engaged in the biggest military build-up since the collapse of the Soviet Union, in keeping with Putin's argument during the campaign that the world was far from safe. Putin had thrived as the 'faction manager', balancing between the various groups within the regime, above all between the *siloviki* represented by Sechin and Sergei Ivanov and the liberals such as Kudrin and Medvedev, but now factional balance was disrupted as the liberals began to defect, reducing Putin's room for manoeuvre.

Of the other candidates, Prokhorov's 15-page manifesto, titled 'Present and Future', echoed the demands of the protestors. He called for new State Duma elections, a return to four-year presidential terms, a professional army by 2015, a visa-free regime for OSCE citizens, the privatisation of state-owned companies, and a 30 per cent cut in state employees by 2014. He also promised to free all economic 'criminals' from jail, foremost among them Khodorkovsky.[25] Neither Zyuganov nor Zhirinovsky had anything new to offer, while Mironov fought an oddly muted campaign. The regime gradually regained the political initiative. Putin's poll ratings began to rise, and the programme of political concessions took much of the wind out of the sails of the opposition movement. Although more protest meetings were planned, divisions among the leadership of the opposition and the lack of a clear alternative strategy allowed the regime to consolidate its wavering support. Putin gradually built up a commanding lead, helped by Medvedev, who returned from the shadows to assert that the political reforms would be implemented, and that he himself harboured ambitions to return to the presidency.

The rival demonstrations on 4 February illustrated the growing split in Russian society. Despite Arctic conditions, thousands marched down Bolshaya Yakimanka down to Bolotnaya Square, yet much of the earlier élan was missing. The various groups could agree on little other than that Putin had to go, and were unable to foster a positive vision of change other than in the broadest terms. The leadership of the movement remained divided, as each jostled for the mantle of leadership. The CPRF was notable by its absence from all street activity. The 'new opposition' lacked a systemic critique of the model of capitalism that had been created in Russia; or even the moral critique of the sort presented by the various 'Occupy Wall Street' movements in the West of this time, protesting against an unbalanced financial system in which profits were private but the risks socialised. Putin's *dirigisme* and paternalism exposed him to critique from the liberal right, but only Prokhorov enunciated (and that only fitfully) a programme for the emancipation of big business from Putin's tutelary regime. Indeed, it was potentially not the protesters who would inherit the post-Putin Russia but the magnates, no longer tainted by the cruder aspects of oligarchic power of the 1990s but shaping a free-market neo-liberal agenda of marketisation of state and society. Already in March 2006 Oleg Deripaska, one of those who had profited most from the Putin stabilisation, argued that the country's leader should be someone under the control of the business community who could 'make decisions to ensure economic efficiency'. The president in this vision was little more that the 'top manager who governs the whole country', which echoed Putin's own view of his role although based on a very different hierarchy. This was another facet of the 'Ukrainisation' of Russian politics that Putin so feared.[26]

As noted, on the same day a massive crowd of Putin supporters gathered on Poklonnaya Hill, the site of the military commemoration park, drawing together some 140,000 people. Many were undoubtedly bussed in or otherwise encouraged to attend by the authorities in the classic Soviet manner of 'voluntary-compulsory' mobilisation, yet a large proportion genuinely feared that a 'Russia without Putin' would be rendered vulnerable externally and prey to internal fragmentation. That certainly was the view of a video of that title which was aired widely on YouTube and other social media.

Ryzhkov warned that the rival demonstrations signalled that both sides were 'walking down a dangerous path of escalation', and asserted that 'the protesters' demands have become stronger as the authorities continue to stonewall'. He insisted that Putin's articles 'dispelled once and for all any illusions some might have had that the authorities were preparing to reach an agreement with the protesters', arguing that Putin 'remains out of touch with reality'.[27] Ryzhkov called the protest movement 'Decembrists 2.0', denoting not just the month in which mass mobilisation began against the Putinite system, but also acknowledging that the struggle for genuine constitutionalism, begun in December 1825, had still not been achieved. Ryzhkov recognised that the 'new Decembrists' lacked a single ideological view but insisted on broad democratic reforms supported by the developing middle class. He admitted that the organising committee was far from being in a position to control what happened in the squares during protest meetings. Ryzhkov was clearly frustrated by the lack of progress, despite four meetings between Putin and Kudrin, and numerous meetings between Kudrin and the opposition. He feared that the struggle was taking on an extended and systemic character, which could be escalated by either side. He feared the 'Lukashenko scenario', when the president of Belarus had violently cracked down on the opposition following the December 2010 presidential election.[28]

Putin responded by engaging with various interest groups. Meeting with political scientists on 6 February, Putin addressed a fundamental question: in his various articles and speeches he identified major shortcomings in the country's economic, political, social and judicial systems, but then why had he not addressed the problems earlier. His response was that 'we are finishing the first steps of the post-Soviet era and can begin making real progress. ... Back then [in his previous presidencies] it was just not possible because we had no resources or facilitative conditions'. This was hardly a satisfactory response, but it at least showed Putin understood the force of the argument: 'Why didn't you do it before?' He went on to defend an open economy, noting that some $60bn of the capital outflow of $85bn in 2011 represented Russian investments into companies in other countries. He ridiculed the programmes of the other presidential contestants, charting a middle path between Prokhorov's proposals to privatise everything, including all TV stations, and Zyuganov's threat to nationalise everything, including most industries.[29]

He also criticised Zhirinovsky's idea of having a political, economic and criminal amnesty: 'Are we talking about releasing all convicts, like they did in 1953? Frankly, I'm not sure what he means when he says political amnesty. I don't think that we have any political prisoners, although they keep talking about them without providing any names. Why don't they show us at least one person who is in prison for political reasons? I don't know any'. Eduard Limonov was mentioned, but Putin did not need to look far – Khodorkovsky obviously came into the category. His comments provoked widespread criticism, with numerous lists of political prisoners bandied about, and in the end a list with 32 names was presented to Medvedev.

Putin added a number of elements to his campaign. Meeting with the RUIE on 9 February, Putin talked about the need to improve the business climate and to close the book on the 'dishonest' privatisation of the 1990s. As Khodorkovsky had repeatedly argued in various missives from jail, the problem of legitimising the property settlement of the 1990s was perhaps the most painful issue facing Russia, and would have to be resolved before the country could set out on the path of normal capitalist democratic development. One measure which Putin suggested could 'draw the curtain' on the issue of the 'unfair privatisation' of the 1990s would be to impose a 'one-off levy' on those businesspeople who had benefited to ensure 'the social legitimacy of private property'. Putin even acknowledged that the idea of a windfall tax had originally been mooted by the Yabloko leader: 'I discussed this with Grigory Alekseevich Yavlinsky ... I agree with him that we should put an end to this period'. Yavlinsky had made the proposal in 2005, but it was unclear how it could be implemented. More to the point, Khodorkovsky had long talked of such a way of legitimising the 'black privatisation' of the 1990s. As Kasyanov tweeted: 'Khodorkovsky and I suggested this. His [Putin's] reaction: I was sacked, Khodorkovsky sent to jail'.[30] The idea of such a tax was probably a decade too late, since much of the property in question had changed hands, some of it several times. In such cases it was not clear who would pay the fine.[31]

Putin also spoke of the introduction of a luxury tax, which would represent a 'publically recognised levy for the refusal to invest in development in favour of over-consumption and vanity', although he promised that this would not affect the middle class. In addition, Putin once again spoke of the need to appoint an ombudsman to monitor the rights of local business people.[32] Soon after, the cabinet website put up a long list of measures that had been undertaken to improve conditions for business in the last year, including a reduction from 90 to 60 days to approve or reject construction projects, streamlined regulations for companies to connect to electricity, water and sewer systems, and the introduction of independent directors for boards of state companies.[33] In an environment with a weak judiciary and a predatory administrative system, there was a grave danger that even a token levy could be exploited by the venal bureaucracy. The attack on the oligarchs represented a populist move in a tough electoral environment.

From his prison cell in Karelia, Khodorkovsky was sceptical. He noted that Putin did not trust the bona fides of the demonstrators, believing that they were either in the pay of western powers or marginals who sought to use the movement for their careerist ambitions. He noted that Putin thought of himself as a successful ruler, and that his methods were correct. It was for this reason any concessions to the protestors would be individual rather than systemic, since the latter would throw in doubt Putin's whole approach. Khodorkovsky argued that the 'new opposition' could only use Kudrin as an intermediary to establish the rules of the game, rather than acting as a substantive negotiator. Putin was now set against the square, and there was no need for a 'new Putin'; what was required was a whole new philosophy of cooperation to replace the archaic 'vertical'. Russia's opposition should hold a dialogue with Putin since the country needed more political cooperation. The demands of the new opposition came down to the need for honest government, which required honest elections, for which independent and fair courts and media were required, as well as intolerance of corruption and a coalition government. Not least, the powers of the presidency needed to be reduced; otherwise a new leader would soon engage in the discredited practices of old. The new opposition in his view needed to escalate peaceful protest until it achieved its goals. However, asked about the acceptable limits to the protest actions, he argued that the authorities had 'not yet crossed the boundary' to become wholly morally illegitimate, even though some of its officials had crossed the line. Asked whether the protest movement could force Putin to make concessions, possibly by releasing him and Lebedev, Khodorkovsky was doubtful: 'I have received no signal from the current authorities associated with the latest changes in society. It is impossible for me to compromise with conscience. I do not wish to speculate on my future.'[34] The tone of the piece was imbued with Solzhenitsyn's demand for self-limitation and self-knowledge, sensitive to the opposition's dilemma of asserting its demands while drawing back from the brink that could escalate into violence.

Putin's return

In the end, through supreme exertions, Putin officially won in the first round on 4 March with 63.6 per cent of the vote, and thus his strategy appeared vindicated. Zyuganov came in second with 17.2 per cent, but Prokhorov gained an impressive third place finish with 8 per cent of the vote, while Zhirinovsky won 6.2 per cent and Mironov trailed in last with a disappointing 3.85 per cent (see Table 7.2). In Moscow Putin's vote was significantly lower than nationally, officially 46.95 per cent (suspiciously similar to United Russia's official vote in the city in the parliamentary election), while Prokhorov won 20.5 per cent of the city's vote. This reflected a contraction in the regime's social base, losing the confidence of much of the more globalised electorate and forced back on to the support of traditionalists and blue-collar workers in the regions and non-metropolitan areas. In the North Caucasus Putin gathered the usual loyalty vote, winning over 90 per cent in four regions, including an impressive 99.76 per cent in Chechnya. Estimates suggest that fraud had

Table 7.2 Presidential election of 4 March 2012

Candidate	Vote	Percentage
Putin, Vladimir	45,602,075	63.60
Zyuganov, Gennady	12,318,353	17.18
Prokhorov, Mikhail	5,722,508	7.98
Zhirinovsky, Vladimir	4,458,103	6.22
Mironov, Sergei	2,763,935	3.85
Electorate	109,860,331	
Number of valid ballots	70,864,974	
Turnout	65.3%	

Source: Central Electoral Commission: http://www.vybory.izbirkom.ru/region/region/izbirkom?action=show'root=1'tvd=100100031793509'vrn=100100031793505'region=0'global=1'sub_region=0'prver=0'pronetvd=null'vibid=100100031793509'type=227.

decreased – instead of the 12 per cent in the parliamentary election it was now about 5 per cent, enough to boost Putin's vote above the 60 per cent needed to reassure his supporters that he retained a firm grip on power.

The OSCE report repeated some of the criticisms made earlier of the parliamentary election, including a deterioration in the process during counting, and 'the conditions for the campaign were clearly skewed in favour of one candidate'.[35] The demand for honest elections by the protest movement prompted greater observation efforts, accompanied by the use of web cameras and new voter technologies, including ballot scanning machines and touch-screen electronic voting systems.[36] The Golos election monitoring NGO reported that 'the RF presidential elections can be characterized as normal in the context of the past decade of Russian elections, with an insufficient level of competition, interference with the electoral process, and some degree of coercion to vote'.[37] Opposition reaction to the vote was divided, and a palpable sense of frustration stymied further coordinated protests. The result demonstrated that support for Putin was much greater than for United Russia, explaining his shift from the party to the Popular Front. At the victory celebration on election night in Manezh Square, a tearful Putin proclaimed 'I promised you we would win. We have won. Glory to Russia.' The western-sponsored enemy had been defeated: 'We showed that no one can direct us in anything! We were able to save ourselves from political provocations, which have one goal – to destroy Russian sovereignty and usurp power.'

The opposition claim that Putin was an illegitimate president was based on two assertions. The first is that the whole electoral process had been fraudulent. The evidence suggests that the presidential ballot had been less flawed than the State Duma election, yet once again the mass media was skewed to support Putin's return and opposition candidates had been filtered out of the race. Golos suggested that Putin had won no more than 50.2 per cent of the national vote, giving a genuine first-round win but with nothing like the margin the official results suggested. Statistical models looking at areas of exceptionally high turnout posited a high level of fraud. To balance this, most authoritative opinion polls had predicted the given outcome, with the Levada agency forecasting that 66 per cent would vote for Putin. The second argument is that the larger pattern of fixed succession, initially from Putin to Medvedev in 2008 and now back to Putin, showed that the electoral process had been suborned to serve the needs of one man. The system assumed the features associated with 'electoral authoritarianism', in which elections (unlike in fully authoritarian systems) retain an element of choice and contingency but are heavily managed. This was challenged by a societal counter-movement calling for genuinely competitive and free elections. The presidential elections were consequently rather cleaner than the parliamentary ones, but this breach in the regime's claim to tutelary management was a warning that Putin took to heart. As so often in Russian history, the regime was most vulnerable during the period of succession. The Medvedev interregnum had fostered a degree of intra-systemic pluralism, while encouraging the belief that society would be a partner in governance. This relative liberalisation and self-fragmentation of the regime alarmed Putin's traditionalist supporters and was something his return was intended to rectify.

On the day before his inauguration, on 6 May, a protest march to Bolotnaya Square ended in disorder, with at least 400 people detained. The authorities had clearly resolved to change tactics, sensing that the tide had turned in their favour. The police imposed maximum inconvenience on the march, forcing a bottleneck that provoked violence. Criminal cases were later opened against some of the leaders and participants (see Chapter 8). The mood was soured, and on 7 May Putin drove through eerily deserted streets to his inauguration in the Kremlin. This was a strangely lacklustre affair with few benign portents. In his speech Putin recognised that the country was 'entering a new stage of national development', but argued that the goals would only be achieved 'if we are one and united'.[38]

Back in the driving seat

Putin's return proved to be far more traumatic than anticipated. When Putin announced his plan to return for a third term on 24 September 2011, he certainly did not envisage that he would have the fight of his political life on his hands. His abrupt repudiation of Medvedev's evident desire for a second term struck many as ill-considered, rendering Medvedev's programme of gradual liberalisation no more than a footnote in history. The cynical way in which the 'castling' move was announced made things worse. Medvedev was to become prime minister and Putin to return to the Kremlin; and both stated that this had long been decided. The elections were thus rendered little more than the formal 'plebiscitary' ratification of what Putin had decided. The mass protests following the flawed parliamentary elections demonstrated that popular tolerance for 'managed democracy' had reached breaking point.

On inauguration day Putin issued over a dozen decrees, the 'May executive orders', dealing with forming a new cabinet of ministers, demographic policy, revising the foreign policy concept, military service, the modernisation of the military industrial complex, inter-ethnic peace, the civil service, housing and improvements to communal services, education and science, health, social policy and economic policy. The overall tone was populist, making spending commitments whose funding was unclear. Nevertheless, as a pragmatic politician, Putin was well aware that there could be no simple return to the pre-Medvedev system. For example, Putin understood that the state corporations fostered in his second term had been ineffective and the breeding ground for monopolistic and corrupt practices.

On 17 May Putin outlined some ambitious economic goals in the decree 'On the state's long-term economic policy', including the creation of 25 million new jobs by 2020, investment to reach 25 per cent of GDP by 2018, a 30 per cent increase in high-tech products, a 50 per cent increase in labour productivity, and an increase in Russia's rank in the World Bank 'ease of doing business' index from 120th place to 50th by 2015 and 20th by 2018. In the event, in the index announced in October 2013 Russia rose to 92nd place, mainly because of improvements in the ease of getting electricity and registering property. Demographic issues were also addressed, including goals to raise the average lifespan to 74 years and birthrate to 1.753 per woman by 2018. The government was to prepare a strategic plan and new budget policies by October 2012, an ombudsman created to defend small business by December, and a review of the state corporations by March 2013.[39] On 21 May Medvedev announced an ambitious programme of privatisation, calling it a priority, but the next day Putin included Rosneft, RusHydro and some other companies on a list of strategic enterprises, blocking their privatisation. Rosneft's takeover of TNK-BP in autumn 2012 in fact sharply increased the state's share of the economy.

After a protracted pause, the new administration was announced on 21 May. In effect two parallel and competing cabinet structures were created, one headed by Medvedev in the White House, and one under the presidency in the Kremlin. The dualism of the tandem era survived in new forms. Three quarters of the ministers in Medvedev's cabinet were replaced, bringing in some young fresh faces. The new communications minister, Nikolai Nikiforov, was only 29 and had strong experience of creating 'online government' in Tatarstan. The new interior minister, Vladimir Kolokoltsev, was the respected former Moscow police chief, a professional who had risen through the ranks and whose reputation was untainted by corruption. Mikhail Abyzov was appointed to develop Medvedev's ideas on open government, while Olga Golodets became the deputy prime minister responsible for social affairs. Medvedev's former top adviser, Arkady Dvorkovich, took over as deputy prime minister in charge of the energy sector, displacing Putin's confidant and head *silovik*, Sechin, who was appointed to head Rosneft, the company that he had done so much to transform into a global energy major by incorporating Yukos. Putin's long-time aide Igor Shuvalov became the sole first deputy prime minister, joined in the cabinet by some other Putin allies, including Dmitry Rogozin (defence industry), Dmitry Kozak (construction and the 2014 Sochi Olympics) and Alexander Khloponin (the North Caucasus). Surkov was promoted to become deputy prime minister in charge of the cabinet staff, where he was joined by the former presidential foreign policy adviser, Sergei Prikhodko. Overall, the tone of the new cabinet was surprisingly liberal and reformist; in other word, 'Medvedevite'.

Many of Putin's former cabinet moved over to join him in the Kremlin, including some of the more controversial figures such as the former interior minister Rashid Nurgaliev, former health minister Tatyana Golikova, former education minister Andrei Fursenko, and former natural resources minister Yuri Trutnev. Putin's reinforced presidential administration represented a type of parallel government, with its staff increasing to 1,600. The new head of the presidential administration, Sergei Ivanov, was associated with no particular faction, although he had a background in the security service. His power derived from his closeness to Putin, seeing Putin almost daily and that on most issues 'we think more or less identically', and helped him maintain factional balance.[40] A new 'tandem' of Putin and Ivanov formed in the Kremlin. The creation of a 'parallel government' was initially interpreted as the creation of two locomotives to push forward reform, but it soon became clear that this was a typical Putinite ruse to counter the danger of the emergence of a threateningly strong and progressive cabinet. The government became a 'technical' one, firmly subordinated to the presidency. The succession crisis had demonstrated that there was no united 'team' at the top, but two contesting visions of Russian development. Now it was clear that the liberal version would operate under severe constraints.

At the same time, Putin appointed Igor Kholmanskikh, a shop foreman from the Uralvagonzavod (Urals Railcar Plant) in Nizhny Tagil, as head of the Urals federal district, breaking every convention in the bureaucratic rule book. At the 15 December 2011 direct line programme Kholmanskikh had offered to come to Moscow with a detachment of workers to 'sort things out' with the protesters, in a manner reminiscent of Ceauşescu's dictatorship in Romania. Putin inherited the changes inaugurated by Medvedev, including the return of the direct election of governors. In spite of all the filters and control mechanisms, the succession crisis demonstrated that elections remain elections, prey to chance and contingency. Over-manage them, and run the danger of a popular backlash, as seen in December 2011; under-manage them, and some uncontrolled individuals and forces could be unleashed. Putin's third term would be devoted to finding ways of resolving this contradiction, rather than thinking of new ways to resolve the country's problems.

Putin had come out fighting, issuing a cavalcade of major campaign documents, and in the end he managed to convince a large majority of the voters that he was the best bet for Russia's future. The electoral process was flawed but not illegitimate. Putin was challenged to build on the impetus of the desire for reform, so that his third presidency would connect with his first from 2000, when he delivered positive judicial and economic reforms. Putin's renewed presidency was paradoxically challenged to dismantle the system that he had so assiduously built up in his classic period in office. The gulf between the administrative regime and the constitutional state would have to be closed, corruption tackled, and the aspirations of the newly-emboldened 'middle class' fulfilled. Under Putin incomes rose but Russia remained one of the few upper-middle-income countries not to be a consolidated democracy. In the event, the crisis forged a new Putin, but not one who would build on the relative liberalism of the tandem years but instead who reinforced precisely the features against which the demonstrators had protested.

Notes

1 Gleb Cherkasov, 'Kandidat nomer odin', *Kommersant*, 20 February 2012.
2 'Russia's Mironov Says Ready to Serve as "Transitional President"', RIA Novosti, 12 January 2012; http://en.rian.ru/russia/20120112/170722531.html.
3 'Three Independents get 2 mln Signatures by Deadline', RIA Novosti, 18 January 2012; http://en.rian.ru/russia/20120118/170827389.html.
4 Chrystia Freeland, 'Battle Raging at Heart of Russian Elite', *New York Times*, 19 January 2012.
5 Prokhorov apparently asked Putin how far he could go in criticising the regime, to which the latter gave a characteristic enigmatic response: 'As far as you think appropriate', which effectively imposed self-censorship on Prokhorov. I am grateful to Ivan Krastev for this account.
6 According to the Levada Center, http://www.levada.ru/22-12-2011/dekabrskie-reitingi-odobreniya-i-doveriya.
7 Leon Aron, 'The Merger of Power and Property', *Journal of Democracy*, Vol. 20, No. 2, April 2009, p. 67.
8 'Clinton Calls Eurasian Integration an Effort to Re-Sovietize', RFE/RL, *Russia Report*, 9 December 2012.
9 *Strategiya-2020: Novaya models rosta – novaya sotsial'snaya politika*, http://2020strategy.ru/data/2012/03/14/1214585998/1itog.pdf.
10 Vladimir Putin, 'Rossiya sosredotachivaetsya: Vyzovy, na kotorye my dolzhny otvetit'', *Izvestiya*, 16 January 2012; http://premier.gov.ru/events/news/17755/.
11 Vladimir Putin, 'Rossiya: Natsional'nyi vopros', *Nezavisimaya gazeta*, 23 January 2012a; http://premier.gov.ru/events/news/17831/.
12 V. V. Putin, 'O nashikh ekonomicheskikh zadachakh', *Vedomosti*, 30 January 2012b; http://premier.gov.ru/events/news/17888/.
13 'Prime Minister Vladimir Putin Takes Part in the VTB Capital "Russia Calling!" Investment Forum', 6 October 2011; http://premier.gov.ru/eng/events/news/16653/.
14 V. V. Putin, 'Demokratiya i kachestvo gosudarstva', *Kommersant*, 6 February 2012c; http://premier.gov.ru/events/news/18006/.
15 V. V. Putin, 'Stroitel'stvo spravedlivosti: Sotsial'naya politika dlya Rossii', *Komsomol'skaya Pravda*, 13 February 2012d; http://premier.gov.ru/events/news/18071/.
16 'Putin Needs to Specify Sources for Ambitious Spending Plans – Kudrin', RIA Novosti, 14 February 2012.
17 Editorial, 'Ot redaktsii: Tarif sberegatel'nyi', *Vedomosti*, 14 February 2012.

18 V. V. Putin, 'Byt' sil'nymi: Garantii natsional'noi bezopasnosti dlya Rossii', *Rossiiskaya gazeta*, 20 February 2012e; http://premier.gov.ru/events/news/18185/.
19 V. V. Putin, 'Rossiya i menyayushchiisya mir', *Moskovskie novosti*, 27 February 2012f; http://premier.gov.ru/events/news/18252/.
20 A summary version of Putin's article was published as 'Guest Post by Vladimir Putin: US-Russia Ties Need Strong Economic Base', *Financial Times*, 27 February 2012; http://blogs.ft.com/beyond-brics/2012/02/27, from where this quotation is drawn.
21 'Russia at the Turn of the Millennium', in Putin, *First Person* (2000), pp, 209–19.
22 'Vladimir Putin vstretilsya s rukovoditelyam rossiiskikh SMI', 18 January 2012; http://premier.gov.ru/events/news/17798/.
23 Stefan Wagstyl, 'Putin to Oligarchs: Watch Out', *Financial Times*, 20 January 2012.
24 Charles Clover, 'Russia: Politics and Uncertainty Return to Russia', *Financial Times*, 25 January 2012.
25 Jonathan Earle, 'Prokhorov's Platform Courts Protesters', *Moscow Times*, 23 January 2012.
26 Felix Goryunov, 'Putin Divides Russian Capitalism', *Russia Beyond the Headlines*, 14 February 2012; www.rbth.ru.
27 Vladimir Ryzhkov, 'We Want Reforms, Not Revolution', *Moscow Times*, 14 February 2012.
28 Vladimir Ryzhkov, 'Putin vzyal kurs na agressivnoe uderzhanie status-kvo', *Novaya gazeta*, 14 February 2012a.
29 'Predsedatel' Pravitel'stva Rossiiskoi Federatsii V. V. Putin vstretilsya s politologami', 6 February 2012; http://premier.gov.ru/events/news/18008/.
30 Konstantin von Eggert, 'Wooing the Oligarchs', *Moscow News*, 13 February 2012.
31 Oleg Nishenkov, 'Investors Skeptical on "Oligarch" Tax', *Moscow News*, 13 February 2012.
32 'Predsedatel' Pravitel'stva Rossiiskoi Federatsii V. V. Putin prinyal uchastie v rabote s"ezda Rossiiskogo soyuza promyshlennikov i predprinimateli', 9 February 2012; http://premier.gov.ru/events/news/18052/.
33 Irina Filatova and Anatoly Medetsky, 'Putin Has Plethora of Business Ideas', *Moscow Times*, 10 February 2012.
34 Yevgeniya Albats, 'Chto zhdat' ot vlasti? Mikhail Khodorkovskii – the New Times', *New Times*, No. 3, 30 January 2012.
35 OSCE, *Presidential Election 4 March 2012: OSCE/ODIHR Election Observation Mission Final Report* (Warsaw, 11 May 2012), p. 1.
36 Ibid., pp. 7–9.
37 'Association GOLOS – Domestic Monitoring of Elections of the President of Russian Federation, 4 March 2012: Preliminary Report', *Russian Analytical Digest*, No. 110, 16 March 2012, p. 8.
38 'Vladimir Putin vstupil v dolzhnost' Prezidenta Rossii', 7 May 2012; http://news.kremlin.ru/transcripts/15224.
39 Peter Rutland, 'The Political Economy of Putin 3.0', *Russian Analytical Digest*, No. 133, 18 July 2013, p. 3.
40 Vladimir Sungorkin and Viktor Baranets, 'Sergei Ivanov: "My s Putinym poznakomilis' v razvedke"', *Komsomol'skaya Pravda*, 5 March 2013.

8 Tightening the screws

Two sides of Putin were in evidence on the evening of his victory on 4 March in Manezh Square. The first spoke of unification, consolidation and social dialogue, projecting himself as the leader of the whole people. However, the second used the rhetoric of crushing power: 'We won today, and thanks to the overwhelming support of the great majority of our voters we secured a clean victory.'[1] There had been much talk of a wiser and gentler Putin returning to the Kremlin, but instead a battle-scarred and traumatised leader engaged in class and cultural warfare came back to the presidency. As the dust settled, Putinism was forced to devise new forms of political management in which these two Putins were clearly at war. Four strategies were central: coercion, constraints, co-optation and conviction. Selective coercion was applied against the opposition. Constraints were imposed on non-official political engagement, with hefty fines imposed for the infringement of tightened regulations governing demonstrations, and a whole gamut of new offences were introduced. Constraints were also imposed on the regime's elites, including their rights to hold accounts and shares abroad. The main co-optation mechanism was through the Popular Front. As for conviction, this came through a range of ideological initiatives, including an accentuated anti-westernism, closer links with the Orthodox Church, and the espousal of conservative cultural and family values. Since the mid-2000s Putin had been articulating an increasingly conservative ideology, drawing on the 'mid-level-KGB-officer consensus' of the mid-1980s asserting that centralised government, targeted political repression, firmly-controlled media and superpower aspirations would allow Russia to thrive, now shorn of the earlier Soviet prejudices against the free market and religion.[2] This Putinite *Kulturkampf* had no solution to the blockage on modernisation or the political stalemate described earlier.

Coercion

The spirit of revenge was not long in making itself felt. In June 2012 a new law was adopted, sharply tightening the legislation on rallies. Over 400 amendments were introduced at the draft stage, accompanied by a filibuster by

Dmitry Gudkov, supported by the Just Russia leadership, yet in the end the harsh measures were signed into law by Putin. Two years earlier Medvedev had vetoed legislation that had stiffened the legislation on rallies, but now it became law. The fine for participating in unsanctioned rallies was raised to a punitive 300,000 roubles ($9,000), and the fine for organising an unsanctioned meeting rose to one million roubles. In effect this was an emergency law that suspended the operation of Article 31 of the constitution.

On 11 June 2012 the police raided the homes of a dozen leading protest activists. These raids were allegedly part of the investigation into the clashes between protesters and police at the 6 May demonstration, but their timing suggested other motives – two days after the 'anti-demonstration' law came into effect and the day before the so-called March of Millions. The apartments of leading opposition figures Ilya Yashin, the leader of Solidarity and head of the Moscow branch of the People's Freedom Party, Udaltsov, Navalny and TV presenter and self-styled 'representative of the younger generation' Ksenia Sobchak (the daughter of Putin's former sponsor and St Petersburg mayor, Anatoly Sobchak) and some others were searched. They were then called for questioning by prosecutors on 12 June, forcing some to miss the rally. The police seized computers, flash cards and other digital devices, and in some cases personal cash savings. The aim clearly was to intimidate the leaders and to scare off rank and file participants.

There are differing estimates of the numbers at the 12 June rally, but at least 60,000 marched in what would turn out to be the last of the major demonstrations provoked by Putin's return. A resolution was adopted calling for Putin's resignation, a new Electoral Code, the disbanding of the State Duma, and new national legislative and presidential elections. The Free Russia manifesto adopted at the rally included classic nationalist arguments, repeating the view that the regime had turned 'the country into a raw materials appendage of the West'. The veteran nationalist Ivan Mironov condemned Putin for destroying Russian industry through WTO membership, poisoning society with alcohol, and committing genocide on the Russian people. The presidency and parliament were declared not only illegitimate but also illegal, and the value of elections in changing the government was questioned, although no alternative to civil initiatives and electoral struggles were advanced. Putin's speech that day marking the Russia Day national holiday adopted a conciliatory tone: 'It is important to listen and to respect each other, to seek mutual understanding and find compromise, to unite society around a positive and constructive agenda.' This apparently suggested a willingness to have dialogue with the opposition, but he went on to insist that 'The unconditional value of an evolutionary development path is obvious for a huge country like Russia, with its multiethnic people and complex federal structure'.[3] His conciliatory tone turned out to be ritualistic, and retribution continued against those who had challenged his authority.

On 21 February 2012 five members of the feminist art collective Pussy Riot, formed in October 2011 in response to Putin's announced return, performed a 41-second 'punk prayer' in the Cathedral of Christ the Saviour, entitled 'Mother of God, drive Putin out of Russia!' This was the culmination of a number of actions – the metro, the roofs of city buses, outside Navalny's cell on 5 December and on Red Square – goading the authorities. The three most active members, Nadezhda Tolokonnikova, Maria Alyokhina and Ekaterina Samutsevich, were arrested and held without bail. The women refused to recognise their guilt, insisting that they had not intended to offend believers but sought to draw attention to the church's unhealthily close relations with Putin. However, dancing on a church ambon singing 'Shit, shit, shit of our Lord!' was at best ill-considered transgressive behaviour. The 'childish and obnoxious publicity stunt' finally provoked the authorities.[4] The Khamovniki court on 10 August 2012 found the Pussy Riot activists guilty and on 17 August imposed two-year terms for 'hooliganism motivated by religious hatred' (Samutsevich, was released later that year with a suspended sentence). The harsh outcome provoked an international uproar, which only confirmed the prejudice of Russian conservatives that the West was going to hell in a handcart.

The Russian members of the international review of the second Khodorkovsky trial, commissioned by Medvedev's Presidential Council for Civil Society and Human Rights, came under attack shortly after Putin's return to the Kremlin. The report consisted of three volumes of closely argued analytical material identifying serious and widespread violations of the law. The experts rejected the court's findings about the illegality of Yukos's operations, arguing that the company's vertically-integrated structure and the use of offshore companies for trading oil and oil products were standard for the industry. The report was scathing about the verdict, which was held to have misunderstood and misapplied basic concepts of Russian civil and criminal law.[5] In September 2012 the Investigative Committee searched the home of Mikhail Subbotin and two of his colleagues, apparently investigating the old charge that Yukos money had been laundered in the West and then channelled back to Russian NGOs in exchange for them reaching 'deliberately false conclusions' about Khodorkovsky's conviction 'under the guise of independent public expertise'. Subbotin was named as a 'witness' in the case; the former Constitutional Court judge, Tamara Morshakova, who had worked with Subbotin on the report, was also summoned for questioning. Three more of the six Russians on the expert commission were called in for questioning: Sergei Guriev, Oksana Oleinik and Astamur Tedeev. Increasing the Kremlin's ire, in April 2012 Guriev donated 10,000 roubles (€220) to Navalny's anti-corruption fund. After two more bouts of questioning, including a visit by a RIC investigator in April 2013 with a warrant to impound his computer hard drive, Guriev in May fled to join his wife and children in Paris. He announced that he would not return to Russia for fear of being arraigned as a defendant in a possible third criminal trial against Khodorkovsky, and at the same time he gave up the leadership of the New Economic School. 'There is no guarantee that I won't lose my freedom', he told *Ekho Moskvy* on 31 May 2013.[6]

The 'experts' case' was part of a larger attempt to intimidate the creative intelligentsia, but it resulted in a growing flow of talent abroad. Like Khodorkovsky, Guriev insisted that 'I am a free person', explaining his right to support Navalny's campaign. 'As long as I don't break the law, nobody can prohibit me from speaking or doing what I want.' But, as a report in the *Moscow Times* put it, 'Or so he thought. Guriev, like all normal Russians, shared Medvedev's banal belief that "freedom is better than no freedom". And that is precisely why he fled to Paris'.[7] From his cell in Karelia, Khodorkovsky noted the 'obvious political motivation' of the Bolotnaya and Navalny cases, intended 'to intimidate and demoralize opponents and politically active voters, and to represent peaceful civil protest and the constitutional struggle for power as something marginal and extremist'. The Kremlin thereby risked inflicting 'a tangible political loss on itself', and warned the business community that 'the political trials of 2013' could have serious consequences for them as well.[8] The lack of criteria for a limit to the repression undermined the regime's support among the 'active classes' and its own elites.

The 'Bolotnaya case' is set to join the Yukos trials as the most ramified act of political repression since the Soviet period. It applied Putin's favoured method of 'fictitious legalism' to crush his enemies, accompanied by a media campaign to discredit opponents and to raise the level of hysterical witch-hunting.[9] Reminiscent of late Soviet practices, the goal was not full-scale repression but a deterrent – *profilaktika* – to forestall the further development of the opposition movement. The RIC created a special 200-member group to investigate the alleged conspiracy behind the 'riot'. The 'anti-inauguration' demonstration on 6 May 2012 ended in violence, but there is considerable evidence that it was instigated by the authorities. Heavy-handed policing funnelled and blocked the demonstrators, exacerbated by the alleged use of *agents provocateurs*. A Public Inquiry Commission established by RPR-Parnas and the '6 May Committee' analysed statements by over 600 eyewitnesses and examined hundreds of videos and photographs of the events.[10] It concluded in a 250-page report in April 2013 that in fact there had been no riot, but only demonstrators defending themselves from police attacks, with the bottleneck created by the police, many of whom wore no identification of their status, as the route of the 60,000-strong march was changed without consultation.[11] Over 12,800 police officers were involved, some flown in from as far away as Mari El and Yakutia.[12] In the end 28 defendants were charged with organising and participating in the 'mass riot'. By the time of the report's publication one, Maxim Luzyanin, had in November 2012 been sentenced to four and a half years in jail, 15 had spent months in pre-trial detention, seven had been barred from leaving the country, two were being hunted, and two others, including Udaltsov, were being held under house arrest. Udaltsov's resolute struggle against the regime is reflected in the title of one of his books: *War on Putin!*[13]

Once again the power of the media was launched against the opposition. The propaganda pseudo-documentary *Anatomy of Protest*, aired on the pro-Kremlin

NTV, accused the opposition of serving the interests of the United States and of bribing participants with the prospect of free biscuits! Navalny was allegedly recruited by the CIA when he took part in Yale University's six-month World Fellows Programme in 2010. In America Navalny allegedly received his secret orders to lead the protests in Russia after the 2011 parliamentary elections to undermine the Putin regime. The rather more professionally made *Anatomy of Protest 2* of 5 October 2012 showed the Left Front activists Udaltsov, Leonid Razvozzhaev and Konstantin Lebedev meeting in Belarus and apparently receiving advice on how to seize power from a Georgian politician by the name of Givi Targamadze. Prompted by its own propaganda, shortly afterwards the RIC charged the three with planning the disturbances of 6 May 2012. Lebedev was arrested in October and sentenced to two and a half years in April 2013. He 'confessed' that he had plotted 'mass riots' and that he and his associates had paid people to participate in the anti-Putin protests, and they had been put up it to by foreign powers. As one of his colleagues put it, 'Had he told the truth, I would have said he'd sold us all out. But his confession is pure fantasy, as far as I know, so this is something else'.[14] Razvozzhaev fled to Kiev in October 2012 and applied for asylum, but apparently was seized by Russian security officials, drugged, and bundled back to Russia. He signed a confession admitting to receiving foreign money to provoke 'mass riots' to destabilise the country, but in court he repudiated the charges. For the left the repression represented the consolidation of 'capitalist authoritarianism'; but whatever the system was called the result was clear: 'All these arrests have demoralised a movement that just a year and a half ago looked as though it could fundamentally alter the Russian political landscape.'[15] The trial of 12 people suspected of taking part in the clashes continued. Ilya Ponomarev was accused of helping organise the riot, but parliamentary immunity prevented a criminal case being opened against him.[16]

There were many signal cases of personal political repression. The Russian billionaire Alexander Lebedev had long faced difficulties, with a raid by masked security officials on his National Reserve Bank, followed by an investigation into the bank's affairs. His attempt to run in the Sochi mayoral election in 2009 was swiftly thwarted when he was refused registration. He called the decision 'insane', and his comparison with elections in Zimbabwe certainly did not win him any popularity in the Kremlin.[17] Navalny joined the board of Aeroflot, in which Lebedev has a 15 per cent stake, to pursue anti-corruption investigations. In September 2012 Lebedev was charged with 'hooliganism motivated by political hatred' and battery in connection with an incident a year earlier when he punched Sergei Polonsky, a property developer, while filming a programme for the state-owned NTV. Lebedev claims he was deliberately provoked into the assault. Lebedev is the co-owner with Mikhail Gorbachev of the liberal *Novaya Gazeta*, as well as the London *Evening Standard* and *The Independent*, and he was an outspoken supporter of Navalny's campaign against corruption.[18] Lebedev had clearly breached the rule in place since Khodorkovsky's arrest in October 2003 that oligarchs should not independently get involved in politics. In a surprising turn of events, the 'hooliganism' charges against Lebedev were dropped in June 2013 and instead he was found guilty of battery and sentenced to 150 hours of community service.

Navalny at this time was charged with economic crimes that carried a potential ten-year sentence. This came in the wake of Navalny's declaration on Dozhd TV on 4 April 2013 that he harboured the ambition to become president of Russia, followed by the threat that 'If I become president, Putin will go to jail'. Earlier that month Navalny had declared that he would seek the presidency, and thus placed himself in the dangerous category of open challengers for the Kremlin throne. Soon after he claimed that Bastrykin held undeclared assets in the Czech Republic, and indeed that he had a residence permit there. Given that the Czech Republic was a member of NATO, Navalny noted that this inevitably raised questions about Bastrykin's security clearance for work at the top level of Russia's law enforcement agencies. Navalny dubbed him 'foreign agent Bastrykin'. Not surprisingly, the Investigative Committee thereafter hounded Navalny.

On 17 April 2013 Navalny's trial began in Kirov. Navalny was charged with embezzling R16m ($500,000) worth of timber from the state-owned Kirovles when he worked briefly between May and September 2009 as an advisor to Belykh. Navalny allegedly forced Kirovles, headed by Vyacheslav Opalev, to sell the wood to Pyotr Ofitserov's Vyatka Lesnaya Kompaniya (VLK) company at 7 per cent below the going rate. Local investigators had already twice dismissed the case, but it was reopened on Bastrykin's direct order. Vladimir Markin, RIC's official spokesman, conceded the political nature of the case when he revealed that the trial had been accelerated because Navalny had been 'taunting the authorities'.[19] 'If a person tries with all his strength to attract attention, or if I may put it this way, teases the authorities saying "look at me, I'm so good compared to everyone else" well, then, interest in his past grows and the process of exposing him naturally speeds up.'[20] Prokhorov exclaimed that 'In any law-abiding state, one such statement would be enough to drop charges against Navalny and charge General Markin instead'.[21]

Navalny's trial moved with unusual speed, helped by the fact that the presiding judge, Sergei Blinov, did not allow the defence to cross-examine Opalev or 13 defence witnesses to testify on Navalny's behalf. The prosecution relied on Opalev, Opalev's stepdaughter and the evidence of the third man in the case, who pleaded guilty to signing a contract with Ofitserov's intermediary firm, VLK, set up on Navalny's initiative, on less than market terms. The deal only lasted for four months, and no one benefited from the venture. When Navalny served as Belykh's adviser in 2009 he recommended that Opalev be fired as director of Kirovles and investigated for corruption since the company had already run up large debts of R200m ($6m). In fact, the timber business runs on tight margins, and Kirovles was forced to charge uneconomic rents on its forests. An audit was commissioned by the regional property fund, the nominal owner of Kirovles, which criticised the deal, while Navalny sought a counter-audit to be conducted by Deloitte. Soon after, with its experienced manager removed, the company went bankrupt. It was one of the major employers in the region, and the loss of jobs was reflected in the lack of local support for Navalny during his trial. There are certainly many questions to be asked about quite what Navalny thought he was doing, and it reveals a frighteningly chaotic state of affairs in the Kirov region.

Opalev was clearly a broken man, and his evidence was at times confused, but the judge nevertheless called it trustworthy and reliable. Opalev is clearly the greatest victim of the intrusion of inexperienced Muscovites onto his territory. Another is Ofitserov, who hoped to put the Vyatka timber business on a firmer commercial basis. Ultimately, the attempt to impose neo-liberal market nostrums onto traditional neo-Soviet relationships destroyed everything. In his closing statement on 5 July Navalny called on the judge not to convict Ofitserov, who had become a 'hostage by accident'. A father of five, already a quarter of his flat in Moscow's suburbs had been sequestered. 'This is why I call on you, even in the context of an obviously political order [*zakaz*], a political trial, not to take steps which are obviously excessive'.[22] Navalny vowed to destroy Putin's 'feudal system of power', in which '83% of the national wealth belongs to 0.5% of the country'. He characterised it as an 'occupying power', pilfering the country of billions of dollars and leading Russia down a path of vodka-fuelled degradation.[23] Prosecutors asked for a six-year sentence, below the possible ten-year maximum, but enough to keep him out of the way for the next series of regional and national elections. In the event, on 18 July he was sentenced to five years, while Ofitserov got four. Some 10,000 Muscovites demonstrated in Navalny's favour on 18 July when news of his conviction came through, and the following day he was released on bail.

The dilemma of what the resistance should do remained. Michael Idov, the editor of *GQ Russia*, argued:

> Just as in September 2011, when Putin's return shocked into protest the Russians lulled by Medvedev's talk of modernisation, my friends and I are realising again how optimistic we had been. Russia has joined the list of countries with an imprisoned opposition leader. The worst-case scenario is, in fact, here. ... All routes to peaceful change have been cut. For now, the overriding feeling is helplessness, tinged with shame for the last year of passivity.[24]

The writer Boris Akunin was equally pessimistic, arguing that there was now little hope of changing Russia by democratic means: 'Lifetime deprivation of elections, this is what the verdict means not only for Navalny but for all those who thought it was possible to change this through elections'.[25] Khodorkovsky was rather more positive:[26]

Until we realise that the trials of Navalny, Bolotnaya and hundreds of thousands of other guiltlessly convicted people are our trials, they are just going to keep on locking us up, one at a time. The era of unbelief and indifference is ending.

The Kirovles case gave Navalny the unique chance to bring together the different strands in the opposition, ranging from liberals to patriots, but Navalny's abrasive style and cutting comments lost him the sympathy of many of his potential supporters. Old guard democrats like Ryzhkov barely remain polite when mentioning Navalny's name. The next day, in an unprecedented move, Navalny and Ofitserov were allowed out on bail while their appeal was pending. The trial had economic costs, with the markets dropping sharply on the news of the imprisonment. Capital flight continued unabated, and according to the Central Bank $54bn left in 2012 and $38bn in the first six months of 2013. Foreign direct investment was relatively low, and although $51bn came in 2012, much of this was money returning from Cyprus and other off-shores. The poor investment climate would not help the new three-year privatisation programme announced by Medvedev at that time. VLK had been engaged in normal brokerage work, and when the court suggested that such activities were outside the law, it struck at the very heart of a market economy. Nevertheless, economic factors have always been secondary in Putin's Russia. Navalny's release revealed the contradictions within the Putin system. Ten years earlier Khodorkovsky had been hounded mercilessly, but now the case exposed the struggles between the Investigative Committee and GPO, between the hardliners seeking revenge on Navalny and those within the regime who understood the massive reputational damage the case inflicted on Russia. Ryzhkov noted that 'The Kremlin elite have split into two warring groups: the *siloviki* and the political strategists'. The former include Bastrykin and the FSB eager to punish the opposition leaders, while the latter encompassed Volodin and those who tried to shift to non-coercive forms of political management.[27] Even Putin, speaking at the Seliger youth camp on 2 August, called it 'strange' that one person – Opalev – had been given a four and a half-year suspended sentence, while a second – Navalny – was given a real term of five years.[28]

Navalny, moreover, had been registered as a candidate in the Moscow mayoral election (see below). Sobyanin was looking for a 'model' clean and legitimate victory, possibly for its own sake and certainly to allow him to position himself as someone with genuine democratic legitimacy in any possible succession struggle. Navalny's removal from the candidate list on dubious economic charges would have long-term damaging consequences. The authorities had no single view on how to deal with the challenge, and these divisions now came to the fore. In the appeal hearing on 16 October the verdict on Navalny and Ofitserov was upheld but commuted to suspended sentences, allowing the defendants to return home. Amendments to the Criminal Code in July 2013 stipulated that convicted people have to wait eight rather than the earlier six years for the 'criminal record' of serious crimes to be expunged, barring Navalny from running for public office for that period. A law signed by Putin in 2012 imposed a lifetime ban on all ex-convicts, including those with suspended sentences, from running for public office, which the Constitutional Court on 10 October found to be unconstitutional, and called on parliament to set a time limit.[29]

Constraints

After the humiliations endured in the succession campaign, the mood of many United Russia deputies in the Sixth Duma was vengeful. One of the most extreme was Yevgeny Fedorov, who argued that real power lay not in Putin's hands but in the State Department in Washington. In his view, the United States occupied Russia and turned it into a colony, and Putin was leading a national liberation struggle to free the country. This was too much even for United Russia, and there were threats to deprive him of his seat.[30] The idea that the Washington 'obkom' (regional committee) was managing Russian affairs became something of an obsession for radical traditionalists. Their paranoia was stimulated by an equally aggressive mood in certain circles in Washington. For example, in its *Freedom in the World 2013* report Freedom House noted that its findings were particularly grim for Eurasian countries: 'Russia took a decided turn for the worse after Vladimir Putin's return to the presidency. Having already marginalized the formal political opposition, he enacted a series of laws meant to squelch a burgeoning societal opposition.' This was fair enough, but the report urged the United States 'to demonstrate leadership in the struggle for freedom'. It criticised 'both the Obama administration and the Republican opposition for a reluctance to provide that leadership'. Russia was categorised as 'Not free', and given a freedom rating of 5.5 (on a scale of 1–7, with 7 the worst), a civil liberties rating of 5, and a political rights rating of 6.[31] Calls for 'leadership in the struggle for freedom' was what the new edition of the *Foreign Policy Concept*, adopted on 12 February 2013, no doubt had in mind when it lamented the 'reideologisation of international relations', noting that this had a negative effect on the 'strengthening of global stability'.[32] The Concept in effect systematised Putin's earlier programmatic article on foreign policy.

In this context, it is hardly surprising that the State Duma passed a raft of repressive legislation. Much of it was initiated by Mikhail Starshinov, a former Just Russia deputy who had gone over to United Russia and there quickly made his name as a backbencher ready to sponsor the harshest measures against non-conformity. He authored the law that allowed opt-outs from gubernatorial elections, the law on the registration of NGOs as 'foreign agents', and he had even tried (with Andrei Lugovoi, allegedly implicated in the murder of Alexander Litvinenko in London) to introduce 'Pozners' law'. This was in response to the legendary talk show host Vladimir Pozner's apparent slip of the tongue on 23 December 2012, when he had called the State Duma the 'State Dura' ('state fool'). The measure would have banned journalists who hold foreign citizenship from working on state television if they criticised Russia, and imposed controls over the salaries of journalists who held another citizenship as well as that of Russia. Fëdorov even submitted a bill to forbid government employees from marrying foreigners, reminiscent of Stalin's similar ban in 1947. These two measures were not adopted, but they revealed the punitive ethos raging in United Russia and allied ranks. It also reflected the legislative bacchanalia reigning in this Duma. At the end of the summer session in 2013, 56 laws were adopted in one go, many of them ill-thought-out and contradictory. For example, one stipulated that men were prohibited from taking on government jobs if they had not first completed their compulsory military service, but since this is not compulsory in the North Caucasus, if the law was applied no police or civil servants would remain.[33]

In November 2012 Putin signed into law provisions that required NGOs in receipt of funding from abroad to register as 'foreign agents' or face fines of up to R500,000 ($16,000). The term in Russian unequivocally suggests working in the interests of foreign powers (in other words, a 'spy'), and evoked an intense reaction among Russia's NGO community. Earlier, on 11 September 2012 the Kremlin ordered the US Agency for International Development (USAID) to close by 1 October, entailing the removal of its 13 officials employed in Russia, and an uncertain fate for the 60 local people employed by the agency. The Ministry of Foreign Affairs bluntly accused USAID of meddling in domestic politics and deviating from its stated goals.[34] The Kremlin had clearly been annoyed by USAID's funding for Golos, the election monitoring NGO that had trained some 50,000 election monitors who provided evidence of widespread ballot-rigging. Since 2000 Golos had received some $9m in western funding, including from the National Democracy Institute and the right-wing International Republican Institute. In February 2013 11 Russian NGOs, including the Moscow Helsinki Group, lodged a complaint with the European Court of Human Rights against the law.

At a meeting of the board of the FSB in February 2013, Putin expressed indignation, on national security grounds, that the 'foreign agents' law was not being implemented even though it had come into effect on 1 January. His statement launched a wave of inspections, and by July 2013 the premises of some 2,000 NGOs across the country had been searched, often in a brutal manner, with 500 violations allegedly found, and legal action was started against 36 of them.[35] Golos was the first NGO to be prosecuted under the new law, and another 60 faced mandatory closure if they refused to incriminate themselves as 'foreign agents'. Some 300 NGOs from March 2013 were subjected to exhaustive checks by tax officials, prosecutors and the justice ministry. The Moscow School of Political Studies, long a training ground for talented young politicians and administrators from across Russia, was one of those forced to register as a foreign agent. On 25 April 2013 the Presnensky Court fined Golos and its head, Liliya Shibanova, for not complying with the NGO law and on 26 June the Justice Ministry closed it down for six months. Both fines were paid, but Shibanova insisted that the verdicts were illegal and that Golos would not register as a foreign agent. Golos appealed to the

European Court of Human Rights, and vowed to continue its work as a temporary NGO. Another leading NGO facing sanctions was Russia's earliest and largest human rights organization, Memorial, as well as the country's major independent polling agency, the Levada Centre. The Centre had broken away from Russia's oldest opinion research institute, VTsIOM, after the regime imposed a new management in 2003.

In an interview with German television on 5 April 2013 Putin claimed that over 28 billion roubles ($870 million) had been transferred from abroad to Russian NGOs in the four months since the law on foreign agents had been adopted, including some $26.5 million through diplomatic missions, but when pressed for a breakdown of these astonishing figures, none was forthcoming. Western foundations were winding up their work in Russia, since NGOs now feared to approach them. The sums earmarked to support Russian NGOs (in 2013, $258 million) were clearly insufficient to compensate, and in any case were subject to budget cuts.[36] The violence attending the expulsion of the Movement for Human Rights from their offices on the night of 21/22 June 2013, including a physical assault on its veteran leader, the 71-year-old Lev Ponomarev, was clearly intimidating. The NGO, created in 1997, defended business people facing trumped up charges, helped resolved disputes with employers, and assisted convicts to find work after their release. The organization had a long record of opposing human rights violations and had forcefully argued that the two trials against Khodorkovsky were politically motivated. At issue was the extension of the lease, and the rent had apparently been paid up to 1 August, so the suddenness and violence of the attack, with offices ransacked and staff humiliated, came as a shock.[37] By August over 60 human rights and other NGOs had been deemed to be 'foreign agents', four had been fined, and 20 more had a month to re-register or face trial.

By characterizing NGOs as potentially disloyal and unpatriotic, the law clearly sought to drive a wedge between society and independent NGOs. The administration insisted that the law was modelled on America's 1938 Foreign Agents Registration Act (FARA), with Putin arguing that 'The new law adopted late last year in Russia stipulates that non-governmental organisations engaged in Russia's internal political processes and sponsored from abroad must be registered as foreign agents. ... This is not an innovation in international politics. A similar law has been in operation in the United States since 1938.' He claimed that there were 654 NGOs in Russia funded from abroad to the tune of R28.3bn, nearly $1bn, a figure questioned by NGOs.[38] In the same interview Putin accepted that opposition was important, but it had to abide by the rules and use peaceful demonstrations and the ballot box, and warned 'Northern Africa is a vivid example of what chaos leads to'. He said nothing about what the opposition should do when the vote is rigged. As for the NGO law, Russian legislation was far more all-encompassing than the American one. Under two dozen criminal cases were prosecuted under FARA during the war, and an amendment in 1966 greatly restricted the meaning of 'foreign agent' to those acting 'at the order, request, or under the direction or control, of a foreign principal' and was engaged 'in political activities for or in the interests of such foreign principal'. There was thus no targeting of NGOs, and even political NGOs based abroad or with foreign funding do not have to register as foreign agents since they do not act 'in the interests of a foreign principal'.[39]

These directly political laws were reinforced by a range of socially repressive legislation, much of it shaped by Elena Mizulina, head of the Duma committee on family, women and children, as well as her close associate, the deputy head of the committee Olga Batalina, couched in the language of 'protection' and the promotion of Russian family values. Mizulina left Yabloko in 2001, before joining Just Russia in 2007. On 11 June 2013 the Duma adopted an 'anti-gay propaganda' law, intended ostensibly to protect children against 'The spread of information directed at minors in the form of non-traditional sexual arrangements, the attraction of non-traditional sexual relations, the distorted perception of social equivalency between traditional and non-traditional sexual relations'. The law did not define what was meant by 'non-traditional', providing broad latitude for the authorities to define it as they saw fit. Already ten cities had adopted laws against promoting homosexuality among minors, the first on 24 May 2006 in Ryazan. The legislation revealed the culture war raging in Russia about sexual and gender diversity, and exposed the homophobia prevalent in United Russia, with the support of the Russian Orthodox Church. Earlier we described the pressure against the LGBT community as evidence of the neo-traditionalist turn in Russian affairs. The law prompted a wave of homophobic vigilantism, but at the same time it stimulated the most profound debate over the issue since Russia decriminalised male homosexuality in April 1993.[40]

On the same day a 'blasphemy law' was adopted, extending Article 148 of the Criminal Code, designed to defend the feelings of believers by banning 'Public actions which convey clear disrespect toward society and absolute in their purpose to offend the religious feelings of believers'. The bill had been introduced following Pussy Riot's 'punk prayer', a performance that infuriated traditionalists and provoked a slew of conservative legislation. The insult to believers' feeling was at the time ranked only as an administrative offence, but now became subject to criminal liability with up to three years in jail. The definition of anti-religious extremism was so vague as to be liable to be used against any type of criticism. Even the Public Chamber refused to endorse the law, arguing that it contradicted the principles of the constitution and international law. More surprisingly, even the Kremlin feared that the screws would be tightened too far. A proposed bill by United Russia deputy Yevgeny Fedorov's to force media publications and TV stations that receive over half of their funding from foreign sources to register as 'foreign agents', as NGOs, was quashed by the authorities.[41] Not all the anti-reforms came from above but expressed genuine revulsion amongst the Putinite rank and file at western-style liberalism.

The spirit of anti-cosmopolitanism was clear, and represented an extension of Putinite 'order' into the personal sphere, an arena into which it had not previously ventured in such a prescriptive manner. The 'epidemic of prohibition' according to Alexander Rubtsov encompassed the ban on smoking and on pavement parking and represented 'disciplinary techniques' intended to encourage a culture of self-limitation, including in politics. It was also designed to give the appearance of regime activity, and thus to forestall comparisons with the stagnation of the Brezhnev years. In fact, the 'unprecedented lawmaking activity mainly of a political and moralising nature' with a smack of ideology only reinforced the ties with Mikhail Suslov's era.[42] The conservative shift in ideology and its alignment with Orthodox values represented an attempt to provide a cultural basis to the regime, but only reinforced the filiations with Tsar Nicholas I's retrograde and ultimately catastrophic reign.

Responding to the widespread concerns about unregulated labour migration, a detention camp was set up outside Moscow for allegedly illegal immigrants in mid-2013. In the first sweeps of markets and other places where labour migrants were concentrated, many Vietnamese citizens were swept up into the camp, many of whom were legally registered to live in Moscow. Not surprisingly, relations with Vietnam sharply deteriorated. There are three levels to the labour migration issue in Russia. External migration from what is conventionally called the 'far abroad' is regulated using the normal gamut of international norms including visas and work permits. Migration from the 'near abroad' can also be regulated in that way, but is made trickier by the range of preferences given to CIS citizens, including for long periods a visa-free regime. This allows a mass influx of labour migrants from Central Asia, many of whom are employed in low-paid jobs in Moscow's booming construction sector. The third is internal migration, with the Russian constitution guaranteeing the right of free movement within the country. A number of incidents in 2013 exposed the volatility of relations. In the small town of Pugachev in the Saratov region the population effectively took the law in their own hands in July following the killing of a young trooper, Ruslan Marzhanov, allegedly by a 16-year-old Chechen youth. In October, nationalist riots followed the murder of a Russian in the Moscow suburb of Biryulovo.

Such incidents, coming on the heels of the Manezh riots of December 2010, fanned xenophobic sentiments and an anti-immigrant backlash. The killing of Spartak fan Egor Sviridov and the release of the alleged Caucasian perpetrators provoked 2,500 far-right activists to gather in Manezh Square, in the shadow of the Kremlin, on 11 December 2010. Following attacks on dark-skinned passers-by, the police intervened, but had to call on reinforcements to win the subsequent vicious battle. The attack by traders in the Matveev market on 28 July on a policeman trying to arrest a Dagestani man suspected of raping a 15-year-old girl led to the detention of all those in the market without the appropriate papers, and exposed the network of corrupt relationships between the police, bureaucrats and traders. Planned legislation to control the so-called 'rubber apartments', in which hundreds of migrants are registered but do not live, would have forced people to live only at their official place of residence, potentially rendering tens of thousands of perfectly honest citizens criminally liable.

At this time the Moscow police chief, Anatoly Yakunin, suddenly announced that 'in Moscow 50 per cent of all crimes are committed by individuals coming from other areas. Out of this number, 22 per cent of crimes occur with the involvement of foreign nationals. 20 per cent of crimes are committed by individuals that mostly come from Central Asia'.[43] Official statistics suggest that one in seven murders and half the rapes in Moscow are committed by immigrants, but others contend that this is not out of proportion with demographic data. By pandering to radical nationalists by opening a temporary detention centre at Golyanovo, which was swiftly dubbed a 'concentration camp', the authorities failed to deal with the underlying problem of managing normal processes of labour migration and population movement. This reflected Putin's own confusion in addressing the 'national question', as in his text on the subject before the presidential election. Nationalism and xenophobia entered mainstream politics, threatening the integrity of the country. As Ryzhkov notes, 'Twice in its history, a surge in ethnic nationalism combined with other systemic problems has led to this country's collapse: once in 1917 and again in 1991'.[44]

The opposition posed little of a frontal threat to the regime, yet it was able to score some victories. In early 2013 Navalny exposed the ownership of properties in Miami worth over $2m by United Russia deputy and chair of the ethics committee, Vladimir Pekhtin, who was forced to resign not only his post but also his parliamentary seat. Pekhtin insisted that he owned 'practically nothing' in the way of property abroad, provoking a wave of sarcastic commentary to the effect that Russian elections are 'practically free' and that 'Khodorkovsky is practically free'. Another two United Russia deputies followed shortly thereafter, for similar reasons. The hypocrisy of State Duma member Alexander Sidyakin was the subject of particular commentary. An avowed America-basher and the author of some of the most notorious of the repressive bills in 2012, the law on public rallies and the foreign agents law, Sidyakin spent his vacations travelling through America. Despite facing a raft of criminal accusations, Navalny was still able to deploy an army of on-line volunteers to expose details of property owned by the Russian elite abroad. The regime was willing to use this information for its own purposes. It had decided on new methods of managing the elite, against the background of intensified power-sharing tensions within the leadership. In conditions of economic slow-down there were fewer rents to distribute, exposing those with unexplained wealth to greater scrutiny. Putin feared the emergence of a more fractious elite and mobilised society.

Putin relied increasingly on an inner guard of loyal subordinates while appealing to a conservative majority in the country. Putin endorsed more populist policies, including attacks on loyal Putinites, to retain mass support. Constraints were imposed on officials, a policy that became known as the 'nationalisation of the elites', and reflected Putin's de-offshorisation programme announced in December 2012. On 19 May 2013 legislation came into effect banning state officials, their spouses and under-age children from holding bank accounts abroad or foreign-issued stocks or bonds. The original proposals envisaged the ban extending to any foreign assets, but this was softened during the passage of the law and now ownership of property abroad is allowed as long as it is declared, as well as the origin of the money used to buy the real estate. Laws on income and spending declarations were also tightened, accompanied by a push to prevent Duma deputies combining their parliamentary status with business activities. The Kremlin feared that if officials kept their money abroad, they would become vulnerable to foreign pressure. This was in line with Putin's call for the 'de-offshoreisation' of the Russian economy announced in his December 2012 address to the Federal Assembly (see below), but it was also about ensuring that officials had an unchallenged stake in maintaining the regime.

The 'nationalisation of the elites' was part of a broader reconfiguration of the power system. Political and property insecurity in Russia encouraged the elite to keep their wealth abroad, creating what Ryzhkov called an 'offshore aristocracy', with much of the money not earned through entrepreneurship but through kickbacks and bribes. The elite treated 'the motherland as a type of colony'.[45] Putin's speech calling for 'de-offshorisation' and subsequent measures forcing officials to repatriate their wealth represented a fundamental change in the rules of the game. With no foreign bolt hole available, those in the elite sympathetic to opposition views were now more beholden to the Kremlin. By August nine senators had resigned, preferring to hang on to their foreign assets than serve the people. Thirty-nine deputies by then had moved their assets to Russia, as had Chubais, who sold his shares in foreign companies. Roman Abramovich responded to the foreign asset ban by relinquishing his post as speaker of the Chukotka parliament, no doubt with a sigh of relief. The ban effectively deprived key political figures and the bureaucracy of independence, since their assets in Russia were always vulnerable to the depredations of the regime and thus their loyalty could now be enforced. The measure was in part a response to the Magnitsky act, but it signalled above all the broader 'conservative revolution' and a return to Russia's patrimonial tradition. Putin reshaped his base, even though this entailed alienating part of his traditional elite supporters. Framed as part of an anti-corruption drive, the initiative was blunted by a spate of divorces, the placing of foreign assets in trusts, and numerous other loopholes.

At the heart of the regime's new political strategy was the attempt to ensure that the elite remained in line, and to deter regime defection. The leadership moreover understood that it was in danger of becoming the object of popular hostility; hence its attempt to be seen disciplining its own officials, while removing a safety hatch for them to bail out if things got tough in Russia. There were three elements to the new strategy. First, the regime understood that perceptions of corruption within the regime threatened the stability of the system in its entirety. For this reason Serdyukov had been jettisoned, and a sustained anti-corruption campaign launched within the bureaucracy. Second, the dominant party was subjected to the sharpest purge, in a pattern that other authoritarian systems had long practised of cleansing its own ranks. Third, the purge encompassed the old generation of leaders, and in the centre and regions a new cadre of loyal Putinists was being forged. With the ban on foreign holdings and bank accounts, Putin sought to 'nationalise' the elites to avoid the threat of defection. This was accompanied by some significant changes in the constellation of power, with some major shifts in the relative standing of some top officials. All this suggests that a new type of Putinism was taking shape.

Co-optation

Faced by a perceived threat from 'colour revolutions', Surkov in 2005 created the Nashi ('Ours') youth organisation, which along with some other such groups was designed to occupy public space and pre-empt an occupation of the streets along the lines of the Orange revolution in Kiev the previous autumn. The regime thereby revealed its own vulnerability, since the conditions for a similar popular mobilisation at that time were absent. The idea of Washington using 'orange techniques' to achieve regime change in Russia was simply fanciful: not that such techniques did not exist, but the internal political configuration, with Putin riding high in the polls, would not allow external influence to shape the political conjuncture. For Medvedev, such militant youth organisations were clearly distasteful, especially when they launched various campaigns of harassment, notably against the columnist Alexander Podrabinek. Volodin for very different reasons disliked Nashi, having disapproved of the previous policy of forcing Nashi members on to United Russia's electoral lists. In keeping with his policy of regularising the elements making up the stability system, Volodin planned to institutionalise the movement. He had no plans to give up the use of para-societal movements to dominate the streets, but would draw on more disciplined bodies such as 'Orthodox' activists and even Cossack volunteers.[46]

The All-Russia People's Front (ONF) had been created in May 2011 as a personal vehicle for Putin in the forthcoming elections, bringing together trade unions, business groups and around 2,000 other organisations, such as Russian Railways, in a loose pact in support of the regime. On 12 June 2013 Putin assumed by acclamation the leadership of the ONF, which at the same congress was renamed the People's Front for Russia (PFR). This was the first time that Putin had joined a political organisation since he had left the Communist Party in 1991, and since then had only identified himself with a political movement at elections. He had taken on the leadership of United Russia without actually becoming a member. Now the Front was focused on Putin personally, and was to act as a general purpose vehicle for mobilisation and as a sounding device to assess popular concerns. The congress resolved that membership henceforth would only be sought on an individual basis. The front's programme and budget remained unclear, but now had a 55-member central staff headed by three co-chairs: film director Stanislav Govorukhin, Delovaya Rossiya co-chair Alexander Galushka and State Duma deputy and TV journalist Olga Timofeyeva. There was a notable representation of younger members and blue collar workers in an attempt to distance itself from the elitist character of United Russia. As with the creation of para-constitutional bodies earlier, PFR was another top-down organisation but with a para-societal orientation (like the Public Chamber). It mimicked the work of bottom-up civil society associations and thereby acted as a spoiler. At the time of the protests it had organised counter-rallies in support of Putin, and then launched an anti-corruption campaign that mimicked the work of Navalny's anti-corruption endeavours.

Above all, the People's Front was to compensate for the declining popularity of United Russia. Although the party held 238 of the 450 seats in the Sixth Duma, its reputation was irredeemably tarnished as little more than a pedestal party for the Kremlin, with no clear programme of its own and with its various platforms united in little more than the search for political advancement and personal enrichment. Putin's popularity was relatively stable at around 60 per cent, but United Russia's approval rating, which four years earlier had also been at that level, now barely exceeded 35 per cent, while in Moscow it struggled to reach the 20 per cent mark. Although the PFR claimed not to be political, 87 of the 238 deputies who entered the Duma on the United Russia ticket in December 2011 had been included on the party's candidate lists through the Front. Reform to the electoral system would once again allow candidates to fight in single-member seats in the 2016 parliamentary election. Pro-regime 'independents' sponsored by the PFR could by-pass United Russia to enter parliament. Sobyanin had been appointed Moscow mayor in September 2010 but only joined United Russia in 2012, and then fought his (re)-election campaign in 2013 as an independent. This was typical of many regime supporters and United Russia members who run as independent candidates in local and regional elections to avoid being tainted by association with the 'party of thieves and swindlers'. The Front targeted the 12 to 16 per cent of the electorate who support Putin but do not vote for United Russia.[47] United Russia remained a key electoral instrument and parliamentary voting machine, but the PFR could position itself as an anti-bureaucratic popular organisation. The aim was to consolidate the conservative Putinite majority against the 'disaffected urbanites'.

Tatyana Stanovaya notes that the PFR is made up of four constituencies. The first is the group of Putin's election proxies, his authorised representatives who are usually stood down after the campaign but which in December 2012 were transformed into a permanent institution. With the declining efficacy of United Russia, this group of well-known figures would mediate between Putin and his electorate. The second group comprises leading cultural and scientific figures. In a practice reminiscent of the Soviet period, representatives of women's councils, trade unions, veterans' association, youth organisations, scientific bodies, blue collar workers and many others would be permanently co-opted to work in the Front. And as in the Soviet period, much of this was formalistic, intended to give an illusion of close communication with the electorate. The PFR established local offices in all of Russia's regions, with the same structure as at the centre, and was explicitly tasked with controlling the government. This was substitutionism taken to the extreme, undermining both elected legislative bodies and now executive bodies as well. It also potentially marginalised the third core group in the PFR, representatives of the dominant party. Key members of United Russia joined the PFR's central staff, including the secretary of United Russia's General Council Sergei Neverov, the head of United Russia's Duma caucus Vladimir Vasiliev, and senior General Council members Olga Batalina and Irina Yarovaya. This was the first step in a potential fusion of the two bodies. The fourth constituency comprised loyalist political parties. The central staff included representatives from the Patriots of Russia, and Rodina, now chaired by Alexei Zhuravlev, but formerly led by Rogozin. By creating the PFR the regime sought to present a fresh face to the public, but reflected the way that all of the existing formal and informal institutions had been sidelined. As Stanovaya puts it, 'The transformation of the ARPF [PFR] into a movement is the regime's reaction to the demolition of key government institutions, the erosion of confidence regarding these institutions, and deep-seated shifts in the public mind'.[48]

The new body represented a corporatist response to the problem of managing political pluralism, and was reminiscent of an analogous body in the GDR, where Putin had spent five years in the late 1980s. The practices of managed democracy typical of classical Putinism now gave way to new forms of political management. The Front's development was yet another instance of the Putinite tendency to create structures that functionally duplicated existing institutions, and thereby reduced their administrative capacity. The creation of public chambers sought to overcome the inadequacy of the representative and feedback functions of elected legislatures at all levels. The ONF now suffered from a critical overloading of functions, acting as 'a party, a government, a presidential council, and think tank', seeking to compensate for the 'dysfunctionality of traditional democratic and administrative institutions'. The problem was not some sort of eternal 'Russian curse' but reflected the absence of competition, 'which gives life to institutions', and for that some 'meaningful dynamics in the "regime-opposition" system' had to be restored; otherwise the attempt to co-opt politicians into 'de facto non-functional institutions', like the ONF, would be of limited utility. 'If opposition is perceived as one of the natural states of the political elite then the regime does not fear losing, it doesn't try to grasp the ungraspable and focuses on establishing contact predominantly with its own electorate, and seeks to implement its own ideas more boldly.'[49]

Conviction

On 25 April 2013 Putin held his eleventh televised 'direct line' question and answer session, setting a record in answering 85 questions in four hours and

47 minutes.[50] This was his first since being re-elected president, since the event was not staged the previous year. The format differed from earlier ones, with fewer outside TV links and most questions came from the studio, including some invited guests. The occasion had long been his favoured mode of communication with the Russian people. Putin dislikes the hurly burly of an election campaign, so the direct line allows him to assume a naturalised position of authority and to speak as the teacher to a class, the patron to the supplicant, and the wise leader to a grateful nation. Notions such as 'sovereign democracy' were now redundant, as was Surkov himself, and instead Putin became the ideologist of the regime as well as its personification, reflected in the shift in his own image from 'effective manager' to 'father of the nation'.

Given the turbulence of the succession, Putin sought to use the opportunity to re-assert his authority on Russian politics. There were repeated references to tensions between the Kremlin and the government. Putin noted that he would not respond to calls to sack the prime minister, Medvedev, but the government would have to adopt stimulus measures to improve economic growth. Commenting on the 15 April Boston marathon bombings by the Tsarnaev brothers that killed three people and injured 282 others, he insisted that 'Russia is a victim of international terrorism too', and condemned what he perceived as double standards: 'I was always appalled when our western partners and the western media described the terrorist, who committed bloody crimes in our country, "insurgents", and almost never "terrorists".' He called on Russia and the United States to increase co-operation over security, but in comments following the session he insisted that Russia is not trying to spoil relations with anyone, but 'It is necessary to respect Russian society, our traditions, our culture and the laws of the Russian Federation'.

In what was clearly a demonstrative gesture, Kudrin was in the audience and Putin twice referred to him in complimentary terms as 'the best finance minister in the world'. The former finance minister condemned the sluggish economy: 'Today we do not have a programme for freeing our economy from its dependence on oil, a programme in which every measure would have its proper place: money, institutional and structural reforms, and the role of the regions. That's the problem, Vladimir Vladimirovich! I am not ready to be in charge of inertial processes and to micromanage the economy. I want to do real work'. In response, Putin called him a fine economist but this did not mean that he was the best 'social development minister' or politician, given the need to temper economic reform with social protection for the vulnerable. Putin jokingly called him a 'slacker'. Another critical voice in the audience was that of Alexei Venediktov, chief editor at the *Ekho Moskvy* radio station. The repressive tone of many of the questions made Putin look relatively liberal. Venediktov noted that 'Your agents are rather bloodthirsty: one is demanding that Serdyukov be jailed, another that Chubais be imprisoned'. He suggested that the imprisonment of Pussy Riot members, the Navalny trial, other prosecutions and the NGO law were reminiscent of the Stalin period. Putin rebutted the charge that the prosecutions were politically motivated. 'These girls from Pussy Riot and these youngsters who desecrate the graves of our soldiers must all be equal before the law and must be held responsible for their actions.' He argued that Stalinism was characterised by the gulag and the cult of personality, whereas there was no such cult in Russia today, although he insisted that the country required order, discipline and equality before the law.

As for Navalny, Putin's sensitivity was once again on display: 'If you fight corruption, you have to be squeaky clean yourself, otherwise it can all turn into self-promotion and political advertising. Everyone must be equal before the law. ... No one should be under any illusion that just because they spend their time shouting 'Stop thief' that they can get away with theft themselves'. Once again, as in the second Khodorkovsky trial, Putin veered towards interference in judicial matters. Putin defended the regime against charges of corruption, although he used the occasion once again to traduce Chubais: 'I am not going to defend Mr Chubais. Moreover, he is my opponent on many issues (although he has told me many times that he does not get involved in politics, I can see that this is not the case)'. He announced that CIA agents acted as consultants to Chubais in the 1990s, and argued that 'intelligence officers' had been prosecuted in the America for illegally 'enriching' themselves. It is not clear what Putin had in mind. Two Harvard USAID academics who had advised the Russian government during the transition, Andrei Shleifer and Jonathan Hay, had indeed been accused of making illegal investments in Russia while working in Moscow, charges that they denied, and there was nothing to link them to the CIA. Putin conceded that 'many mistakes' had been made during privatisation in Russia, but he praised Chubais and the other reformers for their 'courage' in taking what they deemed necessary measures, and rejected calls for their imprisonment.

Much of the session was devoted to bread and butter issues, such as salaries for medical workers, pension questions, as well as rising tariffs for housing and communal services (a matter for regional authorities). The whole show had a staged character. Like a medieval Passion play, it was designed to propagate homilies, to pass judgement on good and evil, and to assert the power of the virtuous over the damned. Direct lines have been held since 2001, and although there was talk in autumn 2012 of abandoning them, the event proved too useful to be dropped. Like all majoritarian leaders, Putin was allowed free rein to assert himself as the 'national leader', displaying dazzling knowledge of arcane matters while demonstrating his closeness to the people, accentuated by a healthy dose of bureaucracy-bashing and attacks on select members of the elite. The concentration of power in the hands of a single 'sovereign' was now made clear. Potential challengers, including paradoxically Medvedev's government, were not only neutralised but delegitimated.

At the St Petersburg Economic Forum on 21 June 2013 Putin insisted that 'Russia's top priority is to create the conditions for sustained economic growth', to be based on the three pillars of 'increasing labour productivity, investment and innovation'. He was obviously alarmed by the sluggish economy, with growth of only 3.4 per cent in 2012. Inflation had fallen to a historic post-communist low of 6.1 per cent in 2011, but thereafter crept up to over 7 per cent in 2013. By announcing a limit to the growth in tariffs of infrastructure monopolies to the inflation rate of the previous year, he hoped both to defuse popular anger at the rising cost of utilities and to curb inflation. Bowing to pressure from the left, Putin announced that $14bn of the resources accumulated in the National Welfare Fund would be invested in infrastructure development. In July 2013 the fund held some $85bn, essentially drawn from oil and gas revenues. In August the economic development ministry announced that half of the Fund would be used for infrastructure projects. Plans included a high-speed train service between Moscow and Kazan, a new Central Ring Road around Moscow between 30–70 kilometres from the existing Moscow Ring Road (MKAD), and an upgrade of the Trans-Siberian Railway, one of the longest in the world that would act as 'a key artery between Europe and the Asia-Pacific region', help develop Siberia and the Far East, and tap into 'fast-growing Asian markets'.

A new bridge across the Amur would stimulate Russo-Chinese trade. There would also be new pipeline developments in the Far East. In a deal worth an unprecedented $270bn signed with the China National Petroleum Corporation (CNPC) at the Forum, Rosneft contracted to deliver up to 45m tonnes of oil a year for the next 25 years. The independent Novatek company also signed an agreement with CNPC to cooperate on the Yamal LNG project based on a long-term contract to supply China. Although shale gas was not on the agenda, its potential 'game-changing' effect was the main topic of informal discussions. Putin concluded with a discussion of governance issues, noting that the People's Front could be used to protect borrowers' rights. He endorsed the proposal by the Commissioner for Entrepreneurs' Rights, Boris Titov (a post whose creation had been announced at the Forum the previous year), for an amnesty on first convictions for economic offenses, for those who agreed to compensate for damages.[51] Titov had been given extensive powers with the right to shape legislation in an attempt to improve the business environment. After considerable discussion leading to the significant narrowing of the categories, the amnesty law came into effect on 4 July 2013. It was to last six months and was expected to cover 6–8,000 prisoners. Titov estimated that 16,000 were serving sentences for economic crimes, but the amnesty only covered first time offenders who agree to compensate the damages inflicted by their crime. Unlike in previous years when the Forum had been dominated by liberal economists, the event was organised by Sechin, with a marked statist economic orientation. A state-sponsored but market-oriented developmental strategy was in the making, accompanied by paternalistic welfare and social policies.

At the forum Putin announced plans for the merger of the Supreme Court and the Supreme Arbitration Court, and in October 2013 introduced a bill to that effect. At the time the arbitration court had only 53 sitting judges out of a maximum of 90 allowed, and the number of judges in the new Supreme

Court would rise from 125 to 170 judges, appointed by a special qualification board. The new court would move to St Petersburg to join the Constitutional Court. The move prompted speculation that the head of the merged body would be an appropriate post for Medvedev, but at the same time the reform weakened Medvedev by removing one of his few remaining top level allies.[52] Just as with 'reform' of the Russian Academy of Sciences implemented at this time, the plan aroused powerful opposition. The two courts had very different functions and operated in different ways. The arbitration court, headed by Medvedev's associate Anton Ivanov, is a model of effective jurisprudence. The plan to create a single supreme judicial body, to deal with civil, criminal and administrative cases as well as to adjudicate economic disputes, was less a merger than a takeover by the Supreme Court, and in effect represented another example of raiding that would destroy one of the few successful instances of judicial reform. It intensified the centralisation of the judicial system that had been under way for over a decade. This was yet another example of a 'reform' that had a destructive character, building on the sharp reduction of jury court jurisdiction, the abolition of the two-chamber structure of the Constitutional Court, and the replacement of the election by the nomination of the chair of the Constitutional Court.[53]

A number of other moments of disarray accompanied Putin's return. Yakunin was head of the board of trustees of the Centre for the Complex Analysis and Public Administration, founded in 2006, which sought to 'help the Russian authorities [*vlast'*] by increasing the efficiency of state management', based on the principles of 'social humanism'.[54] The Centre endured a severe blow to its reputation in 2013 when Stepan Sulakshin, effectively the Centre's director, issued a report 'The Electoral System and Progress of the State' detailing electoral fraud in the December 2011 parliamentary election. Based on sophisticated mathematical modelling, it unequivocally announced that the CPRF had won the election with 25–30 per cent of the total, with United Russia coming in second with some 20–25 per cent, while Just Russia came third with 15–20 per cent. Turnout was significantly lower than official data suggested, at around the 50 per cent mark rather than the 60.2 per cent announced by Churov. By contrast, Putin's election was considered fair, but with only 52 per cent of the vote, while another 13 per cent had been added.[55] The coefficient of fraud had declined between December and March since Putin had fought a vigorous campaign, and he needed for his election to be seen as fair, and thus legitimate. The report was hastily withdrawn and Sulakshin was demoted, but the damage was done.

The neo-traditionalist ideas of the Izborsky club were certainly not unchallenged, especially since the assault on liberalism was accompanied by an attack on capitalism as a social form. The slogan of 'beyond left and right' was reinforced by condemnation of 'the centre', precisely the ground where Putin had long sought to root himself. Other think tanks, such as the Centre for Strategic Research, the Badovsky Centre, and Sergei

Karaganov's Council for Foreign and Defence Policy (SVOP), issued alternative models for Russia's development, and critical reports on Russia's present. The CSR's report of March 2011 had predicted mass protests after the elections, while that of November 2011 warned that the regime was approaching the parliamentary elections in a state of political crisis. The report focused on the 'moving forces' for change, and identified the 'middle class', which formed in the 'fat years' of Putin's rule and now constituted some 20–30 per cent of the population, depending on the region, and would reach 60 per cent by 2020. The decline in trust towards the tandem began in 2010, above all among the middle class, paradoxically, the greatest beneficiary of Putin's rule. However, their political aspirations were not being met, since not a single new party had been registered and the Right Cause project had been abandoned. Moreover, the castling move was executed in the most damaging form, destroying the Medvedev 'brand'.[56]

The report of May 2012 talked of the 'political reaction scenario', the coercive suppression of the protest movement and the end of reforms, while the third in October 2012 outlined three scenarios: mass insubordination provoked by some unpredictable event; the voluntary relinquishment of power by the regime, although the president could remain in power; and the rapid degradation of the population and society, the path pursued in Putin's third term.[57] The Higher School of Economics brought together several scholarly centres that provided critical analysis of developments. The Valdai Discussion Club (of which the present author is a member) sought to provide dispassionate scholarly analysis while engaging with the regime. First meeting at the time of the Beslan hostage crisis in 2004, the Club thereafter gathered annually and sponsored a number of working groups. One of these, for example, issued the visionary plan for 'a union of Europe', in an attempt to transcend the stale antinomies that once again threatened to divide the continent. The Izborsky Club was in part established to counter the liberalism of the Valdai Club. The Valdai Club rejected the axiological politics of both Putin's sharpest detractors and supporters, and instead tried to navigate a path based on the principles of political dialogism.

The war against independent NGOs suggested that Russia had entered a period of reaction. Repressive laws restricting demonstrations, labelling NGOs 'foreign agents', the criminalisation of defamation, amendments to the law on high treason (including harsh punishment, but not yet implemented), a ban on a list of websites, the ban on 'propaganda of homosexuality', and the anti-Magnitsky law, represented for many a 'tactical war' waged by the authorities to divert attention from 'collapsing infrastructure, economic stagnation, corruption and fraudulent elections'. Yuri Dzhibladze, the head of the Centre for the Development of Democracy and Human Rights, considered all this cumulatively as a red line, and he withdrew from work with the regime.[58] As in so many spheres, opportunities for intra-systemic evolution were closing down.

Demedvedisation

In early February 2012 Yurgens suggested that Medvedev would be a 'non-productive' prime minister, and argued that he should become a vice president with responsibility for modernisation.[59] In an interview on 17 February 2012 Yurgens argued that Medvedev should refuse the post of prime minister, since he would not be 'very successful in the job' since Putin's allies would 'tear him apart', and suggested that Kudrin would be a more appropriate prime minister in the circumstances.[60] Medvedev cut off all contact with Insor after the September demarche, leaving his erstwhile supporters isolated. Medvedev was indeed persecuted in his job. Not all of his innovations were reversed, but there was a clear pushback against not only Medvedev's specific reforms but above all the spirit in which they had been enacted. The conservatives held Medvedev responsible for having allowed a 'thaw', which created the social conditions for the protest movement. The key slogan of his rule had been *modernizatsiya* of Russian politics, economy and society, accompanied by the banal yet potent slogan that 'freedom is better than unfreedom'. With the unravelling of his project there were fears that Russia would demodernise.

The regime had to deal with the most dangerous threat of all – that of the intra-systemic reformer. Strange as it may sound, in the Putinite order the Medvedev cabinet became a type of internal competitor because of its semi-autonomous status enshrined in the constitution, and the logic of the system demanded that it be neutralised. Putin's return to the Kremlin was accompanied by Medvedev's political humiliation. The hard-line group clearly felt that Medvedev had betrayed the principles on which the Putinite order had been founded, compounded by his evident desire to return to the presidency, and now sought their revenge. Ministers became the subject of unprecedented attack as the traditionalists sought revenge for their relative marginalisation and humiliation in the Medvedev years. Medvedev's alleged weakness was dissected in ruthless detail in the media, while his liberal ministers became the subject of attacks on their integrity and competence. Nevertheless, Putin was careful not to allow this to go too far, since after all he needed a government that could implement policy. The optimum was an administration that was weakened and recognised its political subordination, yet was still capable of governing. Medvedev was to be weakened but not dismissed.

Medvedev's reform package was voided of much of its democratic content. The proportional system had allowed United Russia to consolidate its parliamentary predominance in 2007 and 2011, but the protests demonstrated that the old system was breaking down and the party could no longer be guaranteed to win over 50 per cent. Medvedev had already talked of a return to a mixed electoral system in 2010, but the proposals advanced in his last *poslanie* on 22 December 2011 proposed 'proportional representation in 225 districts', an incomprehensible binomial system. The proposals sent by Medvedev to the Duma in February were even more confused, with party lists alone without the federal part of the ticket, and with the nomination of candidates from 225 territorial units. The proportional system was preserved, but parties had to divide their candidate lists into 225 groups. In early 2013 Putin advanced a new version of electoral reform, finally restoring the mixed system of the sort that had operated up to 2003. In the event, the bill introduced in October 2013 proposed a 25/75 per cent split in the electoral system in favour of single-mandate constituencies – where Popular Front candidates stood a strong chance of victory. By then over 60 parties had registered, and it was clear that United Russia was in no position to deliver a parliamentary majority. A first-past-the-post system would allow the RPF to advance candidates, and would allow a pre-Kremlin majority in parliament.

A number of new rules shaping the political system came into effect on 1 January 2013. One of these was Medvedev's initiative to reduce the threshold barrier to the Duma from 7 to 5 per cent. Another was the new method to form the Federation Council. Candidates for the post of senator from a regional legislature have to be members of that legislative assembly, with the right of nomination belonging to the chair of the assembly, any of its factions, or one-fifth of its members. The senator would then be chosen by the region's governor from the three candidates nominated to stand alongside the latter in gubernatorial elections. From that date also all state employees had to publish information about their expenses and those of their spouses and children under 18, while another anti-corruption measure entailed the compulsory rotation of federal civil servants every 3–5 years, depending on the seniority of the official.

The anti-corruption campaign would inevitably sooner or later run into fundamental contradiction: dealing with venal forms of corruption was one thing, but many of the regime's senior officials were implicated in meta-corrupt practices, whose extirpation would threaten the regime itself. The systemic privatisation of public funds, above all though exorbitant cost over-runs on public contracts and services, was typical of a middle income country, and impeded Russia's advancement into the ranks of developed societies. Serdyukov's sacking in November 2012 was intended as a signal that the regime was taking the anti-corruption campaign seriously, but as we have seen the authorities were careful not to alienate their own elites. Soon after a probe took place into the finances of Glonass, Russia's answer to the American GPS system and Europe's Galileo project, as well as into the financing of the APEC summit, held in Vladivostok in September. The unpopular former agriculture minister, Elena Skrynnik, was also named in a corruption investigation. Putin endorsed the anti-corruption campaign to the degree that it would not threaten his associates or his system, and would not disrupt the precarious factional balance only tenuously restored after the succession crisis. Experts agree that at the minimum the fight against corruption requires an independent judiciary, a competitive political system and independent mass media, none of which were on the cards.

Medvedev himself remained remarkable insouciant throughout and retained his phenomenal capacity for hard work. He quietly pushed forward his agenda of political reforms announced in December 2011, including the creation of the Public Television of Russia (OTR) in April 2012. In part Medvedev's resilience may be explained by awareness that if he were dismissed, he could go on to become a rallying figure for the opposition. Whatever Medvedev's personal deficiencies, no one had any doubts that his sympathies lay with strengthening of the constitutional state. Medvedev criticised the two-year jail sentence handed down to Pussy Riot, arguing that they should have been set free at their trial. On 22 October 2012 he criticised the possibility of state companies buying stakes in privatised assets, thus criticising Putin's plan adopted in May that allowed state holding companies to acquire stakes in energy assets sold off by the government. Signs of the struggle were everywhere. On 7 December, during an interview with five Russian television channels, Medvedev was caught on an open mike calling Investigative Committee agents who had recently conducted an early morning raid on the house of film director Pavel Kostomarev 'kozly' (literally 'goat', a term dating back to the prison slang of the 1960s referring to a collaborator with the authorities, but is now a demeaning insult). Clearly, Medvedev was uncomfortable with the repressive actions of Bastrykin's Investigative Committee.

Already in an interview with *Le Figaro* on 26 November 2011 Medvedev left open the question of whether he would again run for the presidency, and at a meeting with journalism students at Moscow State University he admitted that some of the Bolotnaya protesters were motivated by anger that he had not run for re-election. In an interview he commented that he may run for the Kremlin. Following widespread ridicule, in February 2012 at Davos he insisted that he would never run against Putin. The regime devoted considerable efforts to discredit the opposition, but the campaign became a personal attack on Medvedev himself. In August 2012, a film called 'The Lost Day' attacked Medvedev for his indecisiveness at the time of the Russo-Georgian war in 2008. Allegedly, 'afraid to give the command', the Kremlin had to be 'kicked' by Putin in Beijing to launch the operation. Then in February 2013, soon after his presidential announcement, another video was posted attacking Medvedev for allegedly selling out Russia's interests by implicitly backing Nato's air campaign against Gaddafy, something that he did, according to the video, against Putin's express wishes. The instigators of these 'provocations' are unknown, but indicated system erosion and a return to '1990s-style mischief and disarray'.[61]

Addressing a United Russia meeting on 27 March 2013 Medvedev sought to make sense of the ideological conflicts in Russia. He argued that conservatives in Russia were not opposed by the liberals but by reactionaries, a view that came as a shock to party stalwarts, especially those in Andrei Isaev's Conservative Club, who had made his party career through attacking the 'liberalists' who are 'under orders from [American ambassador Michael] McFaul'.[62] Thus Medvedev sought to shape a new type of Russian progressive conservatism, opposed to the reactionaries, who tried to pull the country backwards. United Russia was defined as 'the classic party of the political centre', and defined the main threat as coming from the right, and his speech was notable for the absence of any critique of the liberals or the left.

The criminal investigation from April 2013 against Alexei Beltyukov, senior vice president of Medvedev's brainchild, the Skolkovo Innovation Centre, was accompanied by another into the payment of $750,000 to Just Russia Duma deputy and opposition activist Ilya Ponomarev. The latter apparently received the money for delivering just ten lectures and academic research, but is alleged to have been a way of covering up Beltyukov's embezzlement. The case implied that Medvedev, and with him Surkov, were funding the opposition. In a pattern that became all too typical, on 7 May the Investigative Committee's spokesman, Markin, published a scathing condemnation in the pro-Kremlin paper *Izvestiya* of Surkov's comments in London criticising RIC's investigation into Skolkovo. The article was reminiscent of the political denunciations of the Soviet period and represented an astonishing breach of bureaucratic etiquette, since Surkov held a far higher rank than Markin.[63] The incident demonstrated the renewed confidence of the security apparatus following Putin's return. On 8 May, Surkov, once one of the most powerful men in Russia, resigned. The day before Putin had publicly scolded the cabinet while glaring at Surkov for not carrying out his orders. Surkov had been responsible for the implementation of Putin's rather populist inaugural decrees of 7 May 2012. The televised performance was intended to show Putin firmly in command, but it only demonstrated his isolation and governmental disarray.

Surkov left the Kremlin in December 2011 at the time of the mass protests, which he had called 'the best part of society', and entered the government, where he was responsible for overseeing the implementation of presidential decrees and innovation projects. Although Surkov was known as Putin's grey cardinal and the architect of the system of managed democracy, he had no taste for coercion and preferred more sophisticated methods of political management. His successor, Volodin, as well as Sergei Ivanov at the head of the presidential administration, were only too glad to see the back of a wily operator of Surkov's calibre, and his departure represented a victory for the *siloviki*. Surkov openly declared himself for a Medvedev second term, and was then held responsible for allowing the mass protest movement to develop. His departure was accompanied by a shift from the use of political technologies towards targeted repression.[64] Surkov left an administration that he clearly considered flawed, but he continued to argue that God had 'called upon him [Putin] to save Russia from a hostile takeover. He was a white knight, and a very timely one at that', and that he had been considering leaving for some years.[65] Later that year, however, he returned to the Kremlin as an advisor on Abkhazia and South Ossetia, and clearly retained broader influence over Caucasus policy as a whole. Above all, Surkov's return signalled a potential alternative to Volodin and his policy of 'regime reset'.

Medvedev as prime minister was in an even less enviable position than as president. There were elements of genuine partnership in the tandem years, but with Putin's return the Kremlin went out of its way to demonstrate that the tandem form of rule was over. The condition for Medvedev's political advancement was his relationship with Putin, but it also determined the limitations of what he could do in power. His economic policies were mercilessly attacked by Kudrin, who used his close personal ties to Putin to position himself as an unofficial economic adviser, lambasting the work of the government as unsatisfactory. Medvedev's plans for greater governmental transparency ran into the sands, and the work of the minister for open government, Mikhail Abyzov, became increasingly redundant. Putin effectively imposed direct presidential control over the cabinet, with a constant stream of injunctions and invective. In April 2013, in a typically Putinite move, a new informal 'super government' was created bringing together ministers with economic portfolios with the presidential economics team and experts. The latter included Kudrin and the *dirigiste* economist Sergei Glazev, with the first deputy prime minister commissioned to draft proposals on stimulating economic growth. At a 'super-government' meeting in Sochi on 22 April, Igor Shuvalov and Elvira Nabiullina, who in July took over as head of the Central Bank of Russia, were also charged with thinking of ways to stimulate economic growth. While the open government idea was dead, a new super-government was in the making.

This was just one aspect of the cold civil war raging between the Kremlin and the White House. Dvorkovich and Medvedev's press secretary, Natalya Timakova, came under permanent siege from the conservatives. Others who were associated with Medvedev were also attacked. These included Akhmed Bilalov, the vice president of the Russian Olympic Committee and board chair of the North Caucasus Resorts Company (KSK), who sought to implement Medvedev's plan for the economic diversification of the North Caucasus by developing its tourism industry.[66] Charged with corruption, he headed abroad. Fundamental decisions that were formally the responsibility of the cabinet were being made elsewhere, above all within the Kremlin, the Security Council and by representatives of the financial and power factions. This inevitably fostered a climate of reactive and reactionary policy making, blunting coherent plans to fulfil the Kremlin's own initiatives, such as improvements in the investment climate. The anti-Medvedev coalition in the Kremlin was able to achieve the government's functional neutralisation, but this did little to help resolve the country's problems.

Medvedev's wide-ranging programmatic article in October 2013 revealed the dearth of new ideas. Called 'The Time for Easy Solutions Has Passed', he reviewed the difficult economic conditions and his responses, including harsh budgetary discipline, and warned that the state as the major source of investment was only viable as long as oil prices remained high. He admitted that there was an 'absolutely explainable distrust' of public institutions, including the judicial system and the law enforcement agencies, depressing economic activity. He ended by warning that Russia faced a crossroads, and could not continue along its old path, but provided no substance to how to get onto the new path.[67] Neither could Medvedev do much with the party he nominally led, and the gulf between United Russia's revanchist and neo-traditionalist turn and Medvedev's erstwhile liberalism became ever wider. The development of the People's Front only reinforced the point that Medvedev had been placed in charge of an increasingly defunct political organisation. Medvedev could do little to reverse the shift in the balance of factional power to the *siloviki*. By endorsing some of the repressive actions, such as the Bolotnaya case, Medvedev lost the final vestiges of respect in the liberal camp, and increased his vulnerability to the pressure from the conservatives. Medvedev found himself in a trap, unable to criticise Putin or even to advance a distinctive governmental alternative, his premiership rapidly went the way of his presidency, attended by bold liberal intentions but drowned in contradictions not of his own making. The political strains between the government and the Kremlin were clear, and only intensified the stagnation in policy development. This was clearly a dysfunctional way to run an administration, and placed intense strain on personal relations between the two key figures.

Notes

1 Editorial, 'O pobednom kliche', *Nezavisimaya gazeta*, 6 March 2012, p. 2.
2 Vladimir Frolov, '50 Shades of Putinism', *Moscow Times*, 14 October 2013.
3 V. V. Putin, 12 June 2012; www.kremlin.ru.
4 The description is from Patrick Armstrong, *Russian Federation Sitrep*, 10 October 2013.
5 *Report of the Presidential Council of the RF for the Development of Civil Society and Human Rights on the Results of the Public Scholarly Analysis of the Court Materials of the Criminal Case against M. B. Khodorkovsky and P. L. Lebedev (tried by the Khamovnichesky District Court of the City of Moscow; the verdict issued on 27.12.2010)* (Moscow, 2011).
6 Michael Bohm, 'Guriev's Exile is a Huge Loss for Russia', *Moscow Times*, 14 June 2013.
7 Op. cit.
8 Open letter by Mikhail Khodorkovskii, 'Chelovek i zakon: O politicheskikh presledovaniyakh v Rossii', *Vedomosti*, 24 April 2013.
9 Kirill Rogov, 'Vtoroi front Putina: Ot fiktivnogo legalizma k repressyam', *Novaya gazeta*, 27 October 2012.
10 Members included Academician Yuri Ryzhov, Higher School of Economics academic director Yevgenii Yasin, the writer Vladimir Voinovich, human rights activists Nataliya Gorbanevskaya and Valeri Borshchev, and many other respected figures.
11 The report is summarised here: '"Nikakikh massovikh besporyadkov ne bylo" – nezavisimyi doklad po sobytiyam 6 maya 2012 goda', *The New Times*, No. 14–15, 22 April 2013.
12 *Doklad Kommissii "Krugloga stola 12 dekabrya" po obshchestvennomu rassledovaniyu sobytii 6 maya 2012 goda na Bolotnoe ploshchadii*; http://rt12dec.ru/documents/report220413/default.html; Vladimir Ryzhkov, 'Putin's Bolotnoye Show Trial', *Moscow Times*, 25 April 2013.

13 S. S. Udal'tsov, *Putin – Boi!* (Moscow, Algoritm, 2013).
14 Kirill Medvedev, 'Diary', *London Review of Books*, 20 June 2013, p. 39.
15 Ibid.
16 'Ponomaryov Accused of Orchestrating Bolotnaya Riots', *Moscow Times*, 11 July 2013.
17 Luke Harding, *Mafia State: How One Reporter Became an Enemy of the Brutal New Russia* (London, Guardian Books, 2011), p. 132.
18 Miriam Elder, 'Lebedev Charged with Hooliganism over TV Fisticuffs', *The Guardian*, 27 September 2012, p. 28.
19 Aleksandr Grigor'ev, 'Vladimir Markin: "Naval'ny smozhet borot'sya s korruptsiei i iz tyur'mi"', *Izvestiya*, 12 April 2013.
20 Quoted in Fred Weir, 'Anti-Putin Protesters March in Moscow, but Momentum Weakened', *Christian Science Monitor*, 6 May 2013.
21 Blog Mikhaila Prokhorova, 14 April 2013, http://md-prokhorov.livejournal.com/116213.html.
22 David M. Herszenhorn, 'Text of Navalny's Closing Remarks in Russian Court', *New York Times*, 6 July 2013, modified translation.
23 Miriam Elder, 'Opposition Leader Hits Out at "Feudal" Putin from the Dock', *The Guardian*, 6 July 2013, p. 28.
24 Michael Idov, 'We Have Woken Up at Last. But We Are Helpless', *The Guardian*, 19 July 2013, p. 20.
25 David M. Herszenhorn, 'Russian Court Convicts Opposition Leader', *New York Times*, 18 July 2013b.
26 Miriam Elder, 'Protesters Take to the Streets in Moscow as Opposition Leader Navalny Gets Five Years', *The Guardian*, 19 July 2013, p. 20.
27 Vladimir Ryzhkov, 'The Kremlin Is Split Over Navalny', *Moscow Times*, 23 July 2013a.
28 'Putin Questions Jail Term for Opposition Leader Navalny', RIA Novosti, 2 August 2013.
29 Yekaterina Kravtsova, 'Ex-Convicts Regain Right to Run in Elections', *Moscow Times*, 11 October 2013.
30 'Tsenzura v otnoshenii Putina rabotaet zhestko', 22 January 2013; www://lenta.ru/articles/2013/01/22/fedorov/.
31 The quotations come from the introduction, 'Democratic Breakthroughs in Balance', to the annual report, with the substance in 'Russia', January 2013; www.freedomhouse.org/report/freedom-world/2013/Russia.
32 *Kontseptsiya vneshnei politiki Rossiiskoi Federatsii*, 12 February 2013, article 14; www.mid.ru.
33 A point made by Mikhail Fedotov to the Public Chamber, a body that monitors new legislation, 'Kremlin Rights Council Chief Slams Parliament for Hasty Laws', RIA Novosti, 12 July 2013.
34 'Comment from the Russian MFA's Official Spokesman Alexander Lukashevich', Russian Ministry of Foreign Affairs Website, 19 September 2012; *JRL*, 166/4, 2012.
35 'Half of Russians Support Tough NGO Sanctions', *Moscow Times*, 11 July 2013.
36 Yevgeny Gontmakher, 'Fate of Foreign Agents', *Kommersant*, 4 October 2013.
37 Vladimir Ryzhkov, 'Kremlin's New Attack on Human Rights', *Moscow Times*, 2 July 2013b.
38 'Interview to the German ARD', 2 April 2013; http://eng.kremlin.ru/news/5216.
39 Vladimir Kara-Murza, 'FARA and Putin's NGO Law: Myths and Reality', *IMR*, 9 May 2013.
40 Alec Luhn, 'Gay Russians Say They Live in Fear of "Legalised Violence and Humiliation"', *The Guardian*, 2 September 2013, p. 13.
41 Anna Arutunyan, 'Media Bill Controversy', *Moscow News*, 23 July 2012.

42 Aleksandr Rubtsov, 'Metafizika gosudarstva: Chto otkazalas' delat' vlast'', *Vedomosti*, 28 June 2013.
43 Boris Bruk, 'Three Objects of Aggression', *IMR*, 4 September 2013.
44 Vladimir Ryzhkov, 'The Kremlin's Pogrom Mentality', *Moscow Times*, 22 October 2013.
45 Harding, *Mafia State*, p. 145.
46 Tatyana Stanovaya, 'The Fate of the Nashi Movement: Where Will the Kremlin Youth Go?', *IMR*, 26 March 2013.
47 Yulia Ponomareva, 'Putin's Popular Front to Replace United Russia?', *Russia Beyond the Headlines*, 18 June 2013; www.rbth.ru.
48 Tatyana Stanovaya, 'The People's Front: Against Whom Are They Joining Forces?', *IMR*, 27 June 2013.
49 Editorial, 'Narodnyi front i disfunktsiya institutov', *Nezavisimaya gazeta*, 21 June 2013, p. 2.
50 'Direct Line with Vladimir Putin', 25 April 2013; http://eng.kremlin.ru/transcripts/5328.
51 Vladimir Putin, 'Plenarnoe zasedanie Peterburgskogo mezhdunarodnogo ekonomicheskogo foruma', 21 June 2013d; http:/www.kremlin.ru/transcripts/18383.
52 'At Least 7 Judges Quit Supreme Arbitration Court', *Moscow Times*, 10 October 2013.
53 Olga Khvostuna, 'Hostile Takeover: On Putin's "Judicial Reform"', *IMR*, 18 October 2013.
54 The Centre's website is at Rusrand.ru.
55 Tat'yana Stanovaya, 'Stsenarii rospuska Gosdumy i problema legitimnosti', 18 March 2013; http://www.politcom.ru/print.php?id=15504.
56 Centre for Strategic Research, Sergei Belanovskii, Mikhail Dmmitriev, Svetlana Misikhina and Tat'yana Omel'chuk, *Dvizhushchie sily i perspektivy politicheskoi transformatsii Rossii* (Moscow, November 2011).
57 Mikhail Dmitriev and Sergei Belanovskii, 'Kak my teper' dumaem', *Vedomosti*, 24 October 2012, p. 4.
58 Yuri Dzhibladze, '"Foreign Agents" Fight for Survival', 30 July 2013, www.opendemocracy.net.
59 Ivan Rodin, 'Medvedev ostaetsya reformatoram', *Nezavisimaya gazeta*, 7 February 2012a, p. 1.
60 'Expert Reasons Dmitry Medvedev of Premiership', Itar-Tass, 22 February 2012.
61 Brian Whitmore, 'Putinism in Winter', RFE/RL, *Russia Report*, 5 February 2013.
62 Aleksandra Samarina, 'Martovskie tezisy Dmitriya Medvedeva', *Nezavisimaya gazeta*, 28 March 2013, p. 1.
63 Vladimir Markin, 'Glyadya iz Londona, na zerkalo necha penyat', *Izvestiya*, 7 May 2013, p. 1.
64 The new coercive approach is powerfully described by the journalist O. V. Kashin, *Vlast': Monopoliya na nasilie* (Moscow, Algoritm, 2013).
65 Andrei Kolesnikov, 'Vladislav Surkov: "I Was By a Great Man's Side"', *Russkii Pioner*, 27 July 2013; http://ruspioner.ru.
66 For this and attacks on other businesses close to Medvedev, see Tatyana Stanovaya, 'Beware of Medvedev', *IMR*, 6 March 2013.
67 Dmitrii Medvedev, 'Vremya prostikh reshenii proshlo', *Vedomosti*, 27 September 2013.

9 The new traditionalism and regime reset

Putin's statecraft endured its most sustained crisis during the succession operation of 2011–12. Although Putin once again achieved his goal with relatively little collateral damage and avoided a 'colour revolution', the 'white ribbon' movement had an enduring legacy. Putin's rule and the system showed sign of exhaustion. Although in formal terms matters continued much as before, the political and temporal foundations had shifted. Putin's return destabilised the system that he had so assiduously created. Once a process of delegitimation begins, it is very hard to return to the status quo ante. The regime was forced to adapt to the demands of the protest movement, although not conceding any of its fundamental demands. In conditions of political instability and declining economic performance, the regime turned to a conservative cultural agenda, while finding new ways of managing political challenges.

Putin's statecraft in crisis

Back in power, the methods of rule that had worked so well in the period of 'classical' Putinism were not suited for his third term. Four things had changed. First, the overall 'condition' of the country had evolved. There was less political capital to be made from condemning the *smutnoe vremya*, the 'time of troubles', of the 1990s. After all, Putin had been in charge for over a decade, and it was time to take responsibility for what had taken shape. The legitimacy derived from the remedial agenda had to be supplemented by performance. Second, there had been some profound socio-economic changes. A period of unprecedented economic growth and rising living standards had expanded and transformed what Russian commentators like to call the 'middle class'. A large group of urban, educated and professionally confident people, who enjoy their holidays abroad, ownership of property, and career independence, now claimed citizenship rights, above all free and fair elections. They may well vote for Putin and his party, but they would like to do so unconstrained and in conditions where their vote was fairly counted.[1] Third, the circumstances attending Putin's return, with little ceremony in reclaiming the throne, provoked extensive protest mobilisation and some signs of intra-elite splits. This meant that Putin would have to fight to consolidate his power, both at the societal and elite levels. Fourth, the country expected policy innovation and good governance, above all through lifting the burden of corruption, raiding and bureaucratic interference, and in general by imbuing the economy with a new dynamism and the country as a whole with a sense of renewal and positive purpose. Instead, Putin's return was associated with a return to the past and more of the same for many dreary years ahead.

Putinite stability proved enduring for well over a decade, but symptoms of the fragility of the system were clear as he entered his third term. An underlying structural weakness was reliance on high energy prices to maintain budgetary stability, the lack of diversification of the economy, insecure property rights, and the lack of reform in the social sector. In 2011 the economy grew by 4.3 per cent, slowing to 3.4 per cent growth in 2012, which was still better than the western average in a time of recession but far short of the 8 per cent of Putin's first decade in power. The further slowdown to 1.3 per cent in 2013 came as a shock to the authorities. The economic development minister appointed in June, Alexei Ulyukaev, admitted in August that the economy would avoid recession but had entered a period of stagnation caused by high levels of social spending and structural problems. He noted that 'Russia is a middle income country but we have shouldered social obligations higher than those middle income countries usually have'.[2] Such comments only intensified fears that economic 'modernisation' and 'reform' would boil down to little more than a new version of neoliberal shock theory, which had driven so many into poverty in the 1990s.

It was clear that the accustomed growth model was running out of steam. Russia was on course for a current account deficit, the first since 1992. Facing a deficit, Putin admitted that there would have to be expenditure cuts.[3] The slowdown was provoked by a range of structural factors, including the exhaustion of spare industrial capacity, the lack of labour mobility, an aging population accompanied by a decline in the working age population, continued net capital outflow, which in the first half of 2013 exceeded $40bn, an overvalued rouble and above all a falling rate of private sector investment. Domestic investment was running at half the Soviet rate of 50 per cent of GDP, and in the end the state was forced to compensate for the lack of private investment. Above all, the weakness of the rule of law and the vulnerability of companies to 'raiding' attacks inhibited the creation of a vibrant SME sector and stifled entrepreneurship in general. Russia, with per capita income of $16,000 in constant 2005 international prices, was falling into the middle-income trap, exacerbated by weakness in underlying economic activity. Ultimately, from the liberal perspective the structural problems of the economy could only be resolved by the reinforcement of the constitutional state. As Gorbachev argued, 'Stagnation [in the late Soviet period] was not only economic, but also ideological and political'. He noted the disastrous consequences of the fraudulent 1996 presidential elections, and like the rest of the country had welcomed

Putin's rise to power, despite misgivings about the way it had come about, since 'Putin inherited chaos, and it was impossible to do nothing'. Putin's second term opened up the possibility 'of realising a new strategy, but the authorities [*vlast'*] chose another path ... and led the country into a dead end'; hence he called for fundamental political reform to ensure free courts and media and an end to political monopoly of a group or an individual.[4] The catastrophically declining performance of the economy threatened not only the survival of the regime but also the integrity of the country, as regional leaders would potentially seek greater autonomy to deal with problems.

Putinite economic stability would be disrupted if energy prices fell sharply. In 2013 for the first time since 1982 America surpassed Russia in gas production, and oil output was only a short way behind – 10.3 million barrels per day (one barrel is 158 litres) compared to Russia's 10.8 million, with Saudi Arabia still in the lead at 11.7 million barrels. The 'shale gas revolution' and new techniques of oil recovery saw American oil imports decline by 15 per cent from 2008, and gas imports by 32 per cent, releasing the surplus onto the world market. Some 40 per cent of the Russian budget and 70 per cent of export income are derived from the oil and gas sector. If Russia was unable to achieve structural reform of the economy in the boom years, it would in the end be forced to do so in a time of crisis. An increasingly apocalyptic tone entered public discourse at this time.

Even though Putin had delivered unprecedented prosperity and opportunities, Russia was suffering from serious governance problems, including corruption, elite kleptocracy, weakly defended property rights and the lack of an independent judiciary. There are a number of symptoms of political crisis. First, the long-term erosion of the Putinite majority during the succession operation effectively turned into a Putinite plurality. Well before the announcement of the *rokirovka* in September 2011 there had been signs of crumbling support, identified for example by focus groups conducted by Dmitriev's CSR. Russia is not immune to the laws of political gravity, and even Putin's remarkably long period of sustained high public opinion ratings would one day have to come down to earth. In international terms Putin's popularity remained remarkably high, but in comparison with his own past, 60 per cent represented a considerable decrease on his previously unassailable 80 per cent. The nature of the system, built on Putin's pseudo-charismatic leadership, required his ratings to be maintained at stratospherically high levels. The castling move reinforced the personalisation of Russian politics, further alienating the section of the population that considered itself European, above all the dynamic middle strata and professional classes.

Although the fall in Putin's popular support is often exaggerated, there was real decline from the heights enjoyed in his second term and when he was prime minister. His trust rating rose from just below 50 per cent in the early years of his rule until from late 2005 they rose to 70 per cent in 2007 and stayed there until early 2010. From the mid-point of Medvedev's presidency the disillusionment with stalled 'modernisation' began to affect Putin's poll ratings, which started a decline that greatly accelerated, to Putin's surprise, after the announcement of the castling move in September 2011, to reach 44 per cent by the end of the year. They recovered for the presidential election before falling again to 42 per cent in September 2012, and then stabilised at around the 60 per cent mark in 2013. The trend is confirmed by the Levada Centre. According to its ten-point scale, Putin reached the peak of his popularity in August 2007 at 7.21, and thereafter fell to reach 6.3 in 2012 and 5.81 in August 2013.[5] The proportion supporting Putin 'as long as he is prepared to pursue democratic and market reforms in Russia' halved from 2001, from 29 per cent to 16 per cent, thus reducing his capacity to attract different electoral groups, while the number of unconditional Putin supporters over the same time period fell from 19 to 14 per cent. Putin was still seen as representing the interests of the security services, accompanied by a decline in those who considered Putin able to express the interests of 'ordinary people', workers, employees and rural dwellers, falling from 19 to 11 per cent.[6] Above all, when pressed, respondents no longer trusted Putin to deliver stability and order, or considered him to be the energetic and far-sighted person of earlier years. His support was becoming increasingly residual, derived in large part from the lack of alternatives.

The 'Putin majority' had dissolved, and Putin was forced back onto his core electorate, which tended to be more traditionalist and susceptible to antiwestern rhetoric. Putin was still able to achieve a high degree of electoral support, and indeed, in August 2013, 63 per cent of respondents approved of Putin's performance as president, but only 30 per cent trusted the head of state.[7] Putin had now clearly become a divisive figure, with a growing proportion seeing him as a liability rather than an asset. There had long been a gap between support for Putin personally and lower ratings for the regime. There was now a secular trend for the two to converge at the lower level, but as long as the system could deliver stability and other public goods (including now political reform), then barring external shocks it could prove durable.[8] Putin never reacted well to criticism while disliking competitive politics, increasingly believing in some sort of mystical predestination governing his relationship with the people. In a television interview for his 60th birthday on 7 October 2012 Putin admitted that he looked at the sociological research produced for the Kremlin, but more important for him was the sense of inner certainty:

> The main thing is – it's hard for me to get this across. There is some sort of chemistry, an inner feeling of correctness, the truth of what I do. Not just some narrow group of respected intellectuals, but the real Russian people.[9]

Second, the unity of the elite showed signs of fragmenting. In this respect, 28 September 2010, the day that Moscow mayor Luzhkov was summarily dismissed by Medvedev, is as important a date as 24 September 2011. Luzhkov's ouster followed a prolonged media campaign that sought to blacken his character. Although Luzhkov had never been a trusted Putinite, he had certainly been willing to work within the system, joining the governing council of United Russia. Some of the other long-standing regional heavy-weights were purged at this time (notably, in Tatarstan and Bashkortostan), suggesting a coordinated attempt at elite renewal. However, the brutal and incoherent manner in which Luzhkov was sacked prefigured the castling move a year later, and demonstrated how even a senior political figure in the establishment could be treated. Luzhkov now emerged as a leading critic of the regime, and even appealed to the Gorbachevian spirit that 'It is impossible to live like this'.[10] Soon after, Kudrin, the veteran minister of finances, in Krasnoyarsk and other venues called for the forthcoming elections to be free and fair. Prokhorov's short-lived leadership of the Right Cause party in 2011 further exposed the exhaustion of traditional forms of political management.

The creation of the tandem had damaged the coherence of policy-making, but the end of diarchy did not mean that Putin could return to the pre-2007 methods of controlling the elite. Indeed, the slew of repressive legislation and uncoordinated political moves (notably Navalny's conviction and immediate release) suggested that Putin had lost control not only of the elites but of the management of the country as a whole. The outbursts of ethnic tension and the xenophobic campaigns against 'immigrants' all suggested that social and political conflicts were no longer being managed effectively. The system was still able to neutralise any serious potential alternative, but belief in Putin's ability to solve problems was weakening. The loss of faith in his authority was exacerbated by the moral fatigue that inevitably sets in when someone has been in power for so long. Moreover, the efficacy of his rhetoric declined, since despite the correct sentiments that he expressed, the gulf between his words and deeds – between what we have called the 'project' and the 'practices' – simply became unbridgeable. The very existence of a strategy came into question since so few of the problems facing the country were resolved. The mass of literature analysing the new stagnation depicted Putin as drowning in the sea of a self-serving elite that he had in part created.[11] The containment of the elites now became a matter not only of the regime but also Putin's personal survival. The management of factional struggle required above all constant balancing of the powerful factions within the *siloviki*, above all between the FSB and the MVD, and limiting the tensions between the Prosecutor's Office and the Investigative Committee.[12]

Third, the regime lost its best chance of a gradual evolution to some different form of political authority, without threatening the property and power settlement of the Putin years. Medvedev had clearly entertained hopes of a second run at the presidency. He had successfully gained a political identity of his own, aligning himself with gradual political liberalisation, partnership with the western powers, and less statist economic policies. What he failed to do was gain political autonomy. Faction management remained Putin's responsibility. The Medvedev presidency and its liberalising acolytes became no more than just another faction, and not the most powerful one at that, rather than transcending the logic of factional conflict to become a hegemonic force in its own right. The shift of power from the *siloviki*, running the military, the security services and the oil sector, to the '*civiliki*', the liberal modernisers and their supporters in charge of the country's economic and financial institutions, was stalled and in the end reversed. The attempt to provide an evolutionary option from within the Putin system was defeated by the character of the system itself. A faction could not overcome the logic of factionalism. The *civiliki* faction was dealt a stunning, although not entirely unexpected blow, in September 2011, from which it has not yet recovered.

Although the protests worked to this group's advantage, and the package of liberal reforms announced at the end of December 2011 were in part a response to mass mobilisation, the 'modernising' part of the elite feared calling on society for support. This would have been one way for the faction to have become a party, and for politics in general to have become 'normalised' and competition institutionalised, but the risks would have been high. There is no evidence that the Medvedev modernisers seriously contemplated appealing to the people for support, and thus lost their historical opportunity. In any case, popular support for the liberal strategy was relatively limited, and if it came to street politics, the radicals of left and right would win. Part of the protest movement supported the long-term aspirations of the Medvedev 'modernisers', but despite much rhetoric about the growth of the 'middle class', this remains a decidedly minority constituency. Medvedev's personal prestige suffered irreversible damage, despite his own stated ambitions to return to the presidency.

Repression against opposition leaders undermined opposition as a political form, and thereby weakened the potential for political renewal. The package of Medvedev reforms continued, but was eviscerated of any transformational potential. Although it was much easier (and indeed too easy), to establish a political party, the ban on forming electoral blocs remained. This accentuated the spoiler role of the new parties and stymied purposive political alliance building. Of the 58 new parties created by spring 2013, only 16 could be considered serious political organisations, with defined political views and programmes, while another ten were purely leader-centred projects.[13] With the evolutionary path of change impeded, liberals intensified their critique, allowing them to be characterised as dangerous 'radicals'.[14] Instead, Volodin tried to stimulate competition from the top. Meeting with the speakers of regional legislative assemblies on 24 August 2013, he urged them to pay more attention to the opposition and to stimulate political competitiveness to divert street protests into parliamentary channels. United Russia was no longer presented as the party of power and what had been essentially a one-party system was discarded. This pluralist line was in evidence in the Moscow city and regional elections on 8 September, and the strategy was implemented nationally, notably in the Zabaikalsk and Vladimir regional assemblies.[15] Although Volodin lacked Surkov's 'grey eminence' character, he had considerable skills as a political manager.

Fourth, the reform of the party system prompted by the protest movement and sponsored by Medvedev at a time of crisis took on a life of its own. In part this was a response to the spontaneous desertion of elites from the sinking United Russia ship, some leading regional politicians joining Just Russia, and the emergence of Civil Platform and other newly-energised parties.[16] Ambitious politicians now had a range of options to engage in political life that had earlier been lacking. United Russia would not give up its effective monopoly without a fight, yet its status as the party of power was eroding. Many of its functions were usurped by the RPF, and in parliament it had to share leadership of the various committees with the other systemic parties. Volodin's new approach sought to shift protest from non-systemic to systemic channels. A more pluralistic multi-party system gave the administrative regime more options and combinations with which to experiment as part of what would become the 'regime reset'. The days of a hegemonic party system were over.

Fifth, the earlier factional constellation changed. The democratic statists around Surkov lost whatever residual coherent identity they ever had, and other minority sub-factions lost their political salience. Instead, Russian politics now aligned along the lines of two broad constellations, the liberals and the traditionalists, with the latter including a growing band of hard-line nationalists. The Russian nationalist movement hijacked the 4 November national holiday, until in 2008 the march was broken up by the police, accompanied by the arrest of over 1,000 people followed by various trials. The liberal modernisers grouped around Medvedev in the government had to fight for their positions on a daily basis. On the other side, the traditionalists, encompassing the *siloviki*, economic statists and conservatively-inclined nationalists demanded the spoils of victory. Putin's power rested on his ability to manage and constrain factional conflict while at the same time tempering the extremes of Russian politics. He was the 'great moderator', preventing xenophobic nationalists on the side and ultra-liberals on the other from shaping policy, but now he struggled to provide a progressive vision for his centrism. The Putin project was in danger of collapsing into the unprincipled *trasformismo* of late nineteenth-century Italy, drawing eclectically from left and right. The Putin system still sought to maintain factional balance, and for that it needed the liberals, however demoralised, to balance the hard-line statists. The division began to assume overtly political forms, with regime-sponsored ideational programmes giving way to more openly ideological conflict over development strategies and modernisation plans. This remained elite contestation, but both sides at times of stress could appeal to the street. The politicisation of elite competition would deal a death blow to the Putinite technocratic system of political management.

Sixth, an associated aspect of what is increasingly 'mismanaged democracy' is the declining coherence of legislative and policy initiatives. Some of the repressive legislation emerging from the Sixth Duma bears signs of ad hoc independent political entrepreneurship by United Russia and its allies. Pavlovsky identified an 'atmosphere of slight administrative insanity', in which a third trial and new prison sentence on Khodorkovsky was as real a possibility as his release, and in which the 'boundaries of what's possible have expanded dramatically. Things that seemed impossible just a couple of years ago have become quite likely'.[17] At precisely the time when the electoral base of the regime reduced to a plurality, its majoritarian features were accentuated. This was accompanied by enhanced doubts about the system's capacity to react effectively to exogenous shocks. The slow response to the shale gas and tight oil revolutions and the accompanying seismic shifts in energy markets demonstrated the vulnerability of a factionalised economy and personalised political system.

Seventh, Putin's own vulnerabilities now came to the fore. Commentators noted signs of withdrawal and an arrogant dismissiveness towards the ideas of others, accompanied by a turn to a safe conservatism and fortress Russia mentality that was the exact opposite of what reformers, even within the system, advocated. Obama cancelled the bilateral summit planned for Moscow on the eve of the G20 summit in St Petersburg on 5–6 September 2013 and compared Putin to a tiresome schoolboy: 'He's got that kind of slouch, looking like the bored kid in the back of the classroom'.[18] Putin had lost some of his customary vigour, while the 'hoax' dismissal of Yakunin, the contretemps between Surkov and Markin, the arrest and release of Navalny, the removal and reinstatement of Bryansk governor Nikolai Denin, suggested more than irresolution but a rampant factionalism undermining systemic coherence. The United Russia candidate Denin was removed from the elections by the regional court, apparently as a result of an anti-corruption check by Bastrykin's RIC and the MVD. The court ruling came as a surprise to the presidential administration, and after emergency actions at the highest level, the Supreme Court reinstated Denin. Although Putin enjoyed enormous powers, he appeared less engaged in current matters. This meant that 'The country is controlled by everyone at once and no one specifically'.[19] The presidential administration was no longer the coordinating centre that it had once been, with competition between Volodin and Sergei Ivanov for influence over the supreme leader, while Bastrykin's Investigative Committee was pursuing its own agenda, notably the grinding down of Bolotnaya activists, Navalny and the preparation of a possible third Yukos case. Meanwhile, Medvedev remained marginalised, although he still spoke in favour of competitive elections and openness.

The divergence between Putin's political discourse and the cultural expectations of a significant part of society was growing. The cracks in the Putin edifice prompted elites to think about a world without Putin, and thus started to devise personal exit strategies. Putin's own physical condition came under scrutiny in autumn 2012, when he cancelled various trips and had to deal with what was officially admitted to be a health issue, albeit allegedly a minor one. The power *vertikal*, however mythical, relied on the single individual at the apex. Already at the time of the tandem the accustomed hierarchy of power had been divided, provoking policy confusion over how to handle the effects of the global economic crisis, international affairs (notably Libya and Syria), and strategies for development, prompting Putin to return to restabilise the system. The regime had then been shaken by an intra-systemic and societal succession crisis, apparently reinforcing the need for Putin-style personalistic consolidation. This only exacerbated the long-term dilemma of how the system could be preserved when Putin finally stepped off the stage of history. A genuine post-Putin succession crisis would be on a very different scale to anything experienced in post-communist Russia. The prospect sharpened intra-elite personal and factional conflict, and raised fears of a genuine outsider making a bid for power that would threaten the whole Putinite order.

Putin had returned, but the country and the political system had evolved. New forms of political statecraft were introduced, but the rebalancing of the power system was partial and, typically, combined elements of screw-tightening with some concessions to political pluralism. The more tutelary aspects of the system were at war with those who sought a gradual decompression to allow greater competiveness in elections and the easing of repression. In other words, systemic dualism was reflected in day-to-day conflicts over policy and strategy. A positive reinvention of the Russian political order would require an act of unprecedented leadership and political imagination, otherwise Putin's *redux* would become an era of disappointment and stagnation.

The Putin doctrine

Gontmakher has identified a 'Putin doctrine' shaping strategic choices in his third term. Putin's thinking was determined by two factors. The first was the economic crisis from 2008, which revealed the vulnerability of the West and its descent into economic stagnation. There was also a political crisis, with the rise of populist movements, while Russia even at its most accommodating, had been humiliated and marginalised. Rather than deeper integration with the decaying western economic, political security space, a shift in orientation to the East, above all China, and Eurasian integration appeared rational. Second, the civil protest movement indicated that Putin's achievements, including a substantial rise in living standards, had not been reciprocated with gratitude to the 'national leader'. Putin could either ally with the 15–20 per cent of Russians demanding changes, or rely on the more conservative and even fundamentalist strata. Putin tacked towards the latter, entailing a chilly relationship with the West and solidarity with America's critics, accompanied by the danger of suffocating in China's embrace. The 'doctrine' was vulnerable to a resurgence of the West, and the alienation of the most active segment of society was the recipe for permanent conflict, stagnation and the isolation of the regime.[20] Many within the elite were no less alienated by the implications of the new 'doctrine', and persistent pressure from popular 'grass-roots non-violent activism' could be enough to force a change of course.

Putin's return polarised society. On the one hand, there was a ground-surge of resistance to more years of the stifling tutelary regime, which took the immediate form of the 'Bolotnaya' and 'Sakharov' demonstrations against electoral fraud and the regime's claimed prerogative to speak on behalf of society. The resistance was fragmented and unable to agree on a single programme, yet it reflected an appeal to the principles of civic equality and political inclusion. On the other hand there was 'Poklonnaya' and the broader movement in support of Putin and the perpetuation of the old order. Again, Putin's supporters were far from united, and covered a spectrum from constitutional conservatives to radical reactionaries, who exploited Putin's return to push through a slew of repressive legislation to shape their vision of a neo-Muscovite social order, isolated from the degeneration of the West, morally conservative, and reaching deep into the roots of Russian exceptionalism. For them, Putin's third term was to be run as a rectification campaign, to overcome the elements of perceived weakness in foreign policy and the shoots of a new thaw at home.

Putin allowed much of the reactionary agenda to be driven by radicals in the parliamentary United Russia faction. Without the need for explicit instructions, they understood the practicalities of the 'Putin doctrine'. There were superficial indications of a gulf between Putin and 'Putinism', with actions taken in his name that he had not apparently instigated, a classic trope of aging despotisms. When it came to signing, he showed no sign of dissenting with the repressive legislation. Putin it seemed was abandoning his policy of balance between the factions in favour of intensified coercion and a rebalancing of the system in a more conservative direction. As president, Medvedev had been able to block much of the agenda of the reactionaries, including laws on libel and control of the internet; but now these proposals came back with a vengeance. The language of politics also became polarised, with the regime's supporters denouncing the protest movement as lackeys of the West; whereas the liberals considered Putin's supporters as both venal and stupid. The struggle between epistemes was in danger of turning into a physical conflict. The gulf opened up by the castling announcement in September 2011 between the 'creative class' and the traditionalists was widening. The middle ground was disappearing, and Putin's 'centrism' was forced to adapt to polarisation and mobilisation.

In the first *poslanie* of his third term on 12 December 2012, the staleness of the regime's developmental agenda was evident.[21] Putin's speech covered issues of domestic development in great detail, but offered no major policy initiatives and had little to say about foreign policy. The tone was passionless but typically paternalistic, and focused on top-down actions and 'values'. This was a classic pragmatic and technocratic speech, but now imbued with a patina of cultural conservatism. The country, in his view, faced a 'demographic and moral crisis'. Improvements in the country's demographic situation, so that 'Three children per family should become the norm for Russia', Putin argued, were to be reinforced by reform of the health, education and science sectors.

However, in an implicit response to the protesters, Putin warned of the country's 'moral crisis', to be remedied by promoting 'traditional values', above all in the educational system by fostering a patriotic spirit and strengthening national identity. 'We must not only preserve but develop our national identity and soul. We must not lose ourselves as a nation: we must be and remain Russia.' This was the answer to the question that everyone had been asking since September 2011: what was the purpose of Putin's return? The answer appeared to be: to save the nation!

This was accompanied by warnings of the dangers that overt nationalism could pose to Russia's fragile multiethnic social fabric, balanced by the need to prevent the emergence of 'closed ethnic enclaves with their own informal jurisdiction' (a dig at multiculturalism), accompanied by tighter immigration rules. In short, he was for spiritual revival without chauvinism. There was once again to be electoral reform, with a move back to the mixed electoral system (single-member constituencies and party lists) in operation before the 2007 parliamentary elections. Putin passionately denounced foreign funding for domestic political actors, but defended democracy as the only way for the country to develop, but standards could not be imposed from outside but should be based on the country's own traditions. Putin's proposal that the right of legislators and top officials to hold accounts in foreign banks or assets abroad would be limited was, as we have seen, implemented. Putin called for the 'de-offshoreisation' of the economy, to reverse the trend for Russian businesses to register in low tax enclaves. Putin noted that 'Any country sees a surge in public activity in the course of election campaigns, including protest activity', but insisted that even his opponents had to concede that he had won the presidential election in the first round. The decline in protest activity had nothing to do with a 'tightening of the screws', he insisted, since people could still express their opinions legally, but warned against threatening 'the sovereignty of the country'. There was no concession to the substance of the protesters' demands, let alone accepting elements of shared sovereignty through dialogue.

The basic theme was that 'In the twenty-first century, amid a new balance of economic, civilisational and military forces, Russia must be a sovereign and influential country'. He evoked the catastrophe of the First World War as a warning of the dangers emanating from the international system, but overall the stress was on 'stability'. The idea of 'modernisation' had disappeared entirely, replaced by the implicit concept of '*dostroika*' (the completion of building), in contrast to Gorbachev's 'perestroika', rebuilding. Values, vaguely enunciated but pervasive, had become the regime's new ideology. The speech represented a tack towards the traditionalists, balanced by some apparent concessions to the 'angry urbanites', notably in the form of the regime constraining the venality of its own officials. The speech as a whole reflected the broader conservative consolidation of Putin's return. The system was still looking for a centrist niche, although forced to satisfy the demands of increasingly polarised constituencies. The speech suggested that there would be no radicalisation of the regime, but by the same token it was not clear whether it had enough dynamism to offer a clear prospect for effective and convincing leadership for the years ahead.

Shortly afterwards, in his extended press conference on 20 December, Putin reiterated some of these themes.[22] He stressed that 'we have ensured stability as the essential condition for development. ... Yet I cannot call this system authoritarian. ... I think that order, discipline and compliance with the letter of the law do not contradict democratic forms of government'. He noted that he favoured gubernatorial elections in most regions, but left open the option that certain regions could decide for themselves the optimal way of selecting their chief executive. In line with Medvedev's political reforms announced a year earlier, the federal law on direct elections came into force in July, and the first elections were held on 14 October. Putin referred to the dramatic events in Karachai-Cherkessia, where the elections had been accompanied by inter-ethnic tensions, and he cited the positive experience in Dagestan, where power had been shared by different ethnic groups on a rotating basis, a system that he had earlier dismantled when abolishing gubernatorial elections. In a stab against the opposition, he noted that 'Democracy is above all subordination to the law'.

Putin condemned the adoption of the Magnitsky Rule of Law Act, which president Barack Obama signed into law on 14 December 2012. Already in July 2011 the State Department had imposed visa bans on Russian officials associated with the case. Now the Act gave statutory force to the travel proscriptions on 18 officials allegedly associated with the death of Sergei Magnitsky in November 2009. Congress at the same time, after nearly four decades, finally repealed the Jackson-Vanik amendment that had imposed trade sanctions on the Soviet Union because of its restrictions on Jewish emigration, and granted Russia permanent normal trade relations (PNTR). Putin stressed that the Magnitsky Act 'spoils Russo-US relations and pulls them back into the past', and noted 'This act is certainly unfriendly towards the Russian Federation'. 'One anti-Soviet act has been replaced by another, anti-Russian one.' The Russian response was rushed through the Duma, the Dima Yakovlev law (named after a Russian adoptee who had died in America after being left locked in a car in the heat of the day) banning the adoption of Russian children by Americans. Putin signed the law on 28 December and it came into effect on 1 January, and had a supplementary clause allowing Russia to suspend the activities of NGOs if they received money from American citizens and 'present a danger to the interests of Russia' (Article 3), thus broadening the scope of the 'foreign agents' law adopted the previous July. The measure provoked numerous hostile questions, but Putin defended the response as appropriate.

Putin explained his decision not to change the constitution in 2008 to allow a third consecutive term: 'Had I really considered a totalitarian regime preferable, I would have changed the constitution. It could then have been done quite easily'. As for the protesters, he argued that 'I do not think that people should be jailed for participation in mass actions, even if they were accompanied by legal infringements'. He insisted that he had made no 'systemic' mistakes, and thus defended the broad pattern of his rule. He emphatically denied that he had influenced the courts in the Khodorkovsky trials, and equally insisted that no personal or political motives were involved: 'I had no means of influence, and I did not influence the activity of law enforcement or judicial bodies in any way. I stayed away from that affair', Putin stressed. 'You have a mistaken idea of the way our judicial system works' he responded to a question that suggested that the court had reduced Khodorkovsky's prison sentence because the president's view had changed (with the implication that with the succession out of the way, it was now safe to release Khodorkovsky). 'Certain legal amendments were made, and apparently, those amendments were reason enough for the court to take those decisions.' As far as the Khodorkovsky case is concerned, 'There is no personal persecution involved. He insisted that 'in keeping with the law, if everything is normal, Mikhail Borisovich will be set free, and I wish him good health'. Platon Lebedev was due to be released on 2 May 2014, and Khodorkovsky on 25 August. Overall, it was clear that Putin had a high view of his achievements: 'I wish the future leaders of the country and the future president to be even more successful. But I consider, compared with other periods in Russia's development, this period has been far from the worst, and possibly, one of the best.'

Putin's capacity for renewal and reinvigoration was on display at the Valdai International Discussion Club meeting in September 2013. Fresh from his diplomatic triumph in having secured international control over the dismantling of Syrian chemical weapons, and thus averting a western military assault on the country, Putin had a spring to his step. In an op-ed piece published in *The New York Times* on 12 September, Putin warned that 'No one wants the United Nations to suffer the fate of the League of Nations, which collapsed because it lacked real leverage'. He insisted that 'Syria is not witnessing a battle for democracy, but an armed conflict between government and opposition in a multireligious country', and he argued that from the beginning Russia had advocated peaceful dialogue. His final paragraph responded to Obama's statement about American exceptionalism in a speech delivered shortly before. In a comment that enraged many in America, Putin warned 'It is extremely dangerous to encourage people to see themselves as exceptional, whatever the motivation'.[23]

Putin's keynote speech on 19 September was one of his most considered 'ideological' statements, presenting Russia as the keeper of a western tradition that he argued the West itself had lost.[24] He had made the same argument about foreign policy at Munich in February 2007, arguing that Russia was the upholder of the principles of international law and order that the West no longer applied. The Valdai speech had a reflective character and sought to analyse the dynamics of the times in light of the conference's theme of 'Russian national identity'. He made seven key points. The first was the emphasis on the need of new strategies 'to preserve our identity in a rapidly changing world'. He noted that there could be no return to Soviet ideology and sought to find a middle way between current ideas: 'Proponents of fundamental conservatism who idealise pre-1917 Russia seem to be similarly far from reality, as are supporters of extreme western-style liberalism'. He stressed the competitive nature of international affairs, with the world 'becoming more rigid, and sometimes foregoes not merely international law, but also basic decency'. It would be the 'quality of citizens' that would allow Russia to withstand the economic-technological challenges as well as the ideological informational ones, hence 'the question of finding and strengthening national identity really is fundamental for Russia'.

Second, Putin stressed that development paths could not be mechanically borrowed or assumed to emerge spontaneously. Not only globalisation but Russia's recent historical experience of catastrophic breakdowns in the twentieth century and the emergence of a 'quasi-colonial element of the elite ... determined to steal and remove capital', meant that Russia had to devise a developmental ideology of its own. In keeping with his tutelary and *dirigiste* instincts, he argued: 'A spontaneously constructed state and society does not work, and neither does mechanically copying other countries' experiences.' He rejected attempts to 'civilise Russia from abroad', and instead stressed that 'the desire for independence and sovereignty in spiritual, ideological and foreign policy spheres is an integral part of our national character'.

Third, he admitted that identity and a national idea should not be imposed from above and could not take the form of an ideological monopoly, and instead stressed historical and organic creativity: 'All of us – so-called Neo-Slavophiles and Neo-Westernisers, statists and so-called liberals – all of society must work together to create common development goals.' He called for a broad dialogue in which what I have called the contending epistemes should learn to speak with each other and not only with like-minded people. Equally, reprising a theme from his pre-election articles, he stressed not only political diversity but above all that:

> Russia was formed specifically as a multi-ethnic and multi-confessional country from its very inception. Nationalists must remember that by calling into question our multi-ethnic character, and exploiting the issue of Russian, Tatar, Caucasian, Siberian or any other nationalism or separatism, means that we are starting to destroy our genetic code. In effect, we will begin to destroy ourselves. Russia's sovereignty, independence and territorial integrity are unconditional.

This was a powerful indictment of the many currents threatening to erode Russia's integrity, and reasserted Putin's centrist vision of a multi-faceted Russia.

Fourth, he took a swipe at the opposition, arguing that as so often in Russia's history 'instead of opposition to the government we have been faced with opponents of Russia itself'. Thus he returned to one of his persistent themes, namely that critique threatened to bring down the Russian state. He insisted that 'It's time to stop only taking note of the bad in our history', and while admitting that self-criticism was valuable, it had to know the bounds and not become 'humiliating and counter-productive'. He brought in western experience, noting that 'We can see how many of the Euro-Atlantic countries are actually rejecting their roots, including the Christian values that constitute the basis of Western civilisation'. Here his cultural conservatism was on full display, condemning same-sex marriages, the 'excesses of political correctness', and the loss of societies' ability to self-reproduce. Later in the speech he took up the theme again, condemning multiculturalism and praising Konstantin Leontiev's vision of Russia as a 'state-civilisation'.

Fifth, he once again took up the themes of his Munich speech in February 2007, condemning attempts to 'revive a standardised model of a unipolar world and to blur the institutions of international law and national sovereignty'. In a biting indictment, he warned: 'Such a unipolar, standardised world does not require sovereign states; it requires vassals'. He insisted that decisions should be taken on a collective basis 'rather than at the discretion of and in the interests of certain countries or groups of countries'. Russia defended international law to temper the 'right of the strong'. In a historical excursus he stressed that when Russia participated in international agreements, notably the Congress of Vienna in 1815 and Yalta in 1945, a lasting peace was secured, but when Russia was excluded, as at the [Treaty of] Versailles in 1919, which was 'unfair to the German people', the peace proved fragile.

Sixth, he stressed the mutual responsibility between the state and society, extolling the values of responsible citizenship: 'A citizen is someone who is capable of independently managing his or her own affairs, freely cooperating with equals'. His critics would find this a bit rich coming from a man who had systematically stifled independent civic initiative. Nevertheless, Putin went on to extol 'Local governments and self-regulated citizen's organisations', that 'serve as the best school for civic consciousness'. He declared that the government was prepared 'to trust self-regulating and self-governing associations', but warned that 'we must know whom we are trusting'. Thus he defended the 'foreign agents' law.

Finally, Putin stressed that the twenty-first century promised to become an era 'of the formation of major geopolitical zones', hence it was important for Russia to integrate with its neighbours. In his view, 'The Eurasian Union is a project for maintaining the identity of nations in the historical Eurasian space in a new century and in a new world'. Warning of the danger of peripherality, he argued that 'Eurasian integration is a chance for the entire post-Soviet space to become an independent centre for global development, rather than remaining on the outskirts of Europe and Asia'. The union would be built on the principle of diversity.

He ended with the argument that after the many tribulations of the post-communist era since 1991, Russia was 'returning to itself, to its own history'.

Overall, this was a powerful speech, centrist in overall orientation but laden with a tutelary and traditionalist message. Putin's centrism had moved towards a new formulation of conservatism and a developmental strategy that stressed its autonomous values and direction. In detail it was convincing, but when placed in the overall context of the economic and political challenges facing the country, it represented a partial and ineffective model for the future.

Rebalancing the power system

The protest movement revealed the vulnerability and insecurities of the regime. As Navalny put it, 'There is no evil Putin machine, and if you push hard enough it will collapse ... it's all a fiction. That is, they can destroy a single person, like Magnitsky or me or Khodorkovsky. But, if they try to do anything systematically against a huge number of people, there's no machine. It's a ragtag group of crooks unified under the portrait of Putin.'[25] There was no all-encompassing 'sistema', and in Navalny's view, it would take no more than 'ten businessmen [to speak] up directly and openly [and] we'd live in a different country'. Equally, it would take no more than a handful of courageous judges and renegade officials to change Russia. At least, to change the regime; since a 'revolution' would do no more than swap one set of elites for another. To change the country would mean strengthening the constitutional state, to push back on the Soviet and Putinite legacy of *podmena* where the regime substituted for the impartiality and regularity of constitutional institutions. The demand for a 'Russia without Putin' had to be accompanied by a positive idea of how such a country would be run.

Managed democracy endured its most sustained challenge, but regrouped on a new basis following Putin's return. The public oversight of elections improved, but this mainly affected the precinct-level polling stations. Cameras had been installed for the presidential vote and transparent ballot boxes introduced, but it remains extremely difficult to monitor the work of the territorial electoral commissions (TECs), and impossible to oversee the work of the Central Election Commission. For a country of Russia's stature and cultural traditions, and above all with claims to be a democratic European state with a major role in world politics, its position was anomalous. If Botswana, Kenya, and Indonesia could hold reasonably free and fair elections, then why not Russia?

The pressure for change came from above and below. The evolution of Just Russia is fascinating, with periods of critique tempered by sharp retreats. In the run-up to the succession Mironov criticised tutelary politics. Even though he was a long-time friend of Putin, he was unceremoniously stripped of his chairmanship of the Federation Council, and was forced to transfer the formal leadership of the party to his colleague Levichev. Just Russia fought a vigorous parliamentary campaign, emerging with a more clearly delineated programme of political renewal, while Mironov lambasted the inadequacies of the system. The party gained a solid bloc in parliament, although

Mironov's personal vote in the presidential campaign was disappointing, coming bottom with only 3.85 per cent, while even the relative newcomer Prokhorov got more. With the succession over, the party was subject to reprisals. One of its leading activists, the former KGB officer Gennady Gudkov, in September 2012 was stripped of his parliamentary seat for allegedly combining business activities with legislative commitments, but the political motives for his expulsion were clear.[26] He first entered parliament in 2001, and had been loyal to Putin, although in the end his independent spirit turned him into a thorn in the regime's side. He was expelled without a court order and on the evidence of a copy of a document whose provenance was dubious. Shortly afterwards some United Russia deputies fell foul of this rule, so the regime could claim that the norms were being applied impartially.

In an attempt to bring the opposition together, a Coordination Council of the Opposition (CCO) was elected in an internet poll in autumn 2012. The CCO consisted of 45 members, 30 of whom were elected from a 'general' list' and another 15 from three separate streams: liberal, left wing and nationalist. Some 81,000 people participated in the online vote, which, although impressive, was no more than a tiny sample of Russia's population. Navalny came top, and was joined by the writer Dmitry Bykov, the chess player Garry Kasparov, the TV presenter Ksenia Sobchak, as well as Yashin and Udaltsov. One surprising outcome was the relatively low proportion of the vote cast for the left wing and nationalists. Later, members of Just Russia elected to the Council were forced to choose between party membership and participation in anti-systemic activities, and in the end the party leadership chose conformity over opposition. The enormous diversity of the group impeded coherent actions, most of its meetings lacked a quorum, and in October 2013 the body was dissolved.

The political reforms of 2012 blurred the line between the systemic and 'non-systemic' opposition, those groups who were forced to act outside of the sanctioned frame of political action. The CPRF and Just Russia tried to join the demonstrations in December 2011, when the situation looked uncertain, and despite plans later for Zyuganov to attend the September 2012 'March of Millions', in the end the CPRF retreated and criticised the 'orangism' of the protesters. Just Russia's retreat was far more painful. Three of its leading activists, Gennady and Dmitry Gudkov (father and son) and Ilya Ponomarev, enthusiastically joined the protest actions of the non-systemic opposition, threatening a split in the party. The business interests who funded the party insisted that it retain a constructive relationship with the Kremlin. Gennady Gudkov was one of the most popular rostrum speakers, and emerged even as a threat to Mironov within the party. In the end he was unceremoniously stripped of his Duma seat, and in October 2012 Mironov threatened members of the party who cooperated with the opposition with expulsion from the party: 'In such circumstances, playing revolution and provoking the authorities to further tighten the screws is either infantilism, or even worse, a dangerous and wilful provocation aimed at attaining one's own egoistic goals at all costs'.[27] Just Russia voted for the Dima Yakovlev law, and when its activists joined the impressively-large 'March Against Scoundrels' on 13 January 2013 (protesting against the Dima Yakovlev law), the Just Russia leadership stipulated that its members could not participate in rallies organised by other political organisations. On 13 March 2013 the Gudkovs, having refused to comply with the ultimatum either to stop their activities in the Coordination Council or leave the party, were expelled from Just Russia's ranks. Ilya Ponomarev and Oleg Shein were issued with the same ultimatum, and accepted the deal: the former left the Left Front and the latter resigned from the Council.

It was in this context that Prokhorov re-entered party politics. He gained a respectable vote in the presidential election, and after a few months he created Civil Platform. Given his extensive resources, the new party had a strong material base, but it was not clear what role it could play in circumstances of 'managed competition'. It would have no future if it allied too closely with the Kremlin, but how far could it push the bounds of sanctioned opposition? In the event, its attempt to bring together former political heavyweights, former governors and other substantive political figures was quashed by the Kremlin.[28] Instead, the new party focused on regional elections, although in the first major test, the 8 September 2013 regional elections, it was ousted in Yaroslavl, Vladimir and Transbaikal, but did achieve a signal victory in Ekaterinburg (see the next section). The prospects for an independent centre right party depended on unpredictable changes in the political conjuncture.[29] Prokhorov was one of the leaders of the 'elite opposition', along with Kudrin, who would play a crucial role if the regime weakened. In the meantime, Kudrin acted as the voice of technocratic reform, a role endorsed by Putin:

> But generally, Mr Kudrin and the likes of him have a point to make, and we need to listen to them. It's a very useful thing. So I believe that an opposition that has national interest at heart will be in demand.[30]

There was a broad consensus among critics about what needed to be done to 'modernise' the political system. Measures to restore the political subjectivity of the institutions of the constitutional state included reform of the central and local electoral commissions, and an independent judiciary and media. In July 2013 some of the country's leading experts published an open address in which they warned that 'the country's constitutional order is under threat'. The constitutional scholar Mikhail Krasnov, Alexander Obolonsky from the Higher School of Economics and four dozen others argued that 'The basic provisions of the constitution and, above all, the constitution's description of Russia as a rule-of-law state, have essentially become meaningless decorations'. The separation of powers had become blurred: 'How can one speak about the legal nature of the state when the public authorities are apparently waging a war on the country's emerging civil society?'. Modelled on the Gaullist constitution of the French Fifth Republic, the Caesarist features of the Russian polity had become accentuated. The president was not ascribed to any branch of government and instead hovered over them all. The address noted that 'the legislative work of parliament has acquired a distinct prohibitive and repressive character', while 'Law enforcement and intelligence agencies – the Investigative Committee, the police, the FSB, the prosecutor's office – rudely, sometimes deliberately and cynically violate constitutional and other provisions, including by fabricating criminal and administrative cases against those who criticise the authorities'.[31] The experts' case and Bolotnaya affair were notable examples of the 'war' of the public authorities against civil society.

The Centre for Strategic Research revealed a significant shift in the social base of opposition to Putin's regime. In May 2012 a CSR report prepared for the Committee of Civic Initiatives described the situation in the country as a political crisis, warning that the regime 'has lost the trust of the public'.[32] In its fifth report, *New Electoral Equilibrium* of July 2013, the decline in protest sentiments in Moscow and St Petersburg was noted, and instead less educated and poorer people in the regions were more likely to protest. Economic rather than political issues were more likely to trigger protest. Already in 2012, 33,000 protest events had taken place in the country, and now 63 per cent stated that economic grievances would prompt them to take part in actions, whereas in Moscow only 15 per cent said they would take to the streets over economic matters. Approval ratings for Putin had stabilised, once again making Putin the bedrock of stability, but the scale of protest sentiments had broadened. The ratings for Medvedev were also stable, while United Russia had even increased its authority. The 'demand for democracy' was now greater in the regions than in Moscow and the other big cities. This contradiction exposed a fundamental instability in the country. Dmitriev noted that the finding that regional respondents wanted more 'democracy' signalled their sense of powerlessness. In general, given that Russians saw no alternative to Putin, economic, ethnic or ecological issues would be more likely to provoke protest. In the year since the Bolotnaya events of 6 May the regime had managed to 'pacify' the population, with a sharp decline in protests in Moscow, but there had been a steep rise in the incidence of protest actions in the form of ethnic unrest in Russia's regions.[33]

A report from Olga Kryshtanovskaya's sociological laboratory in August 2013 described the shift in the structure of the opposition. The movement had not only ebbed, but its composition had changed. Much of the younger generation had left, and the average age of the protester had risen from the 30–35 to the 40–45 age bracket. Participants were now more educated and more professionally specialised, in other words, more middle class. The masses that had come out earlier now stayed at home, satisfied that they had forced the regime to liberalise or had become utterly demoralised. Above all, the movement's atrophy left the more radicalised and uncompromising vanguard in place. There had been a shift from 'Russia without Putin' to condemnation of the Putin system in its entirety. The aim of the radicals was no longer so much a change of leader as fundamental regime change. There had been a shift in slogans from 'for honest elections' to the call to free political prisoners, the Bolotnaya 28 and Alexei Navalny. There was also a shift in tactics, away from lawful protest to the call to occupy government buildings and to take the fight, violent if necessary, to the streets. The tough regime response to the demonstrations, as on 6 May 2012, meant that many previous participants were now scared of taking part in even legal demonstrations, leaving the field open to the radicals. The report estimated the militant vanguard to number some 8–10,000, deeply divided politically but united in the view that with peaceful protest exhausted, more radical measures were required.[34] Opposition had mutated from protest to militancy.

Elements of this were reflected in increased labour militancy. Shein, the Just Russia activist who had maintained a 40-day hunger strike after the Astrakhan mayoral elections on 4 March 2012, when he had come in second and refused to accept the result, is a leader of the Confederation of Labour of Russia (KTR). He noted that 'Workers in Russia are paid half as much as in the West. In developed countries, the share of wages in GDP is about 50 per cent, and in Russia just 25 per cent'. KTR is the country's second largest trade union, with its two million members encompassing teachers, air traffic controllers, dock labourers, motor manufacturers, sailors and doctors, the most militant sections of the workforce. The KTR leader, Boris Kravchenko, envisaged a strategy of demonstrations and rallies.[35] The official trade unions were deeply implicated into the Putinite corporatist system, and feared that industrial action on their part would lead to the loss of privileges and the network of property inherited from the Soviet period, leaving the field of 'contentious politics' to the independents.

Although critique and contestation returned with a vengeance to Russian politics after September 2011, the opposition was trapped by many of the same dilemmas facing protest movements against the destructive consequences of neoliberal capitalism in the West. The 'political imaginary' of the mainstream protest movement was no longer able to offer radical solutions, such as the renationalisation of the means of production, or a radical wealth tax on the elite. The CPRF did continue to peddle its radical anti-market and anti-western ideology, with some of these themes taken up by Udaltsov and his left-wing radicals, and even by the radical nationalist Eduard Limonov, but these were not central demands of the protest organisers. It is for this reason that the CPRF was left to one side by this new wave of popular mobilisation. Instead, too often the protests seemed to express the concerns of dissatisfied consumers rather than the aspirations of self-confident citizens for the free exercise of their political rights. This is hardly surprising, since unlike the advanced neoliberal states of the West, which largely excluded issues of social welfare from the basis of the legitimacy relationship with their citizens, Putin's social populism meant that these concerns were central to the legitimacy of his rule. Thus the system was vulnerable to both consumerist and civic demands.

Elections in Putin's third term

Between January and June 2012, while the old rules still applied, five governors were appointed, avoiding the need to hold what were likely to be contentious elections. These included Yaroslavl, where United Russia officially won only 29 per cent in December 2011, the lowest proportion in any region, and Sverdlovsk, where United Russia won only 33 per cent of the vote. On 14 October 2012 regime candidates won all five gubernatorial elections and six regional legislative contests. The Kremlin continued to act as the country's electoral regulator. The excessive politicisation of the election commission prompted one of the senior members of the CEC and a former Constitutional Court judge, Boris Ebzeev, to ask 'Are we moving from a civil state towards a party state?'.[36] In each case a different form of electoral management was applied, but in all instances the result was the same. For example, in Ryazan region the main challenger, Igor Morozov (the Pensioner Party's candidate), was offered a senate seat, allowing the incumbent Oleg Kovalev, to be re-elected, even though his chances earlier had been minimal. Ways were found to lower the voter turnout, 'spoiler' parties were deployed to fragment support for opposition candidates, as well as the usual tricks with absentee voter certificates, ballots and pressure on state employees and students. In local elections in Khimki, where there had long been protests in defence of the forest traversed by the planned Moscow–St Petersburg motorway, support for protest leader Yevgeniya Chirikova was diluted by a large number of spoiler candidates, allowing the regime-sponsored incumbent to squeeze through on a turnout of only 27 per cent.

Even this was not enough, and in January 2013 the State Duma adopted the law signalled by Putin earlier allowing regional legislatures to abolish gubernatorial elections and return to presidential appointment. A number of ethnically diverse and conflict-prone regions in the North Caucasus adopted this option, including Dagestan and Ingushetia. In September 2012 the anti-regime candidate in Yaroslavl, Yevgeny Urlashov, had won a landslide victory (70 per cent to United Russia's 28 per cent) to become the city's mayor. He planned to lead Prokhorov's Civil Platform campaign in the regional legislative elections in September 2013. Instead, on 3 July he was detained by the police on suspicion of demanding a bribe from a local company to have their rubbish collection contract renewed, and soon after he and four colleagues were charged. Navalny noted in his blog that about 90 per cent of mayors who won against United Russia candidates had been arrested or removed from office. A notable case was the arrest in June 2013 of the mayor of Makhachkala, the capital of Dagestan, in connection with the murder of a state investigator. On 1 August the Civil Platform was denied registration on a technicality, but RPR-Parnas was allowed on to the ballot, and Nemtsov campaigned tirelessly to win a seat to the regional legislature.

On 8 September 2013 the country once again went to the polls on what is now an annual single election day. Eight gubernatorial, 16 regional legislature, and 11 mayoral elections in regional capitals would be held, once again accompanied by the Kremlin's attempts 'to eliminate competition and guarantee victory for its preferred candidate'. As Ryzhkov notes, where the pre-Kremlin candidate was popular, a plethora of opposition candidates was encouraged to dilute the anti-regime vote; but where the Kremlin's candidate was weak and faced a strong opposition candidate, 'the authorities use their old trick of completely excluding all serious contenders from the elections'.[37] In Ekaterinburg, the country's fourth largest city, the political establishment was challenged by Roizman, the head as we have seen of the 'City without Drugs' foundation, who sought to become mayor. In the 2011 Duma election Just Russia won 27.2 per cent of the vote, to United Russia's 26.6 per cent. In the Moscow region Gennady Gudkov was allowed on to the ballot, having passed through the municipal filter with the assistance of the incumbent, Andrei Vorobyev. With seven million inhabitants, the region is Russia's second largest in terms of population and fourth in terms of aggregate economic output. About 2.5 million commuters pour into Moscow city every day, typically spending 2–3 hours on packed trains. Despite recourse to the old managerial tricks, there were clear signs of disarray in the system.

In June 2013 Sobyanin triggered pre-term elections by resigning. The mayoral elections, the first in Moscow in over ten years, had been scheduled for 2015, but Sobyanin sought to gain legitimacy for his rule now that gubernatorial elections had been restored. A potential Putin successor, the endorsement of Moscow's population would immeasurably strengthen his position. The city's official population is 12 million, but unofficial reckonings range as high as 18–20 million. Either way, it is one of the world's ten largest cities, a major financial and economic centre, with half of Russia's banks registered there as well as hosting the headquarters of most major corporations. The city's GDP is over $300bn, roughly a sixth of the country's entire GDP. The city had clearly fallen out of love with Putin, registering one of the lowest votes for him in March 2012, and was even less keen on United Russia. Sobyanin only joined the party in 2012, but significantly, he chose to fight for the mayoralty as an independent, with the support of the RPF. Navalny entered the lists as his main challenger, even though he was facing criminal charges in Kirov.

Prokhorov's decision not to participate in the mayoral election, referring to problems in transferring his foreign assets to Russia, removed one of the strongest potential candidates. He won 20 per cent of the presidential vote in the city in March 2012, yet he now shied away from standing. He argued that his Civil Platform party would use the contest to prepare for the following year's Moscow Duma elections, but once again it looked as if he was pulling his punches.[38] He could have delegated his sister, Irina Prokhorova, a noted publisher and popular political figure with no foreign assets, to fight the contest, but this solution was refused, reinforcing the impression that 'Mr Prokhorov is involved in the Kremlin politico-technological games'.[39] Mitrokhin, head of Yabloko, entered the lists as the liberal flag-bearer. Mitrokin had served as a Moscow duma member, and thus was familiar with the problems facing the city and was a noted champion of local government. He also stood a reasonable chance of passing the municipal filter since Yabloko had 21 deputies in Moscow's municipal assemblies. Ivan Melnikov, first deputy chair of the CPRF and considered one of its reformers, Levichev of Just Russia and the LDPR's Mikhail Degtyarov joined the six candidates registered to run.

Despite being on trial for embezzlement in Kirov, Navalny entered the mayoral race as the RPR-Parnas candidate. Even here Navalny proved a controversial candidate, with Ryzhkov voting against the Republican Party backing Navalny, but the co-leaders Kasyanov and Nemtsov voted to support him. The 'municipal filter' meant that he needed to collect the notarised signatures of at least 6 per cent of municipal deputies or heads in 110 out of the city's 146 municipal districts. Independent candidates also have to collect the signatures of at least 73,000 ordinary voters, but since Navalny was a party candidate, he did not need to do this. Sobyanin helped Navalny gain the requisite municipal signatures, reflecting his confidence that he would win and to demonstrate the legitimacy of the contest.[40] He fought a western-style campaign, meeting with voters every day, raising funds through individual donations, and mobilising thousands of activists on his behalf. Navalny advanced one of the more thoughtful programmes, although it was short of detailed policies. His 19-page manifesto called for devolution and local solutions to national problems, including immigration, but above all promised the creation of an 'accountable' power system and full transparency. The city was, as Navalny put it, 'the key to change in Russia'.[41] The programme noted the 'archaic management principles' on which the city was run (p. 3), and took a hard line against illegal migration, noting that 'The slavish position of illegal migrants is useful for employers, including municipal agencies', with corrupt officials paying them kopeks and putting the rest of budget funds into their pockets (p. 13).

Navalny's sudden release after his conviction, following a gathering of some 10,000 that evening in Moscow, to allow him to fight the Moscow election prompted endless speculation. One theory was that the regime feared mass disturbances if he had been jailed and removed from the Moscow lists, yet this is unlikely. Although a cautious politician, Putin is not someone who would be intimidated by the prospect of even a 100,000-strong demonstration. Others focused on Sobyanin's need to ensure a genuinely competitive election to ensure his own legitimacy in a potential presidential bid. The opposite view suggested that conservatives in the heart of the Putinite apparatus were playing the 'Navalny card', to check Sobyanin's popularity and political influence to prevent him positioning himself as a potential successor. Putin won only 47 per cent in the city in the presidential election, and the idea now was that Sobyanin could not be allowed to win by a much more impressive margin.[42] Less plausible was the idea that allowing Navalny to participate was a token of the regime's liberalisation. The 'Bolotnaya case' was continuing and across

The new traditionalism and regime reset 213

Russia civil society activists were being imprisoned on trumped up charges. Another theory argued that Navalny was ultimately a put-up job, sponsored covertly by elements within the regime. For the security apparatus, he was another 'special operation' designed to preserve the status quo and to prevent the country sliding into another disintegrative cycle of the perestroika type.[43]

Navalny was characteristically liberal in his abuse and employment of extravagant language, alienating potential voters, above all in the bureaucracy. Many commentators noted that Navalny's team had as little tolerance for the views of others as the authorities had. Navalny's candidature galvanised the campaign and signalled the return of competitive politics and brought the opposition back from irrelevance. In a striking departure from the practice imposed after the Yukos affair that business stays out of openly supporting candidates in elections, 37 Russian internet entrepreneurs signed a 'social contract' supporting Navalny's run for the mayoralty. There were even suggestions that his campaign was being quietly supported by the influential Alfa Bank. It seemed that finally 'the bourgeoisie' was once again tempted to exert its political muscles. Navalny appeared to offer a genuine political alternative, although many questioned his credentials as a 'true democrat'. Desperate to find someone who could lead the opposition to Putin, liberals appeared to turn a blind eye to Navalny's shortcomings, including alleged anti-semitism.[44]

A complementary perspective argues that Navalny was an auxiliary in the regime's campaigns, as with his denunciation of United Russia as a 'party of thieves and swindlers', which suited those factions who favoured the popular front gambit. In other words, Navalny was a reserve force to be played when the regime mutated towards a new style of political leadership. His vocabulary replicated the classic formulations of neo-liberal governmentality, including competition, transparency, accountability and choice, with a technocratic idealisation of the 'free' market as the most rational form of organising social life. The vengeful attitude of his campaign staff to critics mimicked that of the regime. His nationalist sentiments and anti-elitist right-wing populism suited some in the regime perfectly well. These considerations led many to doubt that he could be trusted as a politician.

In the event, Navalny won an astonishing 27.24 per cent of the vote, to Sobyanin's 51.37 per cent, while the CPRF candidate Melnikov came third with 10.69 per cent. Navalny garnered 633,000 votes to Sobyanin's 1.2m, in a city with 7.25m registered voters. Navalny's share was inflated by the very low turnout of only 33 per cent. He was able to mobilise his supporters (mostly the same as the 869,000 who had voted for Prokhorov in 2012), while Sobyanin's constituency stayed at home. Even though he won in the first round (a result challenged by Navalny's team), Sobyanin proved a dour and uninspired campaigner, and his status as a potential presidential candidate was damaged. The liberals could not take much comfort from the result either. In genuinely competitive and fair conditions, Navalny was only able to win 8.7 per cent of the total electorate in Moscow. In the country's most advanced city the liberals represented a rather small enclave. Nevertheless, relatively free elections were the most effective way of averting an 'orange' revolution, typically provoked when people see no hope of change through the ballot box. Russia now witnessed the rebirth of competitive elections and, as Navalny put it, 'A large opposition, a genuine political movement has been born in Russia. ... Today we are witnessing the birth of a genuine political movement and we know what to do next'.[45]

In the Moscow region Vorobyev won a comfortable victory with 75 per cent of the vote, the CPRF came second, pushing Gudkov, the Yabloko candidate, into third place with 4.43 per cent on a 38.6 per cent turnout. In Ekaterinburg, Roizman won the contest as the Civil Platform candidate to become mayor with 33.25 per cent to United Russia's 29.77 per cent. Given the earlier political scandals associated with his name, this was an astonishing vindication of his approach and a striking illustration of the regime's new liberalism. In Petrozavodsk the independent candidate Galina Shirshina defeated United Russia to become mayor. In Yaroslavl region RPR-Parnas crossed the 5 per cent representation threshold, allowing Nemtsov to enter the regional legislature. The Just Russia incumbent acting governor in Transbaikal region, Konstantin Ilyinsky, was confirmed in his post. Overall, United Russia candidates registered strong victories across the country, winning the governorships in Chukotka, Magadan, Khakasia, Vladimir and others, while in Dagestan and Ingushetia the governors were elected by the regional parliaments. United Russia came top in the legislative elections in all 16 regions, securing 636 seats out of 820. Across the country there was no shortage of the usual tricks, with the mobile ballot boxes taken to old people's homes, psychiatric wards and pre-trial detention centres registering nearly 100 per cent of the votes for regime candidates, but in general fewer infringements of electoral procedures were recorded than in the parliamentary and presidential elections. However, many regions objected to the order from above to register opposition candidates. In Khakasia, for example, Churov's direct instruction to do so was ignored and the local authorities stuck to administrative methods, including extensive ballot rigging. Nevertheless, these elections marked a qualitative transformation of Russian politics. Medvedev's reforms were taking root, and the ballot box was restored as a mechanism of political change. But the gains were fragile, especially since there was little evidence of the consolidation of an independent party system. The vote cast in Moscow for the established political parties – the CPRF, LDPR, Just Russia and Yabloko was mostly in single figures, demonstrating their need for renewal. It was the regime that ordered honest elections, and the regime could take them away.

The only real winner was Putin, whose candidate in Moscow won (but not by too much), demonstrating that in conspicuously free and fair elections the regime could triumph. Putin noted that 'work in the political field has become more complicated' because of 'our actions to improve the country's political system', rendering it 'thoroughly competitive'. He praised the elections as the most 'legitimate, transparent and regulated' that the country had ever seen, and urged the victors to work with the opposition, 'bearing in mind that they ... sincerely wanted to win the instruments of power to resolve the problems of our citizens'.[46] Volodin's strategy to create a 'competitive political environment' was being implemented, challenging the opposition to use the new freedom to fight the regime through the ballot box. Those within the system who argued that legitimacy was as important as control were vindicated, although the shift to a more competitive environment cast into doubt the legitimacy of all previous elections. There were new rules to the political game, but the regime could still come out on top. The regime appears genuinely to have engaged in what Petrov calls 'reactive political modernisation'.[47] To ensure its own survival, elements of competitive democracy were incorporated into practices of political management. Not for the first time in history, adaptive evolution to pre-empt societal challenges may be the firmest path to democracy.

Regime reset

The great sociologist Pitirim Sorokin noted that 'It is naïve to assume that the so-called absolute despot can allow himself to do what he pleases regardless of the wishes of and pressure from his underlings. To believe in such an absolute power of despots and in their total freedom from societal pressure is nonsense.'[48] Rivalries and conflicting ambitions within the elite will always constrain the leader, while in the end the voice of 'the people' makes itself heard. In Putin's Russia, where the constitutional state remains a constraining force, the leaderism inherent in regime forms of rule was stunted. However much *primus*, Putin's rule was still embedded *inter pares*. Putin's political genius lay in balancing the factions against each other, and not allowing any primacy over the others, accompanied by the creation of a central corps of individuals, who could be called the Putinite high command.

The dual state as it developed in the Putin years placed a high premium on the concept of 'loyalty' and is one of the central pillars of the semi-institutionalised administrative regime. This rather amorphous concept plays an important role in the shaping of factions and the development of the Russian polity. When independent business leaders threatened the regime they were subject to attack, a system that was consolidated in the wake of the Yukos affair to create obeisant 'state oligarchs'. However, even loyalty was not enough at times of stress, notably during periods of succession at regular four-yearly intervals (hence the extension of the presidential term to six years). In the 2011–12 electoral cycle early victims were Luzhkov, summarily and brutally dismissed on 28 September 2010, and Mironov, the head of the Federation Council and leader of Just Russia, who was unceremoniously dropped from his leadership of the upper house in spring 2011. Despite years of loyal service, when they became superfluous to the over-riding imperative of regime perpetuation and elite reproduction, they were jettisoned. The protest movement against the flawed parliamentary elections of December 2011 was accompanied by intra-elite splits, which in part followed factional lines. Kudrin showed signs of defection from the Putinite consensus already from the beginning of 2011, when he called for free and fair elections, but his personal loyalty to Putin shielded him from recriminations.

The 'hegemonic' presidency was careful to maintain its pre-eminence by standing above factions, and indeed part of its effective power derived from its ability to arbitrate between different elements of the regime. Conflicting groups appeal to the supreme arbiter for support. This was a Bonapartist model of politics, but there is no agreement on what these groups represent. The ruling elite is divided into factions engaged in a permanent 'war' for access to resources and super-profitable output. Those able to wield the 'power' resource are in a particularly strong position, with numerous well-funded security agencies at their back, reinforced by the General Prosecutors' Office and the Investigative Committee. All groups participated in the creation of super-monopolies in the Putin era – energy, shipping, telecommunications, banking and so on, which were susceptible to factional exploitation. The state is one of the players in this field and always wins any fight. However, when the state itself is fragmented, the outcome is more uncertain. The fragmented political terrain in the context of a stalemated political system allowed 'corporate' raids (with the corporation being a combination of state officials and private interests) against Yukos and other companies.

This balancing act was constantly evolving in response to changing circumstances, accompanied by constant modifications to the high command. With Putin's return, a study by the Minchenko consulting agency, based on expert surveys with 60 leading political scientists, business leaders, politicians and practitioners, identified a 'Politburo 2.0' at the heart of the system, an analogue of the old Soviet body of supreme power. This was an inner elite of eight individuals, some of whom had nothing directly to do with politics.[49] Such a delineated core to the Putinite system of rule was something new, although there had always been a côterie of key figures meeting on a regular basis with Putin outside of formal institutions. The key power-holders in contemporary Russia were identified as Igor Sechin, Sergei Chemezov, Gennady Timchenko, Yuri Kovalchuk, Sergei Sobyanin, Sergei Ivanov, Vyacheslav Volodin and Dmitry Medvedev. The politburo does not of course meet as a collective, yet it represents the heart of the informal constellation of power. Its members are trusted by Putin and each has their own portfolio where they can take their own decisions, and they mostly do not compete with each other. For example, Sechin oversees the oil industry, Timchenko the oil and gas markets, Sergei Shoigu the military, Sobyanin the mega-city of Moscow, Sergei Ivanov the presidential administration and the security sector, while Medvedev, constitutionally the second most senior figure in the country, led a group of second-tier liberal ministers and was effectively eclipsed by the other constellations.

A bloc of 'Politburo candidates', or outer elite, was also identified, including Patriarch Kirill, the leaders of the parliamentary parties and, surprisingly,

Mikhail Prokhorov, the businessman who ran as a liberal candidate in the presidential elections. The model suggests that Russia is ruled by a number of clans linked by business interests, common Soviet-era backgrounds, and in certain cases family relationships. The key elite groups were identified as the 'force' (the '*siloviki*'), 'political', 'technical' and 'entrepreneurial' factions. Putin crowns the system, balancing interests and preventing any single one becoming predominant. To do so, as argued above, would threaten his own independence, rendering him potentially hostage to a single faction; but at the same time, he cannot be seen as a mortal threat to any of the groups, since that would render him a liability for all. In other words, he has to have enough power to prevent factional conflict spiralling out of control and becoming a war of all against all; but at the same time this power has to be disguised and shared, to allow key constituencies to retain a stake in the system.

In a follow-up report, based on elite interviews conducted in January and February 2013, Minchenko Consulting traced leadership dynamics since the election.[50] It once again stressed that the Russian regime was a conglomerate of competing clans and groups, with Putin acting as the arbiter and moderator. At the heart of the new report was the observation, shared by many other commentators, that the so-called 'big government', encompassing the presidential apparatus, the government proper, and the Security Council, represented an eclectic mix of different elements. This allowed Putin to retain his personal pre-eminence, but inhibited the adoption of strategic decisions. Regime preservation and Putin's personal power acted as a brake on what Medvedev had called 'modernisation'. The struggle for the post of prime minister acted as a proxy in the battle to succeed Putin, since the premier is the automatic successor in case anything happens to the president. The key point is one that has been made consistently in this book and my earlier work:

> Russian power is by no means a rigid vertical structure controlled by one man. The line of command (Putin's 'vertical of power') is no more than a propaganda cliché. Russian power is a conglomerate of clans and groups that compete with one another over resources. Vladimir Putin's role in this system remains unchanged – he is an arbiter and moderator, but a powerful arbiter who has the last word (at least for the time being) in conflict situations.

The report traced who was up and who was down among the top officials. Shoigu was the clear winner, with a surge in his popularity after he took over as minister of defence following Serdyukov's dismissal. Shoigu had long successfully led the emergency situations ministry, and he now became one of the leading putative contenders, possibly as prime minister in the first instance. However, the fact that he is a Buddhist made him a less attractive leadership prospect to the Putinite conservative majority and the Russian Orthodox

Church, and his age did not help. Others sought to assume the mantle of charismatic leadership. Moscow mayor Sobyanin had consolidated his position, and although he was a loyal Putinite he worked well with other groups. He had the advantage of having earlier been a regional leader as governor of Tyumen, and was thus also well-connected to the powerful energy companies. Sobyanin was one of the few who could assume the mantle of 'faction manager' and appease the contending factions within the regime. The head of the Federation Council, Valentina Matvienko, raised her profile, as had Sergei Naryshkin as speaker of the Duma. The latter positioned himself simultaneously as a moderate reformer and loyalist. Vice premier Dmitry Rogozin, at the head of the military industrial complex, certainly entertained leadership ambitions, but his reputation as a maverick damaged his chances. Nevertheless, Rogozin was a core figure in the new traditionalism, and thus would be a powerful candidate when the succession finally comes.

There were few who could represent different political forces in the country to balance the decaying United Russia organisation. These included some semi-oppositional figures, notably Kudrin and Prokhorov. The key process was the break-up of the 2010–11 model of the 'Medvedev coalition' for gradual within-system change, and there appeared nowhere now for the liberal reformers within the regime to go. Even some within the dominant party felt uncomfortable with the conservative turn. In late May 2013 Alexei Chesnakov resigned as United Russia's deputy secretary, complaining of a democratic deficit within the party, and in particular criticising its media and internet policies.[51] As one of the architects of the Surkov system of managed democracy, his sudden realisation of democratic inadequacies came as a surprise to many. Medvedev was a much diminished figure and his credibility as the leader of the liberal modernising trend in Russian politics was minimal. Medvedev had indicated that the presidency was a river into which one could step twice, but he soon retreated to state that it would be unthinkable for him to compete against Putin. Elite groups continued to fragment, spinning off new players but constrained by the system's reconsolidation on a new basis. Putin remained the linchpin of the system; hence the view among the top elite that Putin would have to remain in power after 2018.

Volodin, the head of the Kremlin's domestic policy administration, was at the heart of managing the political reset. His new approach of 'managed competition' potentially created space for more competitive electoral politics. Moves towards systemic demonopolisation saw 54 of the newly-registered parties participate in the September 2013 elections, and as a result 31 parties were represented in regional and municipal legislatures. At the Valdai Club on 18 September 2013 Volodin insisted that 'The move towards fair elections will intensify, and there will be greater political competition in the future'. This strategy was not just for public display, and Kremlin insiders confirmed that this was the line pursued in the corridors of power. Soon after Oleg Morozov, the head of the presidential domestic policy directorate, congratulated the electoral commissions 'for your success in ensuring that the number of bans imposed on different candidates and different political parties seeking to take part in the electoral process was minimal during the September elections'. He stressed that the era of banning potential candidates 'for no discernible reason' had passed; 'this instrument of "political struggle" is over', he insisted.[52] Permitting Navalny to run in Moscow and the opposition victories elsewhere demonstrated that the regime was willing to experiment with electoral competition, and represented 'a victory for both the government and the opposition'.[53] Putinism is an amorphous and relatively capacious political project, and now the struggle between its various manifestations was to be waged in public. The Rogozin flavour was to go head-to-head with Prokhorov's liberalism, while Kudrin would advance his own model of economic reform. What had formally been the 'non-systemic' opposition would now be systematised and brought in from the cold, as long as it conformed to the Putinite rules of the game.

The protests and United Russia's poor showing in the 2011 State Duma elections prompted changes to the political system, including the return to direct gubernatorial elections, relaxing party registration procedures, the return of the mixed electoral system, prohibitions on the elite holding bank accounts abroad, restructuring the presidential Human Rights Council, accompanied by restrictions on the non-for-profit sector. The Institute for Socioeconomic and Political Studies Foundation (ISEPI) was created in 2011 to prepare programmes for both the People's Front and United Russia. It was headed by the former deputy head of the domestic policy administration, Dmitry Badovsky, with the brief to work with the expert community. In 2013 ISEPI took over responsibility for dealing with applications for presidential grants for research into socio-political issues, including polling, political analysis and election monitoring, while the grants were managed by Ella Panfilova's Civil Dignity foundation. With external sources of funding effectively cut off, the number of applications for presidential grants tripled. At a meeting with experts and political analysts on 9 July 2013 Volodin explicitly linked these changes to the 'regime reset', designed to create a system that did not need manual management and reliance on administrative levers while preserving 'stability and predictability'.[54]

The regime shifted to a new mode of operation, based on disciplining its own elites, incorporating the part of the opposition ready to engage in electoral politics, the absorption into the regime's rhetoric of nationalist concerns, and increases in social payments to wean the socially-motivated part of the protest movement from the opposition. There were even plans, drafted by the presidential Human Rights Council at Putin's request, for an amnesty to mark the twentieth anniversary of the adoption of the constitution on 12 December 1993. Mironov called for the 'broadest possible amnesty', and urged that the Bolotnaya case and Pussy Riot prisoners be released, while others urged that this was an opportunity to give Khodorkovsky and Lebedev their freedom, as well as Navalny.[55] The final decision was taken by the State Duma in December 2013, and saw some 10,000 of Russia's 700,000 prisoners released. Above all, on 19 December Khodorkovsky was pardoned by Putin, and the next day he was released after ten years in jail and flew to Berlin.

The regime reset was prompted by intra-elite splits and pressure from below. A powerful *civiliki* coalition for change remained at the heart of the Putinite system. People like Gref, Chubais, Kudrin and Nabiullina, plus of course the prime minister and a whole group of cabinet ministers, all fought for liberal economic reforms and a degree of political liberalisation. Their aspirations to strengthen the constitutional state were constrained by the continued power of the tutelary administrative regime, defended notably by the statists and *siloviki*. This gave rise to the situation we have described in this book of stalemate and policy drift, but the duality of the state also provided a platform for reform.

Notes

1. This sentiment comes over in innumerable conversations with Russian colleagues; not only academics but also in various other professions, and not only in Moscow but in various provincial towns.
2. 'Russian Economy Stagnating – Minister', RIA Novosti, 12 August 2013.
3. 'Interview to Channel One and Associated Press News Agency', 4 September 2013, http://eng.kremlin.ru/news/5935.
4. Mikhail Gorbachev, 'Razryv mezhdu vlast'yu i narodom bolee neterpim', speech of 9 February 2012, *Novaya gazeta*, 16 February 2012.
5. Maksim Glinkin, 'Vse menee obayatel'nyi lider', *Vedomosti*, 9 August 2013.
6. 'Disappointment in Putin Has Doubled Since 2001', RIA Novosti, 9 August 2013.
7. 'Most Russians Approve of Putin's Performance as President', reporting a Levada Centre poll, 29 August 2013.
8. Rose, Richard, William Mishler and Neil Munro, *Popular Support for an Undemocratic Regime: The Changing Views of Russians* (Cambridge, Cambridge University Press, 2011), p. 173.
9. Charles Clover, 'A Ratings Game with Just One Player', *Financial Times*, 19 October 2012, 'Investing in Russia' supplement, p. 3.
10. Yurii Luzhkov, *I tak zhit' nel'zya ... Besedy s politikom i grazhdaninom* (Moscow, Veche, 2012).
11. For example, Aleksei Chelnokov, *Putinskii zastoi: Novoe politbyuro kremlya* (Moscow, Yauza Press, 2013), and Vladimir Novosel'tsev, *Kremlevskaya vlast': Krizis gosudarstvennogo upravleniya* (Moscow, Algoritm, 2012).
12. Donald N. Jensen, 'Putin's "Praetorian Guard"', *IMR*, 10 October 2013.
13. Arkadii Lyubarev, 'Protsess udlineniya spiskov', *Nezavisimaya gazeta*, 17 April 2013, p. 5.
14. Aleksandra Samarina, 'Liberal'nyi elektorat broshen na proizvol syd'by', *Nezavisimaya gazeta*, 17 April 2013a, pp. 1, 3.
15. Nikolai Petrov, 'Elections Show the End of One-Party System', *Moscow Times*, 27 August 2013.
16. For details, see Vladimir Ryzhkov, 'Regional Elites See United Russia's Stock falling', *Moscow Times*, 27 August 2013.
17. Interview with Gleb Pavlovsky, 'Return of the Refuseniks', Valdai Discussion Club, 25 June 2013; Valdaiclub.com.
18. Quoted by Ian Traynor, 'Putin and Obama Apart in More Ways than One at G20 Table', *The Guardian*, 5 September 2013, p. 1.
19. Oleg Savitsky, 'Sovereign Democracy without the Sovereign', *Osobaya bukva*, 26 August 2013.

The new traditionalism and regime reset 221

20 Yevgenii Gontmakher, 'Rekonstruktsiya nastoyashchei "Doktriny Putina"', *Vedomosti*, 19 October 2012.
21 'Poslanie Prezidenta Federal'nomu Sobraniyu', 12 December 2012, http://kremlin.ru/news/17118.
22 'Press-konferentsiya Vladimira Putina', 20 December 2012, http://kremlin.ru/news/17173.
23 Vladimir V. Putin, 'A Plea for Caution from Russia', *New York Times*, 12 September 2013.
24 Vladimir Putin, 'Meeting of the Valdai International Discussion Club', 19 September 2013a; http://eng.news.kremlin.ru/news/6007.
25 Julia Loffe, 'The Most Dangerous Blogger in the World: How Aleksey Navalny Changed Russian Politics', *The New Republic*, 18 July 2013.
26 For his own account of how he fell out with the 'party of thieves and swindlers' see Gennadii Gudkov, *Za chto menya nevzlyubili 'partiya zhulikov i vorov'* (Moscow, Algoritm, 2013).
27 Cited in Tatyana Stanovaya, 'Opposition(s) in Waiting', www.neweasterneurope.eu, No. 1 (VI), 2013b.
28 Aleksandra Samarina, 'Smert' politicheskikh brendov', *Nezavisimaya gazeta*, 10 September 2013b, p. 1.
29 Tatyana Stanovaya, 'Mikhail Prokhorov: Between the Kremlin and the Opposition', *IMR*, 19 February 2013c; http://www.imrussia.org.
30 'Visit to Russia Today Television Channel', 11 June 2013; http://eng.kremlin.ru/transcripts/5571.
31 'Pravovaya ugroza', 22 July 2013; http://www.polit.ru/article/2013/07/22/letter/. For commentary, see Ekaterina Mishina, 'Let's Say "No" to the Erosion of the Constitution', *IMR*, 29 July 2013.
32 Centre for Strategic Research, *Obshchestvo i vlast' v usloviyakh politicheskogo krizisa* (Moscow, Doklad ekspertov TSR Komitetu grazhdanskikh initsiativ, May 2012).
33 Centre for Strategic Research, *Novoe elektoral'noe ravnovesie: Srednosrochnyi trend ili 'vremennoe zatish'e'* (Moscow, July 2013).
34 Kryshtanovskaya Lab, *The Dynamics of Protest Activity: 2012–2013*, discussed by Pavel Koshkin, 'Russian Protest Movement: Smaller and More Radical?', 13 August 2013, http://russiadirect.foreignpolicy.com/content/russian-protest-movement-smaller-and-more-radical.
35 'Alternative Trade Unions Threaten with Nationwide Action', Itar-Tass, 16 August 2013.
36 Natal'ya Gorodetskaya, 'Izbirkomy depolitizirovat', sbor podpisei prodlit', registratsii ne lishat", *Kommersant*, 19 October 2012, p. 3.
37 Vladimir Ryzhkov, 'Kremlin manipulation of Elections Continues', *Moscow Times*, 16 July 2013.
38 Jonathan Earle, 'Prokhorov to Skip Mayoral Election', *Moscow Times*, 14 June 2013.
39 'Mikhail Prokhorov not to Run for Moscow Mayoral Elections', ITAR-TASS, 14 June 2013.
40 Julian G. Waller, 'Re-Setting the Game: The Logic and Practice of Official Support for Alexei Navalny's Mayoral Run', *Russian Analytical Digest*, No. 136, 16 September 2013, pp. 6–9.
41 *Programma kandidata v mery Moskvy Alekseya Naval'nogo 2013 god*, p. 7; http://navalny.ru/platform/Navalny_Program.pdf.
42 Georgy Bovt, 'Why Navalny Wasn't Removed', *Moscow Times*, 26 August 2013.
43 For a powerful exposition of this view, see Daniil Kotsyubinsky, 'Messiah or false Prophet?', www.opendemocracy.net, 13 August 2013; http://www.opendemocracy.net/od-russia/daniil-kotsyubinsky/messiah-or-false-prophet.
44 Paul Goble, 'Russian Intelligentsia Prepared to Overlook Navalny's Nationalism', Window on Eurasia; *JRL*, 161/7, 2013.

45 'Navalny: This Election Gives Birth to Genuine Russian Opposition', Interfax, 10 September 2013.
46 V. V. Putin, 'Vstrecha s izbrannymi glavami sub"ektov Rossiiskoi Federatsii', 10 September 2013; http://www.kremlin.ru/transcripts/19189.
47 Nikolai Petrov, 'September 8 Election as a New Phase of the Society and Authorities' Coevolution', Carnegie Moscow Center, *Eurasia Outlook*, 5 September 2013.
48 Pitirim Sorokin, *Chelovek, obshchestvo, tsivilitatsiya* (Moscow, Politizdat, 1992).
49 Minchenko Consulting, *Doklad: Bol'shoe pravitel'stvo Vladimira Putina i "Politbyuro 2.0"* (Moscow, Kommunikatsionnyi kholding "Minchenko konsalting", 2012).
50 Minchenko Consulting, *Doklad 'Politbyuro 2.0': Nakanune perezagruzki elitnykh grupp*, 19 February 2013, http://www.minchenko.ru/analitika/analitika_30.html.
51 Brian Whitmore, 'With or Without Putin', RFE/RL, *Russia Report*, 30 May 2013b.
52 'Kremlin Calls Candidates' Groundless Removal from Elections "Yesterday's Instrument"', Interfax, 24 October 2013.
53 Alexei Levinson, 'Cynicism as a Ruling Ideology', 22 October 2013; www.opendemocracy.net.
54 Irina Nagornikh, 'Kreml' prodolzhit perezagruzku vnutrennei politiki', *Kommersant*, 10 July 2013.
55 'Amnesty Proposed by Human Rights Body Could See High-Profile Prisoners Released', Interfax, 16 October 2013.

10 Conclusion: *Respice finem*

Putin's return entailed high political costs, undermining the stability that it was intended to ensure. Putin's focus was on the means, but lost sight of the purpose. The principle of *respice finem* – 'consider the end' – began to elude him. The gulf between the Putin project and Putinite practices began to close, based on a new synthesis of traditionalism and moderated practices of political managerialism, accompanied by Eurasian integration and a sovereignty-oriented approach to international affairs. Whether this would be able to overcome the modernisation blockage and political stalemate was questionable. Unlike China, the restored Putinite system was in danger of delivering neither growth nor democracy. The system engaged in movement without a sense of direction; and when it had purpose, it seemed to be intent on blocking the potential for reform and autonomous development.

Russia is a dual state in which the authoritarianism of the administrative regime is countered by the weak democracy of the constitutional state. Pluralistic and competitive politics is constricted by the power of the administrative system, while the economic regime stifles entrepreneurship and poisons the business climate. Institutions have been gutted of the inner logic that would render them viable in a working system of power and responsibility. The Medvedev presidency offered an opportunity to change the logic of the system without threatening the elites with retribution for their venality and subversion of constitutional authority in the Putin years. This would have been a way of achieving intra-systemic evolutionary change while transforming the fundamental operative code of the system. Instead, the opportunity was squandered, culminating in Putin's 'constitutional coup' of September 2011 and his return to the presidency. Medvedev promised a programme of controlled liberalisation to give more autonomy to the institutions and processes specified in the constitution. This evolutionary potential was smothered by the change. Not only did the 'castling' move evoke popular disgust but, following the flawed parliamentary elections on 4 December, widespread popular protest indicated that the mystical bond (enhanced by rather less than mystical media manipulation) that had united Putin and the people was fraying. For the first time in over a decade the people were forcefully demanding involvement in governance. Putin's reliance on managerial techniques exacerbated the stagnation features of the system.

Putin's return threw a harsh light on the nature of the political system that had developed over the past decade. Rather than a set of independent institutions carrying defined political weight, as laid out in the constitution, the power of one man was determining. Above all, rather than competitive elections shaping the composition of parliament and the presidency, the administrative system decided everything on behalf of the people. Elections became plebiscitary, ratifying decisions already made outside of the electoral process. The contradictions in the Putinite tutelary model of development became manifest at the time of the 2011–12 elections. However, although the Putinite system was highly personalised, the dilemmas facing the country are far larger than the contradictions of Putin's personality. Indeed, the complexities of his political personality are a personification of the dilemmas and strategic choices facing the country. By attributing all the flaws and failures of the post-communist era to Putin, and his predecessor Yeltsin, we lose sight of the structural issues. This is not to deny that agency matters, and the personal choices made by these two leaders did shape Russia's political destiny in these years. Nevertheless, they were not operating in a vacuum, and their personal responses interacted with structural factors to shape the new system.

The key demand of the resistance movement was to bring the administrative regime under social control. This would entail strengthening the autonomy of the institutions of the constitutional state, above all the courts, as well as reducing the power of the sovereign bureaucracy. However, since Putin was not a man of rules but of exceptions, although with the exceptions regulated with fastidious pedantry by rules, with an instrumental and functional view of law (above all, to be used against others and not applied to his friends), then he found himself in a contradictory trap: strengthening the institutions of the constitutional state would undermine his autonomy, the elite structures that he had put in place, and his personalised governmental style in general; but failure to do so risked the whole edifice being swept away by a newly-confident protest movement and sections of the elite pushing for change. By trying to hang on to power too long, Putin risked becoming the instrument of the downfall of the very system that he had so laboriously built.

Worse than this, the regime increasingly boxed itself in. In line with my argument about the historical stalemate in contemporary Russia, Pastukhov argues that the Kremlin finds itself in a 'zugzwang', the term used in chess to describe the position where one or even both sides have no useful or even neutral moves to make, and any move will only worsen the situation. In chess the option of doing nothing is not allowed, and in contemporary Russia stalemate has prompted frenetic activity with little developmental purpose to cover for the lack of substantive ideas. In Pastukhov's view, Navalny's candidature for the Moscow mayoral election 'turned into a referendum on trust in Putin'. There were no good options for the regime: ban him, and the whole electoral process was discredited; let him run, and the contest inexorably turned into a referendum on the Putin system. Pastukhov considers this the first 'strategic blunder' by Volodin since the Bolotnaya violence. For years the Kremlin had tried to stop the clock and to maintain the status quo, whereas Navalny's challenge forced it out of its 'comfort zone'. This, though, was not just an individual mistake but a 'systemic error', one that would inevitably have happened sooner or later. 'Elements of irrationality can build up inside a system for a long time, for whole decades, but not endlessly. There comes a moment when this irrationality starts to "discharge"'. The long-term strategy to marginalise the opposition intersected with the plan to make Moscow a platform for regime development, which earlier led to Luzhkov's dismissal and now to Sobyanin's attempt to fight 'free and fair' elections. The collision of the two strategies raised the risk of system breakdown. Equally, Pastukhov notes that the regime was in another zugzwang with Khodorkovsky: release him, and he could become the rallying point for the opposition; keep him in jail, and all attempts to relegitimise the system would be doomed.[1]

The opposition also finds itself beset by contradictions, determined by the structural and systemic constraints of Russia's current stage of development. Much of the protest against the Putinite system is Putinite in character – depoliticised, mute and gestural – indicating the deep social roots of the present system. Pastukhov argues that Putinism as a historical phenomenon is much larger than Putin the man, and reflects the traditional estrangement in Russia between the state and society.[2] From this perspective, getting rid of Putin would hardly change the structures of power and the fundamental relationships between social actors. This is a powerful argument, but has two possible political corollaries. The first is the encouragement of political passivity, since getting rid of one lot of scoundrels runs the risk only of opening the door to another eager to satiate their hunger, and thus there would be another frenzy of 'redistribution of property'. The second is the precise opposite, the attempt to root out these deep behavioural and cultural attributes could encourage new forms of revolutionary radicalism, a new cultural revolution to destroy the foundations of bureaucratic power and the pathologies of the 'third state'.

Putin displayed remarkably consistent personality traits and approach to statecraft. Suspicious of public politics, Putin was a master of factional balancing and management, yet throughout retained a respectful approach to the formal institutions of governance. The essence of his rule had a profound 'extraordinary' or 'emergency' character, subverting the very constitutional institutions that he formally upheld. This gave rise to the process of sublation, whereby a constitutional body is undermined by an extra-constitutional agency. Classical Putinism had relied on pseudo-competition between United Russia and its various opponents, who were themselves constrained by a range of extra-constitutional limitations, while formally upholding the norms of liberal democracy. No formal 'state of emergency' was declared, yet the whole Putinite system of governance had an inherent emergency dynamic, promoting extra-constitutional institutional innovation and ultimately an exclusivist approach to society and the world at large. The whole system became geared to ensuring that no one could emerge as a viable alternative to personal rule, or no party could challenge the basis of the Putinite system. But this was no longer done with the self-confidence of a system struggling to be born, but with the defensiveness of an order fighting to survive.

The administrative regime nevertheless has deep social and political roots, reaching back well into the Soviet era. In his study based on 34 interviews with leading Russian political figures, Michael Urban traces the moral and political universe of the Russian elite. Urban reveals the intensely 'neo-patrimonial' personalised nature of their understanding of the conduct of politics and social processes in general, with a deeply ambivalent relationship with formal political institutions. This is contrasted with what he calls the 'political community', what we more conventionally call the constitutional state, the established structures of the political order. The latter in Urban's world remains little more than a shadowy presence, an alterity that lacks substance but which is posited as the alternative collective moral order. Urban argues that this individualised discursive orientation is homologous with the broader pattern of social relations in Russia, and represents an enduring nexus that inhibits the country's advance towards a rule-based democracy.[3] This is a sophisticated rendition of the political culture approach, but like most other versions it lacks a mechanism for explaining political change. He concludes that the discursive practices that he has identified reinforce authoritarianism, but he acknowledges that they can also provide a platform for the development of forms of deliberative democracy.

It is precisely this open-endedness of historical outcomes that the dual state model brings to the centre of political analysis. The present balance is not in 'equilibrium', in the sense typically used in political science to describe a situation in which contrary pressures are durably balanced, but one of stalemate. This is a more dynamic situation in which the contrary forces are locked in a permanent endeavour to gain advantage, and it takes all of the leadership's skills to prevent one side or the other prevailing. If Russia were to become a more consolidated authoritarian system, in which the arbitrariness and supra-political practices of the administrative regime were to become locked in, or if the constitutional state was able to bring its own officialdom under control to ensure the impartial and predictable application of rules, then the enhanced role for leadership would become redundant. Medvedev's leadership style, lacking the charismatic elements that made Putin so popular, was precisely suited to the routine management of a constitutional state.

The motors allowing the present stalemate to be overcome include long-term social change (often associated with the consolidation of a Russian middle class), a crisis of one form or another, and the more proximate exhaustion of the present conflicted system to deliver desired public goods, notably personal security, impartial access to law, sustainable and balanced economic growth, and above all the complex 'modernisation' so assiduously proclaimed by the present elite. This does not require another perestroika, but simply the application of the normative principles embodied in the Russian constitution. The shift from 'regime' forms of rule to constitutional governance would entail a profound revolution; but the most revolutionary aspect would be if this was achieved through a passive revolution. We would call the ensuing system democracy.

For good or ill, Putin is one of Russia's most important historical leaders. The cult of Putin is more than propaganda, and although mass acclaim is certainly nurtured by a subservient mass media, it reflects his undoubted genius in reflecting the contradictions of Russia itself. The scale of his historical achievement will no doubt be debated by historians for years to come, but even before the immediate political debates have quietened down it is time for an interim assessment of his leadership. We argued earlier that the essence of statecraft is to leave the country happier, more prosperous and more at ease with its neighbours and itself. Putin's restoration of strong governance was a major historical achievement, but like much else that he did, the legacy was flawed. Governance improved, although deeply torn by the tension between the administrative state and its penumbra of corrupt practices, and the legality of the constitutional state. Tax collection was enhanced, reform and improvements in funding allowed the military to recover from its post-communist decline, the state disbursal of energy rents allowed standards of living dramatically to improve, and Russia consolidated its position as one of the top ten economies in the world. However, it retained the divided polity of the Yeltsin years, and Putin was unable to lead Russia from 'emergency' to 'normal' governance; or put another way, to achieve the desecuritisation of the polity.

Putin was unable to resolve the fundamental contradictions that faced the country, although the specific mechanisms operating in that failure allowed certain problems to be resolved in the short-term. The presentation of Putin as the spiritual father of the nation based on populist ideological stereotypes was a stratagem to disguise the dead-end character of regime rule. In other words, Putin himself began to be advanced as the solution to Russia's problems. Of course, this was even more of a non-solution. In his *Regime of Genius*, Pavlovsky argues that the system itself provoked conflicts that it then needed its power to resolve. The regime created a sense of threat, and then identified and punished the culprits.[4] The regime created emergency situations where it was not bound by norms and rules, and thus reinforced its own sovereignty. Pavlovsky argued that Putin 'feared in some sense becoming redundant in his own system'. He had advocated Putin remaining 'leader', to help Medvedev shape a strategy for his second term. A repetition of the irresolution of the tandem was to be avoided, since 'neither of these half-teams was fully-fledged managerially'. The country had become tired of Medvedev's 'incoherence', and Putin had come forward with not a bad programme, but should he have moved forward and 'regained leadership in the sense of the movement the whole country was waiting for, he would have regained love too'. He condemned the various repressive laws, 'which are rubberstamped and whose enactment is inevitably for show, because there is no centralised repressive apparatus on the scale of the whole country'. For him, these were 'exemplary senseless actions'.[5]

The country remains in a situation of stalemate, where social and political interests and epistemic communities are locked in balance, allowing the Bonapartist political regime extreme freedom of action. The power system (*vlast'*) draws its authority by balancing between factions and the two pillars of the dual state: the administrative regime and the constitutional state. This is a classic stability regime, permanently engaged in the manual manipulation of political processes to ensure pre-eminence. In this context, the transition will end when there is a shift from the stalemate of the stability regime to equilibrium, based on a more or less organic balance of interests and ideas that reflects the dominant consensus in society. The idea of equilibrium is drawn from neoclassical economics and suggests a normalisation in a situation after a period of turbulence. It is precisely this sort of equilibrium that suggests that a transition is over and society has achieved a degree of normality – until the next period of breakdown and transition to a new equilibrium.

Aslund notes that on his return, 'Rather than being a guarantor of stability, Putin has suddenly become a source of destabilization. ... Today, he seems to have lost sense and balance and in reality he has no program'.[6] Putin was in danger of becoming a liability to the legitimacy of the elite. Akunin sketched out four possible futures for Russia. The first was that Putin could turn the tide and win back the trust of the population. The second is that there would be a peaceful revolution, after half a million demonstrators come out into the squares and refuse to go home (comparable to the events that in July 2013 provoked president Morsi's overthrow in Egypt). The third is that the protests turn bloody, leading either to the regime's overthrow or the return of a variant one. The final possibility is that the regime would learn the lessons from protest movements at home and abroad and initiate real reforms, what Akunin called 'perestroika 2'.[7] This model of democratisation without revolution had been a real option during the final period of Medvedev's presidency, but with Putin back in the Kremlin had been decisively rejected. In Akunin's view, Putin had become 'a real obstacle to the development of the country'.

Others noted that Putin was transcending both the regime and the state: 'The state is now part of his domain that depends on his will, which is becoming the main element of law in Russia'.[8] More precisely, his will is above law'. Yuri Shevchuk, the lead singer for the Russian rock band DDT and an active Putin critic, noted that at his concerts he saw many 'radical, sensitive young people. Their eyes are glowing and their dream is to sacrifice everything for the sake of revolution. And I would welcome a spiritual revolution in Russia'.[9] Shevchuk, though, noted the dilemma: 'There's the opinion that we should all band together to get rid of Putin. But what comes next, though? Anything could happen. A radical could come to power who would be a thousand times worse than Putin. We all know our history, how things can turn out in Russia'. He insisted there was no need to rush 'or turn radical'.[10] Equally, Putin gave no indication that he was looking for an 'exit strategy', and when pressed by the former French prime minister François Fillon at the Valdai meeting in September 2013 about whether he intended to run for the presidency in 2018, Putin said 'I do not rule it out' ('ne izklyuchayu').

The political system was kept in a permanent state of emergency, a feature of the totalitarian rule of an earlier era, preventing the consolidation of 'normal' systems of governance where institutions did their job as prescribed by the constitution. To be more precise, the polity under Putin exhibited both normal and emergency features. In the former, the courts work as they should, dispensing justice and adjudicating disputes; and parliament makes laws and reacts to matters of national importance; while the executive rules. However, the interventions of the extra-constitutional administrative regime perpetuate the emergency features of the Soviet system. The old communist party-state had now given way to the regime-state. The system of 'manual management' of elections, not trusting to the rules adopted by the regime itself, undermines constitutionality and inculcates the principle of emergency into political practices. Emergency procedures were at their most vulnerable at times of succession, and as we saw in 2011–12, the attempt to manipulate the system to achieve the outcomes desired by the incumbent threatened the legitimacy of the system as a whole. As so often in Russian and Soviet history, the Putinite order became another 'stability system', achieving a temporary resolution of the immediate crisis, but unable to move beyond short-term reactive management by allowing the polity to work as an autonomous, predictable, transparent and rule-bound system.

Putin remains subject to the natural cycle of leadership. The consolidation phase (in Putin's case, 2000 to 2004) gave way to a phase of maturity (2005–08), followed by a period of decay and disappointment. Rulers who stay in power for too long, such as Leonid Brezhnev's leadership of the Soviet Union from 1964 to 1982, fall prey to this cycle. Putin's return to power for a third term raised fears that the country was entering another terminal phase. If he remains leader until 2024, which is allowed by the constitution, he would have been in power longer than any Russian or Soviet leader since Stalin. Putin's systemic loyalty to a small group of people whom he has known for a long time stymied his freedom of action, but in the long run this loyalty only undermined the legitimacy of his own rule. The institutional mechanisms that could manage a succession have all been weakened. United Russia has its own factions and lacks the authority to choose its own candidate, while the national legislature remains weak. The Medvedev variant was designed to test whether he would make an appropriate successor, but at the first awakenings of independence the plug was pulled on the experiment. Once back in the

Kremlin, the government headed by Medvedev was marginalised from its own sphere of competence, including through the creation of the so-called 'super government', comprising the economic ministers, relevant members of the presidential administration, and trusted experts. Equally, Putin kept a reserve player in position in the guise of a potential replacement in the form of Kudrin, with Putin ostentatiously referring to him as 'the world's best finance minister'. The country was now tired of these endless intra-elite intrigues as Putin became hostage to his old friends and more traditionalist constituencies in the country. His much-prized freedom of manoeuvre was eroding.

The essence of Putinism is the constant absorption by the political centre of policy, personnel and power in general. The Putinite centre is a dynamic constellation that seeks to ensure that all major competing policy orientations are given a degree of influence, but strives to guarantee that none can predominate. Thus macroeconomic policy was broadly liberal, energy policy *dirigiste*, social policy welfarist, nationality policy inclusive but with an ethnic Russian face, and foreign policy statist. All the major constituencies in Russia could feel that they had a stake in the system, even though none achieved the full satisfaction of their agendas. Liberals were disappointed that politics remained manipulative and that elections were flawed, but felt that the system was flexible enough to allow a possible evolution to achieve more of their goals. However, with Medvedev's unceremonious expulsion from the Kremlin, they could no longer have any confidence that the present regime could evolve in a more liberal direction. Equally, nationalists at first were pleased by the restoration of the rhetoric of Russian statehood, the defeat of the Chechen insurgency, and the fist waving at the West, but they began to see a stronger future for themselves in a post-Putin Russia. The division of the spoils of the commodity boom was also distributed adequately to ensure, if not the loyalty, then the acquiescence of major social groups and constituencies. None were entirely happy, but none were so unhappy as to risk losing what they had by rocking the boat and demanding radical change.

George Orwell notes that 'All revolutions are failures, but they are not all the same failures'.[11] To that proposition we may add that in a paradoxical way the most successful revolutions are those that fail. When the immanent logic of a revolutionary process is not taken to its logical conclusion space is opened up for a new synthesis of innovation with the old order, achieving a rebalancing of a political order that maintains the achievements of tradition with the potential for evolutionary development. Thus the unsuccessful 1905 revolution in Russia ushered in a period of constitutional innovation and multi-party politics; whereas the successful Bolshevik revolution (like its Jacobin predecessor) led to terror and the repudiation of many of the principles for which the revolution had been fought. The postulate that failed revolutions provide an impetus for intra-systemic reform applies to Putin's renewed presidency from 2012. The democratisation movement from December 2011 created an ally for intra-system reformers to counter the inertia of the conservative factions, but instead Putin sought to incorporate elements of the insurgency into a rebalanced power system. The potential for change and development was incorporated into the slightly modified system of regime governance. The evolutionary path was not repudiated but became part of the regime's reset, but whether this would be enough to avert a crisis of the regime was unclear. The danger now was that the failure of the Putin system would be destructive rather than creative.

Democracy is seldom granted from above but requires popular pressure from below. The events attending the 2011–12 electoral cycle can be seen as a return to the agenda of 1991 – not just the consolidation of Russian statehood but the empowerment of free and equal citizenship. The regime under Yeltsin and Putin had claimed a tutelary right over the people in the name of various supra-political tasks – above all creating market capitalism, the institutions of statehood and defence of the territorial integrity of the state – and this had given rise to the birth of a dual state. The protests from December 2011 represented the single greatest challenge to the entrenched powers of the administrative regime. The slogan 'Russia without Putin' from this perspective is misguided. The focus instead should be the strengthening of the constitutional state, namely the rule of law, free, fair and competitive elections, a property order effectively defended against raiders and marauders, and reinforcing political institutions. It is certainly far from clear that a Russia without Putin could resolve these tasks better than one with a chastened Putin constrained by the revived institutions of the constitutional state and the pressure of a mature and mobilised political nation. This was the fundamental question that faced Putin on his return.

Notes

1. Vladimir Pastukhov, 'Moskovskii tsugtsvang', *Novaya gazeta*, 12 August 2013.
2. Vladimir Pastukhov, 'Gosudarstvo diktatury lyumpen-proletariata', *Novaya gazeta*, No. 91, 15 August 2012; http://www.novayagazeta.ru/politics/53942.html.
3. Michael Urban, *Cultures of Power in Post-Communist Russia: An Analysis of Elite Political Discourse* (New York, Cambridge University Press, 2010).
4. Gleb Pavlovskii, *Genial'naya vlast'! Slovar' abstraktsii Kremlya* (Moscow, Evropa, 2012).
5. Pavlovskii, 'Bol'she vsego Putin, po-moemu, opasaetsya stat' lishnim', op. cit.
6. Anders Aslund, 'You're a Mean One, Mr Putin', 28 December 2012, www.foreignpolicy.com.
7. John Thornhill, 'Lunch with the FT: Boris Akunin', *Financial Times*, 2 March 2013.
8. Gleb Pavlovsky, 'Putin's Views Become Increasingly Less Compatible with the State', Valdai Discussion Club, 27 December 2012.
9. Yuri Shevchuk: "I Would Welcome a Spiritual Revolution in Russia"', *IMR*, 23 January 2013.
10. Katrina vanden Heuvel and Alec Luhn, 'The Russian Optimist: An Interview with Opposition Rocker Yuri Shevchuk', *The Nation*, 26 January 2013; www.thenation.com.
11. Cited by Timothy Garton Ash, *The Polish Revolution: Solidarity, 1980–82* (New York, Random House), p. 275.

Bibliography

Albats, Evgeniya and Anatolii Ermolin, 'Korporatsiya "Rossiya"', *New Times*, No. 36, 31 October 2011.
Albats, Evgeniya and Andrei Kolesnikov, 'Homo Postsoveticus', *New Times*, 9 February 2009.
Albats, Evgeniya, Ol'ga Osipova and Ol'ga Beshlei, 'Parallel'naya real'nost'', *New Times*, No. 15, (no date).
Albats, Yevgeniya, 'Ne ponimayu, pochemu rukovoditeli strany delayut vid, chto nichego ne proiskhodit', *The New Times*, 20 September 2010; http://newtimes.ru/articles/print/27723.
——, Chto zhdat' ot vlasti? Mikhail Khodorkovskii – the New Times', *New Times*, No. 3, 30 January 2012.
Alyarinskaya, Natalya, Dmitrii Dokuchaev with Irina Zavidonova, 'Ot"ezd s otyagchayushchimi obstoyatel'stvami: Srednii klass bezhit iz Rossii', *New Times*, No. 17, 23 May 2011.
Apter, David, *The Politics of Modernization* (Chicago, University of Chicago Press, 1965).
——*Some Conceptual Approaches to the Study of Modernization* (Englewood Cliffs, NJ, Prentice-Hall, 1968).
Arkhipov, Ilya and Scott Rose, 'Gorbachev Warns of Danger from Putin Return', Bloomberg, 19 July 2011.
Aron, Leon, 'The Merger of Power and Property', *Journal of Democracy*, Vol. 20, No. 2, April 2009, pp. 66–68.
——, 'Nyetizdat: How the Internet is Building Civil Society in Russia', *Russian Outlook*, American Enterprise Institute, Spring 2011.
Arutunyan, Anna, 'Will the Real Vladimir Putin Please Stand Up?', *Moscow News*, 10 May 2012.
——, 'Media Bill Controversy', *Moscow News*, 23 July 2012.
Ash, Timothy Garton, *The Polish Revolution: Solidarity, 1980–82* (New York, Random House, no date).
Aslund, Anders, 'You're a Mean One, Mr Putin', 28 December 2012, www.foreignpolicy.com.
Association GOLOS. 'Association GOLOS – Domestic Monitoring of Elections of the President of Russian Federation, 4 March 2012: Preliminary Report', *Russian Analytical Digest*, No. 110, 16 March 2012, pp. 8–16.
Axworthy, Michael, *Revolutionary Iran: A History of the Islamic Republic* (London, Allen Lane, 2013).

Barabanov, Il'ya, 'Kreml' rabotaet nad novoi ideologicheskoi doktrinoi', *New Times*, No. 34, 28 September 2009.
Bateson, Gregory, 'Culture Contact and Schismogenesis', *Man*, Vol. 35, December 1935, pp. 178–83; in *Steps to an Ecology of Mind* (Chandler, 1972; new edition Chicago, University of Chicago Press, 1980).
BBC News, 'Moscow Mayor Yuri Luzhkov Sacked by President Medvedev', 28 September 2010; www.bbb.co.uk.
Beblawi, Hazem and Giacomo, Luciani, *The Rentier State* (London, Croom Helm, 1987).
Beck, Martin and Simone Hüser, *Political Change in the Middle East: An Attempt to Analyze the 'Arab Spring'*, Hamburg, German Institute of Global and Area Studies (GIGA), Working Papers No. 203, August 2012.
Belanovskii, Sergei and Mikhail Dmitriev, *'Politicheskii krizis v Rossii i vozmozhnye mekhanizmy ego razvitiya'*, Centre for Strategic Research (Moscow, 2011).
Belanovskii, Sergei, Mikhail Dmmitriev, Svetlana Misikhina and Tat'yana Omel'chuk, *Dvizhushchie sily i perspektivy politicheskoi transformatsii Rossii*, Centre for Strategic Research (Moscow, November 2011).
Belkovskii, Stanislav, *Imperiya Vladimira Putina* (Moscow, Algoritm, 2008).
Belkovskii, Stanislav and Golyshev, V., *Biznes Vladimira Putina* (Ekaterinburg, Ul'tra. Kul'tura, 2006).
Belton, Catherine, 'A Realm Fit for a Tsar', *Financial Times*, 1 December 2011.
Belton, Catherine, and Charles Glover, 'Vladimir Putin has Traditionally Balanced Factions, but Tensions are Rising', *Financial Times*, 31 May 2012.
Biryukova, Liliya, 'Vyiti iz zastoya', *Vedomosti*, 13 July 2011.
Bohm, Michael, 'Why Putin Will Never, Ever Give Up Power', *Moscow Times*, 20 January 2012.
——, 'Guriev's Exile is a Huge Loss for Russia', *Moscow Times*, 14 June 2013.
Bovt, Georgy, 'Why Navalny Wasn't Removed', *Moscow Times*, 26 August 2013.
Bratersky, Alexander, 'Luzhkov Goes on Attack in Closed Lecture', *Moscow Times*, 22 October 2010.
Bruk, Boris, 'Three Objects of Aggression', *IMR*, 4 September 2013.
Bunin, Igor, 'Contemporary Russia: The Return of Politics', *Politkom.ru*, 9 April; in *JRL*, 72/15, 2009.
Buribayev, Aydar, 'Russian Corruption at 8-Year Peak', *Moscow Times*, 23 September 2008.
Carnaghan, Ellen, *Out of Order: Russian Political Values in an Imperfect World* (University Park, PA, Pennsylvania State University Press, 2007).
Centre for Strategic Research, *Obshchestvo i vlast' v usloviyakh politicheskogo krizisa* (Moscow, Doklad ekspertov TSR Komitetu grazhdanskikh initsiativ, May 2012).
——, *Novoe elektoral'noe ravnovesie: Srednosrochnyi trend ili 'vremennoe zatish'e'* (Moscow, July 2013).
Chaplin, Sergei, *Tserkov' v postsovetskoi Rossii: Vozrozhdenie, kachestvo very, dialog s obshchestvom* (Moscow, Arefa, 2013).
Cherkasov, Gleb, 'Kandidat nomer odin', *Kommersant*, 20 February 2012.
Chelnokov, Aleksei, *Putinskii zastoi: Novoe politbyuro kremlya* (Moscow, Yauza Press, 2013).
Clover, Charles, 'Medevedev Gains Strength from Power Show', *Financial Times*, 28 September 2010.

——, 'Russia: Politics and Uncertainty Return to Russia', *Financial Times*, 25 January 2012.

——, 'Politics: A Ratings Game with Just One Player', *Financial Times*, 19 October 2012, 'Investing in Russia' supplement, p. 3.

Colton, Timothy J. and McFaul, Michael, *Popular Choice and Managed Democracy: The Russian Elections of 1999 and 2000* (Washington, DC, Brookings Institution Press, 2003).

Cooper, Julian, *Reviewing Russian Strategic Planning: The Emergence of Strategy 2020* (Rome, NATO Defense College Research Review, 2012).

Cowen, M. and R. Shenton, 'The Invention of Development', in J. Crush (ed.), *The Power of Development* (London, Routledge, 1995).

Delyagin, Mikhail, 'The Fight for Control of Bank of Moscow: Isolated Incident or Resurgence of Corporate Raiding?', *RIA Novosti*, 29 April 2011.

Dimov, Alexandre, *Les hommes doubles: la vie quotidienne en Union Soviétique*, translated by Florence Benoist (Paris, Éditions J.-C. Lattès, 1980).

Dmitriyev, Mikhail, 'Vse nachnetsya posle vyborov', *Vedomosti*, 11 July 2011.

Dmitriev, Mikhail, and Sergei Belanovskii, 'Kak my teper' dumaem', *Vedomosti*, 24 October 2012.

Doklad, Kommissii, *'Krugloga stola 12 dekabrya'* po obshchestvennomu rassledovaniyu sobytii 6 maya 2012 goda na Bolotnoe ploshchadii; http://rt12dec.ru/documents/report220413/default.html

Dunn, John, *Setting the People Free: The Story of Democracy* (New York, Atlantic Books, 2006).

Dzhibladze, Yuri, '"Foreign Agents" Fight for Survival', 30 July 2013, www.opendemocracy.net.

Earle, Jonathan, 'Prokhorov's Platform Courts Protesters', *Moscow Times*, 23 January 2012.

——, 'Prokhorov to Skip Mayoral Election', *Moscow Times*, 14 June 2013.

Elder, Miriam, 'Lebedev Charged with Hooliganism over TV Fisticuffs', *Guardian*, 27 September 2012.

——, 'Opposition Leader Hits Out at "Feudal" Putin from the Dock', *Guardian*, 6 July 2013.

——, 'Protesters Take to the Streets in Moscow as Opposition Leader Navalny Gets Five Years', *Guardian*, 19 July 2013.

Fedor, Julie, *Russia and the Cult of State Security: The Chekist Tradition, from Lenin to Putin* (London, Routledge, 2011).

Feifer, Gregory, 'Nominee for Moscow Mayor Set to Impose Kremlin Control', *Moscow Times*, 20 October 2010.

Felshtinsky, Yuri and Pribylovsky, Vladimir, *The Age of Assassins: The Rise and Rise of Vladmir Putin* (London, Gibson Square, 2008).

Filatova, Irina and Anatoly Medetsky, 'Putin has Plethora of Business Ideas', *Moscow Times*, 10 February 2012.

Fossato, Floriana and Lloyd, John, and Verkhovsky, Alexander, *The Web that Failed: How Opposition Politics and Independent Initiatives are Failing on the Internet in Russia* (Oxford, Reuters Institute for the Study of Journalism, 2008).

Freeland, Chrystia, 'Battle Raging at Heart of Russian Elite', *New York Times*, 19 January 2012.

Frolov, Vladimir, '50 Shades of Putinism', *Moscow Times*, 14 October 2013.

Furman, Dmitrii, 'Respublikanets na trone', *Nezavisimaya gazeta*, 9 November 2009.

Gaddy, Clifford G., and Barry W. Ickes, 'Russia after the Global Financial Crisis', *Eurasian Geography and Economics*, Vol. 51, No. 3, 2010, pp. 281–311.

Gel'man, Vladimir, 'Cracks in the Wall: Challenges to Electoral Authoritarianism in Russia', *Problems of Post-Communism*, Vol. 60, No. 2, March–April 2013, pp. 3–10.

Gessen, Masha, *The Man Without a Face: The Unlikely Rise of Vladimir Putin* (New York, Riverhead Books, 2012).

Gleason, J. H., *The Genesis of Russophobia in Great Britain: A Study of the Interaction of Policy and Opinion* (Cambridge, Cambridge University Press, 1950).

Glinkin, Maksim, 'Vse menee obayatel'nyi lider', *Vedomosti*, 9 August 2013.

Goble, Paul, 'Window on Eurasia: Middle Class "Fleeing" Russia, Moscow Experts Say', *JRL*, 93/4, 2011.

——, 'Russian Intelligentsia Prepared to Overlook Navalny's Nationalism', Window on Eurasia; *JRL*, 161/7, 2013.

Golosov, Grigorii, 'Russia's Silent Election Campaign', 29 November 2011, www.opendemocracy.net.

Gontmakher, Yevgeny, 'Rekonstruktsiya nastoyashchei "Doktriny Putina"', *Vedomosti*, 19 October 2012.

——, 'Fate of Foreign Agents', *Kommersant*, 4 October 2013.

Goode, Paul J. *The Decline of Regionalism in Putin's Russia: Boundary Issues* (London, Routledge, 2011).

Gorbachev, Mikhail, 'Razryv mezhdu vlast'yu i narodom bolee neterpim', speech of 9 February 2012, *Novaya gazeta*, 16 February 2012.

Gorodetskaya, Natal'ya, 'Izbirkomy depolitizirovat', sbor podpisei prodlit', registratsii ne lishat'', *Kommersant*, 19 October 2012.

Gorshkov, M. K., Krumm, R., Tikhonova, N. E. (eds), *O chëm mechtayut rossiyane: Ideal i real'nost'* (Moscow, Ves' mir, 2013).

Goryunov, Felix 'Putin Divides Russian Capitalism', *Russia Beyond the Headlines*, 14 February 2012; www.rbth.ru.

Graney, Katherine E., *Of Khans and Kremlins: Tatarstan and the Future of Ethno-Federalism in Russia* (Lanham, MD Lexington Books, 2009).

Grigor'ev, Aleksandr, 'Vladimir Markin: "Naval'ny smozhet borot'sya s korruptsiei i iz tyur'mi"', *Izvestiya*, 12 April 2013.

Gudkov, Gennadii, *Za chto menya nevzlyubili 'partiya zhulikov i vorov'* (Moscow, Algoritm, 2013).

Hahn, Gordon M., *Russia's Revolution from Above, 1985–2000: Reform, Transition, and Revolution in the Fall of the Soviet Communist Regime* (New Brunswick, NJ, Transaction Publishers, 2002).

——, 'Medvedev Makes More Progress on Judicial Reform', *Russia: Other Points of View*, 22 July 2011.

——, 'Reform Lessons for Perestroika 2.0', *Russia: Other Points of View*, 21 August 2011a.

Harding, Luke, *Mafia State: How One Reporter Became an Enemy of the Brutal New Russia* (London, Guardian Books, 2011).

Hellevig, Jon and Latsa, Alexandre (eds), *Putin's New Russia* (Washington, DC, Kontinent USA, 2012).

Hellman, Joel S., 'Winners Take All: The Politics of Partial Reform in Postcommunist Transitions', *World Politics*, Vol. 50, No. 2, 1998, pp. 203–34.

Herd, Graeme P., *Russia's Strategic Choice: Conservative or Democratic Modernization?* Geneva Centre for Security Policy (GCSP), Policy Paper No. 2, May 2010; www.gcsp.ch.

Bibliography

Herszenhorn, David M., 'Text of Navalny's Closing Remarks in Russian Court', *New York Times*, 6 July 2013, modified translation.
——, 'Russian Court Convicts Opposition Leader', *New York Times*, 18 July 2013b.
Hill, Fiona and Gaddy, Clifford, *Mr. Putin: Operative in the Kremlin* (Washington, DC, Brookings Institution Press, 2013).
Huntington, Samuel, *Political Order in Changing Societies* (New Haven, CT, Yale University Press, 1968).
Idov, Michael, 'We Have Woken Up at Last. But We Are Helpless', *Guardian*, 19 July 2013.
Inozemtsev, V., 'Neo-Feudalism Explained', *The American Interest*, March-April 2011.
Insor, *Rossiya XXI veka: Obraz zhelaemogo zavtra* (Moscow, Ekon-Inform, 2010).
——, *Attaining the Future: Strategy 2020. Synopsis* (Moscow, Ekon-Inform, 2011).
Ivanov, Eugene, 'Knocked off the Right Cause', *Russia Beyond the Headlines*, 19 September 2011; www.rbth.ru.
Jensen, Donald N., 'Putin's "Praetorian Guard"', *IMR*, 10 October 2013.
Jones, Tobias, *The Dark Heart of Italy* (London, Faber & Faber, 2007).
Jowitt, Ken, *New World Disorder: The Leninist Extinction* (Berkeley, University of California Press, 1992).
Judah, Ben, *Fragile Empire: How Russia Fell In and Out of Love with Vladimir Putin* (New Haven and London, Yale University Press, 2013).
Kalashnikov, Maksim, *Putin inkorporeited: Kak Putinu obustroi' Rossiyu* (Moscow, Algoritm/Eksmo, 2013).
Kalinina, Alexandra, 'Corruption in Russia as a Business', *Institute of Modern Russia* (henceforth *IMR*), 29 January 2013.
Kamyshev, Dmitry, 'Proekt "Nu, pogodi!"', *Kommersant-Vlast'*, No. 15, 18 April 2011, pp. 24–26.
Kara-Murza, Vladimir, 'FARA and Putin's NGO Law: Myths and Reality', *IMR*, 9 May 2013.
Kashin, O. V., *Vlast': Monopoliya na nasilie* (Moscow, Algoritm, 2013).
Keane, John, *The Life and Death of Democracy* (New York, Simon & Schuster, 2009).
Khodorkovskii, Mikhail, 'Modernizatsiya: Pokolenie M', *Vedomosti*, 21 October 2009.
——, 'Uzakonennoe nasilie', *Nezavisimaya gazeta*, 3 March 2010.
Khodorkovskii, Mikhail, 'Chelovek i zakon: O politicheskikh presledovaniyakh v Rossii', *Vedomosti*, 24 April 2013.
Khodorkovsky, M. B. and Lebedev, P. L., *Report of the Presidential Council of the RF for the Development of Civil Society and Human Rights on the Results of the Public Scholarly Analysis of the Court Materials of the Criminal Case against M. B. Khodorkovsky and P. L. Lebedev (tried by the Khamovnichesky District Court of the City of Moscow; the verdict issued on 27.12.2010)* (Moscow, 2011).
Kholmogorova, Vera, 'Ne nado ottepeli', *Vedomosti*, 10 June 2009.
Khvostuna, Olga, 'Hostile Takeover: On Putin's "Judicial Reform"', *IMR*, 18 October 2013.
Kohli, Harpaul A. and Mukherjee, Natasha, 'Potential Costs to Asia of the Middle Income Trap', *Global Journal of Emerging Market Economies*, Vol. 3, No. 3, September 2011, pp. 291–311.
Kolesnikov, Andrei, 'Vladislav Surkov: "I Was by a Great Man's Side"', *Russkii Pioner*, 27 July 2013; http://ruspioner.ru.
Kortunov, Andrei 'The New Russia', Kennan Institute, event summary, 5 February 2009; *JRL*, 71/10, 2008.

Koshkin, Pavel, 'Russian Protest Movement: Smaller and More Radical?', 13 August 2013, http://russiadirect.foreignpolicy.com/content/russian-protest-movement-smaller-and-more-radical.

Kostin, Andrei, 'Za chestnye vybory Vladimira Putina', *Kommersant*, 13 February 2012.

Kotsyubinsky, Daniil, 'Messiah or false Prophet?', www.opendemocracy.net, 13 August 2013; http://www.opendemocracy.net/od-russia/daniil-kotsyubinsky/messiah-or-false-prophet.

Krainova, Natalya, 'Audit Chamber Lashes Out at Activist', *Moscow Times*, 28 April 2011.

Kravtsova, Yekaterina, 'Ex-Convicts Regain Right to Run in Elections', *Moscow Times*, 11 October 2013.

Kryshtanovskaya, Olga, *Anatomiya Rossiiskoi elity* (Moscow, Zakharov, 2005).

Kuper, Simon, 'What Putin Learnt from Berlusconi', *Financial Times*, 31 May 2013.

Kuvshinova, Ol'ga, 'Tsena demokratii', *Vedomosti*, 23 June 2011.

Kynev, Alexander, presentation at the University of Dundee, 30 June 2013.

Laruelle, Marlène, *Inside and Around the Kremlin's Black Box: The New Nationalist Think Tanks in Russia* (Institute for Security & Development Policy, Stockholm Paper, October 2009).

Latynina, Yulia, 'Putin Divides and Rules', *Moscow Times*, 29 September 2010.

Lavelle, Peter, 'Introduction', in Jon Hellevig and Alexandre Latsa (eds), *Putin's New Russia* (Washington, DC, Kontinent USA, 2012).

Ledeneva, Alena V., *Can Russia Modernise? Sistema, Power Networks and Informal Governance* (Cambridge, Cambridge University Press, 2013).

Levinson, Aleksei, 'Eto ne srednii klass – eto vse', *Vedomosti*, 21 February 2012.

——, 'Cynicism as a Ruling Ideology', 22 October 2013; www.opendemocracy.net.

Light, Matthew and Kovalev, Nikolai, 'Russia, the Death Penalty, and Europe: The Ambiguities of Influence', *Post-Soviet Affairs*, Vol. 29, No. 6, 2013, pp. 528–566.

Lipset, Seymour M., 'Some Social Requisites of Democracy', *American Political Science Review*, Vol. 53, No. 1, 1959, pp. 69–105.

Litvinovich, Marina, *Vlast' semei: 20 klanov, kontroliruyushchikh ekonomiku Rossii* (Moscow, Eksmo, 2012).

Logvinenko, Igor, 'The Dirty Truth about Russia's "Dirty" Money', *Moscow Times*, 10 October 2013.

Loffe, Julia, 'The Most Dangerous Blogger in the World: How Aleksey Navalny Changed Russian Politics', *The New Republic*, 18 July 2013.

Lucas, Edward, *The New Cold War: How the Kremlin Menaces both Russia and the West* (London, Bloomsbury, 2008).

——, *Deception: Spies, Lies and How Russia Dupes the West* (London, Bloomsbury, 2012).

Luhn, Alec, 'Gay Russians Say They Live in Fear of "Legalised Violence and Humiliation"', *Guardian*, 2 September 2013, p. 13.

Luzhkov, Yurii, *I tak zhit' nel'zya ... Besedy s politikom i grazhdaninom* (Moscow, Veche, 2012).

Lynch, Allen C., *Vladimir Putin and Russian Statecraft* (Washington, DC, Potomac Books, 2011).

Lyubarev, Arkady, 'An Evaluation of the Results of the Duma Elections', *Russian Analytical Digest*, No. 108, 6 February 2012, pp. 2–5.

——, 'Protsess udlineniya spiskov', *Nezavisimaya gazeta*, 17 April 2013.
Mackinnon, Rebecca, 'China's "Networked Authoritarianism"', *Journal of Democracy*, Vol. 22, No. 2, April 2011, pp. 32–46.
Markin, Vladimir, 'Glyadya iz Londona, na zerkalo necha penyat', *Izvestiya*, 7 May 2013.
Markov, Sergei, 'Russia Should Create Private Zones for LGBT', *Moscow Times*, 6 February 2013.
——, 'The Myths of Putin's Political Repression', *Moscow Times*, 11 July 2013a.
McFaul, Michael, *Russia's Unfinished Revolution: Political Change from Gorbachev to Putin* (Ithaca and London, Cornell University Press, 2001).
McLaren, Lauren and Cop, Burak, 'The Failure of Democracy in Turkey: A Comparative Analysis', *Government and Opposition*, Vol. 46, No. 4, October 2011, pp. 485–516.
McSherry, Patrice J., *Predatory States: Operation Condor and Covert War in Latin America* (Boulder, CO, Rowman & Littlefield, 2005).
Medvedev, D. A., 'Rossiya, vpered!', 10 September 2009; http://www.gazeta.ru/comments/2009/09/10_a_3258568.shtml.
——, 'S"ezd partii "Edinaya Rossiya": Glava gosudarstva prinyal predlozhenie vozglavit' spisok "Edinoi Rossii" na vyborakh v Gosudarstvennuyu Dumu 4 Dekabrya 2011 goda', 24 September 2011, http://kremlin.ru/transcripts/12802
——, 'Poslanie Prezidenta Federal'nomu Sobraniyu', 22 December 2011a, http://news.kremlin.ru/news/14088/print
——, 'Diary', *London Review of Books*, 20 June 2013.
——, 'Vremya prostikh reshenii proshlo', *Vedomosti*, 27 September 2013a.
Mereu, Francesca, *L'amico Putin: L'invenzione della dittatura democratica* (Rome, Aliberti Editions, 2011).
Merkel, Wolfgang, 'Embedded and Defective Democracies', *Democratisation*, Vol. 11, No. 5, December 2004, pp. 33–58.
Milov, Vladimir, Ryzhkov, Vladimir, and Shorina, O. (eds), *Putin: Korruptsiya – nezavisimy ekspertny doklad* (Moscow, Partiiya Narodnoi Svobody, 2011).
Minchenko Consulting, *Doklad: Bol'shoe pravitel'stvo Vladimira Putina i 'Politbyuro 2.0'* (Moscow, Kommunikatsionnyi kholding "Minchenko konsalting", 2012); http://minchenko.ru/analitika/analitika_27.html.
——, *Doklad 'Politbyuro 2.0': Nakanune perezagruzki elitnykh grupp*, 19 February 2013, http://www.minchenko.ru/analitika/analitika_30.html.
Mishina, Ekaterina, 'Let's Say "No" to the Erosion of the Constitution', *IMR*, 29 July 2013.
Monaghan, Andrew, *The Russian* Vertikal*: The Tandem, Power and the Elections*, Chatham House, Russia and Eurasia Programme REP2011/01, June 2011, p. 2.
——, 'The Vertikal: Power and Authority in Russia', *International Affairs*, Vol. 88, No. 1, January 2012, pp. 1–16.
——, 'Putin's Russia: Shaping a "Grand Strategy"?', *International Affairs*, Vol. 89, No. 5, 2013, pp. 1221–36.
Morozov, Evgeny, *The Net Delusion: How Not to Liberate the World* (London, Allen Lane, 2011).
——, 'Izuchaya fotografiyu: Chto sluchilos' s rezhimom putina?', Radio Ekho Moskvy, 25 July 2013; http://echo.msk.ru/blog/morozov_a/1122606-echo/.
Nagornikh, Irina, 'Kreml' prodolzhit perezagruzku vnutrennei politiki', *Kommersant*, 10 July 2013.

Nemtsov, Boris, and Leonid Martynyuk, *Zhizn'raba na galerakh (dvortsy, yakhty, avtomobili, samolety i drugie aksessuary)* (Moscow, 2012); www.putin-itogi.ru.
Nemtsov, Boris and Martynyuk, Leonid, *Winter Olympics in the Sub-Tropics: Corruption and Abuse in Sochi* (Moscow, 2013).
Nichols, Thomas M., *The Russian Presidency: Society and Politics in the Second Russian Republic* (Basingstoke, Macmillan, 2000).
Nishenkov, Oleg, 'Investors Skeptical on "Oligarch" Tax', *Moscow News*, 13 February 2012.
Nodia, Ghia, 'Putting the State Back Together in Post-Soviet Georgia', in Mark R. Beissinger and Crawford Young (eds), *Beyond State Crisis? Postcolonial Africa and Post-Soviet Eurasia in Comparative Perspective* (Washington, DC, Woodrow Wilson Center Press, 2002).
North, Douglas C., Joseph Wallis, and Barry R. Weingast, *Violence and Social Orders: A Conceptual Framework for Interpreting Recorded Human History* (Cambridge, Cambridge University Press, 2009).
Novosel'tsev, Vladimir, *Kremlevskaya vlast': Krizis gosudarstvennogo upravleniya* (Moscow, Algoritm, 2012).
Oates, Sarah, *Revolution Stalled: The Political Limits of the Internet in the Post-Soviet Sphere* (Oxford, Oxford University Press, 2012).
Odynova, Alexandra, 'Luzhkov Fired Over "Loss of Confidence"', *Moscow Times*, 29 September 2010.
——, 'Mayor Sobyanin to Court Investors', *Moscow Times*, 18 October 2010a.
——, 'Thousands Decry Putin as Public Anger Swells', *Moscow Times*, 1 February 2010b.
Osborn, Andrew, 'Medvedev and Putin at Odds over Moscow Mayor', *Telegraph.co.uk*, 12 September 2010.
——, 'Putin Eyes Presidency as Loyalist Appointed Moscow's Mayor', Telegraph.co.uk, 21 October 2010a.
OSCE, *Elections to the State Duma, 4 December 2011: OSCE/ODIHR Election Observation Mission Final Report* (Warsaw, 12 January 2012).
——, *Presidential Election 4 March 2012: OSCE/ODIHR Election Observation Mission Final Report* (Warsaw, 11 May 2012).
Osipov, Georgii, 'Konservy srednego klassa', *Gazeta.ru*, 23 May 2013.
PACE, *Observation of the Parliamentary Elections in the Russian Federation (4 December 2011)*, Doc. 12833 (Strasbourg, 23 January 2012).
Panyushkin, Valerii, *Vosstanie potrebitelei* (Moscow, Astrel', 2012).
Pastukhov, Vladimir, *Restavratsiya vmesto reformatsii: Dvadtsat' let, kotorye potryasli Rossiyu* (Moscow, OGI, 2012).
——, 'Gosudarstvo diktatury lyumpen-proletariata', *Novaya gazeta*, No. 91, 15 August 2012a; http://www.novayagazeta.ru/politics/53942.html.
——, 'Legenda No 1917', *Novaya gazeta*, 22 August 2013.
——, 'Moskovskii tsugtsvang', *Novaya gazeta*, 12 August 2013a.
Pavlovsky, Gleb, in discussion with Andrei Piontkovskii, 'Chto oznachayut novye slova i ponyatiya, kotorye v poslednee vremya proiznosyat president i ego okruzhenie', *New Times*, No. 34, 28 September 2009.
——, 'Putin's Views Become Increasingly less Compatible with the State', Valdai Discussion Club, 27 December 2012.
——, *Genial'naya vlast'! Slovar' abstraktsii Kremlya* (Moscow, Evropa, 2012).
——, 'Bol'she vsego Putin, po-moemu, opasaetsya stat' lishnim', *Novaya gazeta*, No. 121, 24 October 2012b.

——, 'Return of the Refuseniks', Valdai Discussion Club, 25 June 2013; Valdaiclub. com.

Petrov, Nikolai, 'Elections Show the End of One-Party System', *Moscow Times*, 27 August 2013.

——, 'September 8 Election as a New Phase of the Society and Authorities' Coevolution', Carnegie Moscow Center, *Eurasia Outlook*, 5 September 2013b.

Petrova, Svetlana, 'Andrei Borodin, vozmozhno, sobral blokpaket aktsii Banka Moskvy', *Vedomosti*, 25 October 2010.

Ponomareva, Yulia, 'Putin's Popular Front to Replace United Russia?', *Russia Beyond the Headlines*, 18 June 2013; www.rbth.ru.

Potts, Andy, 'Medvedev in Surprise Plea to Russian Business', *Moscow News*, 13 July 2011.

Preston, Paul, *The Spanish Holocaust: Inquisition and Extermination in Twentieth-Century Spain* (London, HarperPress, 2012).

Primakov, Yevgeny, 'Perception of Russia in the World', Valdai Discussion Club, 29 April 2013.

Programma kandidata v mery Moskvy Alekseya Naval'nogo 2013 god, p. 7; http://navalny.ru/platform/Navalny_Program.pdf.

Putin, Vladimir, *First Person: An Astonishingly Frank Self-Portrait by Russia's President Vladimir Putin*, with Nataliya Gevorkyan, Natalya Timakova, and Andrei Kolesnikov, translated by Catherine A. Fitzpatrick (London, Hutchinson, 2000).

——, 'This Year Was Not an Easy One', *International Affairs* (Moscow), Vol. 51, No. 1, January 2005, pp. 3–5.

——, 'Comments During a Visit to Komi Republic', 28 September 2010; http://premier.gov.ru/eng/visits/ru/12326/events/12336.

——, 'S"ezd partii "Edinaya Rossiya": Predsedatel' Pravitels'stva Rossiiskoi Federatsii V. V. Putin prinyal uchastie v XII s"ezde vserossiiskoi politicheskoi partii "Edinaya Rossiya"', 24 September 2011, http://www.premier.gov. ru/events/news/16552/print/.

——, 'Rossiya sosredotachivaetsya: Vyzovy, na kotorye my dolzhny otvetit'', *Izvestiya*, 16 January 2012; http://premier.gov.ru/events/news/17755/.

——, 'Rossiya: Natsional'nyi vopros', *Nezavisimaya gazeta*, 23 January 2012a; http://premier.gov.ru/events/news/17831/.

——, 'O nashikh ekonomicheskikh zadachakh', *Vedomosti*, 30 January 2012b; http://premier.gov.ru/events/news/17888/.

——, 'Demokratiya i kachestvo gosudarstva', *Kommersant*, 6 February 2012c; http://premier.gov.ru/events/news/18006/.

——, 'Stroitel'stvo spravedlivosti: Sotsial'naya politika dlya Rossii', *Komsomol'skaya Pravda*, 13 February 2012d; http://premier.gov.ru/events/news/18071/.

——, 'Byt' sil'nymi: Garantii natsional'noi bezopasnosti dlya Rossii', *Rossiiskaya gazeta*, 20 February 2012e; http://premier.gov.ru/events/news/18185/.

——, 'Rossiya i menyayushchiisya mir', *Moskovskie novosti*, 27 February 2012f; http://premier.gov.ru/events/news/18252/.

——, 'Vstrecha s izbrannymi glavami sub"ektov Rossiiskoi Federatsii', 10 September 2013; http://www.kremlin.ru/transcripts/19189.

Rodin, Ivan, 'Mironov predlozhil vernut'sya v 1993 god', *Nezavisimaya gazeta*, 13 February 2012.

——, 'Medvedev ostaetsya reformatoram', *Nezavisimaya gazeta*, 7 February 2012a.

——, 'A Plea for Caution from Russia', *New York Times*, 12 September 2013.

——, 'Meeting of the Valdai International Discussion Club', 19 September 2013a; http://eng.news.kremlin.ru/news/6007.

Rogov, Kirill, 'Vtoroi front Putina: Ot fiktivnogo legalizma k repressyam', *Novaya gazeta*, 27 October 2012.

Rose, Richard, William Mishler, and Neil Munro, *Popular Support for an Undemocratic Regime: The Changing Views of Russians* (Cambridge, Cambridge University Press, 2011).

Rosenberg, Justin, 'Basic Problems in the Theory of Uneven and Combined Development. Part II: Unevenness and Political Multiplicity', *Cambridge Review of International Affairs*, Vol. 23, No. 1, March 2011, pp. 165–89.

Rostovskii, Mikhail, 'Neizbezhnost' Putina', Moskovskii komsomolets, 15 July 2011.

Roxburgh, Angus, *The Strongman: Vladimir Putin and the Struggle for Russia* (London, I. B. Tauris, 2011).

Rubtsov, Aleksandr, 'Metafizika gosudarstva: Chto otkazalas' delat' vlast'', *Vedomosti*, 28 June 2013.

Rutland, Peter, 'The Political Economy of Putin 3.0', *Russian Analytical Digest*, No. 133, 18 July 2013, pp. 2–5.

Ryzhkov, Vladimir, 'Konovalov's Ministry of Manipulation', *Moscow Times*, 19 July 2011.

——, 'We Want Reforms, Not Revolution', *Moscow Times*, 14 February 2012.

——, 'Putin vzyal kurs na agressivnoe uderzhanie status-kvo', *Novaya gazeta*, 14 February 2012a.

——, 'Putin's Bolotnoye Show Trial', *Moscow Times*, 25 April 2013.

——, 'The Kremlin is Split over Navalny', *Moscow Times*, 23 July 2013a.

——, 'Kremlin's New Attack on Human Rights', *Moscow Times*, 2 July 2013b.

——, 'The Kremlin's Pogrom Mentality', *Moscow Times*, 22 October 2013c.

——, 'Plenarnoe zasedanie Peterburgskogo mezhdunarodnogo ekonomicheskogo foruma', 21 June 2013d; http://www.kremlin.ru/transcripts/18383.

——, 'Regional Elites See United Russia's Stock falling', *Moscow Times*, 27 August 2013e.

——, 'Kremlin manipulation of Elections Continues', *Moscow Times*, 16 July 2013.

Sakwa, Richard, 'The Regime System in Russia', *Contemporary Politics*, Vol. 3, No. 1, 1997, pp. 7–25.

——, 'Regime Change from Yeltsin to Putin: Normality, Normalcy or Normalisation?', in Cameron Ross (ed.), *Russian Politics under Putin* (Manchester, Manchester University Press, 2004), pp. 17–38.

——, *Putin: Russia's Choice*, 2nd edn (London, Routledge, 2008).

——, 'The Dual State in Russia', *Post-Soviet Affairs*, Vol. 26, No. 3, July–September 2010, pp. 185–206

——, *The Crisis of Russian Democracy: The Dual State, Factionalism and the Medvedev Succession* (Cambridge, Cambridge University Press, 2011).

——, 'Leadership, Governance and Statecraft in Russia', in Ludger Helms (ed.), *Poor Leadership and Bad Governance: Reassessing Presidents and Prime Ministers in North America, Europe and Japan* (Cheltenham, Edward Elgar, 2012), pp. 149–72.

——, 'The Cold Peace: Russo-Western Relations as a Mimetic Cold War,' *Cambridge Review of International Affairs*, Vol. 26, No. 1, 2013, pp. 203–24.

——, *Putin and the Oligarch: Khodorkovsky and the Yukos Affair* (London, I. B. Tauris, 2014).

Bibliography

Samarina, Aleksandra, 'Medvedev iz Germanii dal signal otechestvennomu elektoratu', *Nezavisimaya gazeta*, 20 July 2011.
——, 'Aleksei Kudrin uporstvuet v "erese"', *Nezavisimaya gazeta*, 22 April 2011.
——, 'Martovskie tezisy Dmitriya Medvedeva', *Nezavisimaya gazeta*, 28 March 2013.
——, 'Liberal'nyi elektorat broshen na proizvol syd'by', *Nezavisimaya gazeta*, 17 April 2013a.
——, 'Smert' politicheskikh brendov', *Nezavisimaya gazeta*, 10 September 2013b.
Samarina, Aleksandra and Yan Gordeev, 'Politdistrofiya posle partiinkh kanikul', *Nezavisimaya gazeta*, 22 July 2011.
Samarina, Aleksandra and Roza Tsvetkova, 'Rasstroistvo tandema', *Nezavisimaya gazeta*, 28 July 2011.
Savitsky, Oleg, 'Sovereign Democracy without the Sovereign', *Osobaya bukva*, 26 August 2013.
Schepp, Matthias, 'The Shadow Boxers: Putin and Medvedev Eye the Kremlin – and Each Other', *Der Spiegel*, 18 July 2011; *JRL*, 129/9, 2011.
Sergei, Balanovskii and Dmitriev, Mikhail, Centre for Strategic Research, *Politicheskii krizis v Rossii i vozmozhnye mekhanizmy ego razvitiya* (Moscow, 2011).
Sergei, Belanovskii, Dmitriev, Mikhail, Misikhina, Svetlana and Omel'chuk, Tat'yana, Centre for Strategic Research, *Dvizhushchie sily i perspektivy politicheskoi transformatsii Rossii* (Moscow, November 2011).
——, *Novoe elektoral'noe ravnovesie: Srednosrochnyi trend ili 'vremennoe zatish'e'* (Moscow, Tsentr Strategicheskikh Razrabotok, July 2013).
Sergi, Bruno S., *Misinterpreting Modern Russia: Western Views of Putin and His Presidency* (London, Continuum, 2009).
Shestopal, E. B., *Obrazy vlasti v post-sovetskoi Rossii* (Moscow, Aleteia, 2004).
Shevchuk, Yuri, '"I Would Welcome a Spiritual Revolution in Russia"', *IMR*, 23 January 2013.
Shane, Scott, 'From Success at Putin's Side to Exposing Corruption', *New York Times*, 4 February 2012.
Shishkunova, Elena, 'Vladislav Surkov: "Sistema uzhe izmenilas"', *Izvestiya*, 22 December 2011.
Shlapentokh, Vladimir and Arutunyan, Anna, *Freedom, Repression, and Private Property in Russia* (Cambridge, Cambridge University Press, 2013).
Sieff, Martin, 'What Putin and Thatcher Have in Common', *Moscow Times*, 22 April 2013.
Slater, Dan, *Ordering Power: Contentious Politics and Authoritarian Leviathans in Southeast Asia* (Cambridge, Cambridge University Press, 2010).
Smirnov, Valerii, *Front Putina: Protiv kogo?* (Moscow, Algoritm, 2011).
Soldatov, Andrei and Borogan, Irina, *The New Nobility: The Restoration of Russia's Security State and the Enduring Legacy of the KGB* (New York, Public Affairs, 2010).
Sorokin, Pitirim, *Chelovek, obshchestvo, tsivilitatsiya* (Moscow, Politizdat, 1992).
Surkov, Vladislav, 'Putin ukreplyaet gosudarstvo, a ne sebya', interviewed by Elena Ovcharenko, *Komsomol'skaya Pravda*, 29 September 2004, p. 4.
Stanovaya, Tatyana, 'The Fate of the Nashi Movement: Where Will the Kremlin Youth Go?', *IMR*, 26 March 2013.
——, 'Beware of Medvedev', *IMR*, 6 March 2013a.
——, 'Opposition(s) in Waiting', www.neweasterneurope.eu, No. 1 (VI), 2013b.

——, 'Mikhail Prokhorov: Between the Kremlin and the Opposition', *IMR*, 19 February 2013c; http://www.imrussia.org.
——, 'Stsenarii rospuska Gosdumy i problema legitimnosti', 18 March 2013; http://www.politcom.ru/print.php?id=15504.
——, 'The People's Front: Against Whom Are They Joining Forces?', *IMR*, 27 June 2013.
Strategiya-2020: *Novaya models rosta – novaya sotsial'snaya politika*, http://2020strategy.ru/data/2012/03/14/1214585998/1itog.pdf.
Sungorkin, Vladimir and Viktor Baranets, 'Sergei Ivanov: "My s Putinym poznakomilis' v razvedke', *Komsomol'skaya Pravda*, 5 March 2013.
Sutela, Pekka, *The Political Economy of Putin's Russia* (London, Routledge, 2012).
Taratuta, Yulia, 'Nedeistvitelen', *Vedomosti*, 27 April 2011.
Thornhill, John, 'Lunch with the FT: Boris Akunin', *Financial Times*, 2 March 2013.
——, 'Putin's Corruption Trap', *IMR*, 16 April 2013.
Treisman, Daniel, *The Return: Russia's Journey from Gorbachev to Medvedev* (London, Simon & Schuster, 2011).
Tret'yakov, Vitaly, 'Suverennaya demokratiya', *Rossiiskaya gazeta*, 28 April 2005.
Udal'tsov, S. S., *Putin – Boi!* (Moscow, Algoritm, 2013).
Umland, Andreas, 'The Claim of Russian Distinctiveness as Justification for Putin's Neo-Authoritarian Regime', *Russian Politics and Law*, Vol. 50, No. 5, September–October 2012, pp. 3–6.
Umland, Andreas, 'New Extreme Right-Wing Intellectual Circles in Russia: The Anti-Orange Committee, the Izborsk Club and the Florian Geyer Club', Russian Analytical Digest, No. 135, 5 August 2013, pp. 2–6.
Urban, Michael, *Cultures of Power in Post-Communist Russia: An Analysis of Elite Political Discourse* (New York, Cambridge University Press, 2010).
vanden Heuvel, Katrina and Alec Luhn, 'The Russian Optimist: An Interview with Opposition Rocker Yuri Shevchuk', *The Nation*, 26 January 2013; www.thenation.com.
von Eggert, Konstantin 'Wooing the Oligarchs', *Moscow News*, 13 February 2012.
Voronkov, Konstantin, *Aleksei Navalnyi: Groza zhulikov i vorov* (Moscow, Eksmo, 2012).
Wagstyl, Stefan, 'Putin to Oligarchs: Watch Out', *Financial Times*, 20 January 2012.
Waller, Julian G., 'Re-Setting the Game: The Logic and Practice of Official Support for Alexei Navalny's Mayoral Run', *Russian Analytical Digest*, No. 136, 16 September 2013, pp. 6–9.
Weir, Fred, 'Putin's Next Marquee Event: Russia's Presidency', *Christian Science Monitor*, 29 November 2011.
——, 'Anti-Putin Protesters March in Moscow, but Momentum Weakened', *Christian Science Monitor*, 6 May 2013.
Whitmore, Brian, 'The Powerless Vertical', RFE/RL, *Russia Report*, 10 June 2011.
——, 'Kudrin vs. United Russia', RFE/RL, *Russia Report*, 21 February 2011a.
——, 'Putin's Plan', RFE/RL, *Russia Report*, 19 July 2011b.
——, 'Putinism in Winter', RFE/RL, *Russia Report*, 5 February 2013.
——, 'With or Without Putin', RFE/RL, *Russia Report*, 30 May 2013b.
Wittman, George H., 'Putin's Personal Piggy Banks', *The American Spectator*, 16 December 2011; http://spectator.org/archives/2011/12/16/putins-personal-piggy-banks.
World Bank and the Development Research Centre of the State Council, *PRC: China 2030: Building a Modern, Harmonious, and Creative High Income Society* (Washington, DC, The World Bank, 2012).

Yagodin, Dmitry, 'Blog Medvedev: Aiming for Public Consent', *Europe-Asia Studies*, Vol. 64, No. 8, October 2012, pp. 1415–34.

Yamshanov, Boris and Viktor Vasenin, 'Neposredstvennaya zhizn': Predlozheniya ot Bastrykina – sozdat' edinyi sledstevnnyi komitet I vvesti otchety o raskhodakh chinovnikov', *Rossiiskaya gazeta*, 7 September 2010.

Yanov, Alexander, 'Putin and the "Russian Idea"', *IMR*, 1 July 2013.

Yurgens, Igor and Yevgenii Gontmakher, 'Razvilka-2012: Medvedevu pora pereiti Rubikon', *Vedomosti*, 27 July 2011.

Zakaria, Fareed, 'The Rise of Illiberal Democracy', *Foreign Affairs*, Vol. 76, No. 6, November/December 1997, pp. 22–43.

Zakaria, Fareed, *The Future of Freedom* (New York, W. W. Norton, 2003).

Zlobin, Nikolai, 'Sergei Mironov and the Inter-Party Competition', *Snob*, 24 May 2011; http://www.snob.ru/selected/entry/36001.

——, 'Otvet Medvedeva', *Vedomosti*, 17 May 2011a.

——, 'Bessistemnaya vlast'', *Vedomosti*, 30 January 2012.

Zubarevich, N. 'Chetyre Rossii', *Vedomosti*, 30 December 2011.

Zubov, Andrei, 'Vykhod iz krizisa legitimnosti', *Vedomosti*, 22 December 2011.

Zudin, Aleksei Yu, 'Oligarchy as a Political Problem of Russian Postcommunism', *Russian Social Science Review*, Vol. 41, No. 6, November–December 2000, pp. 4–33.

——, 'Neokorporativizism v Rossii', *Pro et Contra*, Vol. 6, No. 4, 2001, pp. 171–98.

——, 'Rezhim V. Putina: Kontury novoi politicheskoi sistemy', *Obshchestvennye nauki i sovremennost'*, No. 2, 2003, pp. 67–83.

Index

Note: Page numbers in bold refer to tables.

Abhazia 18
Abramovich, Roman 173
Abyzov, Mikhail 155
administrative regime: and business class 56; and constitutional state 2–3, 62–6, 220, 223–31; depoliticisation 34; exceptionality ideology 33–4, 35, 65; factionalism 39; future measures to overcome stalemate 226–7, 228; inner elite 216; Kremlin elite splits 166; legitimacy 18, 35–6, 137; neo-patrimonialism 64, 81; outer elite 216–17; post-2012 reset 215–20; power system 32; Putin as arbiter and moderator 217; stalemate 38–9, 66–7, 77–8, 224–5; super government of economic ministers 186, 230
Agency of Strategic Initiatives 96
Akunin, Boris 228
All-Russia People's Front (ONF) 174
amnesties: economic crimes 179; political prisoners 219
Andropov, Yuri 24
Anti-Orange Committee 76
Arab spring 5, 96, 146
armed forces 145–6
Arutunyan, Anna 39
Aslund, Anders 228
Audit Chamber 54–5
Auzan, Alexander 46

Badovsky, Dmitry 219
Bank of Moscow 39, 54, 91, 93
banking system: capital flight 7–8, 41, 121, 148, 150; currency and gold reserves 148; limited rights for accounts held abroad 173, 200
Barsukov, Mikhail 68
Bashkortostan 88
Bastrykin, Mikhail 72–3, 164
Batalina, Olga 170, 176
Bateson, Gregory 38–9
Baturina, Elena 88, 92
Belarus 18, 138, 150
Beltyukov, Alexei 185
Berezovsky, Boris 30, 32
Berlusconi, Silvio 70–71
Beslan school siege 3, 112
Bilalov, Akhmed 186
Bogdanov, Vladimir 99
Bologna, railway station bombing 68
Bolotnaya Square protest: Dec 2011, 120, Feb 2012, 141, 149, May 2012, 154, 162, 163, 184
Borodin, Andrei 39
Borogan, Irina 70
Bovt, Georgi 97
brain drain 47–8, 107, 162
Brezhnev, Leonid 15, 229
BRICS countries 40–41, 123
Britain, and Russia 71
business: amnesty for economic crimes 179; Commissioner for Entrepreneurs' Rights 179; deprivatisation 3–4, 30; entrepreneurs 47; Medvedev's measures 85, 86, 151; Movement for Human Rights 169; and the regime 56; representative organisations 30; windfall tax 151; World Bank 'ease of doing business' index 142, 155; *see also* state corporations
Bykov, Dmitry 206

246 Index

capital flight 7–8, 41, 121, 148, 150
CCO (Coordination Council of the Opposition) 206
Central Electoral Commission 12, 119, 205
Centre for the Complex Analysis and Public Administration 180
Centre for Strategic Research (CSR) 104, 180–81, 208
Chaika, Yuri 72
Chechnya: 2012 presidential election 152; KGB-organised Chechen wars 68, 70, 71; power transfer 19
Chemezov, Sergei 55, 216
Chesnakov, Alexei 218
Chicherin, Boris 27
children, maternity capital grant 4
China: border dispute 20, 146; modernisation 42; oil and natural gas agreements 179
Chubais, Anatoly 49, 68, 104, 173, 178, 220
citizenship 204
Civic Chamber 3
Civic Force (*Grazhdanskaya Sila*) 96
Civil Initiatives Committee 125
Civil Platform party 125, 207
civil service 7, 168, 183; and military service 168
civil society 31–2
civiliki 74, 122, 195, 220
Clinton, Hillary 126, 138
Commonwealth of Independent States (CIS) 18, 138
Communist Party of the Russian Federation (CPRF): and demonstrations 206; Duma election (2011) 117, **118**, 180; ideology 28–9, 209; lack of ideas 107; Moscow mayoral election 212, 213; pensioner support 66
Communist Party of the Soviet Union (CPSU) 28
Confederation of Labour of Russia (KTR) 209
conservative values 27, 46–7, 199–200, 204
Constitutional Court 180
constitutional state 2–3, 62–6, 207–8, 220, 223–31
consumerism 46
Coordination Council of the Opposition (CCO) 206
corruption 50–55; anti-corruption measures for civil servants 183; and the bureaucracy 173–4; Medvedev's campaign 51, 52, 84; meta-corruption 68; prosecutions 73; Putin's scepticism 144; (Russian) Investigative Committee (RIC) 72–3, 161, 164, 184, 185, 197; and security services 68, 70–72
Council of Europe 9, 119
Council of the Federation 12, 29, 130, 183
CPRF *see* Communist Party of the Russian Federation (CPRF)
crime: electoral candidates' criminal record 99, 166–7; *see also* corruption
CSR (Centre for Strategic Research) 104, 180–81, 208
Customs Union 138; *see also* European Union

Dagestan 210, 214
death penalty 9
decentralisation 86, 129
deep state 68–71
defence 19, 145–6; expenditure **146**, 148
Degtyarov, Mikhail 212
Delovaya Rossiya (Business Russia) 30
Delyagin, Mikhail 76, 93
democracy: and economic development 44, 67; formalities observed under Putin 12; internet democracy 144; managed democracy 18, 27, 63, 205; mismanaged democracy 196–7; Putin's view 143; sovereign democracy 21–2, 22, 27
Democratic Party of Russia 96
demographic crisis 7
Denin, Nikolai 197
Deripaska, Oleg 53, 149
dirigisme 11, 21–2, 30
Dmitriev, Mikhail 104, 208
Dugin, Alexander 76, 123
Dunaev, Andrei 99
Dvorkovich, Arkady 155–6
Dzemal, Geidar 76
Dzhibladze, Yuri 181

East Germany 15
economic crisis (2008) 6, 125
economic development 44, 67
economic policy 6, 95, 142, 155, 178–9, 186
economic regime 39–40
economy 9, 44, 123, 191–2; de-offshorisation 163, 200
Egypt, deep state 69

Ekaterinburg 211, 214
elections: flawed outcomes 12; *see also* parliamentary election (2011); parliamentary elections; presidential election (1996); presidential election (2012); regional elections
electoral system: calls for free and fair elections 74, 95, 125; competition now freely allowed 219; constant changes to regulations 27–8, 64; criminal records of candidates 99, 166–7; electoral commissions 12, 119, 129, 205; Medvedev's proposals 129–32, 144, 182–3; Mironov's calls for reform 101; oversight improvements 205; Putin's 2004 reform 112; Putin's 2013 reform 183; research grants 219; State Council debate on reform (2010) 29–30
elites: fragmentation 193–4; key groups for the future 216–18; Kremlin regime splits 166; moral and political roots 226; nationalisation of the elites 172–3, 174; opposition 125; presidential election intra-elite splits 135–6, 148; property ownership abroad 172; Putin's inner circle and friends 40, 52–4, 55, 229; *see also* security service (*siloviki*)
emigration, brain drain 47–8, 107, 162
Estonia, protests 32
Eurasian Union 7, 77, 138, 204
European Court of Human Rights 130–31, 168
European Union: benefits of membership 57; energy markets 146; enlargement 11
exceptionality ideology 33–4, 35, 65

Fatherland Party 12
federal districts 3
Federal Security Service (FSB) 16, 25, 70, 72
Federation Council 12, 29, 130, 183
Fedorov, Nikolai 139
Fedorov, Yevgeny 167–8, 170
Felshtinsky, Yuri 70
Florian Geyser Conceptual Club 76
Foreign Agents Registration Act (FARA) (US) 169–70
France, 1958 events 112
Freedom in the World 2013 167

FSB (Federal Security Service) 16, 25, 70, 72
Fursenko, Andrei 156

Gaddy, Clifford 23–5, 56
Gaev, Dmitry 54
Galushka, Alexander 175
Gaulle, Charles de 112
Gazprom 52, 54, 142
General Prosecutor's Office (GPO) 72, 118–19, 166
geopolitics, of Russia 48
Georgia: 2008 war 148, 184; NATO membership 18; revolution (2003) 3
Glazev, Sergei 186
Glonas 183
Golikova, Tatyana 156
Golodets, Olga 155
Golos 153–4, 168–9
Gontmakher, Yevgeny 104, 192
Gorbachev, Mikhail 11, 15, 105, 163, 191–2
Gorchakov, Prince Alexander 140
Govorukhin, Stanislav 175
Gozman, Leonid 97
Gref, German 220
gubernatorial elections *see* regional elections
Gudkov, Dmitry 160, 206, 207
Gudkov, Gennady 206, 207, 211
Guriev, Sergei 161–2
Gusinsky, Vladimir 32
Guzzanti, Paolo 70

Hahn, Gordon 102
Hellman, Joel S. 66
Herd, Graeme P. 49
Hilferding, Rudolf 41
Hill, Fiona 23–5
Hobson, John H. 41
homosexuality 170; *see also* LGBT (lesbian, gay, bisexual and transgender) community
hostage incidents, Beslan school 3, 112
human development 145
human rights 169
Human Rights Council 219

Idov, Michael 165
Illarionov, Andrei 148
Ilyumzhinov, Kirsan 88
immigrants: detention camps 171, 172; and ethnic tension 194, 201; from Central Asia and Caucasus 121,

124–5, 171; housing restrictions 171–2; Putin's proposals 141, 145
inequality 42, 45–6
inflation 179
infrastructure projects 89–90, 179
Ingushetia 210, 214
Inozemtsev, Vladislav 50
Institute of Contemporary Development (Insor) 103–4, 106, 182
Institute for Socioeconomic and Political Studies Foundation (ISEPI) 219
international law 204
international relations 10, 19, 146
internet: CCO poll 206; and Medvedev 87, 115; petitions 144; and protest 124
Investigative Committee (RIC) 72–3, 161, 164, 184, 185, 197
Isaev, Andrei 184
Italy 68, 70–71
Ivanov, Anton 180
Ivanov, Sergei 85, 148, 156, 216
Izborsky Club 75, 77, 180, 181

Japan, government 62–3
judiciary 3, 33–4, 72–3, 86–7, 179–80
Just Russia (*Spravedlivaya Rossiya*): election results (2011) 118, **118**, 180; evolution 205–6; Mironov's demotion 101, 106, 205; Moscow mayoral election 212; parliamentary success 205; programme 29, 101–2; and regime pressure 124; regime reprisals 206; regime-sponsored party 28, 100; splits over opposition protests 206–7

Kabanov, Kirill 55
Kalmykia 88
Kamyshev, Dmitry 102
Karimov, Islam 18
Kasparov, Garry 53–4, 206
Kasyanov, Mikhail 52, 97, 124, 151
Kazakhstan 138, 142
KGB 15, 24, 70–71
Khabirov, Radi 99
Khakasia 214
Khimki 210
Khloponin, Alexander 156
Khodorkovsky, Mikhail: arrest 2; and black privatisations 151; challenge to regime 30, 66–7; in correctional camp 115; and destruction of Yukos empire 39, 53; on Medvedev's programme 84; police corruption 72; on political trials 162; on the protest movement 151–2; regime's dilemma 225; release 219–20; trials 78, 161, 169, 202
Kholmanskikh, Igor 156
Kirill, Patriarch 216–17
Kirovles timber 164–5
Kogan, Vladimir 54
Kolesnikov, Sergei 52
Kolokoltsev, Vladimir 155
Korzhakov, Alexander 68
Kostin, Andrei 96
Kostomarev, Pavel 184
Kovalchuk, Yuri 52, 216
Kovalev, Oleg 210
Kozak, Dmitry 53, 156
Krasnoyarsk Economic Forum 95
Kravchenko, Boris 209
Kremlin, Putin as senior official 16
Kryshtanovskaya, Olga 46, 208
Kuchma, Leonid 18
Kudrin, Alexei: criticisms of regime 95, 113–14, 177, 220; and demonstrations 120, 125; and economic reform 125; intermediary for protesters 150, 151; loyalty 216; need for free elections 95, 125; potential replacement for Medvedev 230; and Putin's early career 94; Putin's unofficial economic advisor 186; resignation 114, 146; successful finance minister 16, 125, 177; VTB board member 85
Kurginyan, Sergei 76, 123
Kyrgyzstan, migrants 121

labour migration *see* immigrants
Latynina, Yulia 92–3
Lebedev, Alexander 163–4
Lebedev, Konstantin 115, 163
legitimacy 18, 35–6, 137
Lenin, Vladimir 41, 143
Leninism 34
Leontiev, Mikhail 76
Levada Centre 121–2, 154, 169, 193
Levichev, Nikolai 29–30, 212
Levitin, Igor 85
LGBT (lesbian, gay, bisexual and transgender) community 47, 75, 170
Liberal Democratic Party of Russia (LDPR) 28–9, 106, **118**, 212
liberalism 49, 66, 73–4
Libya 85–6, 96, 184
Limonov, Eduard 209
Litvinenko, Alexander 71
Litvinovich, Marina 54

Index

loyalty 50, 215–16, 229
Lucas, Edward 71
Lugovoi, Andrei 167
Lukashenko, Alexander 18, 150
Luzhkov, Yuri 12, 31, 88–93, 193–4, 215

Magnitsky Act (US) 173, 201
Magnitsky, Sergei 73, 93, 115, 201
Maleva, Tatyana 45
managed democracy 18, 27, 63, 205
Manezh Square riots 171
market economy 26
market forces 9–10, 24
Markin, Vladimir 164, 185
marriage, controls on government employees 168
Matveev market attack 171
Matvienko, Valentina 218
media 32; controls on foreign journalists 167; election coverage 119; proposed foreign funding controls 170; *see also* internet; television
Medinsky, Vladimir 76
Medvedev, Dmitry: anti-corruption campaign 51, 52, 84; business measures 85, 86; and decentralisation 86; desire for second Kremlin term 94, 95; disappointing achievements 5, 35, 82–3; dislike of Nashi 174; eclipsed as inner elite 216, 218; elected president 4; fight against corruption 51, 52, 84; head of United Russia's candidate list 100, 113; and the internet 87, 115; judicial reform 86–7; Kremlin campaign against 127; and Kudrin's resignation 114; and Libya 85–6; and luxury items 52–3; Luzhkov's dismissal 90–93; Magnitogorsk speech 85; modernisation constraints 57, 78–9; modernisation and reform 4–5, 40, 41, 43–4, 57, 81–8, 102–3, 220; police reforms 72; political identity 194–5; political reforms 120, 128–32, 144, 182–3, 201; prime ministerial cabinet 155–6; Putin's chief of staff 4; and the regions 88; Right Cause as support for presidential re-election 29, 97–100; 'Russia Forward!' article 83–4; sidelined as prime minister 182–7; and television subsidy 32; and United Russia 117
Melnikov, Ivan 212
Mereu, Francesca, *My Friend Putin* 70–71
Mezentsev, Dmitry 135

middle classes 45–6, 48, 49, 65, 105, 119–20, 139–40, 190
migrants *see* immigrants
military expenditure 146, 148
military reform 82
military service, and government employees 168
Milov, Vladimir 52, 97
Millennium Manifesto 147
Minchenko Consulting 216–17
Ministry of Internal Affairs (MVD) 51, 69, 72
Mironov, Ivan 160
Mironov, Sergei 29, 100–101, 135–6, **153**, 205–6, 215, 219
Mitrokhin, Sergei 119, 211–12
Mizulina, Elena 170
modernisation programme: constraints 57, 78–9; judicial reform 33–4, 86–7, 179–80; liberal vs conservative 49–50; Medvedev's model 4–5, 40, 41, 43–4, 50, 57, 81–8, 102–3; partial reform equilibrium 66–7; police reforms 72; political reforms 120, 128–32, 144, 182–3; Putin's model 41; retention of conservative values 46–7; Skolkovo Innovation Centre 115; state (democratic) vs business (*dirigiste*) 42–3
Monaghan, Andrew 49–50
Mori, Aldo 68
Morozov, Alexander 116
Morozov, Evgeny 87
Morozov, Igor 210
Morozov, Oleg 218–19
Morshakova, Tamara 161
Morsi, Mohamed 69
Moscow: crimes 172; decline in protests 208; financial centre 211; gay pride marches 89; infrastructure projects 89–90, 179; Luzhkov's achievements 88–9; Luzhkov's dismissal 90–93; mayoral election (2013) 166, 211–14, 224–5; population 211; presidential election result 152; Sobyanin's appointment 91; *see also* Bank of Moscow
Moscow region, elections 211, 214
Moscow School of Political Studies 168
motorists' movement 46
Movement for Human Rights 169
Mubarak, Hosni 35, 65, 69, 96
multiculturalism 141; *see also* immigrants

Nabiullina, Elvira 186, 220
Naryshkin, Sergei 122, 138–9, 218
Nashi ('Ours') youth organisation 32, 174
National Welfare Fund 6, 179
nationalism 121, 124–5, 141–2, 172, 196, 203
NATO, expansion 11, 18
natural resources 67
Navalny, Alexei: alleged CIA recruitment 163; anti-corruption campaign 54, 55, 161, 162, 163; CCO poll 206; Moscow mayoral candidate 166, 211–14, 224–5; nationalism 124; police raid 160; presidential ambitions 164; property owned abroad by Russian elite 172; protest leader 121, 124; Putin's opinion 178; timber embezzling trial 164–6; vulnerability of the regime 205; and Yabloko 124
Nemtsov, Boris 52, 97, 121, 124, 214
neo-patrimonialism 64, 81
neo-traditionalism 74–5, 78, 170, 180, 187
Neverov, Sergei 176
NGOs 31, 75, 168–70, 201
Nikiforov, Nikolai 155
Nodia, Ghia 20
North Caucasus 11, 48, 112, 121, 153, 186, 210
nuclear deterrence 146–7
nuclear disarmament 126
Nurgaliev, Rashid 156

Obama, Barack 197, 202
Ofitserov, Pyotr 164–6
oil and gas 7, 52, 179, 192; *see also* Yukos oil company
oligarchs 1, 39, 148; should not be involved in politics 30, 163; state 39–40; vulnerability of non-insiders 39
Opalev, Vyacheslav 164–5
opinion polls 17, 76
OPORA Rossii 30
opposition: changing social base and tactics 208–9; coercive measures 159–67; Coordination Council of the Opposition (CCO) 206; elite opposition 125; non-systemic 124–5, 206–7; political parties 28–30; systemic 28–30; *see also* protest movement; protests

OSCE (Organization for Security and Co-operation in Europe) 119, 153
Ozero dacha collective 52

Panyushkin, Valery 46
para-constitutional bodies 3, 21, 131
para-constitutionalism 112, 225–6
parliamentary election (2011): flawed outcome 117–19, 180; Just Russia programme 101–2; Medvedev and Right Cause leadership 97–100; Parnas registration denied 97; parties taking part 96–7, 106; Putin's campaign 96, 117; result 117–18, **118**; United Russia's unpopularity 116–17
parliamentary elections: (1993) 27; (2003) 29; (2007) 28
Party of People's Freedom (Parnas) 97, 106, 117
Pastukhov, Vladimir 72, 224–5
paternalism 22–3
Patriots of Russia 97, 176
Pavlovsky, Gleb 25–6, 83
People's Front for Russia (PFR) 174–6
Peskov, Dmitry 23
Petrozavodsk 214
Poklonnaya Hill meeting 123, 149–50
police 72, 160
political institutions: weakening 19; *see also* para-constitutional bodies
political liberalism 73–4
political parties: Duma representation threshold 97, 115, 130, 183; management of 27–8; minimum membership 29–30, 96, 97; new pluralism 195, 196; non-parliamentary 96–7; Parnas registration denied 97; simplification of registration procedures 129, 130; systemic opposition 28–30
political prisoners 150, 219; *see also* Khodorkovsky, Mikhail; Navalny, Alexei
political reform 29–30
Politkovskaya, Anna 71
Ponomarev, Ilya 185, 206, 207
Potanin, Vladimir 53
power, *vertical* of power 50, 53, 89, 102, 112
Pozner, Vladimir 167
prerogative state 63
presidency: extension of term 93; Gorbachev's view 105; Medvedev's election 4; Medvedev's second term

decision 102; Medvedev's second term programme 103–4, 105; Putin's adherence to two terms 4, 29, 34–5; Putin's 'castling' (*rokirovka*) return to presidency 5–6, 57, 112–16, 154; Putin's constitutional coup 112–16; Putin's first election 1; Putin's unofficial campaign 5, 103; Right Cause and Medvedev's re-election campaign 97–100; succession campaign 94–6, 102–7; third candidate demands 104, 105
presidential election (1996) 12, 134
presidential election (2012): candidate list 135–6; fraud 119, 153–4; intra-elite splits 135–6, 148; Putin's programme 139–47; result 152–4, **153**, 180; voter signature requirement reduced 129; webcams and clear plastic ballot boxes 128
Pribylovsky, Vladimir 70
Prikhodko, Sergei 156
Primakov, Yevgeny 89
prisons 115
privatisation 30, 86, 142, 151, 155
Prokhanov, Alexander 76, 123
Prokhorov, Mikhail: Civil Platform 125, 207; dismissed as Right Cause leader 99–100; not a Moscow mayoral candidate 211; outer elite status 216–17; presidency candidate 135–6, 149, 150, **153**; Right Cause leader 98–9
Prokhorova, Irina 211
property, ownership abroad 172, 173
protest movement: and 2011–12 elections 119–26; challenge for authorities 75; Khodorkovsky's view 151–2; mixed composition 121–2; not a prelude to revolutionary change 48; reaction to 57; thank tank analysis 181
protests: blue bucket 46, 120; Bolotnaya Square 154, 162, 163, 184; booing revolution 116–17, 137; counter-demonstration 123, 149; early Putin era 120; economic grievances 208; elections (2011–2012) 53, 120–21, 149; Kholmanskikh's offer 156; Kremlin control efforts 32, 128, 174; March Against Scoundrels 207; March of Millions (June 2012) 160, 206; Moscow gay pride refusal 89; nature of demonstrators 67, 74, 119, 121–2; November national holiday marches 124, 196; Putin's response 126–8, 137;

Ryzhkov's fears 149–50; Strategy 31 124, 160; tougher legislation 159–60
public (civic) chamber 3, 21, 112, 131, 170, 175, 176
public opinion 17, 76, 192–3
public sector, bribery 51
public services, expenditure 7
Pussy Riot 160–61, 170, 177–8, 184
Putin, Vladimir: achievements 227; adherence to two presidential terms 4, 34–5, 201; alleged security service backing 70–71; and Berlusconi 70–71; 'castling' (*rokirovka*) return to presidency 5–6, 57, 112–16, **153**, 153–4; complex political identity 14, 23–6; criticisms of 23, 25–6, 136–7; cultural conservatism 199–200, 204; 'de-offshorisation' speech 173; education 15; election campaign (2011–12) 117, 150–51; election programme (2012) 139–47; executive orders (May 2012) 155; on foreign funding for NGOs 169; FSB head 16, 70; heir-apparent to Yeltsin 16; inner circle and friends 40, 52–4, 55, 229; KGB service 15, 24; and Khodorkovsky trials 202; Kremlin official responsible for the regions 16; Kremlin staff 156; and Kudrin's resignation 114; Leningrad deputy mayor 16; and Libya 85; Luzhkov's dismissal 90, 92–3; personal vulnerabilities 197; presidency for 2018 not ruled out 229; as prime minister 4–5; and protests 126–8, 135, 137; public opinion 192–3; re-election campaign 96; response to 2012 victory 153; rumours of palaces and personal venality 51–3; Russia Day conciliatory speech 160; secretary to the Security Council 16; sense of indispensability 81; state-of-the-nation *poslanie* 4, 17; statecraft 225–6; televised direct line session (May 2013) 176–8; third term *poslanie* 199–201; Valdai Club ideological statement 202–5
Putinism: achievements 6–7; anti-political nature 19–20; anti-revolutionism 17–18; authoritarianism 8; balance between competing policies 230; centrism 76–8; developmental phase (2012-) 5–6; *dirigisme* 11, 21–2, 30; failings 7–8, 13; first remedial phase (2000–2003) 1–2, 146–7;

historical phenomenon 225; and loyalty 50, 215–16, 229; para-constitutionalism 21; paradoxical nature 61–2; paternalism 22–3; and power of the regime 20–21; pragmatism 27; regime consolidation (second phase) (2003–2008) 2–4; repressive measures 159–60, 167–72, 181; tandem modernisation (third phase) (2008–12) 4–5; Thermidor consolidation 18–19; third term conservative doctrine (2012-) 198–201; third term crisis 190–98, 229–30; *see also* administrative regime (*vlast*)

Rakhimov, Murtaza 88
rallies *see* protests
Razvozzhaev, Leonid 163
regional elections: abolition 3, 31, 89, 91, 130; irregularities 210, 214; opt-out law 167; pluralism 195; reinstated by Medvedev 129, 130, 201
regional elections (2009) 29
regional elections (2012) 210
regional elections (2013) 207, 210–215
regional leaders 88–93, 115, 130
regions 16, 31, 112
religion: blasphemy law 170; *see also* Russian Orthodox Church
Remchukov, Konstantin 92
rentierism 56–7
repressive legislation 159–60, 167–72, 181
Reserve Fund 6
revolution, experience of 57, 230
Right Cause (*Pravoe Delo*) 29, 96, 97–100
riots 171; *see also* protests
Rodina 176
Rogov, Kirill 91
Rogozin, Dmitry 156, 218
Roizman, Yevgeny 99, 211, 214
Rosneft 4, 54, 155, 156, 179
Rossiya Bank 52
Rossiya, Delovaya 175
Rotenberg, Arkady 40, 52, 53, 54, 90
Rotenberg, Boris 52, 53, 54
RPR-Parnas 131, 162, 212, 214
Rubtsov, Alexander 171
rule of law 64–6
RusHydro 155
Russia: centrist/intermediate group 49; geopolitics 48; liberals 49; parallel worlds 49; traditionals 49; and US 126, 167

Russian Investigative Committee (RIC) 72–3
Russian language 141
Russian Orthodox Church 74–5, 77, 170
Russian Popular Front (RPF) 96, 107, 117, 138, 153, 159, 174–5, 179, 183, 187, 196, 213, 219
Russian Union of Industrialists and Entrepreneurs (RUIE) 30, 95, 150–51
Ryazan region 210
Ryzhkov, Vladimir 52, 97, 124, 149–50, 211

Saakashvili, Mikheil 3
Sakharov Prospekt protest 120
salaries 145
Sauer, Derk 71
schismogenesis 38–9
Sechin, Igor 85, 122, 148, 156, 216
Security Council, Putin as head 16
security policy 145–6
Serdyukov, Anatoly 55, 173–4, 183
Shaimiev, Mintimir 88, 115
Shamalov, Nikolai 52
Shein, Oleg 207, 209
Shevardnadze, Eduard 3
Shevchenko, Maksim 76
Shevchuk, Yuri 228–9
Shlapentokh, Vladimir 39
Shmatko, Sergei 85
Shoigu, Sergei 216, 217–18
Shuvalov, Ivan 145, 156, 186
Sidyakin, Alexander 172
siloviki: and Chechen war 68; core constituency 2; corruption 68, 70–72; expenditure 69; factions 194; priorities 122, 220; and protests 122; repressive measures 25; salary rises 148; as third state 68–71; under Yeltsin 68; *see also* FSB (Federal Security Service); KGB
Single Economic Area 138
Skolkovo Innovation Centre 115, 185
Skrynik, Elena 183
Skuratov, Yuri 91
Sobchak, Anatoly 15–16
Sobchak, Ksenia 160, 206
Sobyanin, Sergei 91–2, 175, 211–13, 216, 218
Sochi Winter Olympics (2014) 8, 53, 156
social activism *see* protest movement; protests
social benefits 19
social organisations 30
social policy 4, 19, 46–7, 56, 144–5

sociological liberalism 66
Soldatov, Andrei 70
Solzhenitsyn, Alexander 144, 145
Sorokin, Pitirim 215
Soskovets, Oleg 68
South Caucasus 121
South Korea 42
South Ossetia 18
sovereign debt 6
sovereign democracy 21–2, 22, 27
Soviet Union, dissolution 10
sporting events 8, 117, 141; *see also* Sochi Winter Olympics (2014)
Stalin, Joseph 15
Stanovaya, Tatyana 175–6
Starikov, Nikolai 76
Starshinov, Mikhail 167
state: fragmentation 216; prerogative state 63
state corporations: composition of boards of directors 31–2, 85, 87–8; economic significance 9; and energy assets 184; establishment 4; ineffectiveness 155; Putin's view 142
State Council 3, 21, 29, 82, 100, 131
statism 142–3
Stepashin, Sergei 54–5
Stolypin, Petr 27
Storchak, Sergei 73
Strategy 31 meetings 124
Strategy 2020 31, 139
Subbotin, Mikhail 161
Sulakshin, Stepan 180
Supreme Arbitration Court 179–80
Supreme Court 179–80
Surkov, Vladislav: and civil society 31; deputy prime minister 156; Kremlin advisor 185; Kremlin political affairs management 100, 128; moved from Kremlin 128, 138, 185; Prokhorov and Right Cause 99; and the protests 119, 131–2; and sovereign democracy 21–2, 27
Sweden, government 62–3
Syrian uprising 5, 202

Tajikistan, migrants 121
Tatarstan 88, 115
taxation 46, 120, 151
telephone law 78, 87
television: *Anatomy of Protest* programmes 162–3; controls on foreign journalists 167; proposed foreign funding controls 170; Public Television of Russia (OTR) 184; Putin's direct line session 176–8; state control 32, 71
terrorism: Beslan school siege 3, 112; Boston marathon 177; Putin's measures 112
Thermidor consolidation 18–19
think tanks 75–6, 103–4, 180–81
Timakova, Natalya 186
timber trade 164–5
Timchenko, Gennady 40, 52, 216
Timofeyeva, Olga 175
Titov, Boris 97, 179
TNK-BP (Tyumen Oil Company-BP) 56, 155
trade unions 209
traditionals 49
Transbaikal 214
Treisman, Daniel 62
Tretyakov, Vitaly 27
Trotsky, Leon 41
Trutnev, Yuri 156
Turkey, deep state 69

Udaltsov, Sergei 121, 160, 163, 206, 209
Ukraine 3, 18
Ulyukaev, Alexei 191
Union of Right Forces (SPS) 96
United Nations: Convention against Corruption 55; Libyan resolution 85, 96
United Russia: Congress (September 2011) 112–13; creation 12; declining popularity 116–17, 175; democratic deficiencies 218; election results 28, 117–18, **118**, 180; lack of respect for 96; and Luzhkov 89, 90, 92; Medvedev to head electoral list 100, 113; membership 12; and People's Front for Russia (PFR) 176; regional election results 214; support for Medvedev 100
United States: adoption of Russian children 201; bilateral summit cancellation 197; Boston marathon bombings 177; CIA and Chubais allegation 178; European missile defence 19, 146; Foreign Agents Registration Act (FARA) 169–70; Magnitsky Act 173, 201; oil and gas industries 192; and Russia 126, 167, 202; trade relations with Russia 201; USAID 168, 178; war on terror 20
Unity Party 12

Urals federal district 156
Urban, Michael 226
Urlashov, Yevgeny 210
USAID (US Agency for International Development) 168, 178
Uzbekistan 18

Valdai Discussion Club 181, 202–5
Vasileva, Yevgeniya 55
Vasiliev, Vladimir 176
Venediktov, Alexei 127, 148, 177
vertical of power 50, 53, 89, 102, 112
Volodin, Vyacheslav 138, 174, 185, 215, 216, 218–19, 225
Voloshin, Alexander 98
Vorobyev, Andrei 211, 214
VTB Bank 54, 91, 93, 142

Whitmore, Brian 107
World Cup (2018) 8
World Trade Organisation 9–10

xenophobia 171–2, 194

Yabloko 29, 96, 106, 118, 124, 211–12
Yakoleva, Yana 47

Yakunin, Vladimir 52, 180
Yanukovich, Viktor 3, 18
Yaroslavl 210, 214
Yarovaya, Irina 176
Yashin, Ilya 160, 206
Yavlinsky, Grigory 106, 135, 151
Yeltsin, Boris 1, 12, 16, 25, 26–7, 147
young people, Nashi youth organisation 32, 174
Yukos oil company: alternative centre of power 53; assets given to Rosneft 4, 54, 156; illegality charges 161; modern corporation 2; reason for attack 142, 143; regime's economic power 67; vulnerable as non-insider 39
Yurgens, Igor 103, 104, 106
Yushchenko, Viktor 3, 18

Zhirinovsky, Vladimir 29, 106, 135, 150, **153**
Zhuravlev, Alexei 176
Zlobin, Nikolai 101
Zubarevich, Natalya 48
Zubkov, Viktor 55, 85
Zyuganov, Gennady 12, 106, 135–6, 150, **153**